Technology, Work and Globalization

The Technology, Work and Globalization series was developed to provide policy makers, workers, managers, academics and students with a deeper understanding of the complex interlinks and influences between technological developments, including information and communication technologies, work organizations and patterns of globalization. The mission of the series is to disseminate rich knowledge based on deep research about relevant issues surrounding the globalization of work that is spawned by technology.

Mary C. Lacity • Horst Treiblmaier
Editors

Blockchains and the Token Economy

Theory and Practice

palgrave
macmillan

Editors
Mary C. Lacity
Sam M. Walton College of Business
University of Arkansas
Fayetteville, AR, USA

Horst Treiblmaier
School of International Management
Modul University Vienna
Vienna, Austria

ISSN 2730-6623 ISSN 2730-6631 (electronic)
Technology, Work and Globalization
ISBN 978-3-030-95107-8 ISBN 978-3-030-95108-5 (eBook)
https://doi.org/10.1007/978-3-030-95108-5

This Palgrave Macmillan imprint is published by the registered company Springer Nature Switzerland AG.
The registered company address is: Gewerbestrasse 11, 6330 Cham, Switzerland

Acknowledgments

Chapter 4 is based on Cathy Barrera and Stephanie Hurder's paper, "Cryptoeconomics: Designing Effective Incentives and Governance Models for Blockchain Networks Using Insights from Economics," with a foreword by Don Tapscott, published by the Blockchain Research Institute on January 13, 2020, and adapted here with permission.

We thank Haisaini Woods, Administrative Specialist for the Information Systems Department at the University of Arkansas, for her help with manuscript preparation.

Contents

Notes on Contributors

Eric D. Achtmann Eric is an award-winning innovator, entrepreneur, executive, and investor. He started his career fighting fires in the Middle East after Gulf War I before moving on to the US Congressional Lean Aerospace Initiative and McDonnell-Douglas Phantom Works, and McKinsey & Co., where he served as an Aerospace & Defense and Automotive expert and ultimately pioneered the Firm's highly successful product development practice (DTC/DTV). Thereafter, Eric moved into venture capital, serving as a Managing Partner for two pan-European tech and life science venture funds. Following his transition into operational management, Eric proposed, architected, and brought to market the global fresh drinks vending system underpinning Coca Cola's $5.1b acquisition of Costa Coffee and co-founded V-Nova, a London-based software company providing advanced data compression solutions (LCEVC and VC-6). Eric is a Senior Advisor to McKinsey, Arowana Capital, and VivoPower plc; Non-Executive Director of Celdara Medical, Javelin Oncology, TargetArm, and VeriTX; as well as Founding Member of Meggitt PLC's Technology Advisory Board and Expert Advisor to the European Commission. Eric holds degrees from MIT and is Professor of Practice at MIT-cofounded Skoltech.

Tom Barbereau is a doctoral researcher at the University of Luxembourg, originally from Karlsruhe (Germany). He holds a bachelor from the

University of Groningen (Netherlands) and an MSc in Science & Technology Studies from the University of Edinburgh (Scotland). As part of the FINATRAX research group, his research contributions are at the intersection of blockchain governance and management. Current work is on regulatory and political controversies in non-custodial and self-organizing (public permissionless) systems—specifically, in the nascent field of decentralized finance/DeFi—and on decentralized electronic identity management systems.

Cathy Barrera is a Founding Economist at Prysm Group, a leading economic consulting firm in the blockchain and digital asset industry, and the Program Director for the Wharton School's *Economics of Blockchain and Digital Assets* executive education program. She is a frequent keynote speaker and lecturer on economics and blockchain. Her recent speaking appearances include Consensus, SXSW, NBER, and Blockchain Revolution Global. Her research on the economics and governance of blockchain has been presented at Harvard, Stanford, UC Berkeley, University of Cambridge, DARPA, and the Federal Reserve. Dr. Barrera is an advisor to blockchain projects at the World Economic Forum, a collaborator of the MIT Cryptoeconomics Lab, and an industry expert for MIT's executive education course, *Blockchain Technologies: Business Innovation and Application*. She was previously tenure-track faculty at the S.C. Johnson School of Management at Cornell University and was the Chief Economist at ZipRecruiter. Dr. Barrera received her BA from Northwestern University, where she majored in Communication Studies, Economics, and Mathematics. She holds an MSc in Applicable Mathematics from the London School of Economics and a PhD in Business Economics from Harvard University, where she studied under Nobel Laureate Oliver Hart.

Erran Carmel is Professor of Information Technology at the Kogod School of Business at American University in Washington D.C. He is a former dean. Carmel is known for his expertise on the globalization of technology work, especially global outsourcing, and has written three books and well over a hundred articles. Lately, he has been studying Digital Health Passports—and he has nine of them on his iPhone.

Klitos Christodoulou is an assistant professor in the Department of Digital Innovation at the University of Nicosia (UNIC). Klitos obtained his PhD in Computer Science from the School of Computer Science at the University of Manchester, UK. He has been an adjunct staff member at the University of Manchester where he engaged in various research and teaching activities. He is also the Research Manager at the Institute For the Future (IFF) and the Scientific Lab leader of the Distributed Ledgers Research Center (DLRC) at IFF, a Center that aims toward fostering academic research on blockchains. His research interests span both Data Management challenges, with a focus on Machine Learning techniques, and Distributed Ledger Technologies, with an emphasis on blockchain ledgers. He is also a member of the ISO/TC 307 Blockchain and Distributed Ledger Technologies group. Klitos is also an active member for developing the Cyprus National Strategy for Blockchain. He represents Cyprus as an invited expert at the European Blockchain Partnership. Klitos written peer-reviewed articles in prestigious journals and conferences and acts as the Principal Investigator for several EU research grants.

Panayiotis Christodoulou holds a PhD in Computer Engineering and Informatics from the Cyprus University of Technology (CUT), Cyprus. Before pursuing his PhD, he completed his undergraduate and postgraduate studies at the University of Manchester, UK (MEng), and the Frederick University, Cyprus (MSc). He is a faculty member staff in the Department of Computer Science located at Neapolis University Pafos. His main research interests are focused on the areas of Distributed Ledger Technologies (DLTs) and Artificial Intelligence (AI). For the last few years, he has been designing and implementing complex decentralized applications and some of them are currently being used from worldwide organizations. His publications have been presented in top-tier academic conferences and in the *Sensors Journal* and the *Journal of the Knowledge Economy*.

Dale Chrystie is a business fellow and blockchain strategist for FedEx based in the Memphis area. He also serves as chairman of the Blockchain in Transport Alliance (BiTA) Standards Council and is a member of the Blockchain Research Institute. He was awarded the inaugural Enterprise Blockchain Award in Enterprise & Industry Leadership and speaks globally on the business and strategy aspects of blockchain and emerging technologies. His focus on "coopetition" in the blockchain space continues to challenge conventional wisdom and typical corporate and regulatory culture. Dale's career in transportation began more than 30 years ago, and in addition to his work leading the first proof of concept at FedEx using blockchain technology, he has extensive experience in strategy, quality, process improvement, portfolio management, human resources, operations, sales, education, risk, and standards development and is a proud graduate of the University of Arkansas.

Daniel Conway is a teaching professor and associate director of the Blockchain Center of Excellence at the University of Arkansas. He is involved in all Blockchain Center activities, as well as many of the analytics courses at the University of Arkansas. Dr. Conway has been involved in graduate school education for over 30 years and has served on the faculty at USF, Iowa, Notre Dame, Northwestern, Indiana University, Florida, and Virginia Tech. He also has decades of consulting experience in the areas of Data Science, Analytics, and Information Security.

Simon Cousaert is a research associate at the UCL Centre for Blockchain Technologies (CBT). He is also a data analyst and researcher in the decentralized finance (DeFi) industry, providing consulting services for a multitude of companies. After finishing his Business Engineering Master's degree at the University of Ghent in 2020, Simon began focusing his efforts on the opportunities that opened up through public and permissionless blockchain technologies, specifically in the financial industry. His research career is in its earliest stages, containing two preprints, on automated market makers and yield aggregators in DeFi.

Gilbert Fridgen is Professor and PayPal-FNR PEARL Chair in Digital Financial Services at the Interdisciplinary Centre for Security, Reliability, and Trust (SnT), University of Luxembourg. In 2016, he initiated and co-founded the Fraunhofer Blockchain Lab, where he still contributes on selected topics. In his research, he analyzes the transformative effects of digital technologies on individual organizations as well as on the relationship between organizations. He addresses especially decentralized and distributed technologies like Distributed Ledgers, Digital Identities and

Verifiable Credentials, Federated Learning, and the Internet-of-Things. His research involves information systems engineering, IT strategy and (risk) management, as well as regulatory compliance. In his projects and partnerships, he collaborates with partners in financial services, energy, mobility, manufacturing, consulting, as well as with public bodies and governments. His works are frequently published in academic journals and conference proceedings in management, information systems, computer science, and engineering, as well as in outlets at the intersection of these disciplines. He was nominated and received best paper awards at internationally recognized conferences. He edited conference proceedings of the most important German, European, and International Conferences on Information Systems. He is President of the Special Interest Group in Green Information Systems of the Association for Information Systems.

Kiran Garimella, PhD is a visiting associate professor at the Muma College of Business, University of South Florida. His research and teaching interests include blockchain, machine learning, and data analytics. As a Chief Scientist at KoreConX, he advises on the strategy and development of an AI-based blockchain platform for digital securities in the global capital private markets. Previously, he held roles such as Global CIO and Chief Architect at General Electric and VP/Chief Evangelist for Business Process Management at Software AG. Kiran Garimella has a PhD in AI & Machine Learning from the Warrington College of Business at the University of Florida. He is the author of two books on business process management (used as supplemental text at various MBA and EMBA programs worldwide). His latest book is a game changer's guide to AI+Blockchain (foreword by Dr. Vint Cerf, co-founder of the Internet). He has written over 30 articles (including seven academic publications) and delivered over 40 keynote and conference presentations, numerous press interviews, and executive masterclasses in 20 countries.

Stephanie Hurder is a Founding Economist at Prysm Group, a leading economic consulting firm in the blockchain and digital asset industry. She is a frequent keynote speaker and lecturer on economics and blockchain. Her recent speaking appearances include Consensus, SXSW, Hyperledger Global Forum, Crypto Economic Security Conference, and the IBM Columbia University Blockchain Accelerator. Her research on the economics of blockchain has been presented at Harvard, Stanford, UC Berkeley, University of Cambridge, DARPA, and the Federal Reserve. Dr. Hurder is an advisor to blockchain projects at the World Economic Forum and a contributor to the MIT Cryptoeconomics Lab. She runs an opinion column on CoinDesk on the economics and governance of blockchain. She has held economics research positions at MIT Sloan and Merrill Lynch and worked in management consulting at the Boston Consulting Group. Dr. Hurder holds an AB in Mathematics *Phi Beta Kappa* and *magna cum laude*, an AM in Economics, and a PhD in Business Economics from Harvard University, where she studied under Claudia Goldin and Nobel Laureate Al Roth.

Elias Iosif is an assistant professor at the School of Business, University of Nicosia (UNIC), as well as scientific lab co-leader at the Distributed Ledgers Research Centre, Institute For the Future, UNIC. He is teaching MSc in Digital Currency offered by UNIC, which is the first-degree program globally on decentralized digital currencies and blockchains. Also, he is participating in a number of EC-funded projects focused on blockchain technologies. Dr. Iosif has a PhD degree in Electronic and Computer Engineering. His areas of expertise include blockchain and machine learning (with focus on natural language processing and spoken dialogue systems). He has authored/co-authored over 65 peer-reviewed scientific publications.

Oscar A. Jofre is one of the Top 10 Global Thought Leaders in Equity Crowdfunding, a Top 5 Fintech Influencer, Top 10 Blockchain, and a Top 50 InsureTech. He has written an eBook that has been downloaded in over 20 countries and been distributed by partners worldwide. Oscar is a featured speaker on Blockchain, Digital Assets, Digital Securities, Securities Token, Fintech, regulated, equity crowdfunding, compliance, shareholder management, investor relations, and transparency in the United States, Australia, the United Kingdom, UAE, Peru, Germany, France, the Netherlands, Canada, Singapore, Indonesia, and China. He speaks to audiences covering alternative finance, digital securities offerings, equity crowdfunding, DSO, STO, TAO, ICO/ITO, RegTech, insurance, banking, legal, and crowdfunding. Oscar also advises the world's leading research, accounting, law firms, and insurance companies on the impact Blockchain, STO, TAO, ICO, Fintech, RegTech, LegalTech, InsurTech, and OrgTech is having in their business. He is a member of the Crowdfunding Intermediary Regulatory Advocates (CFIRA) in the United States and a contributing author to The Fintech Book, the world's first crowdsourced book on Fintech globally. He writes for Sharewise, Locavesting, Equities.com, Business.com, Crowdfund Insider, Crowdfund Beat, Bankless Times, and Agoracom. Oscar has been recognized as one of the ten most influential Hispanic Leaders in Canada. In May 2010, Oscar A. Jofre Jr. was recognized by the Rt. Hon. Stephen Harper for his accomplishments. Oscar was awarded the Vision 2012 Business Man of the Year by the Toronto Hispanic Chamber of Commerce on September 2012.

Niclas Kannengießer is a research associate with the KASTEL Security Labs and the Institute of Applied Computer Science and Formal Description Methods, Karlsruhe Institute of Technology, Germany. He has authored or co-authored in journals, including *ACM Computing Surveys*, *IEEE Transactions on Software Engineering*, and *Business & Information Systems Engineering*. His research interests include decentralized systems engineering, the analysis of behaviors of distributed systems (e.g., distributed ledger technology systems), and the investigation of human interactions with software systems.

Leonidas Katelaris is a post-doctoral researcher at the Institute For the Future (IFF) at University of Nicosia since 2019. He has previously served as a research assistant at University of Piraeus, where he participated in several EU-IST projects in the areas of cloud computing, e-Health, and information systems. Alongside with his duties as a research assistant, he supported University of Piraeus as a teaching assistant. He served international organizations from different positions including the position of the Research Manager at BTO Research where he participated in various projects both industrial and research. From late 2019 he joined the Institute For the Future (IFF), as a research assistant, participating in EU projects with focus in the areas of Blockchain and DLTs. In addition, he supports the world leading Blockchain and Digital Currency MSc program at University of Nicosia as a teaching assistant. His areas of expertise are Information Systems, Blockchain, DLTs, and lately Non-fungible Tokens (NFTs) where he has authored/co-authored scientific publications.

Johann Kranz is Professor of Digital Services and Sustainability at the University of Munich's LMU School of Management. He was a visiting scholar at Columbia University, Syracuse University, and Copenhagen Business School. From 2019 to 2021, he served as president of the AIS "Green IS" Special Interest Group. Furthermore, he is involved in numerous associations and organizations that aim at fostering sustainable and ethical use of digital technology. His research focuses on IS-business alignment and governance in the digital age, the multi-level impacts of digital technologies and innovation such as blockchain, and information systems for enabling circular economies, smart grids, sustainable mobility, and pro-environmental behavior. His research has been published in *Journal of Strategic Information Systems*, *MIS Quarterly Executive*, *Information Systems Journal*, *Journal of Service Research*, and *Energy Policy*.

Mary C. Lacity is Walton Professor of Information Systems and Director of the Blockchain Center of Excellence in the Sam M. Walton College of Business at The University of Arkansas. She was previously Curators' Distinguished Professor at the University of Missouri-St. Louis. She has held visiting positions at MIT, the London School of Economics, Washington University, and Oxford University. She is a Certified Outsourcing Professional® and Senior Editor for *MIS Quarterly Executive*. She has conducted case studies and surveys of hundreds of organizations on their adoption journeys. She has given keynote speeches and executive seminars worldwide and has served as an expert witness for the US Congress. She has authored 30 books, most recently, *Blockchain Foundations for the Internet of Value* and *A Manager's Guide to Blockchains for Business*. Her publications have appeared in the *Harvard Business Review*, *Sloan Management Review*, *MIS Quarterly*, *MIS Quarterly Executive*, *IEEE Computer*, *Communications of the ACM*, and many other academic and practitioner outlets. According to Google Scholar, her work has been cited over 20,000 times, with an h-index of 59.

Philipp Lesche is heading the Bavarian Center for BlockChain—[bc]^2 at the Bavarian State Ministry of Digital Affairs. The Bavarian Center for BlockChain is the contact point for all governmental blockchain activities in Bavaria. Before joining the ministry, he co-founded CDF Technologies, a company specialized in startup relationship management and was part of the founding team at BLOCKROCKET—the leading accelerator program for blockchain companies in Germany, Austria, and Switzerland. He completed a master's degree from TUM School of Management with stays abroad in Paris and Milan.

Esther Nagel worked as a research associate at the Professorship of Digital Services and Sustainability at the University of Munich's LMU School of Management (Prof. Dr. Johann Kranz). She holds master's degrees from the University of St. Gallen (HSG) and LMU School of Management and has further studied at Keio University, Tokyo, and LUISS Guido Carli University, Rome. She finished her doctoral studies in early 2021 and subsequently joined Munich Re Group's Department of Business Technology as a business analyst involved in various innovative digital projects and publications including the yearly *Tech Trend Radar*. Her research interest spans a range of topics related to blockchain technology applications, including token sales and blockchain-based business models. Striving to highlight socio-technical implications of blockchain technology, she also studied effects on property rights regimes. Her research was published repeatedly at the European Conference on Information Systems and in the journal *Business & Information Systems Engineering*.

Michelle Pfister is a graduate student in the field of information systems. She has worked as a research assistant with the Institute of Applied Computer Science and Formal Description Methods, Karlsruhe Institute of Technology, Germany, and as a research intern at the Computer Architecture and Security Lab, Yale University, USA. Her research interests include technical and political decentralization of distributed ledgers and cross-ledger interoperability.

James Allen Regenor is a serial entrepreneur, technologist, and futurist. He is a recognized SME in digital transformation in the aerospace, medical, and industrial verticals. He recently created The Salacia Project to restore vitality to marine ecosystems. In the spring of 2019, James unlocked the 4th Modality of Logistics…Digital…by merging 3D printing in a distributed edge network and Blockchain provenance. James created a digital commerce marketplace called VeriTX for the B2B supply chain interactions needed to power Industry 4.0. Previously, as Moog's Business Unit Director for Transformative Technologies, he was tasked with creating customer solutions for Industry 4.0 by leveraging Moog's converging Blockchain and 3D printing technologies. Prior to joining Moog, James completed 31 years of military service as a Colonel in the United States Air Force. He commanded at the group and squadron levels and held positions on the Joint Staff, Air Staff, and Strategic Command staffs. Additionally, he served in the White House, Executive Office of the President, as the Deputy Executive Secretary of the National Security Council for the Bush and Obama administrations. James was also an instructor and evaluator pilot with over 4200 hours in the C17, KC-135, T-38, T-37. He is also a Techstars 2020 Cohort member.

Ferdinand Regner is a doctoral candidate at University of Vienna in the Department of Computer Science. His research is focused on blockchain application architecture and engineering. Previously, he has published IS research in international conferences such as the International Conference of Information Systems (ICIS), the European Conference on Information Systems (ECIS), and the *Electronic Markets* (EM) journal.

Alexander Rieger is a research associate at the FINATRAX Research Group at the SnT, the Interdisciplinary Centre for Security, Reliability and Trust at the University of Luxembourg. He leads the scientific advisory team of the FLORA blockchain project of Germany's Federal Office for Migration and Refugees and acts as advisor to the European Blockchain Partnership and various public and private sector partners in Germany and Luxembourg. Prior to joining the SnT, he was the operational lead of the Fraunhofer Blockchain Lab and a doctoral candidate at the University of Bayreuth. Alex has spent several years working in industry and consulting. His research interests include innovative digital technologies such as blockchain, digital identities, and artificial intelligence and, more specifically, their design, governance, and strategic implications.

Philipp Sandner founded the Frankfurt School Blockchain Center. From 2018 to 2020, he was named one of the "Top 30" economists by the Frankfurter Allgemeine Zeitung (FAZ). In addition, he was among the "Top 40 under 40"—a ranking by the German business magazine Capital. Since 2017, he has been a member of the FinTech Council of the German Federal Ministry of Finance.

André Schweizer is the CEO of qbound and Research Fellow at the Centre for Blockchain Technologies at University College London. Previously, he was research assistant at the Fraunhofer FIT and the University of Bayreuth. He holds a PhD in Information Systems from the University of Bayreuth. His research interests include the economic and business implications of blockchain, technology, cryptocurrencies, and fintechs in the fields of Information Systems research. He serves as reviewer for various academic journals and conferences. His research has been published in renowned academic journals and in the proceedings of key international conferences such as the *Journal of Economics and Business*, the *International Conference on Information Systems* (ICIS), the *European Conference on Information Systems* (ECIS), and the *Americas Conference on Information Systems* (AMCIS).

Johannes Sedlmeir is a PhD candidate at the University of Bayreuth and a research assistant at the Project Group Business & Information Systems Engineering of the Fraunhofer Institute for Applied Information Technology (FIT). Before starting his PhD studies, he completed his bachelor's studies in Mathematics at the University of Augsburg and his master's degree in Theoretical and Mathematical Physics at the University of Munich. Johannes has advised several companies and public sector institutions on projects that involve blockchain technology and digital identity management. Accordingly, his research focuses on the adoption of distributed ledger technologies in sectors like energy, mobility, health, and e-government. In this context, he investigates challenges for using distributed ledger technologies from a performance and privacy perspective and designs innovative solutions based on cryptographic methods like zero-knowledge proofs. His research appears in international conferences and journals on the intersection between computer science and information systems research, like the Hawaii International Conference on System Sciences and Business & Information Systems Engineering.

Reilly Smethurst is a doctoral researcher from the FINATRAX Group at the University of Luxembourg. He was born in Australia and previously worked as a lecturer at the SAE Institute in Byron Bay. Reilly's early research publications are dedicated to music-mathematical theory. His research topics include tokenization for digital art and media, the governance of non-custodial financial services (nicknamed "DeFi") that are based on Ethereum, and verifiable credentials.

Ali Sunyaev is Professor of Computer Science at the Karlsruhe Institute of Technology, Germany. His research interests are complex information systems within the scope of information infrastructures, cloud computing services, distributed ledger technology, information privacy, auditing/certification of IT, digital health, and trustworthy AI. His research work accounts for the multifaceted use contexts of digital technologies with research on human behavior affecting information systems and vice versa. His research appeared in journals, including *ACM CSUR*, *JIT*, *JAIS*, *JMIS*, *IEEE TSE*, *IEEE TCC*, and *Communications of the ACM*.

Marinos Themistocleous is the Associate Dean of the School of Business, Director at the Institute For Future (IFF) and the scientific coordinator of the world leading Blockchain and Digital Currency MSc program at University of Nicosia. Before joining University of Nicosia, he worked for Brunel University, London, and University of Piraeus, Greece. He has held visiting positions at Bocconi University, Milan, and IE University, Madrid. He is a member of the Parallel Parliament of Cyprus and president of the Digital Economy and Digital Governance Committee. Marinos serves as advisor or consultant and has collaborated with many organizations in the United States, the United Kingdom, European Union, and United Arab Emirates in areas like blockchain, digital transformation, and information systems integration. His recent collaborations include the Cyprus House of Representatives, Cyprus National Betting Authority, and the NFT marketplace Galaxy of Art. He has authored more than 175 refereed journal and conference articles and 9 books and has received citations and awards of excellence. His research has attracted funding from various organizations. Marinos is on the editorial board of academic journals and conferences, and in the past, he served as managing editor of the *European Journal of Information Systems* (*EJIS*).

Horst Treiblmaier is Professor in International Management at Modul University Vienna, Austria. He received a PhD in Management Information Systems in 2001 from the WU Vienna and worked as a visiting professor at Purdue University, University of California, Los Angeles (UCLA), and the University of British Columbia (UBC). He has more than 20 years of experience as a researcher and consultant and has worked on projects with Microsoft, Google, and the UNIDO. His interests include the implications of blockchain technology, cryptoeconomics, and epistemological problems of social science research. He is a research associate at the UCL Centre for Blockchain Technologies of the University College London. His research has appeared in journals such as *Information Systems Journal, Structural Equation Modeling, The Data Base for Advances in Information Systems, Information & Management, Schmalenbach Business Review, Supply Chain Management: An International Journal*, and the *International Journal of Logistics Management*.

Nils Urbach is Professor of Information Systems, Digital Business & Mobility and Director of the Research Lab for Digital Innovation & Transformation at the Frankfurt University of Applied Sciences, Germany. Furthermore, he is the Co-Director of the FIM Research Center and the Project Group Business and Information Systems Engineering of Fraunhofer FIT as well as the Co-Founder and Director of the Fraunhofer Blockchain Lab. Nils has been working in the fields of strategic information management and collaborative information systems for several years. In his research, he focuses on digital transformation, managing AI, digital identities and blockchain, among others. His work has been published in renowned academic journals such as the *Journal of Strategic Information Systems, Journal of Information Technology, MIS Quarterly Executive, IEEE Transactions on Engineering Management, Information & Management*, and *Business & Information Systems Engineering*, as well as in the proceedings of key international conferences. Nils Urbach is strongly engaged in publicly and privately funded research projects. As a popular speaker, he regularly gives talks for specialists and managers on various aspects of digitalization, strategic IT management, as well as emerging technologies and its application.

Nikhil Vadgama is Assistant Professor of Financial Computing in the Department of Computer Science at University College London (UCL). He is also the Deputy Director of the UCL Centre for Blockchain Technologies and the Programme Director of the MSc Financial Technology at UCL. He teaches on multiple programs at the UCL Department of Computer Science, UCL School of Management, and Peking University. His research focuses on financial technology, decentralized finance, and applications of emerging digital technologies, particularly blockchain, across multiple industries. His experience spans the fintech, real estate, and investment banking sectors. He has worked with some of the largest organizations in the world, including consulting and facilitating innovation activities with Central Banks. He is the Chief Data Officer of a new sustainable challenger bank called Twig, where he helped them launch in the United Kingdom, European Union, and the United States in six months. He is the author of numerous research papers and industry reports and has authored the book *Enabling the Internet of Value: How Blockchain Connects Global Businesses*.

Jiahua Xu is Assistant Professor in Financial Computing at UCL, where she lectures Blockchain Technologies and Machine Learning in Finance. She is an award-winning researcher at the university's Centre for Blockchain Technologies and serves as Programme Director of the MSc Emerging Digital Technologies under the computer science department. Her research interests lie primarily in blockchain economics, behavioral finance, and risk management. She earned her PhD from the University of St. Gallen in Switzerland, MSc from the University of Mannheim in Germany, and BA from Fudan University in China. Prior to her current role at UCL, she performed research and teaching at various institutions, including EPFL, Imperial College London, London Business School, and Harvard Business School. Besides university engagements, she consults for a number of FinTech startups and works pro bono at a not-for-profit organization Development International e.V. which specializes in labor rights research.

Max Zheng is a blockchain enthusiast and Head of Corporate Development at Blockchain Founders Group. As Head of Corporate Development, he advises and builds blockchain startups dealing with digital assets, DLT, and enterprise blockchain integrations. Throughout his professional development, Max has acquired valuable insights about NFTs, tokenized real estate, and the DeFi segment. He also holds a degree from Frankfurt School of Finance and Management, one of the leading business schools in Europe. Combined with his knowledge and experience in managing blockchain-based startup teams, he is an expert in blockchain-related business opportunities and helps turn ideas into reality.

List of Figures

List of Tables

Introduction to the Token Economy

This book explores how innovations in blockchain technologies are creating the "token economy," a market whereby assets are represented by digital tokens, asset ownership is recorded on a distributed electronic ledger, value exchange is peer-to-peer and automated with decentralized computer programs called "smart contracts." The implications of the token economy are profound: imagine a world of true individual empowerment, whereby each person digitally controls their identities, credentials, work products, and assets. Envision all individuals having verifiable claims about their citizenship, education, and skills; unbanked people finally accessing cheap financial services; farmers reaping fair prices for their labors; artists earning the biggest share of fees for their creative works; innovators accessing liquid markets to fund new projects and startups; consumers and buyers having more choices, less friction, and lower transaction costs for their most expensive assets like real estate and insurance, to their least expensive assets, like lottery and event tickets. Moreover, the token economy will enable new incentive models for Environmental, Social, and Governance (ESG) conscious investors, consumers, governments, and enterprises.

The pivot to a "token economy" requires innovative solutions to some very old problems—like the avoidance of double-spending, identity management, credentials verification, asset tracking, bookkeeping, and creating a reliable medium of exchange (i.e., money)—as well as to newer problems like cybercrime. How can we mitigate counter-party risks, the risk each trading party bears that the other party will not fulfill its obligations? Blockchain technologies make the token economy possible. Before blockchains, we rely on centralized institutions such as banks, credit card companies, agents, and notaries to mitigate risks. After the introduction of blockchains, we rely on shared community governance and blockchain technologies to solve these problems. Decentralization is thus a fundamental attribute of the token economy (Tapscott & Tapscott, 2016; Lacity, 2020; Sunyaev et al., 2021).

Blockchain technologies have the potential to disrupt numerous industries, including credentials, energy, financial services, gaming, healthcare, insurance, real estate, supply chains, transportation, tourism, and also public governance (Treiblmaier & Beck, 2019a, 2019b). Indeed, for some services, disruption is already here. Decentralized finance (DeFi) is a perfect example. On public blockchains like Ethereum, people earn interest on their cryptoassets through lending, use cryptoassets for collateral to obtain loans, and place bets on the value of cryptoassets (i.e., derivatives). According to Statista (2021), the DeFi market held $US 70 billion worth of cryptocurrencies per month from November 2020 to May 2021. It reached $98 billion by September 2021 (DefiPulse, 2021; Marketforces Africa, 2021). Compared to the $95 trillion in stocks locked globally (Spendmenot, 2021), DeFi seems small, but it's clearly a new business model that has real advantages, such as not needing to open an investment account—users just download a digital wallet.

While blockchain technologies make the vision for the token economy possible, it will not happen automatically. If decentralization wins, centralized trusted third parties will lose. Disruption of economic and business models will be resisted by dominant individuals, organizations, and governments that fear loss of power, influence, and money. To survive in the token economy, executives from trusted third-party organizations will need to rethink their value-creating activities. Additionally, standards and regulations are desperately needed to keep pace with emerging technical capabilities. The potential business, economic, and social value of a token economy must be large enough to overcome these adoption barriers.

The future of the token economy will emerge based on the actions we take today as individuals, collectives, and societies. We invited foremost academics and practitioners who are leading the efforts to realize the full potential of a token economy. The authors in this collection contribute taxonomies, frameworks, projects, and case studies on the nascent but rapidly evolving token economy. They confirm one important insight, namely, that innovations do not happen in a vacuum; innovations happen by combining, extending, or departing from earlier innovations (Zur & Lacity, 2021). Even Bitcoin's creator, Satoshi Nakamoto (2008), synthesized several prior innovations, such as the idea of a public ledger for timestamping and record-keeping (Massias et al., 1999; Haber & Stornetta, 1991; Bayer et al., 1993; Dai, 1998); cryptographic Merkle trees for security (Merkle, 1980); digital currencies (Back, 2002); and proof-of-work consensus (Dwork & Naor, 1993). Nakamoto brought these prior inventions together to create a peer-to-peer payment application. Similarly, the authors in this collection are combining, extending, or departing from earlier innovations in the blockchain space.

Overview of the Chapters

This book features 13 chapters by 35 authors from both academia and the private sector. The common theme across these chapters is the potential for the token economy to disrupt existing markets. The specific markets examined in this collection include job markets, gaming, real estate, art and collectibles, insurance, fund-raising, and event ticketing. Additionally, the authors also explore entirely new markets for the "metaverse" and propose using non-fungible tokens (NFTs) to save the oceans (see Table I.1).

In Chap. 1, Philipp Lesche, Philipp Sandner, and Horst Treiblmaier develop a rich token taxonomy based on economic purpose, resulting in the categories of *payment tokens*, including pegged, unpegged, and other subcategories; *utility tokens*, including settlement, access, governance, ownership, and other subcategories; and *investment tokens*, including asset-backed, debt, equity, derivative, fund, and other subcategories. The authors also identify business, technical, and legal challenges and

Table I.1 Chapter overviews

Chapter	Topics	Research base
1	Token taxonomy and business, technical, and legal challenges and solutions	Analysis of 254 tokens; 15 expert interviews
2	Myths about blockchains; coopetition	Experience as Blockchain Strategist at FedEx; Chair of Blockchain in the Transport Alliance Standards Council
3	Technical and political decentralization for cross-ledger interoperability	Prior academic literature
4	Cryptoeconomics and governance frameworks	Research done at the Prysm Group
5	Self-sovereign identity and verifiable credentials in job markets and healthcare	Case studies and participant observation in standard-setting bodies
6	Metaverses	Analysis of existing blockchain-based metaverses
7	Asset tokenization of real estate	Twelve expert interviews and analyses of six existing real estate solutions
8	Asset tokenization of art and collectibles	Analysis and design science
9	Token-based insurance solutions	Analysis of six blockchain-based insurance solutions
10	Startup fund raising and token sales	Analysis of past sales
11	Safety and security; private capital markets	Design science
12	Event ticketing	Design science
13	Saving the oceans with NFTs	Design science

potential solutions of tokenization based on expert interviews. In summary they note, "The use of blockchain-based tokens to represent value is a comparatively new idea," and call for more rigorous research. We believe this collection meets that call.

In Chap. 2, readers will hear from one of the foremost practitioner leaders, namely, Dale Chrystie, Blockchain Strategist at FedEx and Chair of Blockchain in Transport Alliance (BiTA) Standards Council. Like many practitioners, Dale started down the route of private-permissioned blockchains but concluded that "consortia efforts will not effectively scale in global commerce due to the increasing level of friction they create." Instead, he now believes that "open is inevitable in the global commerce space." Dale summarizes the lessons he has learned about blockchains over the past few years in the form of dispelling several blockchain myths. These myths, while entertaining to read, suggest a serious route forward. He is a proponent of "coopetition," the idea that competitors should collaborate on shared ecosystem pain points, such as the amount of paperwork required to cross national borders. He also poses provocative ideas, such as the notion that customers of the future may be machines in addition to humans. Smart contracts, for example, might be the primary source of "customer" orders in the future. Most importantly, this chapter teaches readers how to talk about blockchains to the C-suite by focusing on the "why,", not the "what," "when," or "how" of blockchains. He concludes, "If we can't prove business value to the C-Suite, blockchain will remain a new, mysterious, and kind of scary new technology only understood by the R&D or Innovation group at the end of the hallway."

In this preface, we made the simple statement, "Decentralization is the fundamental attribute of the token economy." In Chap. 3, Michelle Pfister, Niclas Kannengießer, and Ali Sunyaev more deeply explore the benefits and challenges of decentralization and do so in a larger conversation about interoperability. The authors describe two types of decentralization in token economies: technical and political. Technical decentralization refers to the distribution of computer nodes in the network; political decentralization refers to the distribution of decision-making rights by humans. They examine three cross-ledger interoperability patterns (manual asset exchanges, notaries, and sidechains) based on degrees of technical and political decentralization and effectively argue that the trade-offs between technical and political decentralization vary based on the respective phase of development—blockchain projects that are still being developed face different trade-offs than established blockchain projects. The authors conclude, "Finding the optimal balance between technical and political centralization and decentralization is mainly determined by the degree to which governance should be automated."

Chapter 4, by Cathy Barrera and Stephanie Hurder, begins with the insight, "Blockchain platforms are mini economies written in code."

Bringing insights from the field of economics, along with their consulting work at the Prysm Group, the authors create a process guide and accompanying frameworks to design effective blockchain goverance models. Their comphrehensive House Framework covers value proposition, funding, incentive, tokenization, and governance layers. One of their most provocative insights is "Many people think that the main economic innovation of blockchain is the use of tokens. That is not true. Indeed, as we discuss in our Prysm Group House Framework, economically sound structuring of transactions, marketplaces, and information all contribute—along with token design—to the functioning of blockchain systems and the value that they deliver to users. A blockchain platform can create significant economic value without having a native token at all." These authors challenge us to think more deeply about the role of tokens in the token economy; it's the shared value creation that will drive organizational adoption.

In Chap. 5, Mary C. Lacity and Erran Carmel discussed self-sovereign identity (SSI), the idea that individuals should possess and control attestations made about them by issuers and, if they choose to do so, prove these attestations cryptographically to verifiers. In addition to user control and digitally verifiable credentials, SSI's design principles also include identity binding, privacy and security, availability to all, interoperability across platforms, data minimization, and transparency about data creation, collection, and use. Many standards-making bodies, open-source working groups, and organizations are working on the key elements to make SSI a reality, such as decentralized identifiers, SSI digital wallets, and trust registries. The authors investigate early applications for job skills and digital health passes and show that early applications meet some, but not yet all, of SSI's principles. They conclude, "Today, verifiable credentials rely on trusted third parties for network services. Interoperability standards, user-generated identifiers, and utility tokens are not yet advanced enough for wide-scale adoption. However, we can more easily see the possibilities."

In Chap. 6, Klitos Christodoulou, Leonidas Katelaris, Marinos Themistocleous, Panayiotis Christodoulou, and Elias Iosif invite readers into the future world of the metaverse, where augmented, virtual, and physical realities converge. This chapter epitomizes our conjecture that innovations happen by combining and extending earlier innovations. The authors show that the metaverse will combine wearable augmented and virtual devices, IoT, holograms, high-bandwidth networks, distributed computing, and data management based on tokenization, distributed ledgers, and peer-to-peer storage networks. The authors analyze six nascent metaverses: Decentraland, The Sandbox, Somnium Space, Cryptovoxels, Axie Infinity, and Neon District, including the launch date, tokens used, blockchains used, and size of the community. They also identify essential features of a metaverse: realism, ubiquity, interoperability, scalability, tokenization, and liquid identity and conclude, "Although we cannot predict whether and when this vision will reach maturity, several downstream technologies are pushing for its evolution."

Moving from the virtual world to the real world, Max Zheng and Philipp Sandner investigate asset tokenization of real estate in Chap. 7. Real estate markets are a major blockchain use case because of its high value—the value of all real estate is estimated to be $280 trillion worldwide (Syrios, 2021)—and because of its high transaction costs, complexity, and existing corruption. The authors analyze six real estate tokenization companies in Europe (Bloxxter, Crowdlitoken, Exporo, Finexity, iFunded/iEstate, and KlickOwn) and seven single asset and entity tokenization projects. Based on expert interviews, they discuss the timing, importance, risks, and benefits of tokenized real estate. From a business perspective, they predict that markets will be disrupted and tokenization increasingly will be used to fractionalize real estate investments. The authors conclude, "The idea of fractionalizing an asset can create greater accessibility to investors because the digital asset itself has no limit to how small it can be fractionalized or by whom it can be acquired. In fact, the buyer could be a low-income individual based in Asia who could buy tokenized asset-backed real estate in Liechtenstein. Thus, with greater accessibility comes greater liquidity, at least, in theory."

Chapter 8 also addresses the use of tokens to fractionalize assets, but in the context of art and collectibles. Tom Barbereau, Johannes Sedlmeir, Reilly Smethurst, Gilbert Fridgen, and Alexander Rieger compare two options for the fractional ownership of physical artworks and collectibles, namely, (1) securitized fractions traded via a company-owned exchange and (2) tokenized fractions traded using a public ledger. The authors note the conflicting values between regulators who want transparency/auditability and individuals who want privacy. The authors design a technical stack to get the balance right and propose that zero-knowledge proofs enable selective disclosure. They foresee the disruption of art and collectible intermediaries and conclude, "DLT offers investors and creators of artworks and collectibles the unique opportunity to exit single-provider, proprietary systems and to interact with global stakeholders from previously disparate, closed systems."

Like real estate, the global insurance market is huge ($5.8 trillion in 2020, according to GlobalNewsWire) and suffers from high transaction costs, fraud, and complexity. Simon Cousaert, Nikhil Vadgama, and Jiahua Xu examine tokenization in the context of insurance in Chap. 9. In this context, blockchains and tokenization have the potential to transfer risk more efficiently, transparently, and securely, as well as increase customization and agility. The authors describe the use of payment, insurance, and governance tokens to meet these objectives. They analyze three decentralized insurance protocols (Nexus Mutual, Etherisc, and inSure) and three insurance-related solutions (fidentiaX, Opyn, and Backd). They, too, foresee the disruption and conclude, "despite being at a nascent stage, the token-based insurance space bears the promise to unseat the incumbent players with more use cases being explored and more user activities."

In Chap. 10, Esther Nagel and Johann Kranz revisit the important topic of blockchain token sales. The first token sales were called Initial Coin Offerings (ICOs), in which the investors bought the tokens, but not the ownership shares, in a company or project. Mastercoin was the first ICO, which raised $5.5 million in 2014, and Ethereum was the second, raising $18 million in 2014 (Griffith, 2017). When regulators around the world started intervening, the ICO market fell precipitously. Where is the market today and where is it headed? The authors answer these questions by identifying seven benefits of token sales, the phases of token sales, new forms of token sales (IEOs, STOs, and IDOs), and the challenges and solutions to building trust when selling tokens to raise funds. They conclude, "We observe that, while the hype surrounding token sales has stalled, they are prospering in regulated forms … Token sales provide a largely disintermediated funding mechanism that could diminish barriers inherent to traditional venture financing and other types of investment. Many regard token sales as a democratization of venture funding and advancement of crowdfunding since investors can participate in projects with little means and supervision."

Blockchain technologies are seen as inherently secure, in part, due to decentralization. In Chap. 11, Daniel Conway, Kiran Garimella, and Oscar A. Jofre deeply explore the challenges of and solutions to designing safe and secure blockchain ecosystems. The authors distinguish the centralization/decentralization of control and the localized/distributed location of nodes. They identify the requirements for safe and secure blockchain ecosystems and illustrate how they can be met with a live blockchain ecosystem called the KoreConX All-in-One. KoreConX is a blockchain-enabled solution that provides private companies access to global capital markets. The platform has been in production since December 2016, and the corresponding blockchain (KoreChain) was launched in October 2019. By summer of 2020, KoreConX had 75,000 private companies on the platform, 1.2 billion shares, 32 million options, and 1.2 million warrants. It is deployed in 23 countries on five different cloud platforms. The solution is built on Hyperledger Fabric, a private-permissioned protocol. The authors conclude that, as of 2021, "Permissioned blockchains are in a position to architect their blockchain applications to meet the unique needs of their digital ecosystems. Since such flexibility is inexpensively available within permissioned blockchains, digital business ecosystems are advised to design their blockchain applications by using the framework we present for a comprehensively safe and secure digital ecosystem that is trusted by all of its participants."

While previous chapters have shown the benefits of blockchain technologies for assets of considerable value like real estate, investment, and insurance, Chap. 12 shows that benefits also apply to lower value products like event tickets. Ferdinand Regner, André Schweizer, and Nils Urbach designed an event ticketing system because these markets are also wrought with fraud, counterfeiting, limited control over secondary transactions, and substantial reliance on trusted third parties. Their solution is built on Ethereum using NFTs. They share the practical challenges and design solutions to create a functional system and point out that "NFTs can help to overcome the weaknesses of existing non-blockchain event ticketing systems, such as susceptibility to fraud, lack of control over secondary market transactions and validation of ownership."

In the final chapter, James Allen Regenor and Eric D. Achtmann propose NFTs to help save the oceans by changing human behavior through positive incentives. The authors designed, built, and will launch the Salacia Project in early 2022. The project is named after Salacia, the Roman goddess of the seas. The solution uses NFTs of marine animals to fund research, innovation, and existing projects and to award prizes for saving oceans. Figure I.1 is an example; it is an NFT of a manatee. The authors donated the NFT to a student who won a blockchain trivia contest sponsored by the Blockchain Center of Excellence at the University of Arkansas in Fall of 2021. Like CryptoKitties, Salacia's NFTs are designed to be cute collectibles that will be valued by holders.

Fig. I.1 One of the Salacia Project's first NFTs

The authors state, "There are many examples of wicked problems being solved when a community unites to tackle them … The Salacia Project is one small effort to raise awareness, fund BlueTech and provide a venue for people, corporations, and governments to make a difference as they answer the call to action."

As the last contribution in this book, we include an overview of blockchain technologies in the Appendix. For readers new to blockchains, this overview aims to quickly bring readers up to speed so they can understand and enjoy the innovations described by authors of this collection.

Conclusion

By the end of the book, we will have succeeded as editors and authors if the readers' thoughts, emotions, and curiosities are heightened. Readers who are currently providing trusted third-party services rightly might be threatened by the coming token economy, but with knowledge comes choice. Those readers should next ask, "What new value can my organization add to the token economy?" This is a question often posed by Dale Chrystie, the author of Chap. 2. Also, the deeper conversations on decentralization and dispersion in Chaps. 3 and 11 show that decentralization comes with significant challenges that might result in the need for centralized services for certain use cases. Certainly, prior research has borne this out for enterprise adoptions as of 2021; trusted third parties (TTP) still exist after blockchains, but they perform different services than before blockchains. For example, TTPs now manage network services such as operating network nodes, protecting digital wallets on behalf of clients, enforcing access rules set up by members, and managing software updates, but no longer need them to validate transactions (Lacity & Van Hoek, 2021).

Beyond the losses from disruption, we hope the majority of readers feel inspired by the possibilities of the coming token economy. It's a beautiful vision of individual empowerment, inclusion, privacy, security, and trust. We can more efficiently use our planet's natural resources and distribute wealth more equitably. Our final thought is to encourage readers to join communities that are working on these innovations to make the world a better place; the future is not predestined, but rather emerges from the actions we take today.

Fayetteville, AR — Mary C. Lacity
Vienna, Austria — Horst Treiblmaier

References

Back, A. (2002). Hashcash—a denial of service counter-measure. http://www.hashcash.org/papers/hashcash.pdf

Bayer, D., Haber, S., Stornetta, W. (1993). Improving the efficiency and reliability of digital time-stamping, in Sequences II: Methods in Communication, Security and Computer Science, 329–334.

Dai, W. (1998). b-money. http://www.weidai.com/bmoney.txt

DefiPulse. (2021). Total Value Locked in DeFi. Retrieved October 20, 2021 from https://defipulse.com/

Dwork, C., & Naor, M. (1993). Pricing via processing: Combatting Junk Mail. Retrieved September 18, 2021 from http://www.hashcash.org/papers/pvp.pdf

Haber, S., & Stornetta, W. (1991). How to time-stamp a digital document. *Journal of Cryptology, 3*(2), 99–111.

Global NewsWire. (2021). Global insurance industry Almanac 2021: Market share, market size value 2016–20, and forecast to 2025. Retrieved October 18, 2021 from https://www.globenewswire.com/en/news-release/2021/05/04/2221983/28124/en/Global-Insurance-Industry-Almanac-2021-Market-Share-Market-Size-Value-2016-20-and-Forecast-to-2025.html

Griffith, E. (2017, May 5). Why startups are trading IPOs for ICOS. *Fortune Magazine*, http://fortune.com/2017/05/05/ico-initial-coin-offering/

Lacity, M. (2020). *Blockchain foundations for the internet of value*. Epic Books/University of Arkansas Press.

Lacity, M., & Van Hoek, R. (2021). What we've learned so far about blockchain for business. *Sloan Management Review*, 63(3), 48–54.

Marketforces Africa. (2021, September 28). DeFi market size soared 335% to $85 Billion. Retrieved October 16, 2021 from https://dmarketforces.com/defi-market-size-soared-335-to-85-billion/

Massias, H., Avila, X., & Quisquater, J.-J. (1999). Design of a secure time-stamping service with minimal trust requirements. In *20th Symposium on Information Theory in the Benelux*, May.

Merkle, R. (1980). Protocols for public key cryptosystems. In *Proceedings 1980 Symposium on Security and Privacy* (pp. 122–133). IEEE Computer Society.

Nakamoto, S. (2008). Bitcoin: *A peer-to-peer electronic cash system*. https://bitcoin.org/bitcoin.pdf

Spendmenot. (2021). Stock market statistics to know in 2021. Retrieved October 20, 2021 from https://spendmenot.com/blog/stock-market-statistics/

Statista. (2021). Amount of cryptocurrency held in decentralized finance, or DeFi, worldwide from August 2017 to May 28, 2021. Retrieved August 14, 2021 from https://www.statista.com/statistics/1237821/defi-market-size-value-crypto-locked-usd/

Sunyaev, A., Kannengießer, N., Beck, R., Treiblmaier, H., Lacity, M., Kranz, J., Fridgen, G., Spankowski, U., & Luckow, A. (2021). Token economy. *Business & Information Systems Engineering, 63*, 457–478. https://doi.org/10.1007/s12599-021-00684-1

Syrios, A. (2021). Here's what $280 trillion of real estate looks like. Retrieved October 18, 2021 from https://www.biggerpockets.com/blog/visualizing-280-trillion-real-estate

Tapscott, D., & Tapscott, A. (2016). *The blockchain revolution: How the technology behind bitcoin is changing money, business, and the world*. Portfolio/Penguin.

Treiblmaier, H., & Beck, R. (2019a). *Business transformation through blockchain—Volume I*. Palgrave Macmillan, ISBN 978-3-319-98911-2. https://doi.org/10.1007/978-3-319-98911-2

Treiblmaier, H., & Beck, R. (2019b). *Business transformation through blockchain—Volume II*. Palgrave Macmillan, ISBN 978-3-319-99058-3. https://doi.org/10.1007/978-3-319-99058-3

Zur, C., & Lacity, M. (2021). The emergence of web 3.0: Tokenization and the internet of value, blockchain center of excellence white paper, University of Arkansas. https://cpb-us-e1.wpmucdn.com/wordpressua.uark.edu/dist/5/444/files/2018/01/BCoE2021_02_POST.pdf

1

Implications of the Token Economy: A Taxonomy and Research Agenda

Philipp Lesche, Philipp Sandner, and Horst Treiblmaier

Introduction

Distributed ledger technology and blockchains as a subset of the former[1] have a substantial impact on the economy by transforming industry sectors and organizational functions such as finance, marketing logistics, energy, tourism, and public administration, just to name a few (Rejeb

[1] In the remainder of the paper, we use the term blockchain to denote all kinds of distributed ledger technologies independent of their underlying data structure.

P. Lesche
Bayerisches Staatsministerium für Digitales, Munich, Germany
e-mail: lesche.philipp@gmail.com

P. Sandner
Blockchain Center, Frankfurt School of Finance & Management gGmbH, Frankfurt am Main, Germany
e-mail: p.sandner@fs.de

H. Treiblmaier (✉)
School of International Management, Modul University Vienna, Vienna, Austria
e-mail: horst.treiblmaier@modul.ac.at

M. C. Lacity, H. Treiblmaier (eds.), *Blockchains and the Token Economy*, Technology, Work and Globalization, https://doi.org/10.1007/978-3-030-95108-5_1

et al., 2020; Treiblmaier & Beck, 2019a, 2019b). Furthermore, immutable, shared, and programmable data structures lead to new forms of governance that fundamentally transform decision rights, accountability, and incentives within and beyond company borders (Beck et al., 2018) and create numerous areas of interest for information systems researchers (Risius & Spohrer, 2017). An especially important use case in this context is corporate finance, in which blockchain enables an alternative form of financing that, similar to crowd investing, opens capital markets to small investors, making it easy for them to divide their assets and sell them as tokens. A *token* in the context of blockchain is defined as "a unit of value issued by a tech or crypto start-up, intended to be a piece in the ecosystem of their technology platform or project" (BitcoinWiki, 2018). *Token sales*, also referred to as token offerings, denote a sales period in which a number of crypto tokens are offered to the public, typically in exchange for major cryptocurrencies or increasingly also fiat money. These tokens can fulfill different purposes, resulting in different forms of tokens, namely, payment tokens, utility tokens, and security tokens.

The first so-called initial coin offering (ICO) was carried out in 2013 by Mastercoin (now: Omni Layer), building on Bitcoin's blockchain and enriching the features of the original cryptocurrency. However, it was not until around 2017 that the market gained traction. According to strategy& (2019), 1753 ICOs took place until the end of 2018. In that year alone, 1132 projects raised a total amount of $19.7bn. However, many token offerings failed or intentionally deceived their investors, and only about one-third of all announced offerings successfully developed their projects (strategy&, 2018). In order to overcome the shortcomings of the largely unregulated ICOs, security token offerings (STOs) were introduced, offering a better compliance with existing securities regulation. These offerings have the potential to significantly transform the economy with implications that go far beyond the financial sector. Within organizations, STOs allow for the seamless connection of the financial system and the STO blockchain (Laskowski et al., 2019) and, from an overarching perspective, might impact the current economy as a whole.

Though token-based fundraising is not yet economically relevant in terms of its overall market capitalization, ICOs and STOs quickly gained importance due to their potential to change corporate finance with far-reaching ramifications. Security tokens are increasingly seen as an alternative to traditional debt or equity fundraising as performed today by venture capital (VC) or private equity (PE) firms and banks. Furthermore, they lay the foundation for a wide range of applications beyond finance. Due to the increasing interest from the industry and in light of the current regulation of the whole crypto ecosystem, the question arises how the future token landscape will look like and what implications it will have. In this paper, we thus investigate the following research questions:

- How will token offerings impact the economy
  - from a business point of view?
  - from a technical point of view?
  - from a legal point of view?

Literature Review

Token-based systems have preceded the rise of blockchain technology by centuries. Tokens were used to count, store, and communicate information representing different forms of economic value. A very early example of the use of token are clay coins. In the early agricultural societies, people exchanged these coins for goods and services, which marked the development from simple barter systems to more complex economies (Schmandt-Besserat & Hallo, 1992). More current examples for tokens include casino chips, bonus points in an airline loyalty program, or entry tokens for a skiing resort represented by a card worn in a jacket. In fields such as psychiatry, clinical psychology, and education, for several decades the term *token economy* has been used to denote operant techniques in treatment and education, with the goal to achieve a certain target behavior (Kazdin, 1977). Carton and Schweitzer (1996), for example, illustrate how a token (i.e., reward) system can be used to reduce noncompliant behavior of a young patient.

Tokens in the Blockchain Economy

In the context of blockchain and DLT research, a commonly accepted definition for "token economy" is still missing. Previous research has identified several constituting features such as reward-based designs, consideration of token issuance, compensation for participation, and users' ongoing service engagement (Lee, 2019). We thus define "token economy" to be an *"incentive system based on cryptocurrencies with the goal to achieve desired behaviors using blockchain (DLT)."* In a nutshell, tokens and blockchain technology are combined to securely, economically, and efficiently trade assets of value.

The changes brought about by the token economy are manifold (Sunyaev et al., 2021; Treiblmaier, 2021). The financial industry can be seen at the forefront of a far-reaching evolution in which assets are tokenized and exchanged between peers, which can potentially trigger substantial structural changes in business and the economy as such (Clohessy et al., 2020). In a narrower sense, the process of fundraising for companies is streamlined and simplified. This especially pertains to the (partial) substitution of venture capital by token sales. Kranz et al. (2019), for example, outline the different stages of a token sale and suggest a comprehensive research agenda. Adhami et al. (2018) specifically investigate companies' motivations to use token sales for raising money and elaborate on the success factors of this process. Similarly, Fisch (2019) scrutinizes the applicability of ICOs to finance new ventures. Recently, tokens, token sales, and the token economy were identified as topics of interest for academia within the bigger framework of blockchain-induced transformation. This includes the identification of design processes of token economy models (Kim & Chung, 2019) as well as the envisioning of a new business ecosystem that provides the legal and institutional basis for a future token economy (Lee, 2019). This development is fueled by several major trends consisting of platform business models, peer-to-peer networks, open innovation, and crowdfunding (Tasca, 2019).

The Token Landscape

Blockchain tokens are built on top of existing blockchains. Beside currencies, they can represent a wide range of assets (Chen, 2018). Previous research has contributed to a greater understanding of token design by categorizing tokens and distinguishing them along a few dimensions that represent token attributes (Euler, 2018). Oliveira et al. (2018), for example, suggested thirteen token parameters, describing the token along with its attributes. Those parameters are class, function, role, representation, supply, incentive system, spendability, tradeability, burnability, expirability, fungibility, layer, and chain.

We distinguish tokens based on the class parameter that divides tokens into three different types: payment tokens, utility tokens, and investment tokens. Payment token, or virtual currency, is a digital representation of value that is not created by a central bank or public authority and does not have to be linked to legal tender, but is accepted as a means of payment (European Banking Authority, 2014). Utility token provides access to a certain product or service and can act as a means of exchange within a certain community (International Token Standardization Association, 2019). In the case of investment token, the emitter issues a token with security-related characteristics. According to the Security Token Standard (2019), these tokens are designed to represent complete or fractional ownership interests in assets and/or entities, and they face several restrictions with regard to jurisdiction, asset category, or identity.

Token offerings democratize the process of fundraising since entrepreneurs are not restricted to specific regions and investors. In traditional fundraising, only professional and accredited investors have exclusive access to early-stage projects. Similar to crowdfunding, token offerings are open to potential investors all over the world, with Internet access being the only prerequisite. Consequently, the reach is bigger than the reach of traditional fundraising means (Chen, 2018), and investors benefit from having access to a highly liquid asset. Tokens can be traded at an exchange and swapped against other cryptocurrencies, in which case they are called "fungible tokens." The invested amount is not locked in equity, but easily tradeable and monetizable by investors without having to wait for the next funding round (Kastelein, 2017). In case of an ICO, one of the biggest advantages for ventures as compared to traditional fundraising is the fact that commonly no equity shares are issued and that there are no special rights, which are common for VC investments (Hahn & Wons, 2018).

An advantage for early-stage start-ups is the support of the crowd that invested in the venture. The buyers of the tokens are often also the initial customers, using their tokens to pay for the product or service of the venture. Based on their early experiences, ventures have the chance to adapt

Table 1.1 Features of token offerings

Token Offering	
Advantages	Disadvantages
✓ Wide reach thanks to digital acquisition of token buyers ✓ Not necessarily a sale of equity ✓ Quick realization of fundraising, faster than traditional means ✓ Token buyers invest based on their product interest ✓ Liquid asset ✓ Reduction of costs for issuance ✓ Cost-efficient trading ✓ 24/7 trading	– Volatility of tokens – Problem of scams – Risk associated with cyberattacks or money laundering – Unclear regulations

Source: Hahn and Wons (2018); Sandner et al. (2019)

their business to find the perfect fit between product and market. This opens up the possibility of building a supportive community around the project which fosters credibility and gains initial traction (Bussgang & Nanda, 2018; Howell et al., 2020). Furthermore, token offerings are usually performed faster than comparable traditional fundraising methods. Table 1.1 summarizes the advantages and disadvantages of token offerings as fundraising mechanisms from a company perspective. In the following sections, we discuss the use and the implications of tokens within an economy.

Methodology

In this paper, we apply a mixed-methods approach and combine the analysis of quantitative data from a comprehensive token database with qualitative findings from expert interviews. This approach is common in IS research to create and validate frameworks (Venkatesh et al., 2013). More specifically, we followed the guidelines from Nickerson et al. (2009) on how to create a taxonomy. In our case, the classification was done based on existing literature, token data, and excerpts from the interviews. First, we gathered quantitative token information from TOKENBASE containing data on more than 800 cryptographic tokens from over 30 exchanges. TOKENBASE builds upon the International Token Classification (ITC) using the International Token Identification Number

(ITIN) and offers extensive time series data of the most important cryptographic tokens that are identified through an ITIN and classified in the ITC. This quantitative data set allowed us to assess the market size of the token economy as well as the relative importance of different token types.

Second, based on the literature review, we designed a questionnaire in a stepwise manner to better understand the implications of the token economy. The aim of the initial step was to collect a multitude of questions in an open brainstorming session, followed by a thorough assessment of their applicability and appropriateness. Finally, the questions were divided into different subject areas and subsumed into lead questions. The final interview guideline can be found in the appendix. In total, we conducted qualitative interviews with 15 industry experts that provided in-depth insights into their underlying motives and expectations. The interviews were designed and conducted as expert interviews based on guiding questions, as shown in the appendix. We selected experts from different areas in our field of interest. The fact that a selected person represents an organization or a company was more important than the person himself (Flick, 2014). Our sample included investors financing start-ups and projects and therefore knowledgeable when it comes to investment terms, processes, and requirements. Legal experts were interviewed to better understand the legal structure and implications of the token economy. Finally, issuers of security tokens and their respective consultants were also included in the sample to better understand the company perspective. Overall, we interviewed fifteen experts—twelve of them via phone and three during a personal meeting.

The interviews were evaluated according to the approach of Mayring (2010), called comprehensive content analysis. In a first step, the individual interviews were transcribed, followed by eliminating all noncontent-bearing text components and the paraphrasing of the significant passages. In a following step, the paraphrased text sections were generalized to a comparable level of abstraction. The generalization was followed by a first reduction, whereby text sections with identical meanings were consolidated. In a second round of reduction, all relevant passages were condensed and integrated, and clusters of related topics were created.

Results

The analysis of the expert interviews revealed three major themes when it comes to transformations induced by token offerings. The first one pertains to the economic purpose of the offering. A multitude of different token types exist that were designed for different purposes. It is therefore not only the case that tokens substitute existing methods of corporate finance, but numerous other use cases exist, which can be supported or newly created through utility, payment, or investment tokens. This classification follows a commonly accepted taxonomy that differentiates between cryptocurrencies that are used as a means of payment, tokens that grant access to applications or services, and, finally, tokens which have a similar role as shares and represent debt or equity security (Tasca, 2019). The second major theme that emerged includes the stakeholders and their respective roles. Existing intermediaries might be substituted, and new functions might emerge as a result of the blockchain's innovative and disruptive capabilities. It is thus crucial to closely investigate and describe the newly defined roles of companies, investors, and intermediaries. Finally, the respective perspective of the stakeholders emerged as a major topic. The implications of token offerings yield a multitude of (partly) conflicting opinions depending on whether the reference point is business, technology, or legislation. These three viewpoints emerged as the result of the clustering of the experts' statements, and each of them simultaneously induces numerous challenges (i.e., obstacles that token offerings can bring about) but also a multitude of potential solutions for existing problems. Figure 1.1 shows a taxonomy in which we summarize the aforementioned major topics (i.e., economic purpose, stakeholder, perspective) as well as the challenges and solutions that arise in case a specific perspective is taken. In the following sections, we discuss the respective parts of the taxonomy in more detail.

Economic Purpose

Our quantitative sample includes the 259 highest valued tokens from the TOKENBASE database as of April 2019 (International Token Standardization Association, 2019). A validation check revealed that five

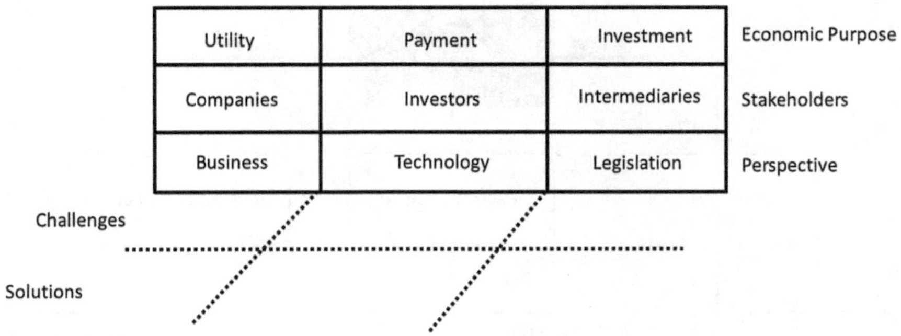

Fig. 1.1 A taxonomy for the token economy

tokens were no longer in existence, and therefore the subsequent analysis is based on 254 tokens. This data set covers 98.8% of the total market capitalization, therefore reflecting almost the total token market. The market capitalization of the 254 tokens included in the ITSA data set was $176.073bn as compared to a market capitalization according to CoinMarketCap.com of $178.257bn. According to ITSA, tokens can be clustered into three different categories: utility token, payment token, and investment token (see Fig. 1.2), the latter of which corresponds to asset/debt token. In terms of numbers, utility tokens constitute the major part (80.7%, n = 205), followed by payment tokens (16.1%, n = 41) and investment tokens (3.1%, n = 8). When it comes to market share, payment tokens have the largest capitalization (62.9%, $110.71bn) followed by utility tokens (37.0%, $65.53bn) and investment tokens (0.1%, $0.13bn). As can be seen in Fig. 1.2, utility tokens can be further divided into five categories. By far the most common token are settlement tokens, which, according to ITSA's token classification, are designed to enable the settlement of transactions, such as the purchase of goods or services in a third-party ecosystem. They represent 71.3% of all tokens with a market capitalization of 35.7% ($62.85bn). Access tokens, which offer the right to use certain services, goods, or resources being offered in the environment that the token was created for, are the second most common utility token representing 5.1% of all tokens. Six tokens in our sample can be classified as governance tokens, having a share of 2.4% of all tokens. These tokens offer rights to participate in the governance of the

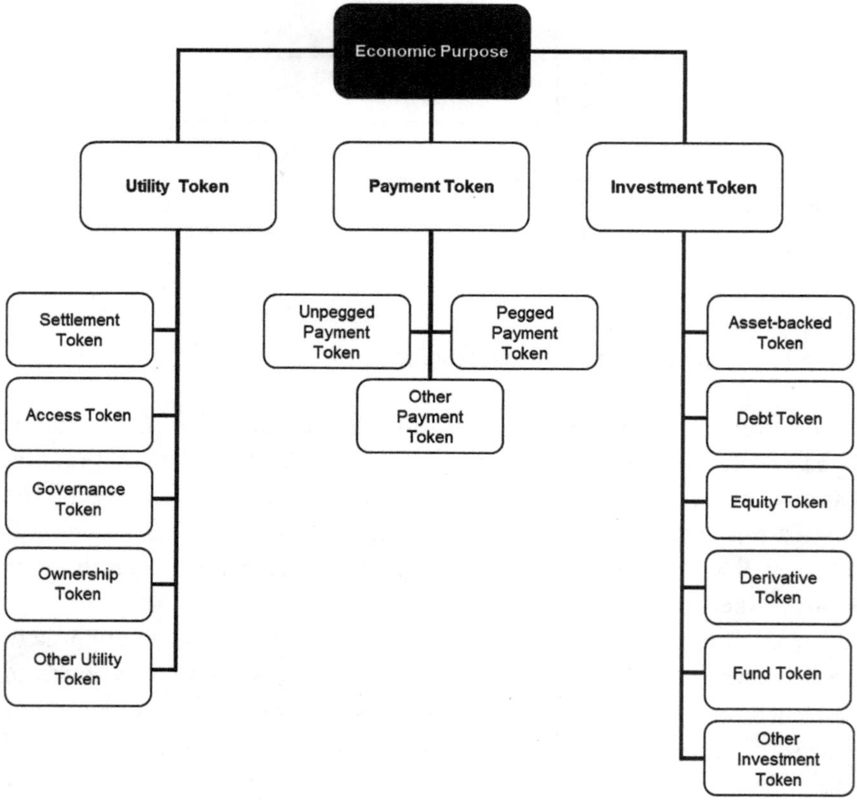

Fig. 1.2 Tokens by economic purpose

environment that the token was created for, such as voting rights. Only 1.2% (n = 3) of all tokens can be classified as ownership tokens with the purpose of managing and transferring the ownership of material or immaterial goods, and two further tokens could not be classified into any of the existing categories.

Payment tokens can be further divided into three different categories: A pegged payment token constitutes a token whose value is intended to remain stable over time in order to better fulfill the classic functions of money as compared to unpegged payment tokens. Pegged payment tokens, which are mostly pegged to a fiat currency, constitute 14.6% of all payment tokens and 2.4% of all tokens. An unpegged payment token's value is determined through supply and demand on the market and thus floats freely over time. Unpegged tokens constitute the biggest payment token category with 85.4% of all payment tokens and 13.8% of all tokens. In terms of market capitalization, unpegged payment tokens have by far the biggest capitalization ($108.33bn, 61.5%) of all tokens. This is mainly due to Bitcoin, which alone has a total market capitalization of 52.5%. In contrast, pegged payment tokens have a market capitalization of $2.38bn, which amounts to a total share of 1.4%. As of 2019, asset/debt tokens only account for 3.1% ($n = 8$) of the total number of tokens and 0.1% ($0.131bn) of the total market capitalization. They can be classified into six categories: asset-backed token, debt token, derivative token, equity token, fund token, and several other tokens which do not fall into one of the aforementioned categories. To date, most investment tokens are debt tokens ($n = 4$), and only one asset-backed token, equity token, derivate token, and fund token exist. In spite of the small number of investment tokens in existence, the expert interviews revealed a huge potential of this token type, which necessitates a further distinction between debt and equity tokens.

An equity security represents an ownership share in a company or in an entity. The holder of the shares has the right to receive a certain amount of the company's earnings, in proportion to the number of owned shares. The most common type of an equity security is the common stock. Furthermore, in case of liquidation, this type of stock gives the right to a share of the residual value of the issuing company. Besides the common stock, there is also the preferred stock. This type is not so common; it provides the holder with a periodic dividend payment but also has other rights that give it a priority over the common stock. Like other types of equity securities, there are also so-called stock options and warrants. Both grant the right to acquire shares at a certain price over a predefined period of time. Other aspects, besides dividend payments, that come with equity securities are control and voting rights. Shareholders have different levels of voting rights in certain matters, like the appointment of a board of directors that should then act on behalf of the shareholders. Equity tokens, therefore, represent an equity position in an underlying asset. The holder of a token that comes in the form of a common stock, therefore, has the same rights as the holder of a traditional stock. The main difference between traditional shares and equity tokens is that the latter records ownership on a blockchain, while traditional stocks are stored in a centralized database and, occasionally, come with a paper certificate. Similar to traditional shares, equity tokens can be divided into common equity tokens or preferred equity tokens. In Germany, a popular form of an equity token is the profit participation right in which the investor participates in profits as well as in losses of the company.

In contrast, a debt security is a debt instrument which represents money that is borrowed by the company and which defines the notional amount, the interest rate, and the maturity as well as the renewal date. Typical debt securities are loans, bonds, certificates of deposit, or collateralized securities such as collateralized mortgage obligations. In general, the holder of debt securities receives a regular payment of interest and the repayment of principal on a specified date or dates. At the end of the term, debt securities can be redeemed by the issuing party. Furthermore, there is the possibility to secure debt, backed by collateral, or to have unsecured debt. In consequence, if the issuing company faces bankruptcy, some types of debt securities are prioritized as compared to other subordinated debt securities. Thus, debt tokens are tokenized assets that represent debt securities that are recorded on the blockchain through a smart contract or a simple ledger format. When setting up a debt token, the underlying smart contract needs to include all terms such as the repayment terms and the need to consider the risk factors of the underlying debt. Table 1.2 contrasts equity tokens and debt tokens.

Stakeholders

The experts pointed out that a token economy will lead to substantial changes in the existing roles and responsibilities of stakeholders, as shown in Fig. 1.3. Most importantly, token sales in the future will change the current financing life cycle of companies, with every stage and stakeholder having their own roles and characteristics. This also includes external consultants who understand the functioning, potentials, and risks of tokens as well as different types of investors who have special requirements that can be served with specialized tokens.

Table 1.2 Comparison of investment tokens (DLT Capital GmbH, 2019)

Criteria	Equity	Debt
Investment instrument	Share (common; preferred), silent partnership, profit participation right	Shareholder loan, venture loan, bonds
Legal position of capital provider	Owner (e.g., shareholder, limited partner)	Subordinated, after creditors like banks, suppliers, or state but before owners
Maximum (Minimum) STO size	€100k[a]/ < €8m (in GER) (€100k)	€2.5m[a] (in GER) (€100k)
Maximum investment amount for private persons[b]	€10,000	€10,000
Payment claim	Performance-based, subordinated claim on profit participation	(Not) performance-based, subordinated claim on profit and predetermined payment
Time horizon	Unlimited or until exit (3–8 years)	(Un-)Limited term or until exit (4–8 years)
Participation and voting rights	Yes, according to voting share	Usually not, unless it is a matter of continuation
Tax burden	Profit tax on the profit of investment	Interest cost is tax-deductible

[a]prospect-free offerings
[b]In accordance with regulatory protection for retail investors

Equity tokens are predicted to become the most important token type for start-ups. At the moment, mainly profit participation rights are represented with equity tokens, which will change in the future when more versatile equity instruments are deployed on blockchain. Today, equity instruments represent ownership interests entitled to dividend payments, but with improving blockchain technology and especially the proliferation of advanced smart contracts, more rights can be tokenized. For corporates, equity and debt tokens present different means of financing. In comparison to start-ups, companies with an existing track record can also raise capital via debt financing instruments. While equity tokens are a risky investment in a company that allows to participate in future growth, debt tokens are more stable, easier to regulate, and expected to gain a

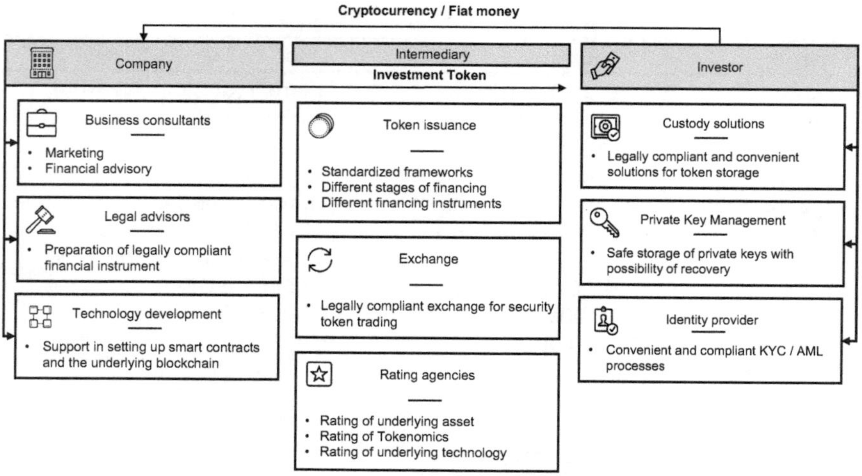

Fig. 1.3 Stakeholder roles in a token ecosystem

higher market capitalization since the debt market in general has a higher market capitalization in comparison to the equity market.

Early-stage start-ups will issue tokens to business angels or VCs in exchange for voting rights, whereas companies that are raising a Series D investment will focus more on financial returns for investors. This entails different tailor-made token standards for different stages of fundraising, such as a "Series A Equity Token," which can be individualized to accommodate the specific needs of a start-up and guarantees an investor some security of the underlying asset. In general, standardization will be crucial for the mass adoption of STOs, which will take place on two levels. First, there are technical token standards. Many different standards already exist, but it is still unclear which one will succeed. The experts, therefore, recommend that functions such as whitelisting or "Know Your Customer" (KYC) should not be part of a token standard. Additionally, they expect various technical token standards to emerge that represent different financing instruments. Second, legal frameworks are needed for issuing distinct types of tokens such as a "Series A Equity Token" or a "Convertible Loan Token." Such frameworks need to clearly define procedures for companies that want to conduct STOs and also clarify which kind of reporting is needed for transparency and investor protection.

Furthermore, it will be crucial for companies to prepare technical reports addressing the underlying blockchain technology and their risks. The goal is the development of financial instruments, ideally in a standardized manner, that are legally compliant and can easily be approved by a financial authority. STOs also bring higher liquidity into the market, which is important for investors, since it ensures higher flexibility and increases the level of risk investors are willing to take. The experts expect that this increased liquidity will have positive effects not only on investors but also for start-ups and their employees. Current employee stock option plans (ESOPs) give employees an illiquid asset, which can take up to ten years if employees want to convert their options into shares. By tokenizing ESOPs, employees can monetize their shares even before the company exit by trading the options on an exchange. The infrastructure around STOs is currently under development, but the experts agree that in the near future we will see solutions for compliant exchanges and safe custody solutions that allow legally compliant and convenient solutions for the storage and trading of tokens, including customer-friendly management of the private keys. There will not be an all-in-one solution; rather, we will see a verticalization of services where specialized players focus on token issuance, custody, secondary market trading, identity, as well as further services. At the moment, it is not clear if there will be first-mover advantages or if traditional players will be able to outperform incumbent market players in the future. Rating agencies, which assess the underlying asset as well the technology and currently only play a minor role in the space, are expected to become more important in the future, once they manage to rate technical assets in a trustworthy manner.

Summarizing those developments, the experts predict that the costs for STOs will significantly decrease. At the moment, the high costs are mainly due to legal and technical support. The existence of standardized technical as well as legal frameworks will help to substantially cut these costs, which will further accelerate the adoption of token sales as a convenient, reliable, and innovative way to finance companies in all stages of their life cycle.

Perspective

Business, technology, and legal perspectives, as shown as the third category in Fig. 1.1, not only emerged as a result of our literature review but also turned out to provide an ideal taxonomy to capture and categorize the respective issues raised by the experts. In the subsequent sections, we summarize the major themes that resulted from the interview analysis, followed by a brief discussion of the challenges and solutions which emerge in the token economy.

Business Model Aspects

The first part of the interviews covered numerous business aspects of the token economy, mainly related to funding. The business case for payment tokens is straightforward, and utility tokens represent the underlying offering of the companies, which leaves the most disruptive potential to investment tokens. The majority of the experts agreed that equity tokens will turn out to be the most relevant type of security token for start-ups, but they also raised doubts because of substantial information asymmetries inherent to this token type. In terms of corporate finance, the interviewees identified equal potential for equity and debt tokens. In comparison to start-ups, corporates have an existing track record that allows them to issue debt financing instruments such as bonds on a blockchain.

All interviewees had similar thoughts regarding the current challenges investment tokens need to address. These include regulatory aspects and missing legal frameworks as well as different aspects of mainstream acceptance. First, users need to be educated about blockchains and tokens. Second, user interfaces and user experience need to be improved in order to ensure trust and enable convenient investing in blockchain-based financial instruments. Current interfaces are not designed for mainstream users and impede fast adoption. Further aspects include the security of the underlying blockchain as well as existing and future KYC and Anti Money Laundering (AML) requirements. Another issue is the lack of liquidity due to missing exchanges. One interviewee mentioned the problem of finding a bank that is willing to place the funds raised by an STO.

When it comes to the implications of security tokens on corporate finance, the interviewees explicitly mentioned the potential inclusion of additional investors. In addition to professional investors, investment tokens allow retail investors easy access to funding. Consequently, the fundraising process will be democratized, opening up novel possibilities for financial backers from all over the world. As a result, the interviewees also expect better and higher liquidity in the market. From a company perspective, financing will be less expensive, more liquid at an early stage, more efficient, and more flexible.

Concerning the infrastructure that it is needed for security tokens, the experts pointed out that compliant exchanges as well as custody solutions for security tokens are needed and in development at the moment. There was some disagreement, however, whether crypto exchanges such as Coinbase or traditional exchanges such as the London Stock Exchange will play dominant roles in the future. Another topic raised was the need for identity providers to comply with KYC and AML regulations and to improve the user experience for investors. The interviewees were unsure when it comes to the future role of rating agencies. Some argued that some sort of rating is needed but that traditional rating agencies will have problems covering all relevant aspects of tokens. Compared to traditional financial instruments, where only the underlying financial asset is rated, rating agencies will need to account also for the technical aspect, such as the underlying blockchain. Furthermore, the numerous possibilities of enriching investment tokens with a utility function will complicate their rating as a token. All in all, there is a strong tendency to disintermediate the middlemen.

The experts disagreed upon the role of tokens for debt or equity financing. Some said that there is a higher potential for debt tokens since they are easier to regulate, more stable, and the debt financing market exceeds the market for equity. Others pointed out that equity tokens will be more relevant as a start-up financing instrument. Additionally, some experts pointed out that it is the underlying financing instrument that matters, independent of the blockchain technology being used, and therefore the current financing life cycle can be mapped one to one with tokens. In other words, the most suitable token depends on the underlying business model and the goals that need to be achieved through the token offering. Some interviewees highlighted the high flexibility of token creation due to smart contracts. This enables the issuance of tokens that are easily tradable for common share investors as well as tokens that are more secure for early-stage investors.

Most of the experts shared the opinion that liquidity is crucial and constitutes the third important aspect of investment tokes besides allowing easy access to financing and creating efficiency gains. Higher liquidity also leads to higher flexibility, which allows VCs to exit their investment earlier. Consequently, they might be more willing to finance risky and early-stage start-ups. However, some experts also mentioned increased competition as a negative side effect of a higher liquidity for VCs. Alternatively, they might follow a predefined strategy that ends with an exit event, and earlier, higher, and better liquidity will not necessarily change this approach.

The final question in the business part was about the costs of investment tokens and their main drivers. The experts all agreed that momentarily the costs of an STO are difficult to predict, since they depend on the underlying financial asset, the jurisdiction, and the targeted group of investors. In general, it is estimated that the cost lies somewhere between €100,000 and €1,000,000. Marketing costs, the legal setup, and the technical infrastructure are the main cost drivers, but these costs are expected to decrease with further standardization. The experts also predicted that the costs associated with STOs will be significantly lower in the near future, which will also help to accelerate adoption of security tokens as a new form of fundraising. Another pending issue that came up during the interviews is the problem of adverse selection. It was mentioned that only start-ups that do not manage to get VC funding are currently doing an STO. Additionally, a lot of projects just swapped from ICOs to STOs, which leads to a proliferation of low-quality projects. Additionally, it is also important for start-ups to find a suitable VC that brings added value to the start-up, which relies heavily on the current stage and the underlying business model. Ideally, VCs also support the STOs of their start-ups.

Technical Aspects

The second part of the interviews focused on the technical aspects associated with token issuance, namely, the underlying issues that need to be tackled to establish tokens as a prime financing and trading vehicle. The major adoption barriers for security tokens included the user interface and experience, but also security aspects which are dependent on the platform. With respect to the underlying blockchain, the importance of interoperability was also highlighted, as were the importance of smooth and convenient processes to perform KYC and AML and the auditing of smart contracts. Additionally, the absence of private key recovery mechanisms was mentioned as a major impediment for the adoption of tokens. To avoid these problems, clear regulations are needed as are mechanisms to avoid a potential loss of private keys and, consequently, a loss of the investment. One interviewee predicted these barriers to disappear followed by accelerated mass adoption once established players enter the market.

The interviewees shared a similar opinion concerning the process of token standardization, such as ERC-1400, a suite of security token standards that includes the core security token standard (ERC-1594), the partially fungible token standard (ERC-1410), the document management standard (ERC-1643), and the controller token operation standards (ERC-1644) (Fries, 2019). As it is the case with utility tokens and the widely used ERC-20 tokens, it will be essential to establish similar standards for tokens categories upon which to build a reliable and functional financial system. The experts agreed that there should not be too many standards, but rather a few very well-thought-out ones. Besides, several interviewees also mentioned the need for standardized legal solutions and the importance of cross-blockchain functionality. Consequently, some experts expressed their concerns when it comes to the ERC-1400 security token standard, which is solely built on the Ethereum blockchain, since it is still unclear whether Ethereum will emerge as the major blockchain solution for the future. One expert doubted its broad application because of its high complexity of resulting in too many implemented functions.

The experts acknowledged the need to have different token standards which depend on the characteristics of the underlying financing instrument, such as stocks or bonds. There is also a pending need for standards for secondary market trading and to account for the different requirements of fungible and non-fungible tokens. An important issue was that there should be few standards that are of high quality rather than a proliferation of numerous different standards. One interviewee argued that the respective use case of a smart contract is the decisive factor for a specific token standard; another one mentioned that every other function, besides raising and transferring money, should be implemented outside of the token smart contract and there should not be any on-chain security regulations.

The question of which blockchain is currently the most suitable for token creation was not answered unanimously by the experts. As of 2020, Ethereum is the most commonly used blockchain for token creation, because of the biggest developer community and the greatest experience. The low probability of a 51% attack is a clear advantage of a popular blockchain with a strong user base. One interviewee mentioned that all STOs he is currently supporting are working with either Ethereum or Stellar. Stellar has clear advantages in terms of speed and cost compared to the relatively slow and expensive Ethereum blockchain. The experts were unsure which one will the leading blockchains in the future, pointing out that this cannot be forecasted in the fast-changing blockchain environment. One expert mentioned the importance of interoperability to combine the best blockchains with respect to tradeability, security, and costs.

The final technical question was about investment token platforms and their role in the future. All interview partners agreed that there will be platforms in order to mainstream the process of token offerings, similar to existing platforms that are standardizing contracts. Furthermore, they all shared the view that it will not be a monopolistic market, but that there will be various platforms coexisting instead, serving numerous use cases and target groups. Alternatively, one expert predicted a one-stop-shop solution, having token creation, custody, and primary and secondary market trading on one platform. The other experts recommended that the different functions should be executed by specialized service providers. Some mentioned that the costs and complexities of regulation and licenses will finally decide on which player will emerge as the most dominant in the ecosystem. They also concluded that it is still unclear if current platforms will survive once established players, such as stock exchanges and investment banks, enter the STO market.

Legal Aspects

The third and final part of the interview dealt with legal aspects of investment tokens. The experts shared similar views on what is needed from a legal point of view for tokens to become a prime financing vehicle for start-ups. The interviewees clearly stated that there is a great need for common European regulatory standards but also for a clear procedure for STOs and legal security. One expert mentioned that regulations should be technology-neutral and that the understanding of the close connection between regulations and technology is a crucial aspect for the success of a token economy. Furthermore, clear guidance by federal banks and financial authorities, as well as best practices, is needed. In order to accelerate the adoption of investment tokens, the legal costs for preparing a prospectus need to be considerably reduced. Another interviewee stated that it is better to implement existing security regulations than to create new ones. Additionally, the benefits of blockchain technology need to be demonstrated to regulators.

The interview partners expressed different ideas when it comes to the reporting requirements for investment tokens, but they all agreed on the importance of reporting in general in order to build trust and transparency. Some experts shared the opinion that the reports from existing financial instruments suffice with no further need for additional reports. However, KYC, AML, counterterrorist financing, and the ownership of tokens need to be covered and clearly outlined. Others mentioned the need for additional information and the issuance of ongoing reports with respect to technical issues. In particular, the security features of blockchain are seen as crucial to build trust for the underlying asset. With respect to security, smart contract and custody audits were mentioned as part of a technical risk report. One expert explicitly highlighted that it will be interesting to see which reporting requirements are needed for securities that are formally not public but act as public securities.

When it comes to the needed changes for law and regulations to accelerate adoption, the experts mentioned the high importance of a standardized legal framework for investment tokens and a significant reduction of costs for issuing tokens. In the end, both investors and startups need legal security. One expert mentioned that programmed tokens need to be accepted in the form of a legal contract and that this needs to be written down in law. Another interview partner pointed out the important role of small countries which rush ahead and can act as role models for other regulators to learn from. In the end, regulation has to be technology-neutral and should not hinder innovation.

In order to conclude the legal part of the interviews, the experts gave their opinions on current best practices in the investment token space. They shared the view that small countries such as Liechtenstein, Switzerland, Malta, Gibraltar, Estonia, and Singapore currently have the best regulations in place for conducting STOs. Some experts even pointed out that countries such as Germany or France should soon issue similar regulations, because investors are still hesitant about investing under the regulations of small countries.

Challenges and Solutions

In Fig. 1.4, we summarize the major challenges and also potential solutions that emerged during the interviews. With regard to business-related challenges, and at the intersection of business and law, one of the biggest issues that companies face is the lack of regulatory clarity, which severely impedes further business development. Another problem, caused by the novelty of the token economy, is the missing infrastructure in the form of exchanges resulting in a market that is not very liquid and therefore volatile. The experts conclude that the latter problem will soon be solved when major players from the crypto industry as well as from the traditional industry work together to develop the needed infrastructure.

Regarding the technical aspects, the biggest emerging problems are the lack of user-friendly interfaces, which impedes achieving mass adoption.

	Challenges	Solutions
Business	• Lack of regulatory guidance limits business development • Missing infrastructure leads to illiquid and volatile markets	• Authorities are working towards regulatory clarity • Infrastructure is rapidly developing, driven by crypto as well as established players
Technology	• UI/UX and inconvenient KYC/AML processes hinder mass adoption • Security and interoperability of the underlying blockchain • Private Key Management	• Startups as well as established companies are working toward human-centric solutions • Solutions for lost Private Keys, similar to "Forgot password" function
Law	• Lack of standardized frameworks • No clarity about legal procedures • High costs for legal documents	• Startups and established players are working on standardized processes • Through standardization costs will be halved

Fig. 1.4 Challenges and potential solutions

Current KYC and AML processes are time-consuming for customers. To reach mass adoption, these processes have to be more convenient and should not have to be repeated for every investment. Consequently, there is a need for identity providers that offer convenient solutions. Furthermore, blockchain technology itself is a field that needs improvements, as is expressed in concerns regarding 51% attacks and other attack vectors. Another important aspect is the interoperability of blockchain solutions such that different blockchains with specific characteristics can easily be combined and their specific advantages be leveraged to build the best solution. Another barrier is private key management and the fact that the loss of a private key prevents access to an investment. This is not a sustainable, long-term solution for financing companies. Solutions using a two-factor authentication, or a "Forgot password" function similar to e-mail services, can help to foster widespread adoption in this regard.

Legal aspects constitute the third big part when talking about current hurdles for the token economy. Specifically, the lack of a standardized framework and the missing legal procedures are pending issues. Furthermore, in order for successful adoption, it is necessary to reduce legal costs, especially for the preparation of a prospectus, which could make token offerings more attractive to companies and help to democratize the fundraising process. Regarding best legal practices, small countries like Liechtenstein, Switzerland, or Malta are currently leading the way. For example, the Liechtenstein Blockchain Act allows to embed a token into current law by defining it as a "container" that can be filled with all kinds of rights. In consequence, all types of securities can be represented as tokens.

Conclusion, Implications, and Further Research

The potential economic and business implications of blockchain technology have led to the suggestion of numerous use cases and pending topics for further research (Beck et al., 2017; Rossi et al., 2019; Treiblmaier, 2018). The emergence of token offerings presents one prominent example of a blockchain-induced transformation that only few researchers so far have investigated in a rigorous manner (e.g., Kranz et al., 2019). In order to account for the far-reaching consequences of token offerings, information systems researchers need to simultaneously consider technological, business, and legal issues. The comprehensive treatment of any application, which is based on blockchain technology, is complicated by the facts that (a) the technology is still under development, (b) legislation is lacking behind, and (c) businesses had little time to implement and test solutions as well as to adapt their business models correspondingly. However, we believe that this should not be seen as an insurmountable obstacle, but instead encourage researchers to build on current findings in order to develop and test theories, frameworks, models, and applications that benefit the industry and drive further development. In this paper, we thoroughly investigate the current impact of blockchain-based tokens and the potential emergence of a token economy. More specifically, we illustrate the purpose and the current distribution of tokens and use expert interviews to delve deeper and uncover pending topics. Our results show that tokens offer manifold potentials in comparison to the current opportunities in place, but they also exhibit numerous shortcomings which pose major barriers for adoption, but which also deserve further investigation.

The use of blockchain-based tokens to represent value is a comparatively new idea that gained a lot of attention in the year 2017 due to the widespread emergence of ICOs as an alternative to traditional financing. The following burst of the bubble revealed numerous shortcomings of the approach due to lack of regulatory oversight and the proliferation of fraudulent companies. However, it was also the case that the potentials of the technology became evident. In line with the call for a rigorous investigation of the impact of blockchain technology, our findings bear substantial implications for both academia and the industry. When it comes to the former, the role of theory is paramount, ranging from analysis, explanation, and prediction toward design and action (Gregor, 2006). In this paper, we have structured the implications of token offerings into three different viewpoints, namely, business, technology, and law, and not only provided the groundwork needed to process the field in a structured and theory-based way but also suggested numerous paths for creative research. More specifically, we have listed advantages and disadvantages of token offerings, each of which deserves further attention and can be investigated from different perspectives. This not only pertains to theories that typically focus on companies and consumers and their manifold issues of adoption but also includes a broader economic perspective which considers the implications of token offerings on national and international levels. Furthermore, we have compared token-based funding with traditional funding procedures, which, again, yields a fertile ground for researchers who want to delve deeper and closely investigate why, how, and under what conditions different funding types might succeed. Finally, we have identified various roles of stakeholders in a token-based economy and derived challenges and their solutions from different viewpoints.

From a managerial perspective, blockchain research is driven by the current technological evolution and by the pending needs of the industry. The token classification presented in this paper not only gives a first glimpse on how the technology has been accepted so far but also allows to identify application gaps that might benefit the industry. Furthermore, all of the identified topics, be it business, technological, or legal issues, are of high relevance to the industry since practitioners will finally decide on the implementation of token-based solutions that help to create value.

The findings of this study, based on experts' interviews and a token analysis, are limited by the current state of the art. Using qualitative content analysis, we have distilled the major research topics, which we believe will be of relevance for the years to come. Given the broad scope of the token economy, we have refrained from suggesting specific theories, frameworks, or models to cope with the questions at hand and leave it up to other researchers to create more elaborate designs. Instead, it is the purpose of our paper to present a starting point for a closer investigation of the token economy. We therefore encourage researchers to elaborate on the concepts in this paper and to come up with theories that can be tested with rigorous empirical research or to develop practical solutions that support the industry by solving some of the pending problems.

Appendix

Business Aspects

- Which type of security token will be most relevant for start-ups/corporates in the future?
- From a business point of view, what are current challenges security tokens need to overcome in order to succeed?
- How will security tokens change the future of financing for start-ups and corporates (SMEs)?
- What type of infrastructure (e.g., exchanges, custody, rating agencies) is needed for security tokens, and what is currently missing?
- Is there a higher potential for debt (e.g., bonds) or equity financing (e.g., profit participation rights)?
  When should equity tokens be used? When should debt tokens be used? When should other tokens be used?
- Will there be different tokens for different stages of financing?
  If yes, how could they look like?
- How important are liquid assets to buyers and sellers?
- How much does an STO cost? What are the main cost drivers?

Technical Aspects

- From a technical point of view, what are barriers that could hinder the adoption of security tokens?
- Do you see a broad application of tokens standards such as ERC-1400?
- Is there a need for different tokens standards, depending on the characteristics of the financing instrument? If so, which standards?
- What are the best blockchain systems for token creation?
- Are there STO platforms that you think will be important in the future?

Regulatory Aspects

- From a legal point of view, what is needed for security tokens to become a prime financing vehicle for start-ups?
- As a company issuing a security token, what needs to be reported?
- How do the current law/regulations need to change in order to accelerate adoption?
- What are current best practices?

References

Adhami, S., Giudici, G., & Martinazzi, S. (2018). Why do businesses go crypto? An empirical analysis of initial coin offerings. *Journal of Economics & Business, 100*, 64–75. https://doi.org/10.1016/j.jeconbus.2018.04.001

Beck, R., Avital, M., Rossi, M., & Thatcher, J. B. (2017). Blockchain technology in business and information systems research. *Business & Information Systems Engineering, 59*(6), 381–384.

Beck, R., Müller-Bloch, C., & King, J. L. (2018). Governance in the blockchain economy: A Framework and research agenda. *Journal of the Association for Information Systems, 19*(10), 1020–1034. https://doi.org/10.17705/1jais.00518

BitcoinWiki. (2018). *Token definition—Cryptocurrency—BitcoinWiki.* https://en.bitcoinwiki.org/wiki/Token

Bussgang, J., & Nanda, R. (2018, November 7). The hidden costs of initial coin offerings. *Harvard Business Review.* https://hbr.org/2018/11/the-hidden-costs-of-initial-coin-offerings

Carton, J. S., & Schweitzer, J. B. (1996). Use of a token economy to increase compliance during hemodialysis. *Journal of Applied Behavior Analysis, 29*(1), 111–113. https://doi.org/10.1901/jaba.1996.29-111

Chen, Y. (2018). Blockchain tokens and the potential democratization of entrepreneurship and innovation. *Business Horizons, 61*(4), 567–575. https://doi.org/10.1016/j.bushor.2018.03.006

Clohessy, T., Treiblmaier, H., Acton, T., & Rogers, N. (2020). Antecedents of blockchain adoption: An integrative framework. *Strategic Change, 29*(5), 501–515. https://doi.org/10.1002/jsc.2360

DLT Capital GmbH. (2019). *Crowdfunding als Finanzierungsinstrument* [Internal Presentation]. DLT Capital.

Euler, T. (2018). The Token Classification Framework: A multi-dimensional tool for understanding and classifying crypto tokens. Untitled INC. http://www.untitled-inc.com/the-token-classificationframework-a-multi-dimensional-tool-for-understanding-and-classifying-crypto-tokens/

European Banking Authority. (2014). *EBA Opinion on 'virtual currencies'* (S. 1–46). https://eba.europa.eu/documents/10180/657547/EBA-Op-2014-08+Opinion+on+Virtual+Currencies.pdf

Fisch, C. (2019). Initial coin offerings (ICOs) to finance new ventures. *Journal of Business Venturing, 34*(1), 1–22. https://doi.org/10.1016/j.jbusvent.2018.09.007

Flick, U. (2014). *An introduction to qualitative research.* Sage Publications. https://us.sagepub.com/en-us/nam/an-introduction-to-qualitative-research/book240398

Fries, T. (2019). *How the ERC-1400 has evolved into a suite of interoperable security token standards.* https://thetokenist.io/how-the-erc-1400-has-evolved-into-a-suite-of-interoperable-security-token-standards/

Gregor, S. (2006). The nature of theory in information systems. *MIS Quarterly, 30*(3), 611–642.

Hahn, C., & Wons, A. (2018). *Initial Coin Offering (ICO): Unternehmensfinanzierung auf Basis der Blockchain-Technologie.* Gabler Verlag. https://doi.org/10.1007/978-3-658-21787-7

Howell, S. T., Niessner, M., & Yermack, D. (2020). Initial coin offerings: Financing growth with cryptocurrency token sales. *The Review of Financial Studies, 33*(9), 3925–3974. https://doi.org/10.1093/rfs/hhz131

International Token Standardization Association. (2019). www.itsa.global

Kastelein, R. (2017). What initial coin offerings are, and why VC firms care. *Harvard Business Review.* https://hbr.org/2017/03/what-initial-coin-offerings-are-and-why-vc-firms-care

Kazdin, A. (1977). *The token economy: A review and evaluation* (1st ed.). Springer.

Kim, M. S., & Chung, J. Y. (2019). Sustainable growth and token economy design: The case of Steemit. *Sustainability, 11*(1), 167. https://doi.org/10.3390/su11010167

Kranz, J., Nagel, E., & Yoo, Y. (2019). Blockchain token sale. *Business & Information Systems Engineering, 61*(6), 745–753.

Laskowski, M., Kim, H. M., Zargham, M., Barlin, M., & Kabanov, D. (2019). *Token economics in real-life: Cryptocurrency and incentives design for Insolar's Blockchain Network*. Social Science Research Network. https://papers.ssrn.com/abstract=3465085

Lee, J. Y. (2019). A decentralized token economy: How blockchain and cryptocurrency can revolutionize business. *Business Horizons, 62*(6), 773–784. https://doi.org/10.1016/j.bushor.2019.08.003

Mayring, P. (2010). Qualitative inhaltsanalyse. In G. Mey & K. Mruck (Eds.), *Handbuch Qualitative Forschung in der Psychologie* (pp. 601–613). VS Verlag für Sozialwissenschaften. https://doi.org/10.1007/978-3-531-92052-8_42

Nickerson, R., Varshney, U., Muntermann, J., & Isaac, H. (2009). Taxonomy development in information systems: Developing a taxonomy of mobile applications. *Proceedings of the European Conference on Information Systems.* https://aisel.aisnet.org/ecis2009/388

Oliveira, L., Zavolokina, L., Bauer, I., & Schwabe, G. (2018). *To token or not to token: Tools for understanding blockchain tokens.* International Conference of Information Systems (ICIS 2018), San Francisco, USA. https://doi.org/10.5167/uzh-157908

Rejeb, A., Keogh, J. G., & Treiblmaier, H. (2020). How blockchain technology can benefit marketing: Six pending research areas. *Frontiers in Blockchain, 3*(3), 1–12. https://doi.org/10.3389/fbloc.2020.00003

Risius, M., & Spohrer, K. (2017). A Blockchain research framework—What we (don't) know, where we go from here, and how we will get there. *Business & Information Systems Engineering, 59*(6), 385–409.

Rossi, M., Mueller-Bloch, C., Thatcher, J., & Beck, R. (2019). Blockchain research in information systems: Current trends and an inclusive future research agenda. *Journal of the Association for Information Systems, 20*(9), 1388–1403. https://doi.org/10.17705/1jais.00571

Sandner, P., Groß, J., Christoph, I., & Labetzsch, C. (2019). *How will security tokens change financing for corporations?* Medium. https://medium.com/@philippsandner/how-will-security-tokens-change-financing-for-corporations-6ca9a1c0de3

Schmandt-Besserat, D., & Hallo, W. W. (1992). Before writing: Volume 1: From Counting to Cuneiform. University of Chicago Press.

Security Token Standard. (2019). *Security token standard*. https://thesecuritytokenstandard.org/

strategy&. (2018). *Initial Coin Offerings: Eine Strategische Perspektive*. https://www.pwc.ch/de/publications/2018/20180628_PwC%20S&%20CVA%20ICO%20Report_DE.pdf

strategy&. (2019). *4th ICO / STO Report*.

Sunyaev, A., Kannengießer, N., Beck, R., Treiblmaier, H., Lacity, M., Kranz, J., Fridgen, G., Spankowski, U., & Luckow, A. (2021). Token economy. *Business & Information Systems Engineering 63*, 457-478. https://doi.org/10.1007/s12599-021-00684-1

Tasca, P. (2019). Token-based business models. In T. Lynn, J. G. Mooney, P. Rosati, & M. Cummins (Eds.), *Disrupting finance: FinTech and strategy in the 21st century* (pp. 135–148). Springer International Publishing. https://doi.org/10.1007/978-3-030-02330-0_9

Treiblmaier, H. (2018). The impact of the blockchain on the supply chain: A theory-based research framework and a call for action. *Supply Chain Management: An International Journal, 23*(6), 545–559.

Treiblmaier, H. (2021). The token economy as a key driver for tourism: Entering the next phase of blockchain research. *Annals of Tourism Research 91, 103177*. https://doi.org/10.1016/j.annals.2021.103177

Treiblmaier, H., & Beck, R. (2019a). *Business transformation through blockchain—Volume I*. Palgrave Macmillan.

Treiblmaier, H., & Beck, R. (2019b). *Business transformation through blockchain—Volume II*. Palgrave Macmillan.

Venkatesh, V., Brown, S. A., & Bala, H. (2013). Bridging the qualitative-quantitative divide: Guidelines for conducting mixed methods research in information systems. *MIS Quarterly, 37*(1), 21–54.

2

Recovering from Blockchain Missteps and Myths with Coopetition

Dale Chrystie

Introduction

The business and technology communities have spent more than a decade either ignoring blockchain—in favor of the bitcoin and/or cryptocurrency discussion—or discussing 'who' ('everyone,' especially in 2017–2018 or so), 'what' ('blockchain'), and 'when' (we all want to know that answer). Or, many have simply been trying to treat it like they did the Internet and immediately monetize it. What they have been missing, to a large degree, is the question of 'why' as it relates to blockchain technology. This is important because 'who,' 'what,' and 'when' force us down a 'this is a brand-new technology' path; but 'why' takes us into the C-Suite. If we can't prove business value to the C-Suite, blockchain will remain a new,

The original version of this chapter was revised. The correction to this chapter can be found at https://doi.org/10.1007/978-3-030-95108-5_14

D. Chrystie (✉)
FedEx Corporate Services, Inc., Memphis, TN, USA
e-mail: dale.chrystie@fedex.com

M. C. Lacity, H. Treiblmaier (eds.), *Blockchains and the Token Economy*, Technology, Work and Globalization, https://doi.org/10.1007/978-3-030-95108-5_2

mysterious, and kind of scary technology only understood by the R&D or innovation group at the end of the hallway.

Tokens are a representation of value managed by programmable smart contracts. We will get into the transformative nature of both peer-to-peer technology and smart contracts. One example could be in the art world, where a token could represent the full amount of a piece of art, or a percentage of the value. The ability to purchase a tiny fraction of a valuable painting could not only change the art world, but the logic is the same for real estate, music, the trusted value of goods moving in the global supply chain that could be used as collateral, and so on. The business models that sit between supply and demand in these areas will likely have to adapt to this new way of thinking.

As a former strategy officer, my approach to blockchain is from the business and strategy angle and not from the technical side. My focus is on how to look at this technology from the C-Suite perspective and translate this discussion into their language. Innovation and R&D labs won't likely be responsible for scaling blockchain; I believe the C-Suites will. Said another way: yes, blockchain **is** a technology discussion, but it is not ***only*** a technology discussion.

In this chapter, I first explore the lessons on early efforts and learnings from FedEx, and then dispel nine early myths about blockchain. My conclusion is that 'open' is inevitable, and that coopetition—working with trading partners, including competitors—is the best route to gaining business and social value from blockchain. 'Open' also includes open source and royalty-free standards, available to all.

The Early FedEx Journey

In 2017, I led the first FedEx blockchain potential use case scenario, where the company focused on a dispute resolution case in the 'big box retail' space. Essentially, it was a three-party scenario with a shipper, receiver, and carrier, and they were getting snagged on 'chargebacks' between the three parties. While the focus was a logistics example, this same scenario works in a number of different industries and examples. In this initial use case, the example was:

- Receiver ordered 100 items on a purchase order from the shipper.
- Shipper fulfilled the order where 40 items fit on a pallet and created two pallets.
- Shipper created a bill of lading (BL) for two pallets.
- Carrier signed BL, picked up the pallets, and delivered two pallets to the receiver in an identical condition as at the time of pickup (for example, no shortages or damage).
- Several weeks later, the receiver issued a shortage notification to the carrier, and a chargeback to the shipper for the missing items.

What they didn't know at the time was that they were speaking different languages—the receiver-to-shipper relationship was in 'purchase order' language and both the shipper-to-carrier and carrier-to-receiver relationships were in 'bill of lading' language. What the carrier also didn't know at the time was that the receiver ordered 100 pieces from the shipper. What the carrier both received from the shipper and subsequently delivered to the receiver was two pallets of 40 each, leaving 20 pieces unaccounted for. These pieces were likely moved by the shipper via some other method because it was less than a pallet and this was the primary source for the 'chargeback' scenario.

Learnings from this initial blockchain use case:

- It is just data
- It creates a common language
- It creates a secure chain of custody
- Peer-to-peer technology will be transformative

Also, in 2017, FedEx became founding member of two blockchain entities. Because the company believes that standards will be critical to global scalability, it became founding member of the Blockchain in Transport Alliance (BiTA) and what is now the BITA Standards Council (BSC). FedEx also joined the Blockchain Research Institute in Toronto, and later, also joined the Hyperledger Project and the Enterprise Ethereum Alliance.

Additional efforts and deep thought started to yield some perspective on this new technology. In the early days, I had a slide that said, "Blockchain is useless and quite boring," which used to get a lot of nervous laughter at a blockchain conference. Blockchain is not yet fast, or scalable, or mature, and it is certainly nowhere near as good as many other databases and technologies. But what it does, it does really well, and where authenticity is critical, I believe it will be transformative.

FedEx spoke publicly about blockchain for the first time in May 2018 at the Consensus New York event. FedEx Founder, Chairman, and CEO, Frederick W. Smith, was joined on stage by Robert B. Carter, FedEx CIO, and Don Tapscott, co-founder of the Blockchain Research Institute. In a wide-ranging fireside chat, Smith said, "(Blockchain is) the next frontier that's going to completely change worldwide supply chains," and he closed with, "If you are not operating at the edge of technology to face up to real threats, you will be disrupted. When you stop innovating or when you stop embracing change, you are really in the process of commoditization at best and extinction more probably."[1] There was immediate buzz in the room, on social media, and in traditional media over those comments.

I include quotes from FedEx executives for one specific reason—blockchain is a topic where there are a lot of companies with a lone evangelist, likely talking about the technology, and likely with limited results. It really separates those who are serious about this when the C-Suite understands not only the technology (back to 'who,' 'what,' 'when') but also the impact of the technology (the 'why') and are willing to speak publicly about it.

In addition to the proof of concept in the big box space, FedEx also built a global supply chain blockchain just to prove that the technology really works (it does). There were also a lot of consortia efforts emerging during that time—in food safety, logistics, pharma, and so on, but the company was also learning how to better understand the magnitude of the discussion.

I have spent many years in process improvement, quality, and strategy. Most of the time, the tendency is to narrow the focus to get to the details

[1] "(Blockchain is) the next frontier that's going to completely change worldwide supply chains," and he closed with, "If you are not operating at the edge of technology to face up to real threats you will be disrupted. When you stop innovating or when you stop embracing change, you are really in the process of commoditization at best and extinction more probably."

Frederick W. Smith—Consensus NYC, May 14, 2018—link—16:48, 21:41

or to the 'root cause.' However, occasionally, I have found it is better to do the opposite, and pull back to see the broader view of the situation. Because I work for a global company that delivers to 220 countries and territories, I never forget the luxury I have of a default position in the blockchain space essentially from the International Space Station (ISS). From that view, there are no companies, there are no industries, and there are no borders. That has provided a very freeing perspective to approach this journey.

There are many consortia efforts that will be successful. And there are a number of industries with a small enough number of participants that could sign up to be on the same private blockchain, which could also be successful. However, from a global commerce point of view, there are millions of entities, ranging from global logistics providers to local bicycle delivery companies. Virtually everyone focusing on blockchain has been trying to treat it like they did the Internet, which has led to private efforts as well as consortia efforts. However, I don't believe those efforts can effectively scale in global commerce, due to the increasing level of friction they create.

FedEx eventually started to see a 'fork in the road,' where almost everyone was heading down the private or consortia path. On the contrary—and from the ISS view—if one party could hang an open license on the door frame of this global virtual conference room and gain agreement from participants prior to coming through that threshold, the company believed this could scale globally. There are many examples of a dominant design emerging in technology, and FedEx believes that will be the case here. This thinking led to my belief that 'open is inevitable' in the global commerce space. To that point, in 2017, I referred to blockchain as a 'team sport,' and then in early 2019, I started referring to this new way of business as a 'coopetition.'

While FedEx had come to that 'open' conclusion well prior to this, the company's CIO, Robert B. Carter, said that publicly for the first time in April 2019 at the inaugural Blockchain Revolution Global conference in Toronto, Canada:

> We think that open—in this particular case (blockchain)—is absolutely what the industry needs. We have got to have a coopetition framework to allow lots of players in supply chain and logistics and manufacturing all be

> a part of this. This technology, if it was positioned as a 'FedEx' technology, would be a bust. It simply wouldn't work.[2]

At that same event, Richard W. Smith (then president and CEO of FedEx Logistics) spoke about the company's ongoing dialogue with U.S. Customs & Border Protection (CBP) and the increased effort to reduce counterfeit items using blockchain. CBP's perspective at that time was that blockchain was not yet widely adopted, to which Richard responded:

> Why not plant a flag in the ground that in the next five years, all importers must be up on blockchain? (If) you want to know that this merchandise is authentic and not counterfeit, blockchain can do that.[3]

Later that same day, FedEx took 'coopetition' to an entirely new level when I (representing FedEx) joined key professionals from the other two members of the Global Express Association (GEA), DHL and UPS, on stage with Don Tapscott moderating. From my perspective, 'coopetition' is not where we have, and will continue, to compete vigorously. It's about where the industry can agree to make the overall supply chain more efficient, in a way compliant with each company's policies and all applicable laws. One such area is that if friction can be reduced across borders, companies win, their customers win, and global commerce wins. In this case, 'friction' means reducing paperwork, delays, resources, and so on. The GEA members further proved later in 2019 that 'coopetition' works by creating a position paper on blockchain and emerging technologies that was provided to World Customs Organization and to the World Trade Organization as both a recommendation and a call to action.

---

[2] "We think that open, in this particular case, is absolutely what the industry needs. We have got to have a coopetition framework to allow lots of players in supply chain and logistics and manufacturing all be a part of this. This technology, if it was positioned as a 'FedEx' technology, would be a bust. It simply wouldn't work."

Robert B. Carter—Blockchain Revolution Global, April 24, 2019—link—18:12

[3] "You're the Government, you could mandate that it (blockchain) is widely adopted. Why not plant a flag in the ground that in the next five years, all importers must be up on blockchain? (If) you want to know that this merchandise is authentic and not counterfeit, blockchain can do that."

Richard W. Smith—Blockchain Revolution Global, April 24, 2019—link—9:11

Myths About Blockchain

While a lot has been learned about blockchain in the past few years, many myths remain. Myths can add color and lore to a topic, but these myths are getting in the way of adoption and the transformative changes blockchain will bring (Fig. 2.1).

- We're all going to get rich with Bitcoin!!
  - Myth: Bitcoin = blockchain
- What's blockchain?
  - Myth: Blockchain is just a technology best left to the technologists.
- Can I sprinkle some blockchain dust on something and it will grow six feet tall?
  - Myth: Blockchain is magic and will fix everything.
- Three of us have a blockchain use case and we're going to sign NDAs and create a consortium.
  - Myth: Consortia are the only way to build blockchains.
- Then, we're going to treat blockchain exactly like the Internet and immediately monetize it.
  - Myth: First, we should monetize blockchain.

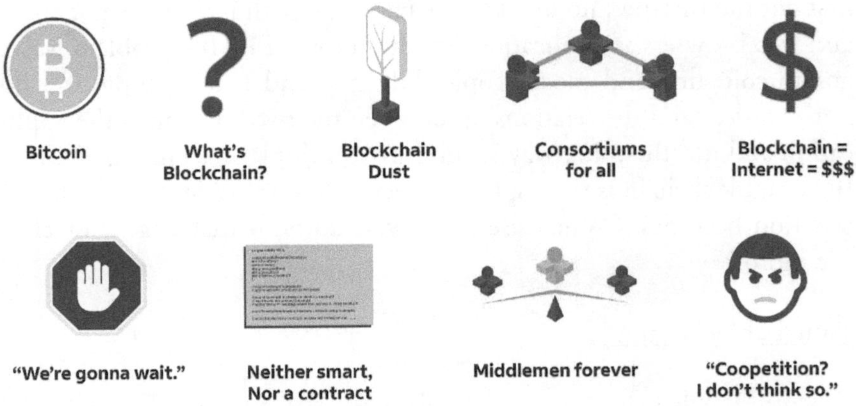

Fig. 2.1 Nine myths about blockchain

- We are going to wait until someone figures out blockchain and then we will jump on board.
  - Myth: It's best to wait.
- Smart contracts are neither smart nor a contract.
  - Myth: Smart contracts are smart and they are legal contracts.
- My business connects supply and demand—peer-to-peer technology won't affect us.
  - Myth: My business cannot be replaced.
- I don't mind 'coopetition' in the blockchain space as long as I don't have to work with other companies.
  - Myth: Coopetition = antitrust

Dispelling Myths About Blockchain

"We're all going to get rich with Bitcoin!!"

- Myth: Bitcoin = blockchain

Some have become rich with Bitcoin, but most won't—and that is a separate discussion from blockchain. With more than a decade of perspective on this, I would argue that Bitcoin blotted out the sun from blockchain for a number of years, slowing down its adoption. When we first got the Internet, no one knew what to do with it until we got email and web browsers as applications to 'sit on top' of it. The problem is, we got Bitcoin first and most people did not—and many people still do not—understand the relationship between the two: Bitcoin is the application and not the other way around. If you think of a shiny new car as Bitcoin, blockchain is the engine or electric motor inside the car and the question becomes, "What else could you do with that engine or electric motor?"

"What's blockchain?"

- Myth: Blockchain is just a technology best left to the technologists.

When I first started gaining interest in blockchain, I remember seeing an online video where a handful of CEOs were interviewed 'live from the conference' style and asked, "What is your definition of blockchain?" First, I didn't learn a single thing from all those smart people because they might as well have been speaking different languages, all the while trying to answer the same question. They meant well, and each of them really did understand what it was. But as the audience member, I got lost in their descriptions. It was then that I realized that if I was going to speak about blockchain, I would need to come up with an 'elevator speech' version from my business and strategy point of view. So, from 2017, my overly simplistic and highly business/strategy-focused definition of blockchain is five words: Digital ledger—permanent, transparent, shared.

"What's blockchain?" also unfortunately leads down the, "Yes, it ***is*** a technology discussion, but it is not ***only*** a technology discussion" path.

- "Yes, it ***is*** a technology discussion"—leads down the 'who,' 'what,' 'when' path, which is almost entirely technology focused, and which limits the scalability and understanding by the broader business community.
  - One of the key challenges is that, as we think of it as 'technology,' we don't yet even have a common definition for blockchain. In his 2021 PhD research, Dr. David Lacek found more than 100,000 definitions for 'blockchain.'[4]
  - For widespread adoption, "in the eye of the beholder" can't be the way that blockchain is defined. And when we think of it only in the 'technology' sense, it does not paint the full picture of the far-reaching potential impact of blockchain technology.
- The "not ***only*** a technology discussion" leads down the 'why' path, which is how this will scale globally.

[4] In his 2021 PhD research, Dr. David Lacek found >100,000 definitions for 'blockchain.'

Lacek, D. A. (2021). *The Definition and Meaning of Blockchain* [Unpublished doctoral dissertation]. The University of Denver.

As mentioned previously, I believe it will be the C-Suite who will ultimately drive widespread adoption of blockchain. Though each member of the C-Suite has their own area of expertise (finance, legal, etc.), what they share is the fiduciary responsibility for the company's risk and opportunity. And, with peer-to-peer technology and smart contracts, entire business models will change. While blockchain may be a new technology, the 'business' language—including risk and opportunity—remains much the same. It is incumbent on us to explain 'why' blockchain will be transformative. We must be bilingual and fluent in executives' (business) language, and not expect them to be fluent in the language of emerging technologies. That transformation also leads to cultural changes as we will see when we get to 'coopetition.'

"Can I sprinkle some blockchain dust on something and it will grow six feet tall?"

- Myth: Blockchain is magic and will fix everything.

The answer is, no, you cannot throw blockchain at just anything and expect results. But that doesn't keep a lot of people from trying. This scenario plays out often with something new in business. It takes a while for people to hear about a new technology or business buzzword. But once someone thinks they understand it, a game of 'Blockchain (or, fill in the blanks—could be 'quality', or another overused business term) Bingo' ensues, where they want to reference it with almost anything—'blockchain this' and 'blockchain that'—when, in fact, virtually none of the early references were a good blockchain use case. And that probably fed into the early hype. It's also not helpful that blockchain really isn't very intuitive, and many are still getting stuck in the 'technology' or 'not ***only*** a technology' discussion.

"Three of us have a blockchain use case and we're going to sign non-disclosure agreements (NDAs) and create a consortium," and then, "We're going to treat blockchain exactly like we did the internet and try to immediately monetize it."

- Myth: Consortia are the only way to build blockchains.
- Myth: First, we should monetize blockchain.

Again, the early understanding and proposed use cases were simply repeating things that had been done (or attempted) with the Internet, or previously in business. While 'working together' in a consortium is a step in the right direction, what most didn't see/still may not have seen is the friction that still exists with private blockchains and consortiums and, in some cases, a for-profit model, which, in the case of global commerce, becomes a limiting factor. This is also a very simplistic and incorrect view that doesn't really demonstrate a true understanding of blockchain technology. If it were that easy to monetize, many people or corporate entities would have already done it years ago, which gets us back to the 'why' of blockchain, and then leads us to 'coopetition.' Also, this splits into two groups: (1) those trying to 'get rich quick' and (2) the rest. Those trying to 'get rich quick' are likely already out of this space, and they took the hype with them. The rest are still working through the difficult aspects of making blockchain work and will likely be responsible for global adoption.

Finally, another important distinction is whether blockchain is considered 'process improvement' (evolution) or 'breakthrough' (revolution). The answer is 'both,' though not a lot of people are currently breaking it down this way. Big entities who can 'improve' processes can see large efficiency gains with even small incremental improvements, which is a great thing. If blockchain can reduce some amount of friction in a multistep process, that is great. However, that also assumes you start with existing processes and 'drill down' into them to see things like root cause and small opportunities. When you 'pull back' from an existing process (back to the International Space Station example) and you see things like peer-to-peer technology and smart contracts completely changing entire business models ('breakthrough'), blockchain will be transformative. That ISS view also helps us gain clarity on the essence of what is in the realm of the possible for this technology; at that level there is no individual company, there is no industry, and there are no borders. Said another way, data knows no geographic borders.

These multiple layers of understanding (and myths) continue to hold back both understanding and adoption of blockchain, including (1) it **is** a technology discussion, (2) it is not ***only*** a technology discussion, (3) we can sprinkle blockchain dust on virtually anything, (4) blockchain is only good for a process improvement initiative, and (5) blockchain is breakthrough technology and will change entire industries.

"We are going to wait until someone figures out blockchain and then we will jump on board," and, "My business connects supply and demand—peer-to-peer technology won't affect us."

- Myth: It's best to wait.
- Myth: My business cannot be replaced.

If you need a ride and I have a car, we could argue that a ride-sharing app could be a better solution than the original taxi/cab model. However, their business model is to play 'matchmaker' and take a slice right off the top of the overall fee. But, if you need a ride and I have a car, **and** we can find each other in a trusted environment like blockchain, we may not need a middleman to essentially introduce us for a price.

This speaks to what was the original 'aha' moment for me in blockchain, and it was a global commerce scenario. To cross one or more borders, you need a series of people (e.g., broker, forwarder, likely multiple other 'middleman' players) that sit between parties. That translates to a lot of friction (delays, paperwork, resources, etc.) in those processes. Interoperability will be key. If we can envision a scenario where each entity can simply provide an anonymized link to a blockchain of the required data (country of origin, etc.) that can be accessed further downstream by the appropriate regulatory/clearing agency as the item moves through the logistics process, that item can progressively clear across borders much more quickly, and with much less friction. Not only do I believe that is the future of Clearance, World Customs Organization, World Trade Organization, and the Global Express Association each have stated similar beliefs:

"Blockchain is a giant leap for Customs in the 21st century".[5]

[5] "Blockchain is a giant leap for Customs in the 21st century."
Unveiling the Potential of Blockchain for Customs, World Customs Organization, June 2018, Yotaro Okazaki

Unveiling the Potential of Blockchain for Customs, World Customs Organization, June 2018, Yotaro Okazaki

"If we succeed in creating an ecosystem conducive to the wider development of Blockchain, international trade could well look radically different in 10 to 15 years".[6]

"Can Blockchain revolutionize international trade?," World Trade Organization, 2018, Emmanuelle Ganne

"Blockchain...can expand international trade by reducing friction at the border." "Call for Action: Development of open standards and interoperability protocols".[7]

Next Generation Border Clearance Through Disruptive Technologies, Global Express Association, August 2019

The issue is that middleman in that multistep process doesn't want to be late to the blockchain (peer-to-peer technology) game. I chose a global commerce/customs clearance scenario, but the point is the same for any company who has a business model that essentially sits between supply and demand.

Again, this portion of the discussion is focused on 'breakthrough' (revolution), and not 'process improvement' (evolution). There are very few true 'my business cannot be replaced' scenarios. In a peer-to-peer technology discussion, the question is, 'What value do you provide?' That is offered as a challenge for businesses to look at themselves in the mirror. The answer to the 'What value do you provide?' question will likely be different in a blockchain and web3 world. That's one of the reasons that 'why' is such a

[6] "If we succeed in creating an ecosystem conducive to the wider development of Blockchain, international trade could well look radically different in 10 to 15 years."

Can Blockchain revolutionize international trade?, World Trade Organization, 2018, Emmanuelle Ganne

[7] "Blockchain...can expand international trade by reducing friction at the border." "Call for Action: Development of open standards and interoperability protocols."

Next Generation Border Clearance Through Disruptive Technologies, Global Express Association, August 2019

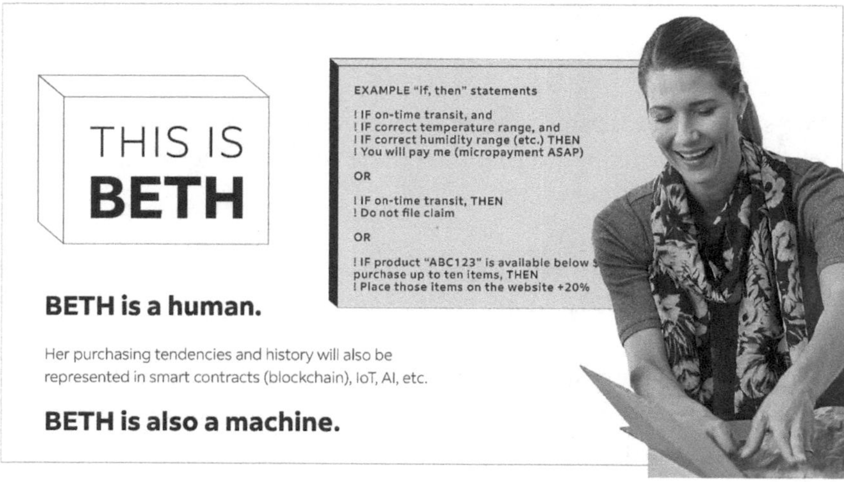

Fig. 2.2 This is Beth

critical discussion point for blockchain, why the C-Suite must be involved, and why—if you are going to sit on the sidelines with this technology—I strongly suggest you do so strategically and not passively (Fig. 2.2).

"Smart contracts are neither smart, nor a contract."

- Myth: Smart contracts are smart, and they are legal contracts.

I heard an attorney make this statement, and it is still perfect. Rather than the current description of 'smart contracts,' I hope and predict that we will come up with something that describes what these do much better (maybe 'code on the cloud,' or similar), because I think these will be transformative as well. Adding confusion to this, there are an increasing number of smart legal contracts that are both smart and also legal contracts, which is essentially a hybrid of the original reference we have been dealing with for many years.

Who is your customer? Today, if I were asked to define what a 'customer' is, I could start by saying, 'human' (in our example, "Beth"), and then maybe split into a shipper or receiver if I stick with a logistics example. However, if you will allow me to refer to a smart contract generically as a 'machine,' there will potentially be more 'machine' customers than 'human' customers within a few years, and many of them will have wallets. So, rather than a binary 'shipper' or 'receiver' (and human) today, we end up with a quadrant, with both human and machine shippers and human and machine receivers, and there will be a 'parent (human)-child (machine)' relationship and the children will have money to spend (though the parents will tell them where to spend it for the foreseeable future).

Fundamentally, that will change a lot of things about existing business models. Again, staying with a logistics example, a current sales model that defines a customer at a physical shipping or receiving location and then combines some geographic territory or total number of customers into a sales territory will be extinct when smart contracts become common. 'Beth' doesn't exist in some traditional industrial park. She may live at the end of a residential street and potentially could be controlling purchasing and shipping from her home, along with her smart contracts, and that current sales model is still looking for store fronts and industrial parks for the majority of their business base.

So, 'Beth' is a human. 'Beth' is also a machine. 'Beth' is invisible. 'Beth' is a customer. Go figure that one out, and don't wait because someone else is already working to solve it and the solution may bypass you entirely (Fig. 2.3).

Fig. 2.3 Coopetition

Diagram: Blockchain represented as a 'futuristic city' on the right. We are on the left—"Come on, let's get there right now." Unfortunately, there is a canyon between us, and most people are trying to cross that canyon alone by building a toll bridge. In the global commerce space, we think this will take a global village (a 'coopetition') to build the toll-free bridge, allowing everyone to build business models on the right ('futuristic city') after it is in place.

"I don't mind 'coopetition' in the blockchain space as long as I don't have to work with other companies."

- Myth: Coopetition = antitrust

'Coopetition' is ***not*** an antitrust discussion. The fine print on the graphic says, "Cooperating to develop the pro-competitive, open source platform on which blockchain will be based."

There are few absolutes in business, but one of those has been that you don't work with your competitors. The current U.S. antitrust laws have been in place for more than 100 years, and in the 'don't get your hand too close to a hot stove' scenario, most entities (and rightly so) stay far away from anything even remotely close to something that might be considered as antitrust.

Remember, we didn't lead with 'coopetition,' it was the inevitable realization from an ongoing journey. No, we can't just monetize blockchain. No, we can't just join a consortia and scale it globally. So, what could scale globally? An 'open' interoperable solution. And how do we contemplate such a thing? We must have a global effort—a 'coopetition'—to work through the creation of standards and protocols that will allow the world to take advantage of the transformative properties of blockchain, and beyond. This will be inter-enterprise, for the first time allowing enterprises to safely share applicable data, in a way compliant with antitrust laws. And there are few rules in this space, not only in terms of actual efforts but also culturally. Harvard Business Review included "The Rules of Co-Opetition" in their Jan-Feb 2021 publication, including "it's not unusual for rivals to team up to set standards and interoperability protocols."[8] However, their focus was more on true competitors working together on a competitive item or product. Yes, that is still 'coopetition,' but that isn't the reference I am making here. I'm focusing more on the 'what do we share in common' side of the discussion.

Another tangible example of 'coopetition' is the Blockchain Revolution Global panel discussion in 2019 where FedEx, DHL, and UPS—the members of the Global Express Association (GEA)—all shared the stage and discussed how reducing friction across borders was a benefit to each of them, their customers, and global trade. The GEA authored and provided a recommendation and a call to action to the World Customs Organization and the World Trade Organization on blockchain and emerging technologies. Again, within all applicable laws, it's not about where individual companies compete, it's about where they can agree to make the overall supply chain more efficient, to the benefit of each company's customers.

A good example of coopetition outside of blockchain was in March 2019 when the leaders of Germany's big three automakers—VW, Daimler, and BMW—all agreed that the future of German cars would be electric. [9] The point is, by agreeing that future German automobiles would be electric, they were also agreeing not to compete at the charging level—the infrastructure level—but at the model level. Rephrased, Germany can have a charging system for a wide range of autos that is common, but VW, Daimler, and BMW can each create their own electric vehicles and still compete at the model level.

Finally, we also saw coopetition immediately when the pandemic hit. In *Dealing in Security*,[10] authors Vinay Gupta and Mike Bennett created a 'target' visual using concentric circles, starting in the center of the

---

[8] "It's not unusual for rivals to team up to set standards and interoperability protocols."

The Rules of Co-Opetition, Harvard Business Review, Jan–Feb 2021, Adam Brandenburger and Barry Nalebuff

[9] A good example of coopetition outside of blockchain was in March 2019 when the leaders of Germany's big three automakers, VW, Daimler, and BMW, all agreed that the future of German cars was electric.

The 'Tesla Effect' hits Germany as VW, Daimler, and BMW fully commit to EVs, teslarati.com, March 24, 2019—link

[10] 'Target' reference around coopetition

Dealing in Security, Vinay Gupta, July 2010

'target' with the individual, and then expanding out to home, village, town, region, country, and, finally, world. Prior to the pandemic, we were all arguing across the back fence about our favorite sports teams (or pick a subject), essentially at the 'individual' level; but—sticking with the concentric circles example—we instantly changed the 'Where do we agree?' all the way to the 'world' level, and people and entities started to work to find PPE, ventilators, and so on for those around the world who they would never meet, but who were in need.

Psst...Whether or Not You Know It Yet, the Rules Have Changed

To date, most of the discussion around blockchain involves 'who,' 'what,' and 'when.' Unfortunately, that continues to take us down the 'blockchain is ***only*** a technology' path, which is not a scalable solution. Much more important is the discussion surrounding 'Why blockchain?' which moves this subject into the C-Suite and takes us down the path that 'blockchain is ***not only*** a technology.'

Just two examples of why blockchain is '***not only*** a technology' are peer-to-peer and smart contracts. We are truly at a 'disrupt, or be disrupted' moment. On the peer-to-peer front, if you and I can find each other, and do so in a trusted environment like blockchain, we may not need a middleman. For instance:

- Example: Party 'A' (supply), 'B' (middleman), 'C' (demand)
- 'A'—You can disrupt if you don't need to know 'B' (middleman) to meet 'C' (demand)
- 'B'—You can be disrupted if you are no longer needed to sit between 'A' (supply) and 'C' (demand)
- 'C'—You can disrupt if you don't need to know 'B' (middleman) to meet 'A' (supply)

With smart contracts, let me introduce you to your new (and ultimately your largest) customer segment, which I referred to earlier in the 'Beth' example as a 'machine.' I don't know of many companies who are currently structured to even comprehend an automated essentially invisible 'customer' segment, let alone to take advantage of the impact or, conversely, to react to another entity who jumps into that space.

The magnitude of these impacts to current business models is enormous:

"(Blockchain is) the next frontier that's going to completely change worldwide supply chains."[11]

– *Frederick W. Smith, FedEx Founder, Chairman and CEO, 2018*

"For blockchain to be transformative, it must be bigger than us."[12]

– *Robert B. Carter, FedEx CIO, 2019*

If open is inevitable, this technology won't scale if we are all trying to 'win' at the application layer and there is no foundational level in place. It will only scale by us working together to create the pro-competitive open source platform on which blockchain will be based. That helps us to collectively bridge the canyon depicted in the coopetition diagram.

That leads to 'coopetition'—it's not about where we compete, it is about where we can agree. We must focus on where we can 'all' win, and that paradigm shift may mean the difference between success and failure in the years to come.

As we discussed, the pandemic is an excellent and recent example of coopetition outside of blockchain, going from good-natured arguing with neighbors about our favorite sports teams to instantly working selflessly with people we will never meet to move PPE around the world to other people we will never meet, because it was the right thing to do, for example, it's about where we can agree.

Traditionally, 'coopetition' hasn't been taught in business schools or on your first day of work. It is a layer of unrealized opportunity. In this case, it could be thought of as both process improvement (evolution) and

[11] "(Blockchain is) the next frontier that's going to completely change worldwide supply chains." Frederick W. Smith—Consensus NYC, May 14, 2018—link—16:48

[12] "For blockchain to be transformative, it must be bigger than us."

Robert B. Carter, FedEx CIO, 2019—I think this was created internally but has been made public and I have quoted it since it came out. Not sure about the footnote references.

'breakthrough' (revolution). It is also a cultural challenge. In the earlier example, the members of the Global Express Association (FedEx, UPS, and DHL) each conclude that if we can reduce friction across borders, we win, our customers win, and global trade also wins.

Another question to consider moving forward is, where else in business do we 'agree,' even though it might mean working with nontraditional partners, or even (under the right circumstances) with our competitors in a pro-competitive way compliant with antitrust law? Safety is one example of this, but many others exist as well. I believe this is one of the key growth opportunities in the next decade and beyond for many entities, rather than only their traditional approach to mostly internal quality process improvement initiatives. Again, what kinds of inter-enterprise opportunities exist?

This discussion would not be complete without including the critical nature of standards. If we are developing a pro-competitive open source platform on which blockchain will be based, we need to establish and play by the same rules. Most key areas in our world involve standards of some type. When we think of standards, we can include the late 1800s when we got to the current railroad track gauge, or even the alphabet. Standards help get us to increased network effects, which also increases adoption.

The BITA Standards Council (BSC) is focused on providing the open-source and royalty-free standards for blockchain and web3-enabled global commerce. Focus areas to date include standards around tracking, location, bill of lading, equipment, purchase order, repair, return, and IoT metadata. Many of the BSC learnings are similar to key points in this writing and represent the 'change agent' mentality I have covered. 'Where can we agree?' (coopetition) rules the day on the Board, Technical Committees and Working Groups, and the broader value of BSC will be to work with other standards bodies to truly create global standards to help accelerate adoption of blockchain technology, so we can all 'win.'

Conclusion

Blockchain ***is*** a technology discussion, but it is ***not only*** a technology discussion, and that has significantly complicated and delayed both understanding and adoption of uses we can envision around this technology. Most people in the space have tried to figure it out and slap a logo on it and try to monetize it, but blockchain has changed the rules, and there is no going back.

'Who,' 'what,' and 'when' are interesting, but it's not until we get to 'why' that we really start to get traction, especially with those who will ultimately have the greatest impact on scaling blockchain and emerging technologies—the C-Suite.

C-Suite executives speak the language of business so they approached blockchain the same way they approached many other business scenarios, by reflexively trying to apply a common language they all speak to a completely new way of thinking. They've asked the question, "What's the ROI?" R&D came back with, "but you don't understand, this is a completely new way of thinking," to which the C-Suite said, "That's great—come back when you have an ROI," and we have been repeating that for multiple years, to the detriment of adoption. The technical side is coming along, and amazing things have been done in the past five years, but we are virtually still stuck in neutral on the business discussion.

Almost no one understands how a cell phone works, but they all know how to use it. So, let's take that approach to our C-Suite discussion. As an example, if the CFO is responsible for the average days outstanding for receivables, which currently sits around 40 days, let's explain that a smart contract could create a 'net-zero days' scenario. My sense is we now have the CFO's attention with an actual business example, and something the CFO is measured on annually. Then, in order to support the CFO's (now) request for the use of smart contracts, the CIO will need people to create smart contracts, the Chief Legal Officer will need bilingual attorneys, essentially fluent in both paper and smart contracts and smart legal contracts, and we are now half-way around the C-Suite. The sooner we come up with legitimate business use cases to solve for existing business issues and where waste and friction currently exist, and use the new technology, such as peer-to-peer and smart contracts, to contemplate both opportunity and risk, the sooner business leaders will expect these capabilities, which will drive both innovation and adoption.

Tokenization has been a difficult concept to break down into simple terms to date. Today, value is frequently controlled at the top of a business model. However, with blockchain, peer-to-peer technology, and tokens, that value will shift to those actually creating the value to a much greater extent, such as the artist who actually wrote a song, or the photographer who actually took the picture that is being copied and pasted by everyone on the internet, or each of us owning the data we choose to share on social media.

The transformative nature of peer-to-peer technology, smart contracts, and standards also means it isn't just each of us competing against each other to 'win' in this space, it actually means our success in this area will be measured by how we work together as a global team, in a 'coopetition' mindset.

If it is correct that most people are still trying to jump to the monetization of blockchain without the broader foundation being built, and they have not yet concluded that 'open' in global commerce is inevitable, those people are inadvertently holding back the widespread global adoption of blockchain technology. As such, the sooner we can get them over to the 'open' side of things, the sooner blockchain will scale.

Finally, whether we ever realize the promise of blockchain is no longer important. It has already changed the way we think of what is in the realm of the possible, and it has already changed the rules.

3

Finding the Right Balance: Technical and Political Decentralization in the Token Economy

Michelle Pfister, Niclas Kannengießer, and Ali Sunyaev

The Token Economy and the Need for Cross-Ledger Interoperability

Decentralization of Token Economy Instances

By increasing the automation of business processes, favoring economies of scale, and enabling improved customer outreach, digital platforms have become a backbone of business ecosystems. A business ecosystem is

---

M. Pfister
Institute of Applied Informatics and Formal Description Methods, Karlsruhe Institute of Technology, Karlsruhe, Germany
e-mail: michelle.pfister@alumni.kit.edu

N. Kannengießer (✉) • A. Sunyaev
Institute of Applied Informatics and Formal Description Methods, Karlsruhe Institute of Technology, Karlsruhe, Germany

KASTEL Security Research Labs, Karlsruhe, Germany
e-mail: niclas.kannengiesser@kit.edu; sunyaev@kit.edu

M. C. Lacity, H. Treiblmaier (eds.), *Blockchains and the Token Economy*, Technology, Work and Globalization, https://doi.org/10.1007/978-3-030-95108-5_3

an "economic community of interacting actors (here: individuals and organizations) that all affect each other through their activities" (Jacobides et al., 2018, p. 2257). Among the various uses of digital platforms in business ecosystems (e.g., for information exchange in supply chains), digital platforms are often involved in managing ownership of assets, such as fiat money and stocks in online banking or electronic money systems (e.g., DigiCash; Camp et al., 1995), where assets are represented as tokens (i.e., sequences of characters). In this context, asset ownership management refers to the *creation of tokens* that reference real-world assets (e.g., fiat money) and the use of these tokens to *prove* and *transfer asset ownership* (Sunyaev et al., 2021). The concept of using digital tokens for asset ownership management is called the token economy. A token economy instance is an application of the token economy concept in a business ecosystem and comprises the digital platforms used for asset ownership management, the actors providing these digital platforms as well as actors consuming services available via these platforms, and the political means to operate a token economy instance (Sunyaev et al., 2021). There can be multiple token economy instances that use the same digital platform, and individual instances can use multiple digital platforms, such as when companies in one business ecosystem transfer money through the independent but interconnected online banking platforms of different banks to other business ecosystems. The actors and means enabling interoperability between digital platforms are also part of token economy instances.

Today's digital asset ownership management is usually mediated by central actors, such as banks and notaries, which provide digital platforms to other actors (e.g., for online banking). One of the major tasks of central actors in asset ownership management is the prevention of fraud, which includes the manipulation of account balances and double-spending. Double-spending refers to using the same tokens in multiple transactions (Karame et al., 2012; Nakamoto, 2008). For example, actor *A* owns USD 100, represented as a number in online banking. *A* transfers ownership of that USD 100 via an online banking transaction, using "USD 100" as a token, to actor *B*. After the transaction, *A* must not be able to transfer the same USD 100 to another actor, *C*. Otherwise, the USD 100 would have been double-spent, and *B* and *C* would each own the same asset. Token economy instances that mainly rely on central actors represent centralized instances.

In centralized token economy instances, central actors usually enable interoperability with other central actors so that tokens can be transferred between them across digital platforms. To this end, central actors agree on technical and political standards (e.g., as proposed by the Society for Worldwide Interbank Financial Telecommunication; short: SWIFT). By using standards, actors can easily interact with other actors, independent of the digital platforms used, increasing flexibility in business relations and actors' ability to reach other actors (e.g., to transfer assets for products; Panurach, 1996) and enabling large network effects (Scott et al., 2017).

A strong reliance on central actors, however, can lead to technical and political drawbacks. Technically, asset ownership management often relies on digital platforms controlled by central actors (e.g., in terms of maintenance and security). Such centralized digital platforms can be prone to vulnerabilities regarding data integrity because only the central actors controlling a platform have control over the stored data and can be able to tamper with it because the processes executed via the platform cannot be verified by other actors. Politically, the central actors can accumulate decision rights for the governing of provided digital platforms, dependencies on the central actors can be increased, and all individual actors must trust in the honest and reliable behaviors of the central actors (Chen et al., 2020). For example, the decisions regarding the specifications of application programming interfaces (APIs) offered for interactions with digital platforms are made by the central actors providing the platforms, which can limit the flexibility in asset ownership management for actors using the digital platform. Moreover, actors must trust that the central actor will not stop providing services on a digital platform or increase service fees.

Decentralizing token economy instances can address drawbacks associated with the involvement of central actors in asset ownership management by decreasing dependencies on central actors and their digital platforms. Instead, various actors jointly operate a digital platform and share the associated responsibilities, such as for platform maintenance. In this chapter, we focus on two perspectives on the decentralization of token economy instances: *technical* and *political*. Technical decentralization refers to the "degree that increases and decreases with the number of distributed, interconnected nodes that operate independently without a central authority" (Sunyaev et al., 2021, p. 3). Political decentralization refers to "the degree of equal distribution of permissions and responsibilities across all agents [actors] that independently act according to their individual incentives" (Sunyaev et al., 2021, p. 4).

Decentralizing token economy instances can enable direct transactions between actors without mediation (e.g., by banks; Beck, 2018), improve cost efficiency (Catalini, 2017), and prevent performance bottlenecks. Moreover, the equal and independent engagement of actors in the advancement of token economy instances can be increased (e.g., Chen et al., 2020), for example, by allowing actors to propose new asset representations through tokens to increase flexibility in managing asset ownership.

To decentralize token economy instances, multiple actors should be able to participate in decision-making for the crucial tasks in asset ownership management that are currently performed by central actors. In summary, the main challenges to be addressed in decentralized token economy instances are as follows:

1. Prevention of the double-spending of tokens.
2. Storage of account balances and transactions in a tamper-resistant way.
3. Coordination of actors to reach agreements.

Decentralized Token Economy Instances That Are Based on Distributed Ledger Technology

To decentralize digital platforms for asset ownership management in token economy instances, distributed ledger technology (DLT) can be used. DLT allows for the automation of crucial tasks of the central actors involved in centralized token economy instances (e.g., the prevention of double-spending and the manipulation of balances; Sunyaev et al., 2021) and makes these task executions verifiable for any actor with access to the used distributed ledger. For example, each actor with access to the distributed ledger can verify that transactions have been correctly processed and detect fraudulent transactions (e.g., in double-spending attempts) which shifts the trust of actors from a central actor to a set of actors that jointly govern and operate the digital platform and the ledger.

A DLT system comprises a network of computing devices (i.e., nodes), where nodes are usually controlled by various actors. Nodes jointly operate a replicated distributed database (i.e., a distributed ledger; Sunyaev, 2020). Each node maintains a local replication of the ledger, which stores a set of transactions between actors via the DLT system, and executes the same DLT protocol. A consensus mechanism is used to achieve consistency across all versions of a ledger stored by individual nodes. Many consensus mechanisms used in DLT (e.g., Nakamoto Consensus in Bitcoin) are Byzantine fault tolerant (Lamport et al., 1982), as they resolve double-spending and prevent retroactive manipulations of asset ownership by storing transactions in a tamper-resistant way, which resembles the tasks of central actors.

In DLT-based token economy instances, tokens can be created and managed in two principal ways: *first*, via the DLT protocol; *second*, via smart contracts. Tokens created via the DLT protocol are native tokens and are often used in DLT systems to incentivize nodes to contribute computational resources to the operation of a DLT system. For example, nodes in the Bitcoin network can receive newly created tokens as rewards for participating in the consensus mechanism process (Nakamoto, 2008). Using smart contracts, actors can implement custom business logic to create and manage tokens representing arbitrary assets on top of DLT protocols. Smart contracts are software programs that are deployed to a distributed ledger and can be called via transactions (Kannengießer et al., 2021). Tokens created and managed via smart contracts can be acquired by using native tokens of the respective distributed ledger. Smart contracts increase flexibility in token economy instances by enabling the development of customized tokens and logic for asset ownership management (e.g., conditional payments). Several smart contracts offer functionalities for buying customized tokens in exchange for native tokens. Actors transfer native tokens to the smart contract by issuing a transaction to the DLT system. The transaction needs to call a specified function of the target smart contract. After processing the transaction, the smart contract keeps the received native tokens and updates the balance of custom tokens associated with the actor, who transferred the native tokens, in its persistent storage. For example, CryptoKitties is an application based on an Ethereum smart contract that creates customized tokens representing collectables, called *cats*. *Cats* can be bought via the CryptoKitties smart contract and are paid for in Ether. The CryptoKitties smart contract retains the tokens and assigns ownership of the purchased *cat* tokens to the actor who paid for them. The flexible specification, creation, and management of DLT-based tokens allow multiple decentralized token economy instances to coexist on the same DLT system. However, the formation of decentralized token economy instances comprising different DLT systems is still a challenge, for example, due to a lack of technical standards for DLT protocols and the uncertain applicability of prior governance mechanisms in the decentralized connection of decentralized systems.

There are a variety of DLT-based token economy instances (e.g., in decentralized finance) where actors can benefit from the customizability of terms for automated payments, for example, in decentralized crowdfunding and offerings for fractional shares. To provide such services, business ecosystems pose individual technical requirements on DLT protocols (e.g., energy-efficient transaction processing).

While requirements for DLT protocols strongly vary between business ecosystems (e.g., large scalability and high transaction throughput is often required for IoT use cases; Lücking et al., 2021), trade-offs between DLT characteristics prevent DLT systems from simultaneously meeting all these requirements. Those trade-offs that cause an improvement in one characteristic (e.g., availability) can lead to the decline in another (e.g., consistency; Kannengießer, Lins, et al., 2020). To meet the various technical requirements of business ecosystems, despite the trade-offs between DLT characteristics, numerous specialized DLT protocols have been developed, such as Quorum for connecting banks for international payments and VeChain for tracking and tracing in supply chain management. Specialized DLT protocols use individual consensus mechanisms, data structures (e.g., blocks including transactions or only transactions), and protocols for communication between nodes and have different smart contract capabilities regarding expressiveness and capabilities for interacting with information systems external to a DLT system (Kannengießer et al., 2021). As token economy instances use DLT protocols or even combinations of DLT protocols suitable to the requirements specific to the business ecosystems, the technical heterogeneity across DLT systems used in token economy instances increases, which complicates the connection of DLT systems (e.g., because individual APIs must be considered), thus hindering asset ownership management across token economy instances. As long as actors using one DLT system cannot transact with actors using another one, network effects and flexibility in business relations can hardly increase beyond individual DLT systems (Sunyaev et al., 2021; Zhou & Zhu, 2006). To overcome these drawbacks and enable actors using different DLT systems to interact with each other in token economy instances, asset ownership management across DLT systems is required.

Cross-ledger interoperability (CLI) offers the technical capabilities to connect isolated DLT systems and overcome drawbacks, such as limited network effects and flexibility in business relations. CLI can enable the following three principal functionalities (Kannengießer, Pfister, et al., 2020; Lacity, 2020): *cross-ledger token transfer*, *cross-ledger token exchange*, and *cross-ledger smart contract execution*. Cross-ledger token transfers comprise unidirectional transactions that transfer tokens from one DLT system to another. Cross-ledger token exchanges require at least two dependent token transfers, one on each of the relevant DLT systems, to exchange tokens between actors. Tokens are only exchanged between two actors *A* and *B* if both actors own accounts on both DLT systems and agree on making a specific number of tokens on their distinct DLT systems accessible to their corresponding exchange partner. Cross-ledger smart contract execution refers to the execution of a smart contract on DLT system *B* via a transaction issued to DLT system *A*, but the transaction does not necessarily transfer tokens. Smart contract execution across DLT systems, moreover, allows actors to execute business logic in targeted DLT systems (e.g., to receive tokens created by smart contracts).

CLI is achieved through CLI protocols that are executed in CLI systems (e.g., BTC Relay, Fusion, and Kusama). CLI systems are designed to secure cross-ledger asset ownership management (e.g., by preventing double-spending) and to coordinate interactions between actors of different DLT systems. CLI systems can be centralized (e.g., managed by central actors) or decentralized (e.g., managed by a set of actors), which affects the degree of the decentralization of token economy instances incorporating different DLT systems. In a cross-ledger token economy instance, for example, a CLI system provided by a central actor can recentralize the interactions of actors from one DLT system with another one, thus reintroducing drawbacks of centralized token economy instances, such as decreased availability, censorship resistance, and fraud resistance. However, a too high degree of political decentralization (e.g., caused by the engagement of too many actors into the governance of a CLI system) can slow down decision-making, whereas the delegation of decision rights to a central actor can lead to the neglect of other actors' interests. To enable DLT-based token economy instances in which actors can use different DLT systems while preserving the benefits of decentralization (e.g., the verifiability of transactions by each actor), approaches to the technical connection of DLT systems as well as the governance of CLI systems and connected DLT systems must be incorporated by actors. Only with appropriate governance can the technical and political decentralization of token economy instances that encompass different DLT systems be reconciled.

The rest of this chapter explains principal approaches to technically connect and politically manage token economy instances comprising multiple DLT systems. In the next section, it is explained how DLT-based token economy instances can interact via CLI by presenting patterns of CLI systems. For each pattern, it is described how the degrees of the technical decentralization of connected DLT systems can be affected. "Political Decentralization in Token Economy Instances That Comprise Different Distributed Ledger Technology Systems" section elucidates political decentralization of token economy instances comprising multiple DLT systems in the context of decentralized governance. In "Drawing

Conclusions from the Technical and Political Perspectives on Centralization and Decentralization of CLI Systems" section, certain ways to balance the centralization and decentralization of token economy instances comprising different DLT systems to synergize the benefits of centralized (e.g., fast decision-making; Chen et al., 2020) and decentralized systems (e.g., direct transactions between actors; Beck, 2018) are discussed.

Technical Decentralization in Token Economy Instances That Comprise Different Distributed Ledger Technology Systems

Various CLI protocols have been proposed (e.g., atomic cross-chain swap and XCLAIM; Herlihy, 2018; Zamyatin et al., 2019) and implemented as CLI systems, such as BTCRelay and Kusama. CLI systems comprise both actors and technical components, which have different designs to provide CLI functionalities (i.e., *token transfer*, *token exchange*, and *smart contract execution*). These designs strongly impact CLI systems' degrees of technical decentralization because they specify the actors and nodes involved in operating a CLI system and how DLT systems communicate (i.e., direct or indirect, see Fig. 3.1; Sunyaev et al., 2021). DLT systems are directly connected by CLI systems when nodes of different DLT systems can communicate with one another without mediators. In indirect connections, nodes in DLT systems are not able to directly communicate with each other but communicate via mediators, such as notaries (see *N* in Fig. 3.1). CLI systems enabling indirect communication between DLT systems can technically centralize the connection between DLT systems and a CLI system, which can reintroduce drawbacks of centralized token economy instances (e.g., the dependence on central actors for asset ownership management across digital platforms).

The following sections describe that different typologies of the communication between DLT systems via CLI systems exist and how

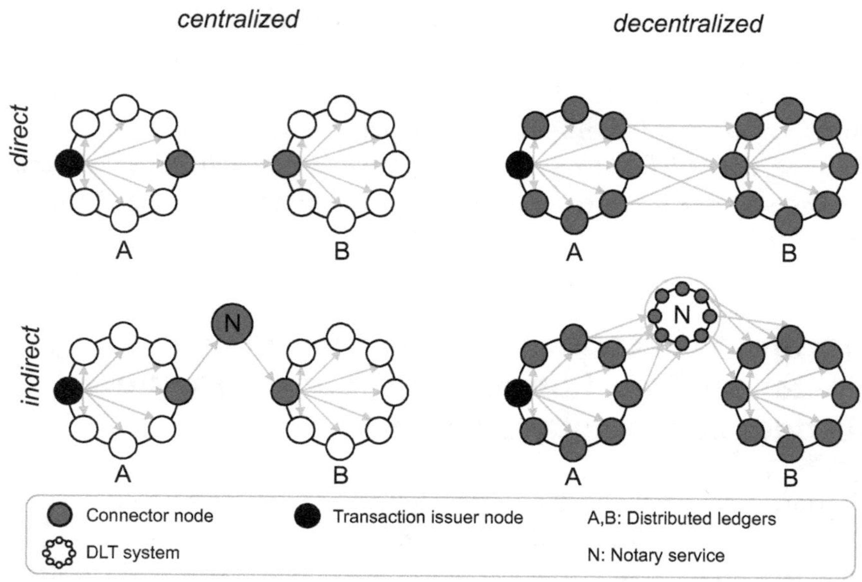

Fig. 3.1 Overview of methods for communication between nodes (adapted from Sunyaev et al., 2021)

these typologies can affect the corresponding degree of technical decentralization of token economy instances, which comprise different DLT systems.

Cross-Ledger Interoperability Patterns and Their Degrees of Technical Decentralization

Cross-ledger token transfers usually require that the tokens to be transferred are not accessible to actors in a source DLT system once a corresponding number of tokens in a target distributed ledger has become accessible to them. If the tokens in the source DLT system remain accessible after new tokens have been created in the target distributed ledger, tokens referring to the same value could then be spent in both DLT systems, allowing for cross-ledger double-spending.

To prevent cross-ledger double-spending, the atomicity of CLI functionalities must be guaranteed (Herlihy, 2018). CLI functionalities are usually executed based on sequences of transactions in DLT systems that are involved in cross-ledger asset ownership management. Atomicity in CLI functionalities refers to the capability of a CLI protocol to guarantee that either all transactions required for a CLI functionality are successfully processed in all relevant DLT systems or that no transaction takes place (Herlihy, 2018). If a CLI protocol does not guarantee atomicity, asset ownership management using that protocol can become prone to theft and cross-ledger double-spending.

To achieve atomicity of CLI functionalities, transactions required in CLI functionalities must be verified in all DLT systems that exchange tokens with one another. Such verifications prove whether transactions have been successfully processed in a DLT system or not. If a verification fails, the asset exchange is aborted. CLI systems can require actors to verify their transactions themselves through direct communication or employ a central actor, who verifies transactions on behalf of the actors exchanging tokens across DLT systems, for indirect communication.

Among a variety of CLI system designs three principal patterns of CLI systems have emerged (Kannengießer, Pfister, et al., 2020): the *manual asset exchange (MAE) pattern*, the *notary pattern*, and the *sidechain pattern*. In the following section, these patterns are explained, and their individual degrees of technical decentralization are discussed. In the descriptions of the CLI patterns, the steps for cross-ledger interactions illustrated in Fig. 3.2 are referenced to illustrate the basic functioning of each pattern.

Manual Asset Exchange Pattern

The MAE pattern enables cross-ledger token exchanges and can be applied manually by at least two actors without software artifacts, except for the involved DLT systems and optional tools for the communication between actors needed, for example, to agree on the number of exchanged tokens (Buterin, 2016; Kannengießer, Pfister, et al., 2020). After the actors have agreed on exchanging tokens, two principal actions are executed: *token locking* and *token provision.* First, exchange partners lock their tokens in their respective source-distributed ledger. Tokens are locked to actors when an access control mechanism prevents these actors

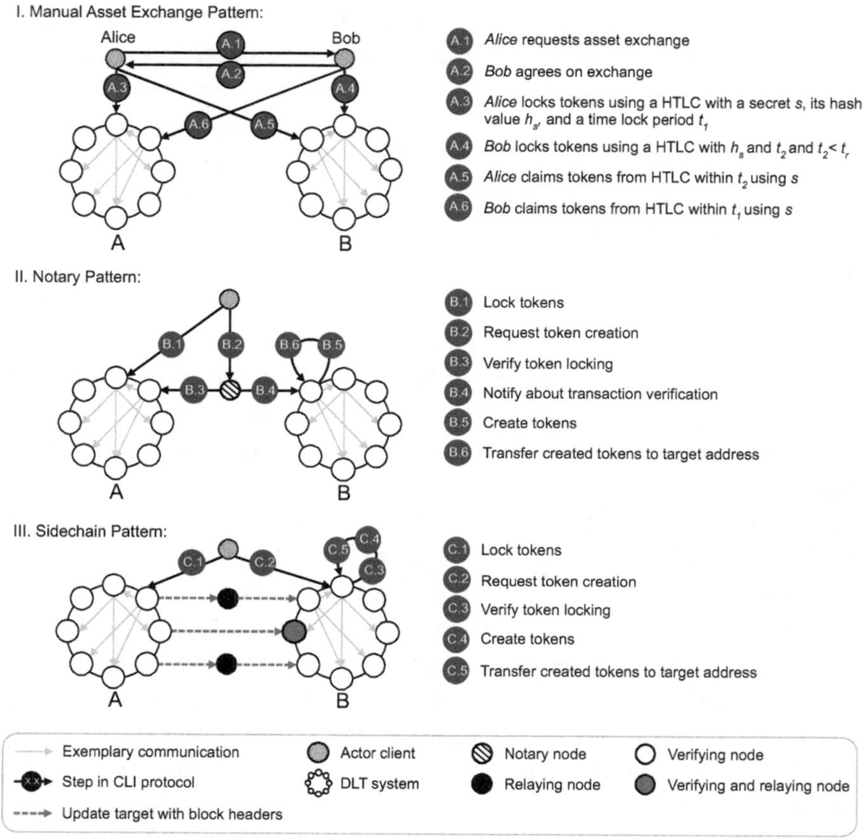

Fig. 3.2 A schematic overview of CLI patterns and their protocols

from accessing the tokens. In *token provision*, the tokens are unlocked by the exchange partners in their respective target distributed ledger (e.g., by using a secret).

For locking and unlocking tokens, the MAE pattern often applies the atomic cross-chain swap protocol, which is based on hashed timelock contracts (HTLCs). HTLCs are smart contracts that allow for payments that are conditional on a hashlock and a timelock. The hashlock stores a hash value h_s, computed by a hash function h from a secret value s. The hashlock grants access to tokens after receiving $\hat{s}$, when $h(s) = h(\hat{s})$ applies. A timelock has a value t, which specifies the maximum time during which tokens are locked. When t elapses, locked tokens are then automatically returned to sender. To unlock tokens locked in an HTLC, a transaction must be sent to the HTLC and execute its hashlock function with an argument $\hat{s}$, with $h(s)=h(\hat{s})$ within t (Herlihy, 2018). The probability for an attacker to find an $\hat{s}$ with $\hat{s} \neq s$ and $h(s)=h(\hat{s})$ within t must be negligible to achieve a high level of security for an HTLC.

The following example illustrates the functioning of an MAE pattern that uses the atomic cross-chain swap protocol based on HTLCs (Buterin, 2016): In Step I.1, Alice asks Bob to exchange her tokens from DLT system A with his tokens from DLT system B. Bob agrees on the exchange in Step I.2. Alice creates s and then computes h_s. In Step I.3, Alice deploys her HTLC to DLT system A, with the hash value h_s and a timelock t_1, and locks the number of tokens she wants to exchange by using the HTLC. In Step I.4, Alice shares h_s with Bob. After Bob has verified that Alice's HTLC has been deployed and the tokens are locked, Bob deploys an HTLC in DLT system B, where the hashlock also uses h_s, but with a timelock $t_2 < t_r$; t_r corresponds to the time remaining for the timelock t_1. Bob locks the tokens to be exchanged with Alice's tokens by using his HTLC (Step I.4). Alice knows s and can claim the tokens locked in Bob's HTLC before t_2 elapses (Step I.5). After t_2 has elapsed, Bob can face two situations. In the first situation, Alice claimed the tokens from Bob's HTLC using s, thus disclosing s to Bob. Using s, Bob can claim the tokens from Alice's HTLC before t_1 elapses (Step I.6). In this case, both transactions are completed. In the second situation, Alice does not claim the tokens that are locked in Bob's HTLC, and the HTLC transfers the locked tokens back to Bob after t_2. Because Bob does not know the secret value s, he cannot claim the tokens from Alice's HTLC, and they are also returned to her after t_1 elapses. In this case, neither of the transactions is completed.

Assuming that both actors act rationally, the HTLC-based atomic cross-chain swap protocol guarantees that either both transactions in the token exchange are successfully executed or that neither are (Herlihy, 2018). Atomicity can only be violated when actors act irrationally, for example, when Alice shares s with Bob without claiming her tokens, and Bob claims the tokens from Alice's HTLC. Alice then loses ownership of her own tokens to Bob on ledger A, while Bob keeps the ownership of his tokens on ledger B.

MAEs exhibit a high degree of technical decentralization in token exchange because no central actor is required, and actors can communicate directly. Exchange partners are found in manifold ways, for example, through decentralized exchanges. However, the MAE pattern is only applicable if actors from different DLT systems agree on tokens to be exchanged. Using the MAE pattern, cross-ledger token exchanges are the only CLI functionality that can be provided to actors (Koens & Poll, 2019).

Notary Pattern

CLI systems associated with the notary pattern can enable token exchanges, token transfers, and smart contract executions across DLT systems (Koens & Poll, 2019) and can automate certain processes in CLI systems that apply the MAE pattern (e.g., transaction verification). Multiple DLT systems are connected via a mediator, called a notary, which passes on information (e.g., for transaction verification) about one distributed ledger to another (Buterin, 2016). In this way, notaries can coordinate manual processes (e.g., finding an exchange partner and transaction verifications) performed in MAE-based CLI systems to a certain degree. Notaries can be centralized (i.e., a single central actor, as in Binance) or decentralized (i.e., a set of notaries that collaborate in a decentralized manner, as in the Interledger Protocol; Deng et al., 2018).

Notary-based CLI systems execute cross-ledger token transfers from DLT system *A* to DLT system *B* in two steps: *token locking* and *token provision.* In token locking, a transaction is sent to lock tokens in *A* and ensure that these tokens cannot be spent again (Step II.1). The tokens can either be locked indefinitely or can be unlocked in future cross-ledger token exchanges. For token exchanges, Notary-based CLI systems can apply the atomic cross-chain swap protocol, as in MAE, but can also automate the manual actions (e.g., order matching and transaction verification). After the tokens are locked, the token provision on *B* can be requested (Step II.2). To prevent cross-ledger double-spending, the transaction for token locking must be confirmed in distributed ledger *A* before the corresponding tokens on *B* are provided (Step II.3). In token provision, either new tokens (e.g., native tokens or tokens created by a smart contract) representing the tokens locked in *A* are created in DLT system *B* (Back et al., 2014), or tokens previously locked in *B* are unlocked and made accessible to the respective actor (as in MAE-based CLI systems). The notary then verifies transactions in both DLT systems and notifies nodes in *B* that the tokens in *A* have been reliably locked (Step II.4). Then, the corresponding tokens are provided in *B* (Steps II.5 and II.6).

A notary-based CLI system is easily customizable (e.g., compared to sidechains); it can be used to connect most DLT systems. Therefore, the notary pattern offers large flexibility to achieve CLI. However, the notary pattern relies on indirect communication and introduces the notary as a potential single point of failure. Actors depend on the notary for cross-ledger interactions because they must rely on the timeliness and correctness of the employed notary's notifications. Therefore, the degree of technical decentralization decreases, and central actors can emerge, as in current centralized token economy instances.

Sidechain Pattern

CLI systems that implement the sidechain pattern can enable token exchanges, token transfers, and smart contract executions across DLT systems in an automated yet decentralized way (Koens & Poll, 2019). In the sidechain pattern, there are two DLT systems, where one or both can play the role of a sidechain (Back et al., 2014; Buterin, 2016). Sidechains are DLT systems in which a smart contract is used to verify that transactions are stored in a distributed ledger. For verification, a smart contract usually uses the block headers of a target ledger (Back et al., 2014). Transaction verifications are cryptographically secured and do not require trust in central actors. After successful transaction verification, the intended CLI functionality is performed on a sidechain (e.g., transferring tokens to a specific actor's address). Two exemplary CLI systems associated with the sidechain pattern are BTC Relay (Buterin, 2016) and Cosmos (Kwon & Buchman, 2016).

Like in the notary pattern, tokens are transferred between DLT systems *A* and *B* in two steps: *token locking* and *token provision.* In token locking (Step III.1), tokens are locked in *A*. Then, the provision of corresponding tokens is requested in *B* (Step III.2). Tokens are provided by creating tokens for one-way asset transfers or unlocking tokens (Steps III.4 and III.5). Instead of having a notary vouch that token locking has been completed in *A*, *B* can verify the transaction for token locking with a mechanism, such as simple payment verification (SPV; Step III.3), implemented in a smart contract (Back et al., 2014). If only one of the multiple DLT systems has smart contract capabilities sufficient to verify transactions, then only that DLT system can become a sidechain. That sidechain is called one-way pegged (Back et al., 2014). If multiple DLT systems have the capability to verify transactions in other distributed ledgers, bidirectional transaction verifications are possible between these ledgers. Each of the distributed ledgers can become a sidechain. Both are considered two-way pegged sidechains.

An example of a one-way pegged sidechain is BTC Relay, where only Bitcoins can be used to pay for Ethereum tokens but not vice versa. BTC Relay uses the Ethereum blockchain as a sidechain and implements a mechanism to verify transactions on the Bitcoin blockchain using an Ethereum smart contract (*BTC Relay*, 2018). The Ethereum blockchain can play the role of a sidechain for the Bitcoin blockchain. For transaction verifications, the BTC Relay smart contract stores the current block headers of the Bitcoin blockchain. To this end, the latest Bitcoin block headers are issued to the BTC Relay contract by nodes, called relayers. Relayers can be set up by any actor with access to the Ethereum and Bitcoin blockchains. Relayers do not need to be trusted like notaries because the correctness of data they issue to the BTC Relay smart contract can be cryptographically verified (Buterin, 2016). In this way, transactions in the Bitcoin blockchain can be verified by smart contracts in the Ethereum sidechain via the BTC Relay contract.

Sidechains exhibit a high degree of decentralization because transactions in another distributed ledger are verified without a central actor. Instead, nodes of sidechains directly communicate with nodes of other DLT systems (e.g., Cosmos) or via various relayers (Buterin, 2016). Sidechains use the built-in lightweight verification mechanisms of DLT systems, executed by smart contracts deployed to the distributed ledger, and the execution directly on-chain enables sidechains to largely automate CLI functionalities. Despite the potential to largely automate CLI functionalities in a decentralized way, CLI systems applying the sidechain pattern pose technical requirements on DLT systems, limiting flexibility in the application of the sidechain pattern compared to the MAE pattern and the notary pattern. For example, DLT systems must support specific smart contract capabilities to execute verification mechanisms. DLT systems that do not meet these requirements cannot be fully integrated into a network of decentralized token economy instance by using the sidechain pattern.

Dependencies Between Technical Decentralization and Security and Performance Characteristics

In the following section, dependencies between DLT properties (e.g., performance and security) and the degree of technical decentralization of token economy instances based on multiple DLT systems are illustrated in the example of cross-ledger token transfers. In isolated DLT systems, trade-offs between DLT properties, such as security and performance, can impact the degree of technical decentralization of a DLT system (Kannengießer, Lins, et al., 2020). In public-permissionless DLT systems (e.g., Bitcoin and Ethereum), any node can join or leave a DLT system and can participate in the consensus mechanism. If a large number of independent nodes participate in a DLT system, the DLT system can achieve a high degree of decentralization, which is desirable in terms of security (Gojka et al., 2021; Kannengießer, Lins, et al., 2020). To achieve a high degree of technical decentralization, all nodes in a DLT system should be able to directly communicate with each other and to participate in consensus finding with equal influence.

Consensus mechanisms can achieve two types of finality: *immediate* or *probabilistic*. Finality is reached when a transaction is included in the distributed ledger and cannot be altered or reversed (e.g., by excluding the transaction from the main branch of the distributed ledger). Most consensus mechanisms with immediate finality, such as Practical

Byzantine Fault Tolerance (PBFT; Castro & Liskov, 1999), cannot scale to a large number of nodes due to the increasing communication complexity. This limited scalability can decrease the possible degree of decentralization of DLT systems because only a limited subset of nodes in a DLT system can be considered in consensus finding (Kannengießer, Lins, et al., 2020). Consensus mechanisms that allow for a high degree of decentralization (e.g., Nakamoto consensus in Bitcoin) mostly relax consistency assumptions to allow for the consideration of more nodes in consensus finding. These consensus mechanisms often achieve probabilistic finality, which is why it can remain uncertain whether a transaction issued to the DLT system will eventually be stored in the distributed ledger (Nakamoto, 2008). Over time, inclusion of transactions becomes more likely to be confirmed by all nodes in a DLT system so that the transaction will remain in the ledger (Kannengießer, Lins, et al., 2020).

The type of finality affects the number of nodes that can be included in a consensus mechanism, and thereby, the degree of technical decentralization in a DLT system. In addition to the degree of technical decentralization, the type of finality also influences the atomicity and processing time of cross-ledger operations. To guarantee atomicity in cross-ledger transactions, CLI systems require actors to initially send a transaction to lock tokens in a DLT system *A* and then wait until that transaction is confirmed. Next, the corresponding tokens are created or unlocked in a target DLT system *B*. In DLT systems that implement consensus mechanisms with probabilistic finality, a reasonable time (i.e., confirmation period) must pass to ensure that transactions will not be excluded from the main branch before the corresponding tokens can be created or unlocked securely on *B* to prevent cross-ledger double-spending (Back et al., 2014). For example, a confirmation period of one to two days is recommended for cross-ledger transactions from the Bitcoin blockchain through the probabilistic Nakamoto consensus (Back et al., 2014). In contrast, consensus mechanisms allowing for total finality do not require such a confirmation period, and tokens can be created almost instantly or unlocked on *B* without the risk of cross-ledger double-spending. The finality type (i.e., immediate or probabilistic finality) affects the processing time of cross-ledger token interactions. Thus, design decisions, such as the choice of consensus mechanisms, can influence the security (e.g., preventing cross-ledger double spending) and performance (e.g., processing time) of CLI.

DLT protocols and CLI protocols represent technical core components for token economy instances that comprise multiple DLT systems. The protocols must be cautiously selected and configured to suit token economy instances' individual requirements (e.g., regarding confidentiality, confirmation latency, and throughput). To better understand how DLT systems and CLI systems are governed by actors (e.g., to specify requirements), the following section discusses the political perspective on decentralization.

Political Decentralization in Token Economy Instances That Comprise Different Distributed Ledger Technology Systems

Political decentralization refers to the coordination of actors in business ecosystems and how actors govern digital platforms. Among various governance types (e.g., corporate governance or environmental governance), this chapter focuses on IT governance. IT governance is a "framework for decision rights and accountabilities to encourage desirable behavior" among actors (Weill, 2004, p. 3) and describes a set of policies and rules for decision-making that supports IT management.

IT governance comprises three principal dimensions: *decision rights*, *accountabilities*, and *incentives* (Beck et al., 2018). Decision rights incorporate two kinds of rights (Beck et al., 2018; Fama & Jensen, 1983): decision management rights and decision control rights. Decision management rights encompass actors' rights to make proposals (e.g., for updates) and implement decisions (e.g., implementation of updates; Fama & Jensen, 1983). Decision control rights refer to the rights required to participate in decision-making regarding the implementation of proposals of actors with decision management rights and how to measure and monitor decision outcomes (Fama & Jensen, 1983). Decision management rights and decision control rights can be assigned independently to different actors in a token economy instance. In token economy instances using the Bitcoin system, for example, decision management rights regarding the integration of software updates in the Bitcoin protocol are assigned to a small group of actors (e.g., core developers; De Filippi & Loveluck, 2016). Additionally, the majority of improvement proposals are made by a few actors, although any actor within token economy instances using the Bitcoin system has the decision management rights to make proposals (Azouvi et al., 2019). Decision control rights are assigned to actors who control the nodes of DLT systems who can vote on proposals and independently decide whether to update their nodes or not (Arruñada & Garicano, 2018).

Decision rights can strongly affect the degree of political decentralization in a token economy instance (Beck et al., 2018; King, 1983). In a token economy instance with a low degree of political decentralization, decision rights are concentrated among a few actors. Thus, permissions and responsibilities regarding decision-making are distributed unequally across actors in such instances and two-level hierarchies can emerge through the unequal distribution of decision rights. In token economy instances with high degrees of political decentralization, decision rights are distributed among many actors, assigning permissions and responsibilities more equitably.

Accountability refers to whether actors are required to justify their decisions and suffer corresponding consequences (Beck et al., 2018). For example, if nodes include an invalid transaction in their ledger, they must forego their rewards. In the presence of a set of rewards (e.g., financial bonuses) and penalties (e.g., compensations of damages) that is applied to decision outcomes, the assignment of accountabilities to actors can make them incorporate the consequences of their decisions into their decision-making processes, thereby incentivizing actors to align their interests with the goals of a token economy instance.

Incentives comprise a set of rewards and penalties that are put in place to encourage actors to align their interests with a particular goal and to act toward attaining that goal (Beck et al., 2018). For example, a bank can be penalized for manipulating actor balances by revoking its licenses. While in centralized token economy instances the central actors can often be held accountable by authorities that are external to a token economy instance (e.g., by courts), holding actors accountable in a decentralized token economy instance can be more difficult if actors' real-world identities are unknown. Encouraging desirable behaviors of actors in decentralized token economy instances means ensuring accountability (e.g., by signing of transactions) and designing incentives (e.g., monetary rewards) that must be enforced within a token economy instance.

Usually, multiple governance mechanisms are put in place to coordinate a token economy instance. Governance mechanisms are the means (e.g., controls, guidelines, and policies) to manage a token economy instance (e.g., the assignment of decision rights to actors) and comprise a set of rules and procedures that are applied by actors to make decisions. For instance, elections are governance mechanisms in democracies. Through elections, decision rights are assigned to the actors elected by most actors. The decision rights are only assigned for a predefined time (i.e., the duration of an election period) and are redistributed by means of reoccurring elections. The actors can be held accountable for their decisions by courts and by the population (e.g., through reelections). An election is an example of a governance mechanism that can reduce the degree of political decentralization by transferring decision-making rights from many actors (i.e., a voting population) to a few actors (i.e., board members). The prospect of reelection also serves as an incentive for actors to perform desirable behaviors. Analogous to the governance mechanisms used in a society, a variety of governance mechanisms are applied in token economy instances to ensure their seamless operations. For example, token economy instances employ consensus mechanisms, which, similar to elections, assign decision rights to include transactions in a distributed ledger to different actors.

Governance in Token Economy Instances That Are Based on Distributed Ledger Technology

In the following, common governance mechanisms employed in DLT-based token economy instances and the principal phases token economy instances move through are described. Subsequently, the implications of the respective governance mechanisms for the degree of political decentralization among token economy instances that comprise multiple DLT systems connected by CLI systems will be discussed.

Token economy instances move through two principal phases, across which their degree of political decentralization can increase: the *creational phase* and the *operational phase*. The creational phase refers to the design and implementation of a digital platform for a targeted token economy instance and the acquisition of actors to participate in the respective business ecosystem. Moreover, initial decision rights are assigned to actors, and governance mechanisms are specified. At the end of its creational phase, a business ecosystem has specified an initial governance system (including governance mechanisms, processes, and involved actors) for a token economy instance and has created a functioning digital platform for managing asset ownership in the operational phase. The operational phase comprises everyday operations in token economy instances (e.g., validating and verifying transactions between actors) and decisions regarding the development of a digital platform and the business ecosystem, including the associated processes. Corresponding to the dynamics in business ecosystems (e.g., actors that join or leave the system), governance mechanisms for a token economy instance can change in the operational phase to adapt to a varying number of actors. In a token economy instance with only a few actors, decisions regarding changes in the DLT system can be discussed by actors in person until agreements are reached. With an increasing number of actors in a token economy instance, in-person discussions can become too cumbersome, and governance mechanisms can be changed to be supported by a digital platform. The digital support of governance mechanisms can facilitate the involvement of a larger number of actors in governance processes, compared to purely manual execution, because processes, such as voting procedures, can be automated.

Decision-making in governance mechanisms of DLT-based token economy instances is often performed through voting. In the Bitcoin system, for example, updates of the digital platform are based on votes by actors in DLT systems (Hsieh et al., 2017). Thereby, Bitcoin system can reach a high degree of political decentralization because the required decision control rights to participate in voting are assigned to all actors in the Bitcoin network (Hsieh et al., 2017). To allow voting among only a few actors, the requirements for certain decision control rights can be specified and directly assigned to specific actors using governance tokens (Jensen et al., 2021), or indirectly assigned via technical (e.g., a computational contribution to the DLT system) or economic capabilities (e.g., the number tokens owned by an actor; Hsieh et al., 2017).

In addition to increasing the number of actors involved in decision-making, digital governance mechanisms can automate the execution of governance processes (De Filippi & Loveluck, 2016). Especially, governance processes for recurring decisions in the operational phase lend themselves to automation (e.g., finding a consensus on the transactions to be included in a distributed ledger). If actors manually operate a distributed ledger (e.g., by taking notes), transactions must be validated and verified by any actor, and consensus finding can take a very long time because actors need to manually agree on each transaction. DLT-based token economy instances automate transaction validation and verification as well as consensus finding for transactions by using a consensus mechanism. Each actor operates a node to process transactions on their behalf. The Nakamoto consensus mechanism (i.e., the consensus mechanism used in the Bitcoin blockchain), for example, assigns decision management rights to propose a new block for the distributed ledger to an actor, who is randomly selected as a leader through a leader election process (Nakamoto, 2008). The leader proposes a block to be included in the distributed ledger. The leader is held accountable if invalid transactions are included in the block and will receive a reward if most nodes agree on storing the block (Nakamoto, 2008). In this way, actors are incentivized to make their nodes propose blocks that are likely to be accepted by other nodes. Decision control rights remain with all the actors controlling nodes in the Bitcoin network because they will not accept blocks containing invalid transactions (Nakamoto, 2008).

Cross-ledger governance is needed to coordinate the design decisions associated with CLI systems. These design decisions affect how CLI systems and DLT systems are connected, for example, to enable transaction processing for cross-ledger asset ownership transfers (Sunyaev et al., 2021). The mechanisms for cross-ledger governance are specified in the creational phase. CLI systems with a high degree of political decentralization in cross-ledger governance (e.g., in Kusama, Cosmos, and Polkadot) often use voting mechanisms for governance. For example, Kusama is a CLI system that has multiple voting mechanisms, which are implemented to distribute decision rights to actors in the CLI system. As in the Bitcoin community, actors in the Kusama system can propose and vote on improvement proposals. Actors vote by locking their tokens on a distributed ledger. The votes are weighted by the number of tokens locked and the time for which actors lock their tokens (Wood, 2019). In this way, actors can increase their voting power for proposals by increasing either the number of tokens locked or the time for which their tokens are locked. Beyond voting on improvement proposals, on-chain institutions (i.e., institutions composed of members with accounts on-chain) are also created, consisting of members that are elected by token holders and assigned additional decision rights (e.g., proposing emergency proposals; Wood, 2019). Establishing the governance mechanisms for CLI systems may produce additional difficulties compared to the governance mechanisms for token economy instances comprising a single DLT system due to the dependencies between connected CLI systems and a lack of technical standards. For example, not all connected DLT systems support on-chain voting mechanisms. In particular, technical incompatibility can pose a challenge for connecting already existing DLT systems. Additionally, in the creational phase of CLI systems, only a few actors of token economy instances may envision the connections between the relevant DLT systems. The identification of the set of actors that should be involved in governing a CLI system can be challenging in the creational phase.

Cross-ledger governance is an emerging research topic, and there are only a few concepts that are already used by actors in productive CLI systems (e.g., in Kusama or Polkadot). However, the impact of governance mechanisms on the degrees of political decentralization of token economy instances comprising a single DLT system allows us to draw analogies to the impact of governance mechanisms on instances comprising multiple DLT systems.

Political Decentralization of Token Economy Instances and Cross-Ledger Interoperability

Governance mechanisms can be applied by actors to assign the decision rights required for governance processes to few or many actors, leading to a correspondingly low or high degree of political decentralization in these processes. For example, decision rights can be concentrated among the core developers of a digital platform, causing a low degree of political decentralization. In contrast, assigning decision rights equally to all actors, and thus achieving a high degree of decentralization, prevents an abuse of power by central actors. Moreover, in token economy instances with a higher degree of political decentralization, decisions that maximize overall welfare become more likely than decisions that favor only a few actors (Chen et al., 2020).

While a high degree of political decentralization is desirable, governance mechanisms involving many actors are associated with increased coordination efforts and longer discussions (Arruñada & Garicano, 2018; Chen et al., 2020). The involvement of multiple actors in decision-making reduces even the likelihood of reaching agreements (Chen et al., 2020), which can cause stagnancy or a separation of token economy instances (De Filippi & Loveluck, 2016). Stagnancy can occur if no compromise can be found to which all actors agree and can be especially harmful when token economy instances need to respond quickly to environmental changes (e.g., changes in laws or regulations) or emergencies (e.g., a discovery of major bugs). An example of stagnancy is the Bitcoin community's debate on the proposal for increasing the block size limit, when the community could not reach an agreement for a long time (De Filippi & Loveluck, 2016; Hsieh et al., 2017). A separation of token economy instances can occur when disputes cannot be resolved. For example, after an unknown actor stole approximately USD 50 million in Ether (Zhao et al., 2017) from the decentralized autonomous organization (DAO) by exploiting smart contract vulnerabilities, the actors controlling nodes in the Ethereum network could not reach an agreement on whether to reverse the transaction history to undo the exploit (DuPont, 2017). Finally, a part of the Ethereum community reversed the transactions stored on their nodes, while a minority refused to do so. The community then separated into the current Ethereum that reversed the transactions and the Ethereum Classic communities, which did not reverse the transactions (DuPont, 2017).

In the creational phase of token economy instances, requirements must be refined and implemented frequently (e.g., when vulnerabilities in a codebase are discovered; Beck et al., 2018). To decrease the risk for stagnancy or separation, decision rights are often concentrated among a few actors to allow for faster decision-making (e.g., in the Bitcoin and Ethereum communities; De Filippi & Loveluck, 2016; Azouvi et al., 2019).

Connecting DLT systems via CLI builds dependencies between actors of token economy instances. For example, prior to updating a DLT protocol that is part of a token economy instance comprising multiple DLT protocols, actors of that DLT protocol must consider the compatibility of connected DLT protocols and the relevant CLI systems. If compatibility cannot be achieved using an existing CLI system, that CLI system must be refined accordingly, involving the actors of all connected DLT systems and, potentially, the actors that operate the CLI system. Therefore, CLI can complicate decision-making between actors. To better understand the dependencies introduced by CLI, the following section discusses how to find a balance between centralization and decentralization from both the technical and political perspectives.

Drawing Conclusions from the Technical and Political Perspectives on Centralization and Decentralization of CLI Systems

The introduction of CLI comes with additional dependencies between the technical and political degrees of decentralization. Like isolated token economy instances using a single DLT system, CLI systems move through two principal phases (i.e., creational and operational), and each phase is accompanied by individual challenges that are influenced by the dependencies shared by the technical and political perspectives on CLI systems (see Table 3.1). In the creational phase of CLI systems, often only a few actors envision the connection of DLT systems. These actors must identify the set of actors that should be involved in governing the CLI system to be used. The number of actors to be involved can become very large because DLT systems are operated by a multitude of actors who may be affected by a CLI system. To consider the large number of actors in governance mechanisms, a digital support of these mechanisms is desirable. However, a digital support of governance mechanisms for the

Table 3.1 Benefits and challenges of different degrees of technical and political decentralization

		Creational phase	Operational phase
Degree of technical decentralization	High	*Benefits:* • Transparent and verifiable execution of governance mechanisms by technical protocols (e.g., on-chain voting)	*Benefits:* • Increased availability of digital platforms • Prevention of dependencies on central actors • Prevention of performance bottlenecks • Verifiability of data stored on nodes by actors
		Challenges: • Design of technical protocol to digitally support governance mechanisms in a decentralized way (e.g., due to the lack of technical standards for DLT systems)	*Challenges:* • Design of incentives that prevent the recentralization of automated governance mechanisms (e.g., mining pools in consensus mechanisms)
	Low	*Benefits:* • Automation of governance mechanisms by technical protocols • Digital support of governance mechanisms	*Benefits:* • Fast transactions processing • Low confirmation latency for transactions
		Challenges: • Trustful consideration of the interests of different actors (e.g., vendors, users) in decision-making processes	*Challenges:* • Actors must trust in the honest behaviors of central actors • Dependencies on central actors in token economy instances

(continued)

Table 3.1 (continued)

		Creational phase	Operational phase
Degree of political decentralization	High	*Benefits:* • Many actors' interests can be included in decisions regarding the initial designs of token economy instances *Challenges:* • Lack of digital support makes it difficult to include many actors in the creational phase regarding initial design decisions	*Benefits:* • Many actors can democratically make decisions through digitally supported governance mechanisms (e.g., consensus mechanisms) *Challenges:* • Increased risks for stagnancy and separation of token economy instances in the case of disputes • Measures for mediation and conflict management need to be included in automized governance mechanisms
	Low	*Benefits:* • Fast and frequent decision-making, such as responding to emergencies • Reduced risk of stagnancy and separation of actors in token economy instances in the event of disputes *Challenges:* • Dependencies on central actors holding decision-making rights • Increased risk for central actors making self-serving decisions	*Benefits:* • Acceleration of decision-making • Reduced risk of stagnancy and separation of actors in token economy instances in the event of disputes *Challenges:* • Dependencies on central actors holding decision-making rights • Increased risk for central actors making self-serving decisions

introduction of CLI systems is challenging. Since CLI does not exist prior to the introduction of a CLI system, actors must either use software applications deployed in one of the DLT systems to be connected, requiring the actors of all DLT systems to have access to that DLT system; use external digital platforms (e.g., a DLT system accessible to all relevant actors), where either no or all actors will have equal decision rights; or employ a central actor who manages the introduction of a CLI system on behalf of all the actors involved (e.g., banks in centralized token economy instances). All the named options have drawbacks regarding the equal consideration of actors because governance must first be defined to achieve the inclusion of all actors. Defining governance in a decentralized way is difficult to automate when actors are scattered across different DLT and CLI systems because of a lack of technical standards. Deciding on technical standards for a variety of decentralized systems (e.g., DLT and CLI systems) can involve a large number of actors from different communities. Automation is desirable to enable this large number of actors to participate in the definition of standards in a decentralized way. While technical standards are necessary to enable digital support of governance mechanisms, a definition of governance mechanisms is necessary to create technical standards. Mutual dependencies between the definition of governance mechanisms and the presence of technical standards pose a major challenge for CLI governance.

Governance mechanisms are designed and automated during the creational phase to coordinate decisions through technical protocols during the operational phase. To act and participate independently despite automation, the corresponding decision rights (e.g., deciding which cross-ledger transaction to pass on) must be assigned to nodes. The assignment of decision rights to actors through automated governance mechanisms influences the degree of technical decentralization in CLI and connected DLT systems. For example, DLT systems typically execute consensus mechanisms to agree on whether transactions will be included in a distributed ledger. To agree on transactions that will be included, a consensus mechanism redistributes decision rights to make a proposal (e.g., for a block) to one actor through a specified process (e.g., a leader election process). Similarly, CLI systems must specify governance mechanisms for tasks, such as transaction verification, for other distributed ledgers.

When balancing centralization and decentralization in token economy instances comprising multiple DLT systems, the dependencies arising in the creational and operational phases should be considered. Both the technical and political perspectives on decentralization show that decentralization favors transparency and an engagement of actors or nodes in decision-making, at the cost of performance in token economy instances that use different DLT systems. Moreover, achieving a high degree of decentralization becomes possible by utilizing technology to automate those governance mechanisms that can be executed by the underlying CLI and DLT systems. However, actors should not decentralize token economy instances comprising multiple DLT systems at all costs because additional governance overhead can be associated with decentralization, which may exceed the benefits obtained from decentralization. Finding the optimal balance between technical and political centralization and decentralization is mainly determined by the degree to which governance should be automated. For automation, actors should first be aware of the degree to which they want to be involved in governance processes within a system because technical decentralization largely entails automating these governance processes by mapping them to a technical system. By providing these insights, this chapter supports actors by specifying governance processes which balance centralization and decentralization, from a political perspective and from a technical perspective.

References

Arruñada, B., & Garicano, L. (2018). Blockchain: The birth of decentralized governance. *Pompeu Fabra University, Economics and business working paper series, 1608.*

Azouvi, S., Maller, M., & Meiklejohn, S. (2019). Egalitarian society or benevolent dictatorship: The state of cryptocurrency governance. In A. Zohar, I. Eyal, V. Teague, J. Clark, A. Bracciali, F. Pintore, & M. Sala (Eds.), *International conference on financial cryptography and data security* (pp. 127–143). Springer Berlin Heidelberg.

Back, A., Corallo, M., Dashjr, L., Friedenbach, M., Maxwell, G., Miller, A., Poelstra, A., Timón, J., & Wuille, P. (2014). *Enabling blockchain innovations with pegged sidechains.* https://web.archive.org/web/20200511053353/http://kevinriggen.com/files/sidechains.pdf

Beck, R. (2018). Beyond bitcoin: The rise of blockchain world. *Computer, 51*(2), 54–58. https://doi.org/10.1109/MC.2018.1451660

Beck, R., Müller-Bloch, C., & King, J. L. (2018). Governance in the blockchain economy: A framework and research agenda. *Journal of the Association for Information Systems, 19*(10), 1020–1034. https://doi.org/10.17705/1jais.00518

Btc relay: github repository. (2018, October 25). https://web.archive.org/web/20210119163450/https://github.com/ethereum/btcrelay

Buterin, V. (2016). *Chain interoperability.* https://web.archive.org/web/20210809163415/https://allquantor.at/blockchainbib/pdf/vitalik2016chain.pdf

Camp, L. J., Sirbu, M., Tygar, J. D., Jean, L., Marvin, C., & Tygar, S. J. D. (1995). Token and notational money in electronic commerce. *Proceedings of the first USENIX workshop on electronic commerce.*

Castro, M., & Liskov, B. (1999). Practical byzantine fault tolerance. In *OSDI'99. Proceedings of the third symposium on operating systems design and implementation* (pp. 173–186). USENIX Association.

Catalini, C. (2017). How blockchain technology will impact the digital economy. *Blockchains Smart Contracts Internet Things, 4*, 2292–2303.

Chen, Y., Pereira, I., & Patel, P. C. (2020). Decentralized governance of digital platforms. *Journal of Management, 47*(5), 1305–1337. https://doi.org/10.1177/0149206320916755

De Filippi, P., & Loveluck, B. (2016). The invisible politics of bitcoin: Governance crisis of a decentralized infrastructure. *Internet Policy Review, 5*(4), 1–28.

Deng, L., Chen, H., Zeng, J., & Zhang, L.-J. (2018). Research on cross-chain technology based on sidechain and hash-locking. In S. Liu, B. Tekinerdogan, M. Aoyama, & L.-J. Zhang (Eds.), *EDGE computing—EDGE 2018* (pp. 144–151). Springer International Publishing.

DuPont, Q. (2017). Experiments in algorithmic governance: A history and ethnography of "the DAO," a failed decentralized autonomous organization. In *Bitcoin and beyond* (pp. 157–177). Routledge.

Fama, E. F., & Jensen, M. C. (1983). Separation of ownership and control. *The Journal of Law and Economics, 26*(2), 301–325.

Gojka, E.-E., Kannengießer, N., Sturm, B., Bartsch, J., & Sunyaev, A. (2021). Security in distributed ledger technology: An analysis of vulnerabilities and attack vectors. In K. Arai (Ed.), *Intelligent computing: proceedings of the 2021 computing conference* (pp. 722–742). Springer International Publishing.

Herlihy, M. (2018). Atomic cross-chain swaps. In *Proceedings of the 2018 ACM symposium on principles of distributed computing* (pp. 245–254). Association for Computing Machinery. https://doi.org/10.1145/3212734.3212736

Hsieh, Y.-Y., Vergne, J.-P. J. P., & Wang, S. (2017). The internal and external governance of blockchain-based organizations: Evidence from cryptocurrencies. In *Bitcoin and beyond* (pp. 48–68). Routledge.

Jacobides, M. G., Cennamo, C., & Gawer, A. (2018). Towards a theory of ecosystems. *Strategic Management Journal, 39*(8), 2255–2276. https://doi.org/10.1002/smj.2904

Jensen, J. R., von Wachter, V., & Ross, O. (2021). *How decentralized is the governance of blockchain-based finance: Empirical evidence from four governance token distributions.* http://arxiv.org/pdf/2102.10096v2

Kannengießer, N., Lins, S., Dehling, T., & Sunyaev, A. (2020). Trade-offs between distributed ledger technology characteristics. *ACM Computing Surveys, 53*(2), 1–37. https://doi.org/10.1145/3379463

Kannengießer, N., Pfister, M., Greulich, M., Lins, S., & Sunyaev, A. (2020). Bridges between islands: Cross-chain technology for distributed ledger technology. *Hawaii international conference on system sciences.*

Kannengießer, N., Lins, S., Sander, C., Winter, K., Frey, H., & Sunyaev, A. (2021). Challenges and Common Solutions in Smart Contract Development. *IEEE Transactions on Software Engineering,* 1–1. https://doi.org/10.1109/TSE.2021.3116808

Karame, G. O., Androulaki, E., & Capkun, S. (2012). Double-spending fast payments in bitcoin. In *CCS'12, Proceedings of the 2012 ACM conference on computer and communications security* (pp. 906–917). Association for Computing Machinery. https://doi.org/10.1145/2382196.2382292

King, J. L. (1983). Centralized versus decentralized computing: Organizational considerations and management options. *ACM Computing Surveys, 15*(4), 319–349. https://doi.org/10.1145/289.290

Koens, T., & Poll, E. (2019). Assessing interoperability solutions for distributed ledgers. *Pervasive and Mobile Computing, 59,* 101079. https://doi.org/10.1016/j.pmcj.2019.101079

Kwon, J., & Buchman, E. (2016). *Cosmos whitepaper.* https://web.archive.org/web/20210805201418/https://v1.cosmos.network/resources/whitepaper

Lacity, M. (2020). *Blockchain foundations for the internet of value.* Epic Books.

Lamport, L., Shostak, R., & Pease, M. (1982). The Byzantine Generals Problem. *ACM Transactions on Programming Languages and Systems, 4*(3), 382–401.

Lücking, M., Kretzer, F., Kannengießer, N., Beigl, M., Sunyaev, A., & Stork, W. (2021). When data fly: An open data trading system in vehicular ad hoc networks. *Electronics, 10*(6), 654. https://doi.org/10.3390/electronics10060654

Nakamoto, S. (2008). *Bitcoin: A peer-to-peer electronic cash system.* https://bitcointalk.org/bitcoin.pdf

Panurach, P. (1996). Money in electronic commerce: Digital cash, electronic fund transfer, and ecash. *Communications of the ACM, 39*(6), 45–50. https://doi.org/10.1145/228503.228512

Scott, S. V., van Reenen, J., & Zachariadis, M. (2017). The long-term effect of digital innovation on bank performance: An empirical study of swift adoption in financial services. *Research Policy, 46*(5), 984–1004. https://doi.org/10.1016/j.respol.2017.03.010

Sunyaev, A. (2020). *Internet computing*. Springer.

Sunyaev, A., Kannengießer, N., Beck, R., Treiblmaier, H., Lacity, M., Kranz, J., Fridgen, G., Spankowski, U., & Luckow, A. (2021). Token economy. *Business & Information Systems Engineering, 63*(4), 457–478. https://doi.org/10.1007/s12599-021-00684-1

Weill, P. (2004). Don't just lead, govern: How top-performing firms govern it. *MIS Quarterly Executive, 3*, 1–17.

Wood, G. (2019). *Kusama rollout and governance.* https://web.archive.org/web/20210504015020/https://polkadot.network/kusama-rollout-and-governance/

Zamyatin, A., Harz, D., Lind, J., Panayiotou, P., Gervais, A., & Knottenbelt, W. (2019). XCLAIM: Trustless, interoperable, cryptocurrency-backed assets. *2019 IEEE symposium on security and privacy (SP)* (pp. 193–210). https://doi.org/10.1109/SP.2019.00085

Zhao, X., Chen, Z., Chen, X., Wang, Y., & Tang, C. (2017). The DAO attack paradoxes in propositional logic. In *2017 4th international conference on systems and informatics (ICSAI)* (pp. 1743–1746). IEEE. https://doi.org/10.1109/ICSAI.2017.8248566

Zhou, Z. P., & Zhu, K. (2006). Platform battle with lock-in. *ICIS 2006 proceedings*. https://aisel.aisnet.org/icis2006/20

4

Cryptoeconomics: Designing Effective Incentives and Governance Models for Blockchain Networks Using Insights from Economics

Cathy Barrera and Stephanie Hurder

Introduction

Blockchain and the Paradox of Choice

Blockchain platforms are mini economies written in code. The distributed data ownership and decision-making processes of blockchain enable groups of stakeholders to collectively create and distribute value among themselves in new and more decentralized ways. Blockchain is being used to reimagine and restructure economic activity in markets as varied as freelance labor, art sales, real estate, financial services, and supply chains.

This chapter is based on Cathy Barrera and Stephanie Hurder's paper, "Cryptoeconomics: Designing Effective Incentives and Governance Models for Blockchain Networks Using Insights from Economics," with a foreword by Don Tapscott, published by the Blockchain Research Institute on January 13, 2020, and adapted here with permission.

C. Barrera (✉) • S. Hurder
Prysm Group, Miami Beach, FL, USA
e-mail: info@prysmgroup.io; info@prysmgroup.io

M. C. Lacity, H. Treiblmaier (eds.), *Blockchains and the Token Economy*, Technology, Work and Globalization, https://doi.org/10.1007/978-3-030-95108-5_4

In creating more decentralized economic institutions, blockchain-based platforms face a quandary of *choice*. Without central decision-makers such as executives or corporations at the helm, blockchain projects rely on the various groups of stakeholders—be they users, vendors, miners, or companies participating in consortia—to behave in ways aligned with the goals of the platform. These behaviors fall into three types.

- *Adoption*: Stakeholders must choose to adopt the platform. They must find that it delivers more value than competing options.
- *Contribution*: Stakeholders must take appropriate actions and contribute specific resources when using the platform so that it delivers value to themselves and others.
- *Participation*: Stakeholders must participate in good faith to decision-making processes that allow the platform to adapt and evolve over time.

For many early projects in the blockchain and cryptoeconomics space, some—or even all—of these behaviors have been beyond reach. Sustained adoption has been a famous challenge for both start-up and enterprise projects. R3's Corda platform quickly lost numerous high-profile participants, including Goldman Sachs and Santander, prior to even initial stages of development (Hackett, 2021). Singapore Airlines' blockchain-based KrisPay loyalty program offered poor consumer value, as participating retailers happily accepted the program's marketing data but refused to award goods and services in exchange for loyalty points (Andrew, 2018). And shipping company Hapag-Lloyd for months showed limited interest in Maersk and IBM's TradeLens due to poor governance design. Hapag-Lloyd CEO Rolf Habben Jansen explained:

> Technically the solution (by Maersk and IBM) could be a good platform, but it will require a governance that makes it an industry platform and not just a platform for Maersk and IBM. And this is the weakness we're currently seeing in many of these initiatives, as each individual project claims to offer an industry platform that they themselves control. (Andersen & Vogdrup-Schmidt, 2018)

Why (Crypto)economics Can Help

Through the study of *choice*, economics brings essential insights for blockchain platforms as their creators seek to push the boundaries of what economic structures can achieve. Economists have spent decades understanding how individuals made decisions in various environments and with varied information. They have developed scientific processes for using these insights to develop new, more effective economic systems and to help us to understand how different relevant stakeholders are likely to behave in a particular system.

Cryptoeconomics draws from a wide variety of economic fields, each recognized with numerous Nobel Prizes:

- Contract theory: how economic actors, generally in the presence of asymmetric information, construct contractual arrangements to align their interests (e.g., Hart, 2001).
- Market design: how to design well-functioning markets for goods and services, including search, matching, and pricing, using the tools of game theory, algorithm design, and experiments (e.g., Roth, 2018).
- Economics of information: how information and information systems affect economic decisions and markets (e.g., Stiglitz, 1989).
- Monetary economics: the study of currency in its functions as a medium of exchange, store of value, and unit of account (e.g., Friedman, 1948).
- Social choice: how to combine individual opinions, preferences, and interests to reach optimal collective decisions (e.g., Ostrom, 2000).

We can use these insights to achieve the three types of behaviors required for successful blockchain projects.

The Prysm Group, an economic consulting firm founded in New York in 2017, specializes in incentive design, token economics, monetization, and governance for blockchain and digital assets. Our frameworks allow projects ranging from blockchain-native networks backed by top venture capital firms to national governments and consortia of major corporations, to attract and retain stakeholders who participate in the evolution of the network over time.

In this paper, we first present three proprietary frameworks for effective economic design. We then present components of economics used at each stage of the design process. The Prysm Group House Framework outlines the levers used to shape incentives in any economic system. The Prysm Group Wheel Framework identifies the elements required in any functioning governance system. Finally, the blockchain 3Cs framework indicates the levers by which blockchain-based systems can deliver economic value to their participants. By using the 3Cs framework, consortia can explain their value to potential members and grow their networks.

Our research shows that blockchain creators cannot copy and deploy the infrastructure designed for one particular use case to another use case, even if it is closely related. We use economic design to customize infrastructure for each deployment so that it maximizes the value delivered to stakeholders of a network.

Framework for Economic Design

People often say to us, "Blockchain is a new industry. My platform has never existed before. How can you know what the economic design should be?"

This conundrum is not new. Economists have spent decades designing institutions and incentives for new environments. In doing so, they follow a well-developed process combining academic research, data analysis, and experimentation to arrive at successful economic designs. Before we delve into the process, let's consider a classic example of successful economic design—what William Safire called "the greatest auction in history" (1995).

Pioneers of Economic Design: The FCC Spectrum Auction

In 1993, the United States Congress passed a law allowing the Federal Communication Commission (FCC) to use an auction to sell licenses for broadband personal communications service spectrum (FCC, 2017).

Before that, the FCC had allocated spectrum licenses through comparative hearings: potential licensees made their case for a license before the FCC, and the FCC would grant licenses case by case. As the cost and time required for hearings became untenable, the FCC attempted to allocate spectrum via lottery, which was a disaster. Over 400,000 entities entered the lottery, but licenses rarely went to those who could make the best use of them. A Boston cellular license, for example, went to a consortium of dentists. In theory, a well-designed auction could allocate licenses to users who valued them most and take only months rather than years.

There was one problem. "Nothing like this had ever been run at scale," according to former chief economist at Microsoft Dr. Preston McAfee, then a Professor of Economics at Caltech and a core member of the auction design team (R.P. McAfee, personal communication, March 15, 2019). The variations on the potential auction design were almost limitless. Would the auctions run simultaneously or sequentially? Would bids be ascending or sealed? Would package (combinatorial) bids be allowed? Should bidder identities be concealed or revealed? The FCC would need to make and implement these decisions within a year, and then use the resulting auction to allocate the equivalent of over $12 billion of licenses (FCC, 2020). According to the FCC, the first spectrum auction produced $7 billion in bids in 1994 dollars (FCC, 2020).

The FCC, as well as major bidders, turned to economists with expertise in auction design, including Dr. McAfee of Caltech, Professors Robert Wilson and Paul Milgrom of Stanford, and Professor John McMillan of the University of Western Ontario, to advise on the design of the auction and optimal bidding strategies (McAfee et al., 2012, p. 169). The economists started by outlining four goals. First, the auction design should be *simple*: bidders would be interacting with the auction for the first time, and so it would be best for all participants if the optimal bidding strategies were relatively easy to calculate. They also wanted to raise significant *revenue* for the government and to fulfill *diversity* goals prescribed by the FCC (McAfee et al., 2012, p. 170).

The fourth goal—*efficient* allocation of licenses to users—provides an illuminating example of the challenges presented by this design project. When economists discuss an efficient allocation, they generally mean that the users with the highest values for the licenses should obtain them. In a simple, one-item auction—think of a typical auction at Sotheby's or Christie's—efficiency simply means that the bidder with the highest value for the item wins the auction (McAfee et al., 2012, p. 173). But for spectrum, finding the efficient allocation of bandwidths and geographies to users was a complex combinatorial problem; they could not determine a solution before the auction. In the words of Dr. McAfee:

> The biggest issue was that we didn't know how the spectrum should be allocated. Let me give an example. If you look at the earlier licenses that had [been traded in the previous system], there were aggregations along interstates. For Interstate 10, a single company owned the spectrum from Texas, all the way to California. You could drive I-10 and never have to go off your carrier. But what's the right allocation? Well, you can't really sit in a room and think about this. Everybody involved in the process who wanted to buy spectrum had a different preferred allocation. We wanted to use market forces to figure out what was the efficient allocation. (R.P. McAfee, personal communication, March 15, 2019)

The economists used a structured process including economic and game theory, observational evidence, and lab and field experiments to arrive at the eventual auction design. The economists began by forming hypotheses for viable designs. While the application of auctions to spectrum was new, previous studies of auctions in other areas—from cartels to government procurement—provided insight about the design levers that would matter most and the impact of various choices on outcomes. Combining the findings from these models with game theory sharpened the set of candidate designs.

Next, the team joined with Caltech Professor Charles Plott who specialized in using laboratory experiments to test game theoretic models. Using Caltech students, and then a wider array of individuals, as subjects, the economists tested which designs were understood by bidders, and which achieved outcomes closest to those desired. [The team also leveraged the student body to ensure the code was bug free. Any undergrad who found a bug in the software implementing the auction received $100 (now $175)].

Having arrived on a leading candidate, the team's final test was to implement the design in a smaller, more contained, but real market for second narrowband (i.e., paging frequency) spectrum licenses. Their auction mechanism was a success—it sold 30 licenses—and so they recommended its design to the FCC.

The first full spectrum auction, which ran from December 1994 to March 1995, raised nearly $8 billion (Safire, 1995). The auction mechanism, now known as the FCC auction, has been used to allocate over $100 billion of spectrum worldwide (McAfee et al., 2012, p. 169).

More importantly for blockchain, this high-stakes example of economic design inspired decades of business applications.

The Phases of Practical Economic Design

The FCC spectrum auction illustrates the phases of practical economic design. Here we discuss each phase.

Phase 1: Value Proposition and Strategy

The foundation of any successful project is a clear value proposition, strategy, and intended user base. Having a clear idea of the various stakeholder groups, their preferences and outside options, and their constraints lays a foundation for a successful economic design.

In most cases, having a general idea of the value proposition is not enough. Just as the economists designing the spectrum auction did, a founding team will need to articulate precisely the goals of the platform and the trade-offs among them. These goals could relate to the product or service, the customers, and the nodes as well as a potential token.

For example, the founding team may need to decide whether it prioritizes maximizing profits or ensuring equal distribution of services. Or, if the platform will include a token, whether the token will increase in value to reward holders and investors or keep a stable value to be used as a medium of exchange. The goals themselves are up to the founding team; yet, they must be mutually consistent, and there must be a clear priority about which will be fulfilled when conflicts between goals arise. The subsequent design of all economic elements will be in pursuit of satisfying these trade-offs in a way that maximizes the objectives of the founding team for the network.

Phase 2: System Architecture

Because blockchain platforms include multiple, coexisting economic systems, we suggest developing an economic architecture first before working out details of design. Otherwise, the team risks designing a system where each subsystem is effective, but the interaction of the various economic mechanisms yields unexpected, undesirable consequences for the platform as a whole.

Such an architecture should include (a) an overview of the top economic issues that the project will need to address, (b) preliminary recommendations for economic design and structure, (c) an outlined plan of action for economic design, and (d) a proposed timeline for economic design. Such an architecture sets up the team to structure an effective economic model that will support the stated goals of the platform and the founding team.

The architecture process begins with the Prysm Group House Economic Framework, which outlines various levers used to shape incentive and economic systems. Designers start with the architecture of the smallest unit of interaction—the transaction—and work outward to ensure that the various elements of the system will work in synchrony. The process ends by applying the Prysm Group Wheel Governance Framework to ensure that the platform has effective governance that allows it to adapt to changes in the environment. We discuss these frameworks in more detail in their respective sections.

Phase 3: Economic and Governance Design

After completing the high-level economic architecture, the detailed economic design can begin. This step includes fully specifying any mechanisms and generating network parameters that can be implemented in code if needed.

Prysm Group follows a structured four-step approach to finish the economics and governance design. These steps have a foundation in the history of economic design, including, but not limited to, the FCC auction. They are as follows:

1. Build models using economic and game theory

Economic research provides a host of considerations and design guidelines for any given system. An economic designer combines their knowledge of current research with the critical goals of the project (from Phase 1), along with any constraints from the architecture (from Phase 2) to derive which potential designs might work well. At this point, there may be a suite of potential designs, or key parameters that are not yet specified.

2. Collect observational evidence

Rather than jumping directly from economic theory to system implementation, it is helpful to collect any observational evidence that might support or disprove any key hypotheses in the design. For an auction design such as FCC auction, this involved looking at how similar auctions had been designed, and the extent to which the outcomes were in line with what the designers intended. Even if the settings are not identical, these types of studies can point out obvious flaws and themes in design.

3. Run lab and field experiments

The use of laboratory and field experiments to test the impacts of economic institutions is one of the main advances of economics in the last half century. The FCC auction is a powerful example of this. Depending on the scope of the final project and the stage of the design, economic designers may choose to have a horse race of mechanisms in a laboratory setting, looking at the trade-offs between subtle differences in design choices and how users interact with the mechanisms. Later on, the team may run a contained field experiment at a smaller scale than the full implementation—such as the pager spectrum auction—to see if unexpected consequences arise when they put the design out in the "real world."

In many cases, effective lab and field experiments result in economic designers returning to the drawing board to rethink fundamental aspects of their design. That is to be expected, and the same steps can be followed to revise the design.

4. Implement and adapt in the real world

Once there is enough lab and field evidence in support of an economic design, it can be implemented in the full system. Critically, there must be processes by which the mechanisms can adapt over time, as it may take many iterations for users to fully understand the ways that mechanisms can be gamed. For example, in the FCC auction, bidders eventually learned how to strategically undercut each other. As users learn more about the system, there may need to be design tweaks to fix any final holes.

Phase 4: Value Verification

All the economic design in the world is of limited use if—at the end of the day—the platform does not deliver value to its various stakeholders. As discussed above, a solid design process begins by understanding the value proposition and stakeholders of the project. Keeping in mind the needs and preferences of the different players, and how they will be fulfilled, must be a consistent focus of the design team.

Many teams choose, upon completion of the economics and governance model design, to complete a benefit analysis for each of the various stakeholder groups. This final check ensures that the system that is obtained is in line with the initial vision and that the preferences of all required participants have been considered. It also provides a basis for marketing the project to key additional stakeholders considering joining the project.

Prysm Group 3Cs of Economic Benefits of Blockchain

Many people think that the main economic innovation of blockchain is the use of tokens. That is not true. Indeed, as we discuss in our Prysm Group House Framework, economically sound structuring of

Fig. 4.1 3Cs of blockchain economic benefits. (© 2021 Prysm Group. Used with permission. All rights reserved)

transactions, marketplaces, and information all contribute—along with token design—to the functioning of blockchain systems and the value that they deliver to users. A blockchain platform can create significant economic value without having a native token at all.

One of the most effective ways to deliver value to participants in a market or economy is to reduce *inefficiencies*. Inefficiencies arise when parties engaging in trade are prevented from reaching the best possible collective outcome, either due to frictions such as search costs or due to incentive problems that prevent value from being created. While the specific applications of blockchain are numerous, the underlying drivers of value creation occur through three levers: coordination, commitment, and control (see Fig. 4.1).

Coordination

Blockchain allows a group of stakeholders to coordinate on a shared database for their common use. It creates a source of instantly verifiable information among this group, reducing the frequently large costs of communicating and reconciling data across different sources.

Commitment

Blockchain, together with decentralized applications, allows participants to commit to future actions and outcomes using code to enforce them. This reduces the risk of one of the parties reneging on a previous agreement and the cost of enforcing these agreements.

Control

Blockchain enables stakeholders to retain local control of their data, thereby balancing bargaining power among participants. It better allows these stakeholders to capture the value they create, improving incentives for participation and investment.

The specific benefits of employing blockchain in a given setting depend on the context at hand, and the relative costs and benefits of addressing various inefficiencies. These benefits highlight use cases for blockchain in an enterprise setting, and all can be accomplished without incorporating a platform-specific token. Understanding these benefits is essential for enterprises building blockchain platforms because they show areas where the ROI is likely to be highest and where gaining adoption by stakeholders will likely be easiest.

Prysm Group House Economics Framework

A core challenge of economic design for blockchain is determining which fields of insights from economics should be applied and in what order to maximize the probability of success for the project. When designing an effective blockchain platform, designers can leverage many areas of economics, each backed by decades of research and multiple Nobel Prizes.

The Prysm Group grounds system architectures and economic designs in proprietary frameworks. For economic design, it follows its *House Framework* (see Fig. 4.2). While the framework is comprehensive, it is most essential for guiding the design of the incentive layer and the token layer of the platform. The goal of these design choices is to produce

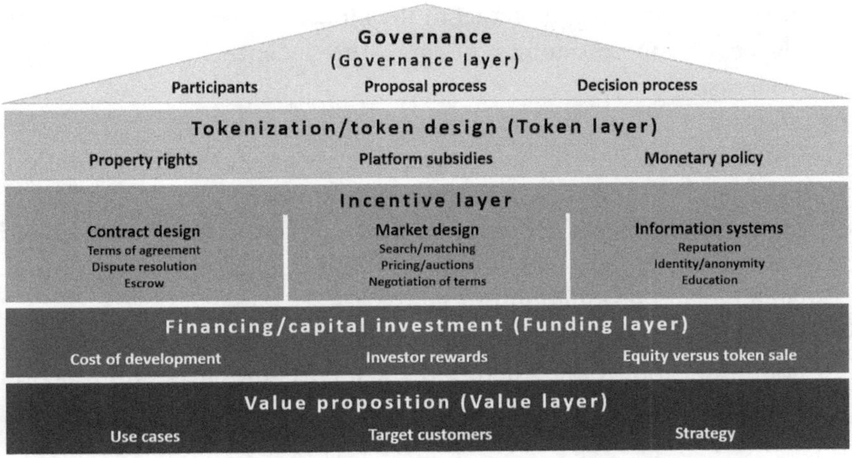

Fig. 4.2 House framework: Blockchain economic design. (© 2021 Prysm Group. Used with permission. All rights reserved)

incentive-compatible systems—systems where stakeholders are properly incentivized to join the platform and engage in value-generating behaviors.

Overview of the Components of the House Framework

As we discussed in our *process of economic design*, any building (or blockchain platform) needs a strong foundation. Before any economic design takes place, the *value proposition* of the platform including its use cases, target customers, and strategy must be clear. The executive team must specify this based on the vision and goals of the project.

Secondly, the executive team will need to allocate or raise funds to support the development of the technology and the design of the economic mechanisms of the platform through *financing and capital investment.* If the project requires external investors, the executive team has the option of raising capital through the sale of a financial stake, like equity, in the platform, or to secure capital against the sale of native tokens.

The three columns in the center of the House are the core of the **incentive layer** of any economic design. The incentive layer has three components:

- *Contract design*: This includes terms of agreement, dispute resolution, escrow, and other transaction-level institutions.
- *Market design*: This is the study of how markets should be structured so that valuable transactions form. This includes pricing, search, matching, and negotiation procedures.
- *Information systems*: These include reputation, identity, and education / communication infrastructure that supports the successful function of the platform.

After the platform design is laid out, one or more tokens may be integrated, if needed, into the platform. In the **token layer**, the property rights, monetary policy, supply, and uses are designed to facilitate the goals of the founding team and the platform design. Tokens are never a means unto themselves on a blockchain platform. Any token should be designed to support the overall functioning of the platform.

The last step is to design the **governance**. The appropriate governance design depends on the incentive and token designs of the platform, along with a determination of which parts of decision-making the founding team would like to decentralize.

The Incentive Layer

When many people think of *incentives*, they think of compensation and tokens. What is the miner's reward for successfully validating a transaction? How much will that reward—perhaps a native token—be worth in the future? While the terms of any contract are an essential lever in shaping the incentives of participants, they are but one lever. In designing the incentives layer of any platform, the founding team must consider how all the many environmental factors come together to shape the economic decision-making of users.

For example, a start-up wishes to build a decentralized, blockchain-based competitor to eBay. Users will arrive either to sell goods or to buy goods. For this new platform to fulfill its goal—to become a marketplace where millions of users buy and sell a wide variety of goods—the platform must develop a reputation as a place where buyers and sellers act in good faith. They honor transaction terms and are pleased with their experience. That outcome is most probable if the platform's founding team put incentive structures in place that encourage good faith behavior.

How might such a platform discourage, for example, sellers of low-quality goods that disappoint buyers? One lever is through compensation: buyers who receive a good not in line with what was advertised may opt to get part or all of their money back. Dispute resolution services can help arbitrate these types of disagreements. The risk of losing revenues is an incentive for sellers to behave properly in the marketplace.

But it is not the only lever available. This eBay substitute could set these terms: if sellers cheat buyers, the platform will drop such sellers to the bottom of any future search inquiry that applies to the sellers' products. If sellers behave badly, then future buyers will have a harder time finding and transacting with such sellers. While not an incentive in a particular transaction, the potential loss of business in the future encourages good behavior in the present.

Finally, the platform may wish to warn buyers of badly behaved sellers through reputation or other information systems: "Cheat a buyer, and your star rating—which is displayed next to your user name in every interaction—goes down." This could be paired with the search change discussed above, but has a similar effect: "How much do you value the future benefits from a good reputation, compared to what you can earn from cheating someone today?"

This example illustrates why a holistic view of incentive design is essential for any platform. Obviously, the levers used in each situation vary with the value proposition and user base of the platform. We delve further into each of the components of the incentive layer in turn. Because of the close relationship between market design and information systems, we discuss them as a single unit.

Contract and transaction design highlights the contract theory and transaction design issues that will be most important to the platform's functioning and success. In a typical transaction, one party pays another party to provide a good or service. There are a variety of problems that can arise in the execution of contracts, such as the buyer not sending payment or the supplier not providing the service as described. Typical problems arise from moral hazard (the inability to properly share risk and track behavior) and adverse selection (asymmetric information about the quality of goods or services).

Blockchain is often touted as a trustless system which helps to ease these sorts of problems; yet, actually ensuring that a contract is executed as agreed and that all parties receive the benefits they expected requires careful design of the contract and related mechanisms. A comprehensive contract and transaction design ensures that they sufficiently align the parties who will enter into them. This can include contract terms, performance verification, dispute resolution, and escrow.

Economic design can be implemented in the following aspects of transactions:

- Contract terms: Who is agreeing to provide what products or services, and in exchange for what?
- Performance verification: How do we prove that what was agreed to in the contract has taken place?
- Escrow design: What escrow should each party provide so that all feel safe entering in the transaction?
- Dispute resolution design: If the contract terms are not fulfilled, how is it decided what will happen?
- Information structures: What information must the platform provide to support these systems?

Depending on the specific context in which a transaction takes place, what is traded, and the behaviors required of participants in order for the transaction to be fulfilled, some of these elements may be more or less important. But there are two goals of economic design common to all types of transactions:

1. To increase the chances that each party behaves as expected, thereby increasing the probability of a successfully completed contract.

2. To increase participation in this type of transaction by increasing the confidence of potential participants that the transactions will be successful.

Market design and information systems highlight the market design and information system issues that will be most important to the platform's functioning and success. Before they can execute transactions, buyers and sellers must be able to find each other on a platform and negotiate mutually beneficial transaction terms. Designing well-functioning marketplaces is a complex endeavor. Some of the many issues that can arise in marketplaces include congestion (buyers and sellers not being able to find each other), unraveling (users choosing to opt out of the market), inefficient matching (users would be better off transacting with alternate trading partners), suboptimal pricing mechanisms (one or both parties do not receive the appropriate surplus), and inefficient or ineffective procedures for negotiating terms.

These two sections together lead the design of the platform's market mechanisms and information systems to provide they will successfully facilitate the marketplace the platform hopes to serve. These sections include buyer and seller matching, pricing mechanisms, and supporting information systems. Economic design can be implemented in the following aspects of marketplace design:

- Matching of transaction partners: How do buyers and sellers find each other (search, recommendation engines, etc.)? Is the process centralized or decentralized?
- Pricing: How is price determined (posted, bargaining, auctions, etc.)?
- Transaction terms: If other contract terms besides price are flexible, how do parties negotiate them?
- Reputation systems: What information does each side need about the other to find high-value transaction partners? How should the information be aggregated and displayed?
- Education: Do participants need instruction on how the platform functions to participate?

The relative importance of each of these elements depends on the specific setting at hand. An online e-commerce platform such as eBay, which sells many highly differentiated goods and has thousands of users, relies heavily on effective matching of transaction partners and reputation systems. In contrast, a procurement auction may depend less on matching and focus more on the design of the pricing mechanism. However, the goal for all marketplaces is that they facilitate the creation of transactions that are mutually beneficial to buyers and sellers.

The Token Layer

The single most important misconception in the blockchain industry is that tokenization determines the incentives of users in a blockchain platform. Introducing a token is very similar to introducing a new currency or a new share of equity. While workers may care deeply about the currency in which they are paid or the stock rewards they receive, it is not the only factor that affects their daily job activities. Many tokens are similar to air miles for airlines—part of an overall marketplace with many aspects of design.

A blockchain-based platform need not have a native token. Introducing a new token is time- and capital-intensive and should be motivated by a genuine need.

Token economics and design examines the economic trade-offs inherent in creating a token and the implication of the token design for the functioning of the broader platform. A well-designed token is more than a means of exchange or a store of value. It must be designed so that it supports the incentive, market, and transaction design of the platform, as well as fulfilling the needs of those who use it for traditional currency purposes. Designing appropriate token economics involves creating a token that fulfills the fundamentals required by the platform, and then verifying that equilibrium token values will sufficiently compensate any platform participants who receive their compensation in tokens. This layer ensures the design of the native token to be used on the platform meets the goals of the executive team and the needs of the potential platform participants. In most cases, this focuses on the role that the token plays in participant incentives and markets for goods and services. The critical design choices in the economics of tokens include the following:

- The fundamental drivers of the token value: What goods or services does the token grant the rights to?
- Token monetary policy: Who are the intended users of the token, and what rate of growth supports their adoption of the token?
- Initial token allocation: Who will receive tokens, and for how long are they vested?
- Distribution mechanisms: Through which channels will inflationary funds enter circulation?
- Token burning: How to remove tokens from circulation, and what are the incentives to do so?
- Impact on incentives and compensation: Does the token design ensure that participants are sufficiently compensated for their contributions to the platform?
- Are participation constraints satisfied?

Designing appropriate token economics involves creating a token that fulfills the fundamentals required by the platform, and then verifying that equilibrium token values will sufficiently compensate any platform participants who receive their compensation in tokens.

Prysm Group Wheel Governance Framework

In our view, the design of governance is the most important decision that any blockchain-based platform will make. Without a credible means for adapting to changes in strategy and environment, a blockchain project will not gain traction. Mark Radcliffe, partner at DLA Piper, agreed: "Blockchain projects are by their nature collaborative, requiring cooperation among multiple participants. The governance of these collaborative organizations is critical to the success of these projects" (DLA Piper, 2019). To assist in decision-making, the Prysm Group developed a comprehensive framework for the design of governance (Fig. 4.3).

Fig. 4.3 Wheel of blockchain governance design. (© 2021 Prysm Group. Used with permission. All rights reserved)

The goal of a blockchain-based platform or ecosystem is to unite a group of stakeholders around a set of resources to create and share value. To understand the design of governance, designers must understand the difference between *governance* and *operational structures*.

Operational structures are the agreed-upon rules and processes that manage the daily functioning of the platform or ecosystem. For most platforms, these include the mechanisms of the incentive and tokenization layers such as the provision of security and the payment of validators and other contributors, and any pricing and market structures.

Governance is the set of mechanisms by which the community makes changes or updates to its operations and decides on a plan of action of shared resources when unanticipated events arise. Operational rules cover the black-and-white platform decisions, whereas governance addresses the gray area. Examples include the process used when compensation schemes need to be altered, when protocols need updating, or when a system-threatening code bug must be fixed. Professor Oliver Hart, Nobel Laureate in economics, stated:

> When you think about the protocols of a blockchain, who gets to change them? I think it's a mistake to think about all these things as being complete contractual transactions. There's always going to be stuff missing, and you may want to change the rules of the game. And who gets to decide that is why governance of blockchain is so important. (O. Hart, personal communication, May 13, 2019)

Prysm Group has developed a framework for guiding the design of a governance system. These components are all interrelated; the design of one component affects the ideal design of the others. Therefore, we recommend working through the steps of this process at least twice:

1. Scope of decisions: Identify the types of decisions that will need to be made.
2. Stakeholders: Identify the stakeholders whose views or wishes should be represented and how their different positions should be balanced to achieve ecosystem-wide goals.
3. Policy research and development: Establish resources and processes for policy research and development.
4. Proposal process: Establish a clear proposal process so that intended stakeholders can propose changes to the system.
5. Information distribution systems: Determine what information is necessary to distribute in order to make high-quality decisions, who has access to that information, and what resources disseminate it requires.
6. Decision-making procedures: Craft decision procedures that engage the relevant stakeholders.
7. Implementation and property rights: Determine who implements decisions and what property rights they have.

All governance processes must be *fully specified at launch*. While the design of the process is important, having shared buy-in to the process itself is equally important. We caution against leaving governance to be designed "on the fly" or not fully communicating the governance design to all users.

While we discuss governance separately from the incentive and token layers of a platform, governance has a profound impact on stakeholder incentives. Any user, particularly one making investments in the long-term health of the platform, will want to know how the rules will evolve over time and whether users will have a say in that evolution. This collective decision-making—precisely the role of governance—works jointly with the various economic levers to attract and retain stakeholders.

Implementation Challenges

As we saw in the FCC auction example, implementation is as important to success as design. In advising dozens of projects and interviewing many more, we have found that these challenges can derail even the best-laid economic plans.

Lack of understanding of what blockchain is. Many potential consortium participants and platform users still have a nebulous concept of what blockchain is and what value it can provide. Mark Radcliffe of DLA Piper said, "There's still this conflation in people's minds about what blockchain means. So much of the press has been oriented on Bitcoin that you can certainly understand why that is" (M. Radcliffe, personal communication, Aug. 21, 2019). This fuzziness must be addressed before any future decisions—or investments—are made.

Disagreeing about who may or may not enter. Particularly in blockchain consortia, the participants must agree whether to use a permissioned or permissionless blockchain. Most corporate consortia will end up being permissioned implementations. As Mr. Radcliffe said, "Participants generally want to know who the players are, and, frankly, would feel better if they if they had control over who joins." However, permissionless systems in an enterprise setting are certainly applicable.

Choosing code and a community that are unstable. Blockchain innovators often base their projects on existing talent and codebases. Especially for corporate projects, the time horizon of the base technology must match the timeline of the project. As Mr. Radcliffe said,

> When choosing a blockchain protocol, you want to make sure that you've got something that is going to be around for a while, and you understand how changes will be made. … The blockchain world will be very different five years from now. The question is, how do people enable decisions to be made to make those changes? If it's not transparent, then it's difficult to have the confidence you want to have to build on top of it. (M. Radcliffe, personal communication, Aug. 21, 2019)

Failing to specify a governance system. As we discussed, governance is the system by which operational processes are updated and when decisions outside the operational rules need to be made. Given the difficulties of agreeing on a governance system, many projects are tempted to forego governance design until needed. But not developing a well-structured governance system before system launch is a way to tank a project—and scare away potential contributors.

Ignoring relevant insights from social science experts. Social sciences—from psychology to sociology to economics—have decades of scholarship on social systems relevant to blockchain. We encourage designers to leverage existing insights—especially contract theory, market design, and the economics of information—to predict and head off potential problems in system design. Although systems must learn and evolve through mistakes, minimizing unnecessary mistakes can help to build user confidence at the outset.

Copy-pasting economic design from other settings. Economic design is a bespoke exercise. Joshua Gans, Jeffrey Skoll Chair in Technical Innovation and Entrepreneurship at the Rotman School of Management, University of Toronto, said, "The one thing we've learned from economic design and market design is it's a bit fiddly. If you miss a key element, the whole market just doesn't work. Things do not take off" (J. Gans, personal communication, May 13, 2019). Copy-pasting incentive systems across platforms doesn't work—the founding team must consider how changes in stakeholders, environment, and system goals might change the economic design.

Disclosures

Prysm Group and the authors of this paper received no compensation from the companies studied for this paper.

Acknowledgments The authors thank Joshua Gans, Oliver Hart, Eric Maskin, Preston McAfee, and Mark Radcliffe for helpful conversations and interviews, and the editorial team at the Blockchain Research Institute for its support.

References

Andersen, O., & Vogdrup-Schmidt, L. (2018, May 15). Rivals reject blockchain solution from Maersk and IBM. *ShippingWatch*. Retrieved June 23, 2021, from https://shippingwatch.com/carriers/Container/article10602520.ece

Andrew. (2018, July 25). *Singapore Airlines launches KrisPay – Poor value redemptions aplenty*. Mainly Miles. Retrieved June 23, 2021, from https://mainlymiles.com/2018/07/24/singapore-airlines-launches-krispay-poor-value-redemptions-aplenty/

Barrera, C., & Hurder, S. (2020, January 13). *Cryptoeconomics: Designing effective incentives and governance models for blockchain networks using insights from economics*. Foreword by Don Tapscott. Retrieved June 23, 2021, from https://www.dropbox.com/s/ckfcxkeb27whasc/Barrera-Hurder_Cryptoeconomics_Designing%20Effective%20Incentives%20and%20Governance%20Models_Blockchain%20Research%20Institute_CC%20release.pdf?dl=0

DLA Piper. (2019, August 23). *Blockchain governance: Key issues in governance for blockchain consortium 2019*. Retrieved June 23, 2021, from https://www.dlapiper.com/en/us/insights/publications/2019/08/blockchain-governance-key-issues-in-governance-for-blockchain-consortium-2019/

Federal Communications Commission. (2017, April 13). *Broadband personal communications service*. Retrieved June 23, 2021, from https://www.fcc.gov/wireless/bureau-divisions/mobility-division/broadband-personal-communications-service-pcs

Federal Communications Commission. (2020, August 26). *Auction 4: Broadband [personal communications service] A and B block*. Retrieved June 23, 2021, from https://www.fcc.gov/auction/4

Friedman, M. (1948). A monetary and fiscal framework for economic stability. *American Economic Review, 38*(3), 245–264.

Hackett, R. (2021, June 15). Why Goldman Sachs and Santander are bailing on R3's blockchain group. *Fortune*. Retrieved June 23, 2021, from https://fortune.com/2016/11/21/goldman-sachs-r3-blockchain-consortium/

Hart, O. (2001). Norms and the theory of the firm. *University of Pennsylvania Law Review, 149*(6), 1701.

McAfee, R. P., McMillan, J., & Wilkie, S. (2012). The greatest auction in history. In J. J. Siegfried (Ed.), *Better living through economics* (pp. 168–187). Harvard UP. Retrieved June 23, 2021, from https://vita.mcafee.cc/PDF/GreatestAuctionHistory.pdf

Ostrom, E. (2000). Collective action and the evolution of social norms. *Journal of Economic Perspectives, 14*(3), 137–158.

Roth, A. E. (2018). Marketplaces, markets, and market design. *American Economic Review, 108*(7), 1609–1658.

Safire, W. (1995, March 16). Essay: The greatest auction ever. *New York Times*, p. A25.

Stiglitz, J. E. (1989). Markets, market failures, and development. *American Economic Review, 79*(2), 197.

5

Verifiable Credentials in the Token Economy

Mary C. Lacity and Erran Carmel

Overview of Credentials

Modern life requires that we prove our identities and credentials to others. Proving our credentials involve three roles that comprise a "trust triangle": the issuer, the holder, and the verifier (see Fig. 5.1). Consider these common trust triangle scenarios: A border control guard (the verifier) asks a traveler (the holder) to show her passport, which was issued by her country's government ministry (the issuer). A potential employer (the verifier) asks the job applicant (the holder) to see his diploma from his university (the issuer). A liquor store cashier (the verifier) asks the customer (the holder) to prove her legal drinking age with her ID issued by

M. C. Lacity (✉)
Sam M. Walton College of Business,
University of Arkansas, Fayetteville, AR, USA
e-mail: mclacity@uark.edu

E. Carmel
American University, Washington, DC, USA
e-mail: carmel@american.edu

M. C. Lacity, H. Treiblmaier (eds.), *Blockchains and the Token Economy*, Technology, Work and Globalization, https://doi.org/10.1007/978-3-030-95108-5_5

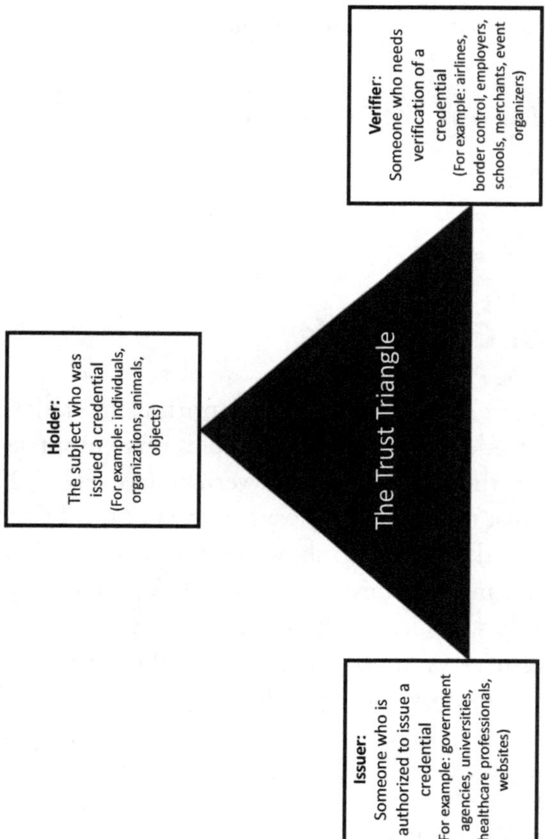

Fig. 5.1 The trust triangle's three roles needed for credentials

her government (the issuer). A school principal (the verifier) asks parents for their child's (the holder) vaccination records from the pediatrician (the issuer).[1] Today, in many of these everyday scenarios, the trust triangle still relies on physical (paper-based) proofs of our credentials, such as diplomas, passports, driver's licenses, and vaccination records. While it may seem archaic in today's digital world, at least these physical documents are portable. We carry wallets and purses, in part, to transport our credentials.

A *verifiable credential* can represent all of the same information that a physical credential represents. The addition of technologies, such as digital signatures, makes verifiable credentials more tamper-evident and more trustworthy than their physical counterparts (W3C, 2019). The DHPs described in this article are "passes"—which display only a subset of the credential—only the data that are necessary for verification.

With the Internet so widely available, why aren't all credentials proven digitally? The Internet, it turns out, has a poor architecture for automating a trust triangle. The Internet was originally designed for sharing information among parties who already knew and trusted each other. As the Internet grew, standards for sharing messages (like TCP/IP) provided a way to identify the growing number of machines connected to the Internet, but they do not verify the individuals or organizations who are sending messages from those machines (Campbell-Kelly & Garcia-Swartz, 2013; Rosenzweig, 1998).

To enact a trust triangle in the digital world, we need an identity layer. The two most common identity solutions are the centralized and federated approaches. Both approaches give complete control over a holder's credentials to the organizations with whom the holder transacts (Preukschat & Reed, 2021).

Centralized identity models are account-based, requiring users to create logon IDs and passwords. By 2015, the average United Kingdom

[1] Each role may be enacted by an individual, organization, or object. For example, holders can be animals, such as certifications about the conditions under which they were raised, handled, processed, transported, and stored. Holders can be organizations, such as credentials pertaining to incorporation date, incorporation jurisdiction, and tax status. Holders can be objects, such as attestations on physical dimensions and composition; entitlements like access rights for self-driving cars and drones; and certifications like fit-for-use, energy-efficient, or sustainably produced.

(U.K.) Internet user had 118 online accounts (Allan, 2015); by 2017, the average United States (U.S.) Internet user had 150 online accounts (Caruthers, 2018). More recently, some organization allow federated logon IDs and passwords, where users access multiple accounts through a single account managed by companies such as Facebook, Google, Amazon, and LinkedIn. While this reduces the number of accounts users need to manage, it increases the power over users' data by these companies. Many people believe there is a better way.

Principles for Self-Sovereign Identity (SSI) and Verifiable Credentials

Many standards-making bodies, open source working groups, organizations, and individuals are working on standards for self-sovereign identity (SSI) and verifiable credentials. The creation of a set of guiding principles is core to the effort. Such principles have been proposed by the Trust Over IP Foundation (2020) managed by the Linux Foundation, ID2020 (2018), the World Economic Forum (2020), the Sovrin Foundation (2020a), and the W3C Verifiable Credentials Working Group (2019); Christopher Allen (2016), author of "The path to Self-Sovereign Identity"; Kim Cameron (2005), author of "The laws of identity"; and Kaliya Young (2020), author of "The domains of identity," are notable individuals. In addition to working on general principles, some groups and individuals are working swiftly to create principles specific to health passes, a particular type of verifiable credential that is urgently needed because of COVID-19. The Good Health Pass Collaborative (GHPC) (2021), the Vaccination Credential Initiative (2021), the Ada Lovelace Institute (2021), and the World Health Organization (2021) are examples.

Many of these groups and individuals share ideas and cross reference each other's work to aid in the development of principles. Overall, they generally agree on the following principles of SSI and verifiable credentials:

1. Credentials should be created by an authorized issuer, shared with holders, and proven to verifiers (verifiable credentials).
2. Credentials should be proven to belong to the holder (identity binding) (Gao et al., 2018).
3. Holders should control their credentials (user control).

The solution should:

4. ensure data privacy and security,
5. be available to and accessible for all,
6. be interoperable across platforms,
7. require user consent,
8. minimize data so that holders share the minimum amount of information required for verification, and
9. be transparent about data creation, collection, storage, and usage.

Other principles commonly mentioned include portability of credentials, a clear governance framework, persistence of credentials over time, and a consistent and user-friendly experience.

Several key concepts and technologies are needed to enact these principles.

Concepts and Technologies for Verifiable Credentials

Trust registries and decentralized identifiers are core concepts that describe *what* verifiable credential solutions need to include. Digital wallets, utility tokens, and blockchains are core enabling technologies that determine *how* verifiable credential solutions might be implemented.

Trust registries. According to the Trust Over IP Foundation (2021), a trust registry is defined as: "A network service available from one or more service endpoints specified in a governance framework that can be queried to determine if a party is authorized to perform a specific role or action. A common example is a verifier querying a trust registry to determine if the issuer of a verifiable credential is an authoritative issuer for a specific verifiable credential type. Another example is a holder querying a trust registry to determine if a verifier is authorized to make a specific presentation request." W3C calls such a database a "verifiable data registry" (W3C, 2019). Trust registries will largely be used as the new decentralized public key infrastructure to verify signatures, particularly from issuers. The actual verifiable credentials will be stored on the holders' digital wallets.

Digital wallets. Holders likely will use a new type of digital wallet, called an "SSI" wallet, to control access to their credentials. Digital wallets are software applications that store the cryptographic private keys that control verifiable credentials. Digital wallets[2] may be noncustodial (held by the holder) or custodial (managed by a trusted third party).

Decentralized identifiers. All roles (issuers, holders, and verifiers) need unique and decentralized identifiers. Standards are coalescing around decentralized identifiers (DIDs). According to the W3C (2020), "DIDs are designed to enable individuals and organizations ***to generate their own identifiers*** using systems they trust. These new identifiers enable entities to prove control over them by authenticating cryptographic proofs such as digital signatures. Since the generation and assertion of Decentralized Identifiers is entity-controlled, each entity can have as many DIDs as necessary to maintain their desired separation of identities, personas, and interactions." Anything can be a DID subject: a person, group, organization, physical thing, digital thing, logical thing (Trust Over IP, 2021). Most of the DIDs will be used for peer-to-peer communications, such as between issuers and holders, between holders and verifiers, and verifiers and issuers.

Utility tokens. Decentralized SSI and verified credentials need an economic model to pay for the development and operations of the network. Those who gain economic value from verifying credentials should be willing to pay for services. Rather than pay for SSI/verifiable credentials with conventional payment networks that rely on a trusted third party, a decentralized network could be paid for with transactions fees using utility tokens. As one specific SSI example, the Sovrin Foundation (2018) proposed a Sovrin utility token to pay for transactions on the Sovrin

[2] The security of the digital wallet is also being considered in work by the Decentralized Identity Foundation (DIF).

network. Sovrin recognized that there is real economic value in reducing risks by verifying credentials before transacting. The greater the risk being taken, the greater the value of the verifiable claims. Using utility tokens, holders could pay issuers a transaction fee, just as some alumni pay universities small fees for copies of diplomas. Verifiers could pay holders fees to gain permission to verify the holders' credentials. Verifiers could pay fees to issuers for the actual verification. Sovrin launched a test token for public experimentation in February of 2020 (Sovrin Foundation, 2020b).

Provided the utility token is not used as an investment instrument, it should not be treated as a security under most government laws. In the U.S., for example, Wyoming was the first state to codify a legal definition of a utility token. The law states, in part: "The token has a consumptive purpose that is available at or near the time of sale and can be used at or near the time of sale for a consumptive purpose. The developer or seller did not market the token to the initial buyer as a financial investment" (State of Wyoming, 2019).

Blockchains. Blockchains are designed for peer-to-peer transactions and are thus well suited for decentralized control of verifiable credentials. A blockchain's distributed ledger would serve as a trust registry. A distributed ledger is a time-stamped, permanent record of all valid transactions that have occurred within a given blockchain application. Each authorized node of the blockchain network has an identical copy; no node is in charge. A smart contract, that sits on a blockchain, stores and executes rules agreed upon by trading partners on when and how to update the trust registry (Lacity, 2020). Smart contracts could also manage the issuance and payments of utility tokens to finance the network.

Minimal Viable Products

The availability of production solutions that adhere to principles for decentralized identity and verifiable credentials is still emerging, with much activity still in R&D and proof-of-concepts (PoCs) (Fry & Renieris, 2020). But some pilots are underway, providing an opportunity for learning. The pilots are minimal viable products (MVPs), an initial version of a product that has enough functionality to attract early adopters, who provide rapid feedback to improve the product, such as adding new features and functionality (Vartan & Brinkerhoff, 2021).

We explore two types of MVPs.

iDatafy's SmartResume is the first example. It illustrates the automation of the "trust triangle" in the context of a job talent platform. A SmartResume is a digital resume where issuers create an individual's credentials, but the individual controls access rights. So far, iDatafy has spent three years building the Arkansas-based ecosystem of issuers, holders, and verifiers, and over 125,000 smart resumes have been generated (but not necessarily activated) by Summer 2021. The case study is based on participant observation and multiple interviews with holders, issuers, and the platform provider over a three-year period.

Digital health passes (DHPs) are the second solution we examine. DHPs expand the concept of a "trust triangle" to a "trust diamond" by including a governing authority. The governing authority determines which types of credentials are allowed, which issuers are allowed to issue credentials, and which verifiers can request access to credentials. The discussion is based on our interviews with DHP leaders and decision makers in 2021 at technology companies, organizations bringing workers back to the office, standards-making communities, airport administrators, as well as individual users. As of this writing in the summer of 2021, we have examined several DHPs, but all were MVPs that had been recently launched.

As we describe the solutions, we assess each against the principles for digital credentials and describe how issuers, holders, and verifiers are incentivized to join the platforms. Table 5.1 summarizes the analysis.

SmartResume

Talent acquisition is a common example of a trust triangle. Universities, professional organizations, training programs, testing facilities, and other sanctioned *issuers* create verifiable credentials about a person's education, skills, and qualifications. Job applicants are the *holders* of these credentials. Potential employers are the *verifiers* that require proof of credentials. Despite all of the advanced human resource (HR) practices, investments,

Table 5.1 Comparison of first-generation solutions: SmartResume and DHP

Assessment of first-generation solutions		
	SmartResume	Digital Health Passes
Purpose of the solution:	Certified job talent platform designed to solve three problems in the job talent acquisition market: (1) fraudulent credentials, (2) selection bias, (3) data leakage and misuse.	Platforms designed to verify one's health so that individuals may fly, cross borders, and access facilities.
Evidence of verifiable credentials principles		
1. Credentials are digitally verified by issuers?	**YES:** Only authorized issuers can create credentials; verifiers can independently verify the credential by querying the blockchain.	**VARIES:** Some DHPs still relied on holders to upload digital copies of their physical paperwork—they were not pulled from a trust registry; some DHPs relied only on self-attestations. One exception was N.Y.'s Excelsior pass; it pulls verified credentials from N.Y. trust registries.
2. Identity binding?	**IN PROGRESS:** Holders activate their SmartResumes using the information held by the issuers, such as last name, organization name, student ID, email on file. This is not yet a strong application of identity binding, but ease of use is a priority for the beta test.	**VARIES:** Airline DHPs have strong identity binding by requiring government ID; New York's Excelsior: our research subjects reported that no one asked for proof of identification at events until a law went into effect in August 2021.
3. User control over their credentials?	**YES:** Holders control access to their SmartResumes. In the beta version, iDatafy serves as the custodian of private keys to prevent holders from losing them. iDatafy is working on a digital wallet where users can download and control their own credentials.	**YES:** In the DHPs we examined, holders must download and activate a DHP wallet. The wallets store the private keys that control access.

(*continued*)

Table 5.1 (continued)

Assessment of first-generation solutions		
	SmartResume	Digital Health Passes
4. Privacy and security?	**YES:** The solution complies with all privacy laws. In May 2021, SmartResume was certified by IMS Global Learning Consortium for Data Privacy.	**YES:** Overall, the solutions we examine comply with privacy laws within the jurisdictions they operate; blockchains are used to secure credentials and to limit access to only authorized parties. Several DHPs use permissioned blockchains for added data security and privacy, such as IATA, N.Y.'s Excelsior.
5. Availability to all?	**IN PROGRESS:** The initial focus is on the Arkansas job talent ecosystem. In addition to scaling the talent indexing in Arkansas, iDatafy is also beginning to work with national partners.	**NO:** While anyone may download a DHP wallet app, populating it with verifiable credentials requires an ecosystem of issuers, verifiers, and a governing authority.
6. Interoperability?	**IN PROGRESS:** iDatafy has demonstrated that multiple Arkansas-based education partners could direct certified awards to a singular SmartResume. As a next step, iDatafy also wants to make the SmartResume interoperable with verifiable credentials from other emerging solutions from across the world. In preparation for this, SmartResume was certified in May of 2021 by a standards group, the IMS Global Learning Consortium, for its Comprehensive Learning Record (CLR) and Digital Open Badges.	**NO:** DHPs belong to one of several groups focusing on standards, such as Good Health Pass Collaborative (GHPC) (2021), the Vaccination Credential Initiative (2021), and the World Health Organization (2021). Fully interoperable ecosystems do not exist yet.

(continued)

Table 5.1 (continued)

Assessment of first-generation solutions		
	SmartResume	Digital Health Passes
7. User consent?	**YES:** Holders have to opt-in.	**YES:** In the solutions we examined, holders have to opt-in.
8. Data minimization?	**YES:** This is a key feature of the platform. Verifiers can only see verified skills, not any protected personal information (PPI) data.	**VARIES:** Some DHPs process rules to minimize data and show a "pass"; some display digital versions of the entire credential to verifiers.
9. Transparency about data creation, collection, storage and use?	**YES:** Policies are clear as to who generates credentials (only authorized issuers), who has access to what data, and the data actually stored on the blockchain (people can examine the source code).	**SAME OLD MODEL:** The DHPs we examined have pages of complicated legal text on terms and conditions that users must accept.
10. Other principles?	• User-friendly • Portability (too early to tell) • Persistence (too early to tell)	• User-friendly: Digital wallets are easy to download, but loading them with credentials has not always been smooth in MVPs.
Value propositions for participants		
Value to issuers	• Protect and promote their brands • Deepen relationships with alumni • Efficiencies by verifying once instead of multiple times during a person's career • Ease of data upload • No cost to use	• Reduces the number of calls to issuers to verify credentials for verifiers or to holders who lost their documents • No cost to use
Value to holders	• Access to a pool of hiring organizations • Control over job search • Assurance that organizations base acceptance on qualifications • No cost to use	• Prove one's health • Access to travel, entry, services, workplaces, etc. • No cost to use

(continued)

Table 5.1 (continued)

Assessment of first-generation solutions		
	SmartResume	Digital Health Passes
Value to verifiers	• Access to a pool of qualified talent • Minimize selection bias • Assurance of applicants' qualifications • Reduce the costs of vetting applicants	• Protect public health • Make customers feel safe • Smoother processing of verification • Prevents costly processing errors (e.g., for airlines: a passenger denied entrance at the destination country and then having to fly them back).
Value to governing authority	• N/A	• Protect public health • In the case of COVID-19, open the economy more safely

and technology innovations, talent acquisition still is wrought with challenges, including these three:

1. Applicants inflate their skills or make fraudulent claims on their resumes. Job sites and social media platforms like CareerBuilder, Indeed, LinkedIn, and Monster do not verify credentials. Subsequently, fraud and inflated resumes remain problematic. One survey found that 75 percent of employers caught at least one applicant lying on their resumes (CareerBuilder, 2017). Hiring companies spend significant resources to investigate a job candidate's claims. Verification slows down the talent acquisition process and increases costs. On average, it costs companies $4129 per hire, but costs can be as high as $40,000 per position for highly skilled workers (National Student Clearing House, 2022; Turczynski, 2020).

2. Hiring organizations and recruiters struggle with selection bias. Social media and many job site platforms reveal people's race, gender, age, religion, affiliations, and life-style choices. Recruiters may (in)advertently dismiss candidates based on this data rather than based on their qualifications. Social media and job site platforms are not the only sources of selection bias; relying on referrals from current employees creates a homogeneous applicant pool because people tend to refer people who are similar to them (Fatemi, 2019).

3. Data privacy protection is another concern for all parties. Hiring organizations—particularly those 60 percent of companies that outsource recruiting—need to make sure applicant data is properly handled. In the U.S., for example, the Family Educational Rights and Privacy Act (FERPA) protects the privacy of student education records. Generally, schools must have written permission from the parent or eligible student before releasing any information about a student's education record. Increasingly, data privacy regulations like the European Union's General Data Protection Regulation (GDPR) and the California Consumer Privacy Act (CCPA) have increased data protection more broadly. Despite these regulations, many job sites and recruiters routinely collect information on applicants like email addresses, phone numbers, age, ethnicity, photos, and other personal information (Smits, 2018).

iDatafy, an American company that was founded in 2011 by David Wengel in Little Rock, Arkansas, created the SmartResume platform and career network to fix these problems. The platform prevents fraudulent claims by applicants, eliminates selection bias, and ensures data privacy compliance. The SmartResume platform is similar to LinkedIn or Upwork, but with *verifiable* credentials secured by blockchain technology.

To launch the career network of issuers, holders, and verifiers, Wengel focused on his home base in the state of Arkansas.

Issuers. In the SmartResume platform, only a credentialing organization may create a SmartResume on behalf of an individual. ***Verifiable credentials*** include educational degrees, coursework, honors, activities, awards, experiences, licenses, affiliations, research, skills, reference letters, and other certifications. The certifications appear on an individual's SmartResume as a tamperproof badge that is secured by blockchain technology (see Fig. 5.2).

The pilot project launched with the first credentialing organization, the Sam M. Walton College of Business at the University of Arkansas, in 2018. Within 18 months, the consortium included the University of Arkansas at Fayetteville, Little Rock, Fort Smith, Community College at Morrilton, *e*Versity, and Pulaski Technical. By summer of 2021, the entire University of Arkansas system had signed a memorandum of

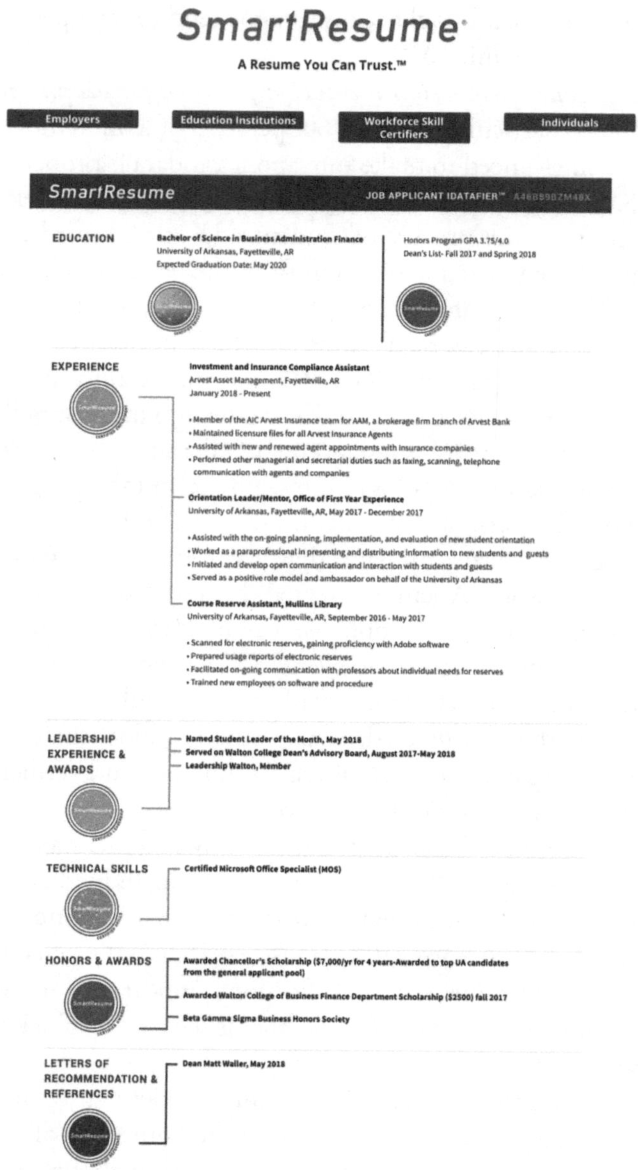

Fig. 5.2 An example of a SmartResume as viewed by a hiring organization. (Source: iDatafy)

understanding, as well as University of Central Arkansas, Arkansas Tech University, North Arkansas College, Arkansas Baptist College, Shorter College, and Philander Smith College. Workforce skills issuers, such as Goodwill and the Forge Institute (trains and certifies cybersecurity skills), also joined.

Incentivizing issuers: The SmartResume platform prevents users from claiming credentials they did not earn, thus protecting the issuer's brand. Issuers also gain efficiencies by credentialing a person *once*, rather than reaffirming credentials every time a person changes employment. For educational institutions, an additional benefit of joining the SmartResume platform is that it serves as a meaningful way to connect with alumni. For workforce skill certifiers that train and certify truck drivers, steamfitters, pipefitters, sprinkler systems installers, and heating, ventilation, and air conditioning (HVAC) technicians, the platform better connects their graduates to employers. Issuers do not pay to participate in the SmartResume platform. Issuers do need to expend time and resources to pull data from existing systems of records, but iDatafy has simplified this process so that issuers can send a batch of records on a spreadsheet. iDatafy assumes the burden of formatting and uploading the spreadsheet data to the SmartResume platform. Issuers just need to review and verify the upload was done correctly.

Holders. Students, alumni, current job holders, and job seekers are holders of credentials. Once an issuer creates a verifiable credential, the holder exists in the system automatically in a dormant state and it is not accessible by any third party. Individuals must opt in to the SmartResume platform. ***Identity binding*** happens by requiring the holder to activate their SmartResume using the information held by the issuers, such as last name, organization name, student ID, and email on file. During the beta test, iDatafy wanted to create a ***user-friendly experience*** and did not want to erect barriers to adoption by making identity binding too onerous.

After opting in, individuals are in control of their job matching preferences and may grant or deny full access rights to particular hiring organizations. These policies enact the principles of ***user control*** and ***user consent.*** This was the right decision to protect users' privacy and to get a more engaged user, even though it slowed the rollout.

Each individual gets one integrated SmartResume, which may contain verifiable credentials from many different issuers. The SmartResume platform does this by creating a unique holder identifier, called a Job Applicant IDATAFIER. (The solution is not using DIDs.) iDatafy only stores a minimum of information (***data minimization***) on the blockchain ledger associated with each credential, including the unique Job Applicant IDATAFIER, credentialing organization, certification type, date, and timestamp to ensure ***privacy and security***.

Individuals who activate their resumes can supplement their personal SmartResume with additional information, such as career objectives, hobbies, and interests.

Incentivizing holders: The SmartResume platform is free to holders. The value to holders includes access to a pool of hiring organizations, control over which organizations can view their resumes, and assurance that organizations base selection on qualifications, not on demographic data. Holders can also have a permanent record of their credentials if an issuer goes out of operation (property of ***persistence***).

Verifiers. Hiring organizations (or outsourced recruiters) are the verifiers. Verifiers search for qualified candidates based only on their skills, as all demographic and personal information like name and gender are masked to prevent search bias. If an organization is interested in connecting to an individual, the platform sends the individual an email request for access. The individual may grant access or may anonymously decline the invitation. This also enacts the principles of ***user control*** and ***user consent***. The verifiers can verify the credential by clicking on the badge to ping the blockchain (***verifiable credential***.) Hiring organizations can ascertain which credentials were verifiable by issuers by the presence of the blockchain badge and which entries were added by individuals.

The hiring organizations were the last group invited to the platform. iDatafy wanted to wait until there was a population of certified job talent first. For the pilot phase, hiring organizations will not be charged to use the platform. To make hiring organizations aware of the platform, Northwest Arkansas Council will point hundreds of employers to the platform. In the long run, iDatafy will charge hiring organizations when they hire talent recruited from the platform. For now, iDatafy is financing the platform, and it received (with partners) a competitive "Reimaging Workforce" grant from the U.S. Department of Education. The CEO commented: "We're foregoing potentially larger short-term revenues to attract hundreds and hundreds of employers to get feedback that will help us build a much larger business in the long run."

Incentivizing verifiers: Wengel aims to index all of Arkansas's job talent, thus providing hiring organizations with a comprehensive pool of verified talent. Hiring organizations can demonstrate that they are creating applicant pools in an unbiased manner because all demographic data is masked. Instead, verifiers can show that they selected candidates based on their skills and qualifications. Moreover, verifiers gain efficiencies by no longer having to call each organization on a candidate's resume to verify credentials. This potentially saves verifiers between $4000 and $40,000 per position (National Student Clearing House, 2022; Turczynski, 2020).

Enabling technologies. The SmartResume platform is a hybrid platform that includes a web-based interface, traditional technologies, and a permissioned blockchain ledger. Traditional technologies allow for fast searches. Blockchain technology provides the ability for multiple parties to verify and trust that credentials are valid, secure, and traceable. Moreover, the platform is compliant with FERPA regulations. From a user perspective, the components are seamlessly integrated on the web-based portal to provide a ***user-friendly experience***. People maneuver through the platform based on their roles, such as employers, educational institutions, workforce skill certifiers, and individuals. The user interface is constantly evolving and improving.

Dave Wengel, the CEO, is also focused on standards to provide long-term ***interoperability***. In May of 2021, SmartResume was certified by IMS Global Learning Consortium for its comprehensive learning record (CLR) and digital open badges. Wengel said: "Industry certification means that SmartResume does not have to be the only provider coordinating credentials. Our hope is that hundreds of trusted education partners can be combined onto one SmartResume." Wengel is also working on a digital wallet so that there is ***portability*** and ***persistence*** of verifiable credentials.

Digital Health Passes

Digital health passes (DHPs) are software applications that help to securely create, store, and share an individual's health credentials. DHPs are not a new idea, but COVID-19 ramped efforts to prove our health so that we can get back to work, travel, school, and play. Examples include IATA's Travel Pass (MVPs tied by multiple airlines), Daon's VeriFLY (tried by airlines including American Airlines), CLEAR's Health Pass (tried by airlines, pharmacies), the U.K.'s Covid Pass by the National Health Service (NHS); Denmark's CoronaPass; Korea's Pass&Go; and New York's Excelsior Pass.

To explain how DHPs work, we must expand the concept of the "trust triangle" to add governing authorities, thus creating a "trust diamond" (see Fig. 5.3). For the context of healthcare credentials, a governing authority (e.g., Ministry/Department of Health) determines which types of health credentials are allowed (which vaccines, which tests) and which issuers (labs, pharmacies, healthcare professionals) are allowed to issue credentials and specifies the rules for credentials (such as expiration dates, required credentials) and which verifiers can request access to credentials.

In an ideal "trust diamond" ecosystem, governing authorities ensure that only authorized issuers (step 1) create and write authorized healthcare credentials to the trust registry (step 2). Issuers notify holders that their credential is available to them to download to a digital wallet (step 3). Only holders can control who is allowed to read their healthcare credentials. A holder must grant permission to verifiers to access their data (step 4), such as displaying a QR code and allowing the verifier to scan it. A holder also needs to prove her identity to bind the healthcare credential to the holder. Verifiers query the trust registry for independent verification, typically by checking that the issuer's public key was used to create the credential (step 5). Depending on the rules established by the governing authority, a verifier might only get an indication of health, say with a green circle to indicate "passes health requirements" or a red circle to indicate "does not pass health requirements." Assuming the pass indicates health, the verifier grants the holder access to the service requested, such as boarding a flight, crossing a border, or entering a stadium (step 6).

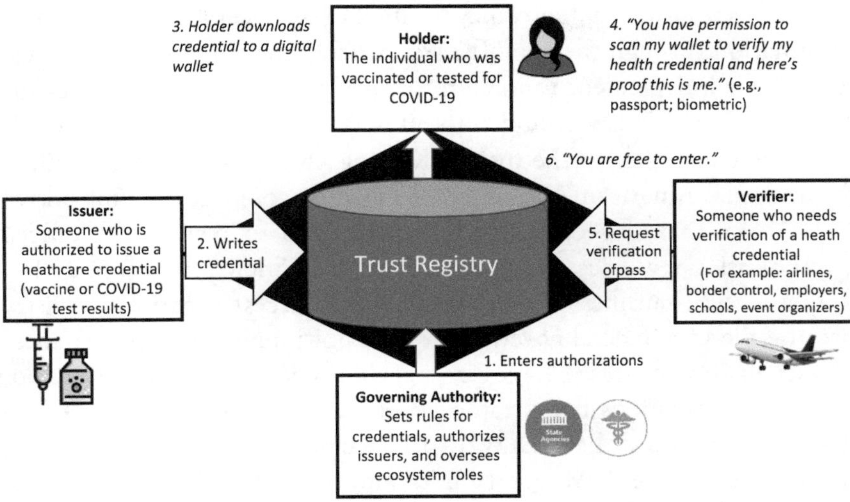

Fig. 5.3 The trust diamond's four roles needed for healthcare credentials

There are a number of important features to note from the trust diamond. First, the solutions are called "digital health passes" instead of "digital health passports" for a reason. A "pass" signals the principle of ***data minimization***—verifiers should only see a minimum of data. In contrast, a "passport" might suggest that a verifier views the entire healthcare credential. In addition to violating DHP principles, it may also violate healthcare data ***privacy*** protection laws. Second, although these systems are based on digital records of healthcare credentials, nearly all DHPs offer paper-based alternatives to meet the principle of ***accessibility***. Instead of displaying a QR code on a phone, for example, a holder might display a QR code on a ticket.

As of the summer of 2021, DHPs are still in the experimental phase. Here, we briefly cover two examples.

VeriFLY. American Airlines offers international travelers the option of using VeriFLY, a DHP created by the American company Doan. Travelers indicate their origin and destinations, and VeriFLY tells travelers which healthcare credentials are required. Travelers upload photos of their COVID-19 vaccination cards and test results to the application (American Airlines, 2021). The verifier team reviews the submission. If the team is unsure of a test's authenticity, they notify the passenger to send additional information through the app. The step where the verifier pings the trust registry for independent validation is missing (step 5 in Fig. 5.3) in the MVP, but VeriFLY is working with 30 major testing facilities to provide verifiable credentials in the future (Keesing, 2021). In August of 2021, for example, American Airlines announced it would accept uploads of New York's Excelsior Pass, which is connected to New York's official immunization registries, as explained below (CBSnews, August 5, 2021).

In the U.S., airlines (the verifiers) cannot access a national registry because the U.S. federal government does not intend to keep a database of vaccination records. Moreover, the U.S. federal government cannot mandate vaccinations because the Federal Drug Administration (FDA) has only authorized three COVID-19 vaccines for emergency use only, not permanent use. Given that limitation, the U.S. federal government has not pushed for DHPs, and instead leaves DHP decisions to states and the private sector (CNBC May 22, 2021). Airline DHPs do have strong ***identity binding***, as it is part of the normal process for boarding a flight to scan passports, government-issued driver's licenses, or national ID cards.

Incentives: For the verifiers, airlines are incentivized to use DHPs, particularly for international travel. Airlines are responsible for making sure passengers have the proper documents to meet the entry requirements of their destination countries. Airlines are stuck with the cost of transporting individuals who are refused entry, and DHPs are valued as one way to minimize this risk.

For the holders, American Airlines offers these value propositions to passengers: "The VeriFLY app takes the confusion out of COVID-era travel" and "Customers using VeriFLY can use expedited check-in lanes at most U.S. hub airports" (American Airline, 2021). As of July 2021, American Airlines have dedicated lanes at 5 U.S. airports and 6 international airports.

N.Y. Excelsior Pass. One U.S. state, New York, adopted a DHP called Excelsior, which is built on IBM's digital health pass platform. The platform utilizes blockchain technology. As of Summer 2021, the Excelsior pass verifies three types of healthcare credentials: COVID-19 vaccination, PCR test, and antigen test. The Excelsior DHP is connected to the

New York State Immunization Information System (NYSIIS) and to New York City's Citywide Immunization Registry (CIR). All New York providers (issuers) must report COVID-19 vaccinations/test results to these registries as of January 2021 (New York Department of Health, 2021). Thus, issuers are creating ***verifiable credentials***. Citizens of New York are encouraged to have this DHP to enter public facilities and events (Carmel & Lacity, 2021). Venues (the verifiers) who accept the pass use a separate app, called Excelsior Pass Scanner. The scanner app reads a QR code which reveals the holder's name, birthdate, and COVID-19 healthcare credential of "pass" or "not pass." Verifiers cannot access the actual healthcare credential (***data minimization***). Verifiers are supposed to ask for a photo ID for ***identity binding*** (State of New York, 2021). At first, compliance appeared spotty. We investigated one event at a major stadium in Summer 2020 and found that identity binding did not occur (no employee asked to see proof of identity), and thus, the verification loop (step 5) was not closed yet. Imagine the thousands of people who enter an arena at the start of an event—what stadium has the capacity to scan a ticket, a DHP, and an ID to connect the three?

On August 3, 2021, NYC mandated proof of vaccination for indoor dining, fitness, and entertainment by September of 2021, requiring every guest (and employee) have proof of vaccination and a government ID (for identity binding) or face fines (New York City, 2021). The lead author was in NYC during September and observed that employees and guests of every bar, restaurant, museum, and office complied with the regulation. Most native New Yorkers used their Excelsior app.

Incentives: The application is free to use; it's paid for by the government: N.Y. State. N.Y. State offers these value propositions to citizens (holders): "streamline entries into public venues" and "protect sensitive personal health information." In New York, at the time of this writing, proof of vaccination can be used to eliminate social distancing and mask requirements. For the Excelsior Pass Scanner, businesses (the verifiers) are encouraged to adopt to "aid compliance with state reopening guidelines." For example, New York required proof of vaccination or a negative test at large indoor venues that seat over 5000 people (State of New York, 2021).

Even with the limitations we describe, these DHP experiments are important. Providers of DHPs are gathering feedback from users to improve product features. Issuers, holders, and verifiers are gaining exposure and experience with using DHPs. Ultimately, DHPs need to rely on a reliable trust registry, and DHP providers have little influence in this regard; governments control these decisions. Within the U.S., given that the national government has shirked support for DHP, this was one advantage the N.Y. Excelsior Pass had over airline apps—at least this app pulls from government healthcare registries.

Conclusion

The SmartResume and DHP solutions aim to create verifiable credentials, one in the context of a job market and one in the context of public health. The SmartResume solution began in 2018, so it was further along its development journey than DHPs that began with the pandemic and accelerated with the vaccinations in 2021. But the key findings were similar:

1. First-generation solutions cannot subscribe to all of the principles envisioned for fully decentralized self-sovereign identity and verifiable credentials. So far, holders do not create their own identifiers (DIDs); it is simply too early. Moreover, trusted third parties still are needed to manage the network, providing services like data uploads, user support, search engines, access management, custodial protection of private keys, and software upgrades—to name a few. First-generation solutions are self-contained, meaning that verifiable credentials are not yet accessible to all; they are not interoperable or portable across platforms. Dave Wengel, creator of the SmartResume, summed it up as follows: "This idea of a decentralized world offers so many benefits. But for now, I guarantee you if SmartResume was a completely autonomous decentralized system and you had a problem with one of your credentials, there would be no one to help."

2. Minimal viable products are not designed to be perfect. We should expect glitches, it is how these systems will improve. Digitizing complex ecosystems like job markets and digital health passes requires live experiments with rapid feedback loops to improve the MVP over time. Dave Wengel said it best, "Focus on good enough, learn from feedback, and aspire to be great." We heard similar same messages from DHP providers.

3. The technology was the easier part, while building the ecosystem was the harder part. SmartResume and N.Y. Excelsior Pass make use of permissioned blockchain technologies. N.Y. Excelsior Pass also uses digital wallets. Neither makes use of DIDs or utility tokens. If a solution's adoption is voluntarily (and most were), a clear value proposition for issuers, holders, and verifiers is needed. All members of the trust triangle/diamond must be incentivized to join the solution. In both sets of solutions, the issuers and holders were not being charged during the experimental pilots; they are paid for by verifiers or governing authorities.

Today, verifiable credentials rely on trusted third parties for network services. Interoperability standards, user-generated identifiers, and utility tokens are not yet advanced enough for wide-scale adoption. However, we can more easily see the possibilities by learning from standards-making bodies, open source working groups, organizations, and individuals that are working on self-sovereign identity (SSI) and verifiable credentials as well as from first-generation solutions. Utility tokens, in particular, could provide a way to finance completely decentralized solutions.

References

Ada Lovelace Institute. (2021). *Checkpoints for Vaccine Passports*. Retrieved on May 8, 2022 from https://www.adalovelaceinstitute.org/report/checkpoints-for-vaccine-passports/

Allan, D. (2015). *We all have too many online accounts – And can't remember the passwords*. ITProPortal. Retrieved July 10, 2021, from https://www.itproportal.com/2015/07/23/we-all-have-too-many-online-accounts-and-cant-remember-the-passwords/

Allen, C. (2016). *The path to self-sovereign identity*. Retrieved July 12, 2021, from http://www.lifewithalacrity.com/2016/04/the-path-to-self-sovereign-identity.html

American Airlines. (2021, May 20). *Press release*. Retrieved July 11, 2021, from https://news.aa.com/news/news-details/2021/American-Airlines-Customers-Can-Now-Choose-Convenient-Vaccine-Verification-Option-in-VeriFLY-OPS-DIS-05/default.aspx

Cameron, K. (2005). *The laws of identity*. Retrieved July 12, 2021, from http://www.ict-21.ch/ICT.SATW.CH/IMG/Kim_Cameron_Law_of_Identity.pdf

Campbell-Kelly, M., & Garcia-Swartz, D. (2013). The history of the internet: The missing narratives. *Journal of Information Technology, 28*(1), 18–33. https://doi.org/10.1057/jit.2013.4

CareerBuilder. (2017). *75% of HR managers have caught a lie on a resume*. http://press.careerbuilder.com/2017-09-14-75-of-HR-Managers-Have-Caught-a-Lie-on-a-Resume-According-to-a-New-CareerBuilder-Survey

Carmel, E., & Lacity, M. (2021). *Digital health passes: It's not the technology but the ecosystem that matters*. Walton Insights. Retrieved July 11, 2021, from https://walton.uark.edu/insights/digital-health-passes.php

Caruthers, M. (2018). World password day: How to improve your passwords. *Dashlane Tech News*. Retrieved July 10, 2021, from https://blog.dashlane.com/world-password-day/

CBSnews. (2021, August 5). *New York State announces launch of Excelsior Pass Plus*. Retrieved August 9, 2021, from https://cbs6albany.com/news/local/new-york-state-announces-launch-of-excelsior-pass-plus

CNBC. (2021, May 22). *Covid vaccine passports: Everything we know so far*. https://www.cnbc.com/2021/05/22/covid-vaccine-passports-everything-we-know-so-far.html

Fatemi, F. (2019, October 31). How AI is uprooting recruiting. *Forbes*, https://www.forbes.com/sites/falonfatemi/2019/10/31/how-ai-is-uprooting-recruiting/#43c6540f46ce

Fry, E., & Renieris, E. (2020). *SSI? What we really need is full data portability*. Retrieved July 10, 2021, from https://womeninidentity.org/2020/03/31/data-portability/

Gao, Z., Xu, L., Turner, G., Patel, B., Diakko, N., Chen, L., & Shi, W. (2018). *Blockchain-based identity management with mobile device*. CryBlock'18: Proceedings of the 1st Workshop on Cryptocurrencies and Blockchains for Distributed Systems, June 2018, pp. 66–70.

Good Health Pass Collaborative. (2021). *Good health pass: A safe path to global reopening*. Retrieved July 12, 2021, from https://www.goodhealthpass.org/wp-content/uploads/2021/02/Good-Health-Pass-Collaborative-Principles-Paper.pdf

ID2020. (2018). *The Alliance Manifesto*. Retrieved July 13, 2021, from https://id2020.org/manifesto.

Keesing. (2021). *VeriFLY mobile health passport takes flight*. Retrieved on July 20, 2021, from https://platform.keesingtechnologies.com/headline-verifly-mobile-health-passport-takes-flight/

Lacity, M. (2020). *Blockchain foundations for the Internet of value*. University of Arkansas Press.

National Student ClearingHouse. (February 28, 2022). *Press release. National Student Clearinghouse, iDatafy Partner to Build Certified Comprehensive Learner Record Solution on the SmartResume Certified Talent Platform*. Retreived on May 8 from https://www.studentclearinghouse.org/blog/national-studentclearinghouse-idatafy-partner-to-build-certified-comprehensive-learner-record-solution-on-the-smartresume-certified-talent-platform/

New York City. (2021). *Vaccination proof for indoor activities (Key to NYC)*. Retrieved September 15, 2021, from https://www1.nyc.gov/site/doh/covid/covid-19-vaccines-keytonyc.page.

New York Department of Health. (2021, May 28). *Important reminder for all health care providers*. Retrieved July 14, 2021, from https://coronavirus.health.ny.gov/system/files/documents/2021/05/nysiis_cir_requirements_for_covid-19_vaccinationprogram_5-28-21.pdf

Preukschat, A., & Reed, D. (2021). *Self-sovereign identity: Decentralized digital identity and verifiable credentials*. Manning Publications.

Rosenzweig, R. (1998). Wizards, bureaucrats, warriors, and hackers: Writing the history of the internet. *The American Historical Review, 103*(5), 1530–1552. https://doi.org/10.2307/2649970

Smits, J. (2018). *Privacy in recruitment – Securing your candidate's data*. https://cammio.com/blog/privacy-in-recruitment/

Sovrin Foundation. (2018). *Sovrin: A protocol and token for self-sovereign identity and decentralized trust*. Retrieved July 26, 2021, from https://sovrin.org/wp-content/uploads/Sovrin-Protocol-and-Token-White-Paper.pdf

Sovrin Foundation. (2020a). *The principles of SSI*. Retrieved July 13, 2021, from https://docs.google.com/document/d/1GhcLeZEujX9h5gqrFNP-C1dMrS71EdCY4Uc1hGQbqI0/edit#heading=h.u4d08qmj8eyz

Sovrin Foundation. (2020b). *Sovrin Foundation launches test token for decentralized identity network*. Retrieved July 26, 2021, from https://sovrin.org/sovrin-foundation-launches-test-token-for-decentralized-identity-network/

State of New York. (2021). *Excelsior pass*. Retrieved July 14, 2021, from https://covid19vaccine.health.ny.gov/excelsior-pass

State of Wyoming. (2019). *HB0062 – Wyoming Utility Token Act-property amendments*. Retrieved July 26, 2021, from https://www.wyoleg.gov/Legislation/2019/HB0062#:~:text=This%20act%20classifies%20certain%20open,subject%20to%20a%20securities%20exemption.

Trust over IP Foundation. (2020). *Governance stack design principles*. Retrieved July 13, 2021, from https://wiki.trustoverip.org/pages/viewpage.action?pageId=71755&preview=%2F71755%2F71758%2FGS+Design+Principles.docx

Trust over IP Foundation. (2021). *Glossary for the good health pass ecosystem governance framework*. Retrieved July 13, 2021, from https://docs.google.com/document/d/1Kznth0dRg2xdFe9MX0p4rE-FLI0w_Nmt1ceip9gdMmo/edit#heading=h.qiggy558slen

Turczynski, B. (2020, January 9). 2020 HR statistics: Job search, hiring, recruiting & interviews. *Zety*. https://zety.com/blog/hr-statistics#job-search-statistics

Vaccination Credential Initiative. (2021). The VCI™ Charter. Retrieved July 18, 2021, from https://vci.org/about

Vartan, A., & Brinkerhoff, J. (2021). *Minimum viable product: A maximally misunderstood idea*. Retrieved July 20, 2021, from https://www.slalom.com/insights/mvp-maximally-misunderstood-term

W3C. (2019). *Verifiable credentials implementation guidelines 1.0*. Retrieved July 11, 2021, from https://www.w3.org/TR/vc-imp-guide/

W3C. (2020). *Decentralized Identifiers (DIDs) v1.0*. Retrieved on July 12, 2021, from https://www.w3.org/TR/did-core/

World Economic Forum. (2020). *Presidio principles foundational values for a decentralized future*. Retrieved July 13, 2021, from http://www3.weforum.org/docs/WEF_Presidio_Principles_2020.pdf

World Health Organization. (2021). *Smart vaccination certificate working group*. Retrieved July 12, 2021, from https://www.who.int/groups/smart-vaccination-certificate-working-group

Young, K. (2020). *The domains of identity: A framework for understanding identity systems in contemporary society*. Anthem Press.

6

NFTs and the Metaverse Revolution: Research Perspectives and Open Challenges

Klitos Christodoulou, Leonidas Katelaris, Marinos Themistocleous, Panayiotis Christodoulou, and Elias Iosif

Introduction

Since its advent, the Web has passed from several evolution cycles and evolved from a static medium of Web resources into a dynamic medium of information sharing. The ability to interlink data sources with semantic metadata, the generation of large volumes of data from interlinked devices—with the emergence of the Internet of Things (IoT), and the ability to use artificial intelligence (AI) and machine learning (ML)

K. Christodoulou (✉) • L. Katelaris • M. Themistocleous • E. Iosif
Department of Digital Innovation, University of Nicosia, Nicosia, Cyprus
e-mail: christodoulou.kl@unic.ac.cy; katelaris.l@unic.ac.cy; themistocleous.m@unic.ac.cy; iosif.e@unic.ac.cy

P. Christodoulou
Department of Computer Science, Neapolis University Pafos, Pafos, Cyprus
e-mail: panayiotis.christodoulou@nup.ac.cy

M. C. Lacity, H. Treiblmaier (eds.), *Blockchains and the Token Economy*, Technology, Work and Globalization, https://doi.org/10.1007/978-3-030-95108-5_6

techniques to infer useful insights from data sources—has transformed the Web into an enabler technology toward digital transformation.

Nowadays, the Web is experiencing a new evolution cycle in which the boundaries between digital content, physical objects, and their digital representations will be eliminated. In the literature, this evolution cycle is referred to as the *Spatial Web* (René & Mapes, 2019), which can be described as the coupling of virtual and real worlds through the user of advanced technologies. The Spatial Web introduces a multidimensional perspective to the Web fabric where digital information is interlinked, integrated, and fused with the physical world, generating a *unified reality*. Previous Web evolution cycles are mainly characterized by the layer of interconnected computers, the network of interlinked Web pages (e.g., text and media content), and the Semantic Web layer with the use of linked data and ontologies (Christodoulou et al., 2015; Lytras et al., 2003). The Spatial Web promises the creation of a dynamic "living" network, a virtual information layer on the Web, that merges the physical with the digital perspective for the user. Through the use of the next generation of user interfaces (e.g., holograms, smart wearables, or voice), users will be able to interact with real-time data and create interconnections with a virtual environment under some extended reality.

The vision of the Spatial Web will be fully realized by the unification of emerging technologies and the convergence of their ecosystems. Such technologies include virtual and augmented reality (VR/AR), geolocation, advanced cellular networks (e.g., 5G), IoT, AI/ML, and distributed ledger technologies (DLTs) (i.e., blockchain).

Although the opportunities for the Spatial Web are likely to be unprecedented both in scope and scale, this vision is still at the early stages. Many supporters of this idea argue that the Spatial Web should embody an open, interoperable, and democratic environment through the establishment of open standards and decentralization (Keller & Simon, 2002; René & Mapes, 2019). They argue that the "universality" property of the Web, as this was proposed by Tim Berners-Lee in the early days of the Web (Berners-Lee et al., 1992), has faded out and that today's Web comprises of centralization, walled gardens, and proprietary services governed by a small number of companies.

It is envisioned that the Spatial Web is set to create new experiences of reality to a degree that we have not imagined before. Such experiences are likely to create highly contextualized and personalized data; therefore, the Spatial Web should consider an infrastructure that can reliably store digitized objects, track their history, verify the authenticity of data within the virtual world, prevent the alternation of previously archived data, and, at the same time, enable users to freely collaborate, explore, and interact in mixed reality spaces (Ryskeldiev et al., 2018).

Setting the Scene

Although the realization of the Spatial Web is still under development, several downstream technological advances have been pushing for its evolution. Figure 6.1 summarizes the categories of emerging technologies that are considered as enablers toward the evolution of the Spatial Web.

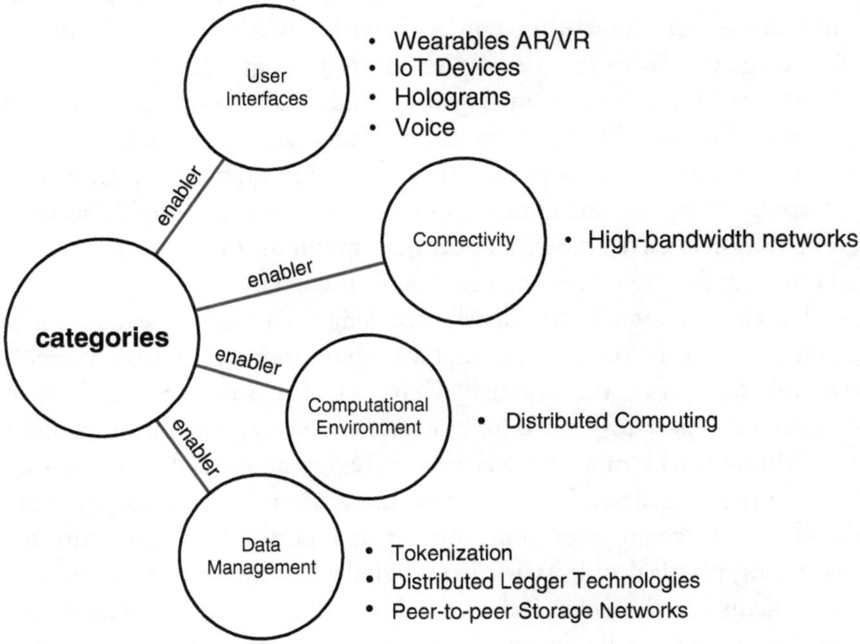

Fig. 6.1 Convergence of enabling technologies toward the Spatial Web

Next generation of user interfaces such as smart devices (interconnected with the IoT), wearables (e.g., haptic wearables), AR/VR devices (e.g., AR glasses) are offering new interfaces for user interaction and access to data.

On the other hand, the digitization of physical objects with computer vision and natural language processing (Malandrakis et al., 2013) generates large volumes of data that require significant processing power. Thus, technological advances in optimized AI/ML techniques are considered vital for supporting such an environment. Another technology which contributes toward the development of the Spatial Web is the advancement in network connectivity. Delivering to the user a seamless interaction experience over a mixed reality environment requires fast connectivity and high-bandwidth networks (e.g., 5G).

Furthermore, the development of browser-based 3D modeling and gaming rendering engines has matured into entire software ecosystems. Currently, several 3D modeling applications are utilized to capture entire cities (Billen et al., 2021). These applications offer 3D geolocation features and advanced real-time rendering with VR/AR and the ability for Web usage (i.e., with the use of WebGL technology). Lastly, at the core of this Web, evolution data management and data integration techniques are very important. Data generated by the process of digitization is structured and modeled with various types and high granularity. Therefore, the ability to handle such volumes of data will require a highly scalable computational environment, optimized methods for storage, and an architecture for preserving the integrity of the data.

This chapter argues that distributed ledger technologies like blockchain (Nakamoto, 2008) could enable a ubiquitous and persistent architectural layer for the Spatial Web. Blockchains combined with decentralized peer-to-peer (p2p) storage networks can enable a medium for a virtual world (or a "metaverse") where digital ownership, authenticity, identity, transferability, and data integrity are preserved. In more detail, a blockchain layer could offer a standardized infrastructure for tokenizing physical objects to their digital footprint in a manner that such tokens can be exchanged and shared. Tokens that represent virtual objects can be digitally owned, identified with unique digital identities, composed with other virtual objects, and characterized by a set of unique attributes and interaction rules. The activity of each object will be made persistent on the Web layer, and its history will be verifiable and traced over a blockchain layer.

The explosion in the development of blockchain-based metaverses (Tapora, 2021) triggered an explosive growth of the non-fungible tokens (NFTs) space (Wang et al., 2021) with top gaming platforms joining the space. Examples are the Atari gaming company, which announced a collaboration with Decentraland[1] and The Sandbox ecosystem[2] for creating a retro arcade. The first arcade station filled with classic Atari games will be offered to Decentraland users (Chaudhari et al., 2019), while Roller Coaster Tycoon, Centipede, Super Breakout, and other intellectual properties (IPs) owned by the Atari portfolio will be offered to The Sandbox. Similarly, Skybound Entertainment, which owns an estate in The Sandbox virtual environment, aims to enable users to experience The Walking Dead adventure. Such examples indicate that the portfolio of IPs of such game platforms will empower the development of theme-based NFTs, including game items, and other digital objects to characters. Such theme based NFTs will offer to players a completely new experience to play, create, socialize, and interact within a multiplayer gaming virtual world.

Blockchain networks are empowering the next generation of community-owned metaverses, obviating the need to trust opaque and centralized platform operators. Blockchains will play an integral role in supporting the economy layer over the virtual world where at the same time they provide a standardize and ubiquitous way to represent virtual items over a natively digital world. To the best of our knowledge, there is limited literature on blockchain-based metaverse, virtual worlds, and non-fungible tokens (NFTs), which leaves plenty of room for study and novel contribution. With this perspective in mind, this chapter aims to contribute by: (i) presenting and analyzing the current status of virtual worlds with a particular focus on the emerging blockchain-based metaverse and tokens, and (ii) articulating open challenges and research perspectives for the emerging space of blockchain-based metaverses.

[1] https://decentraland.org/blog/announcements/dcl-x-atari/.

[2] https://bit.ly/3mkKIrp.

The rest of this chapter is structured as follows. The next section introduces the reader to existing blockchain-based metaverse environments by presenting and comparing the most frequently used environments. The analysis leads to the artifacts inferred from blockchain-based metaverses as well as to a synopsis of the features of a blockchain-based metaverse. Thereafter, the main tokens standards used in this ecosystem are summarized followed by the research perspectives and open challenges. Monetizing opportunities are then discussed, and challenges related to the governance, generation, and minting processes are identified and explained. The chapter concludes with conclusions and contribution.

Virtual Worlds Toward a Blockchain-Based Metaverse

With the emergence of augmented and virtual reality, researchers have been referring to the development of a unified virtual space as the *metaverse* for years. The vision of having a unified virtual world where a 3D virtual space is co-constructed by the interactions of many users was first expressed by the science-fiction writer Neal Stephenson in 1992[3] (Dionisio et al., 2013). The term metaverse refers to the creation of a "meta" (which means "beyond") to capture the creation of a virtual world beyond the physical reality and "verse" (which refers to a back-formation from "universe") to refer to a virtual utopia or nonplace (Greek: Οὐκ τόπος). At the technical level, a metaverse implements a computer network that supports an interactive "virtual reality" where users can join from multiple locations and interact in real time. The virtual environment comprises simulations of the physical world and digital representations of objects in 3D.

Existing metaverse platforms digitize objects (e.g., people, buildings, art) within a virtual world, enabling their monetization and utility (Terpstra & Huisinga, 2020). Virtual worlds predate computers

[3] The reader is referred to the novel titled *Snow Crash*. Activeworlds (http://www.activeworlds.com) describes a virtual world that is based on the vision described by the novel.

(Schnipper, 2017); however, their origins are disputed due to the difficulty to formulate a definition for an alternative existence. The first attempt that is characterized as the closest to the modern vision of virtual reality goes back to the fifties with the project known as the Sensorama machine. Many attempts for the creation of independent virtual worlds followed since then, including the development of a prototype virtual world known as Activeworlds. This virtual world expresses the vision described by the Neal Stephenson's novel. Other attempts proposed the creation of WorldsAway (Lyman & Wakeford, 1999), which led to a richer user experience, and the commercial virtual world called Second Life (Rymaszewski et al., 2007). Second Life presented a virtual world with enhanced in-world user interactions. More specifically, users utilized content creation tools to enrich content and co-create the virtual environment. Furthermore, Second Life introduced the development of a virtual economy and proposed several improvements to the computer-generated 3D environment. Similarly, CryEngine 2, proposed by Avatar Reality, attempted to provide a richer realism to the virtual environment. However, due to the demanding gaming engine and increased system requirements, the project was not fully adopted by the user base.

Following Second Life and CryEngine, the next generation of virtual worlds introduced features of openness and decentralization. For instance, Solipsis was the first virtual world that was built over a p2p architecture (Keller & Simon, 2002; Frey et al., 2008), followed by the development of open projects like Open Wonderland (Open Wonderland Foundation 2011). The decentralized feature introduced with such systems has led to the emergence and development of open-source viewers and server-side engines for virtual worlds. The decentralized character and open-source developments pushed toward the development of the next state-of-the-art of virtual worlds.

With the emergence of blockchain networks, a new fundamental layer to the creation of virtual worlds is introduced—a layer that provides support for the creation of digital identities, a universal and standardized representation layer for digital objects, and a layer that supports the digital ownership of data with the use of fungible and non-fungible standards. Additionally, blockchains offer a layer for the establishment of a self-sovereign financial system for the creation of a decentralized economy within the virtual environment.

Blockchain-Based Metaverse

Although the development of a blockchain-based metaverse is under heavy development, many attempts to build independent virtual environments have been explored. Yet, there is a lack of literature to present and analyze these environments. In an attempt to bridge this gap and enhance the body of knowledge and the reader understanding, we summarize and analyze the most popular virtual worlds with a focus on the emerging blockchain-based metaverse, namely, we discuss (i) Decentraland, (ii) The Sandbox, (iii) Somnium Space, (iv) Cryptovoxels, (v) Axie Infinity, and (vi) Neon District.

Decentraland proposes a decentralized virtual world that is evolved by its users (Ordano et al., 2017). It is considered as the "first fully decentralized virtual world," since the virtual environment is co-created by the users, and it is not controlled by any central authority. Decentraland was launched in 2017 and provides a virtual world which is built exclusively on the public Ethereum blockchain. In Decentraland, users can create their own avatars, interact with other users, and participate in social activities such as concerts and art shows. Furthermore, users can develop buildings and other structures on their digitally owned plots and monetize their creations. Decentraland's virtual world is divided into a limited number of parcels (i.e., 90,000, each measuring 16 × 16 meters). Parcels are represented as virtual content represented by ERC-721 non-fungible tokens (NFTs) known as LAND. Users can purchase LAND parcels using the MANA (ERC-20) token and have full control over the environment and applications they create within their land. All unique assets are made persistent through Ethereum smart contracts that enable users to prove the digital ownership of any virtual asset using the blockchain ledger. Through the available marketplace (i.e., market.decentraland.org), users can trade and manage their on-chain assets used by Decentraland's ecosystem. A recent update of the platform enables users to associate two or more directly adjacent parcels of LAND to create a LAND estate.

Furthermore, the platform enables users to create their own 3D models and import them in the virtual environment. Each piece of land or item in Decentraland is an NFT. Decentraland's governance is managed by a decentralized autonomous organization (DAO), which holds the smart contracts and Decentraland's assets (e.g., LAND contract, estate contract, wearables, content servers, marketplace). Decentraland's DAO governs issues like upgrades of LAND and Estates, dates for future LAND auctions, size of marketplace fees, and others. Such proposals are exposed to the community for voting. Decentraland's DAO is used in multiple cases like policy updates and future LAND auctions through voting by the community. The DAO in the Decentraland virtual world handles the voting through governance interface provided by Aragon. An abstract overview of Decentraland's profile is summarized in Table 6.1.

The Sandbox proposes a blockchain-based virtual world that provides a unique gaming experience to the players. The gaming platform comprises of a suite of integrated products: (i) the Voxel editor, (ii) the marketplace, an open market that allows the trading of in-game NFT assets, and (iii) the game maker. The latter enables users to build, share, and monetize 3D games. The game maker provides a set of visual scripting tools that requires no coding and allows users to develop 3D games for free. The Voxel editor is used for modeling, animation, and NFT creation and

Table 6.1 Decentraland

Decentraland	
Type	Decentralized Virtual World
Launched	2017
Marketplace	The marketplace enables the trading and managing of all on-chain assets. Accessed on: market.decetraland.org
Token types supported	MANA: ERC-20 token which is used to make in-world purchases. MANA holders can buy or exchange LAND parcels. Max supply: 2,644,403,343 MANA LAND: A scarce, NFT-based (ERC-721) token to represent the virtual plots (i.e., parcels)
Chains supported	Ethereum public blockchain
Community	9300+ active monthly users

[a]Data collected from https://www.dapp.com/ for the last 30 days (August 2021)

supports to develop 3D objects like humans, animals, vehicles, foliage, and tools.

The Sandbox ecosystem is based on the Ethereum blockchain. Digital creations are stored using the Inter Planetary File System (IPFS), and their digital ownership is registered onto the blockchain ledger. The platform users (i.e., players, creators, curators, and landowners) can populate the virtual world with their creations that are encapsulated by several token types that comprise the economy of The Sandbox. All assets are represented as fungible or non-fungible tokens with the use of the ERC-20, ERC-721, and ERC-1155 standards. In more detail, the utility token SAND (ERC-20) is used for transactions and interactions within the ecosystem. On the other hand, the LAND token (ERC-721) is used to represent a real estate parcel (96 × 96 meters) in The Sandbox. Each LAND can be populated with games, assets, and interactive experiences. Multiple LANDS can be combined to an ESTATE. Lastly, ASSETS represent a token that is created by players who build user-generated content (UGC). Such tokens utilize the ERC-1155 standard and can be traded on the marketplace. Currently, around 1 million active users have been interacting with The Sandbox metaverse since its inception. Similarly to Decentraland, The Sandbox platform is governed using a DAO where SAND holders can exercise their voting rights on various key elements of the platform. Sandbox's profile is summarized in Table 6.2.

Somnium Space (Somnium Space Ltd, 2021) introduces an open, social, and persistent VR metaverse built over a blockchain architecture. Compared to Decentraland and The Sandbox, Somnium Space offers a more realistic environment, and it is enhanced with VR where people can do almost everything similarly as in real life. A recent update enables access to Somnium Space from every Web browser.

Somnium Space metaverse was founded in 2017, and it is empowered by the Ethereum blockchain for tokenizing in-game assets and land parcels. The long-term vision for the Somnium Space project is to create a realistic user-generated virtual environment which will add a rich virtual layer to reality (Somnium Space Ltd, 2021). Economy in Somnium Space has three cornerstones: (i) tokenization of virtual land, (ii) tokenization of digital assets and experiences, and (iii) decentralized marketplaces. The in-world currency is CUBE, an ERC20 token with a total

Table 6.2 The Sandbox

The Sandbox	
Type	Decentralized Gaming Ecosystem
Launched	2018
Marketplace	Open market environment that allows trading of in-game tokenized assets (e.g., upload, publish, and sell NFTs).
Token types supported	• SAND: ERC-20 token used for all the transactions and interactions within The Sandbox ecosystem. There is a finite supply of 3,000,000,000 SAND. • LAND: Digital piece of real estate within The Sandbox metaverse. LAND is portion of the metaverse open to player ownership. Each LAND is an NFT based on ERC-721 standard. • Max Supply: 166,464 LANDS • ESTATE: Is a combination of multiple LANDS. • ASSET: Token created by players—user-generated content (UGC). ASSETS utilize the ERC-1155 standard. • GAMES: Represent bundles of ASSETS and scripting logic form an interactive experience. Also represented with the ERC-1155 standard.
Chains supported	Ethereum public blockchain
Community[a,b]	15,000+ users have connected their wallets to the project 750,000+ followers support the franchise across social media (e.g., Facebook, Discord, Telegram) 1400+ active monthly users

[a]Data collected from https://www.dapp.com/ for the last 30 days (August 2021)
[b]Data collected from https://medium.com/sandbox-game

supply of 100,000,000 tokens. CUBE allows users to issue transactions between each other or spend them for purchasing in-world assets and activities (e.g., visit museums, participate in arcade games). Various types of NFTs are generate in Somnium Space such as wearables for the in-game avatars, tickets that allow access to certain land parcels, land tokens, world tokens that can be dropped onto land, treasure hunts, or CUBE prizes. Somnium's client provides the ability to create and tokenize custom VR avatars.

NFTs in Somnium Space are encapsulated using the ERC-721 standard. Considering the p2p economy and the high gas fees in Ethereum, due to the multiple trading transactions, several features are implemented on the polygon layer 2 (L2) blockchain, which offers improved transaction speeds and close to zero transaction costs for in-world transactions.

Table 6.3 Somnium Space

Somnium Space	
Type	Decentralized virtual world with enhanced VR
Launched	2018
Marketplace	NFTs for Somnium Space world are available through OpenSea under: opensea.io/collection/somnium-space
Token types supported	• CUBES: In-word ERC-20 token which could be used to trade assets in Somnium Space or exchanges between in-word users. • WORLDS: Independent instances as blockchain-based NFTs (ERC-721) which allow users to upload certain amount of content on Somnium Space's servers (e.g., small-75MB, medium-200MB) • PARCELS: Represent digital plots in Somnium Space world as NFTs (ERC-721) • ETH: Used to buy in-world NFTs such as land PARCELS, WORLDS, ESTATES, and collectibles used to customize their digital avatars and digital world. • DAI: This ERC-20 token is available for Somnium Space users to trade their Blockchain Avatars on OpenSea
Chains supported	Ethereum public blockchain and Matic (L2)
Community[a]	200+ active monthly users

[a]Data collected from https://www.dapp.com/ for the last 30 days (August 2021)

The digital assets of the Somnium Space world are available through the OpenSea digital marketplace. Somnium Space is developed on UnitySDK, offering multiple tools for the users to create content and extend the virtual world with numerous options (e.g., Somnium Space Web, Builder SDK, Worlds SDK, and Blockchain Avatars). The Builder SDK allows users to upload their creations to their land parcels, and the Worlds SDK enables them to upload complete interactive and programmable scenes. An abstract overview of Somnium's profile is summarized in Table 6.3.

Cryptovoxels is a user-owned virtual world which runs over the Ethereum blockchain. Cryptovoxels offers a virtual environment like a Minecraft look and feel. Users in the Cryptovoxels metaverse can buy land where they are able to build buildings, stores, and art galleries. The Cryptovoxels virtual world was first released as a secret beta version in May 2018. The Cryptovoxels universe consists of a city referred to as the "Origin City" where users own their NFT parcels. Similar to other well-known virtual worlds, ownership of digital items is recorded over the

Table 6.4 Cryptovoxels

Cryptovoxels	
Type	Decentralized Virtual World
Launched	2018
Marketplace	Land parcels for the Cryptovoxel metaverse are available through their shop at OpenSea martketplace opensea.io/assets/cryptovoxels and collectibles that can be used to customize in-world avatars
Token types supported	ETH: Used to buy in-world NFTs such as land parcels (digital plots) and collectibles used to customize their digital avatars
Chains supported	Ethereum public blockchain
Community[a]	130+ active monthly users

[a]Data collected from https://www.dapp.com/ for the last 30 days (August 2021)

Ethereum blockchain using the ERC-721 standard. Parcel owners can add and remove blocks from their parcels, which are called "voxels." Voxels represent a value on a grid in three-dimensional space. During its early days, Cryptovoxels's environment used a native token $COLR to attribute color to voxels and images. $COLR is not used anymore in Cryptovoxels universe as it was deprecated in June 2020. Currently, users can buy parcels of land in different districts of the "Origin City" or collectibles to decorate their avatars (Cryptovoxels, 2021). An abstract overview of Cryptovoxel's profile is summarized in Table 6.4.

Axie Infinity: This virtual environment is an example of how the metaverse can offer unique opportunities for gamification and not just a digital realization of some virtual world. Axie offers a decentralized economy that is shaped by its players. In brief, users acquire tokens through gameplay and contribution to the Axie's ecosystem. Users are breeding their digital NFT pets (referred as "axies") and get compensated for their gameplay (e.g., battle, collect, raise, and build land-based kingdoms). Axie's metaverse was introduced in 2018, and since then Axie's user base increased to 250K+ daily active players. Sky Mavis is the company behind the development of the Axie Infinity Universe. Axie Infinity Shards (AXS) are an ERC-20 governance token used within the Axie Universe, enabling users to shape the future of the ecosystem by voting for upgrades, while Ethereum (ETH) is also used for purchasing in-world NFT tokens (e.g., Axies, land, items, and bundles). The total supply of AXS is 270M with almost 61M in circulation. The demand of AXS is driven by the Community Treasury, which aims to create base value for AXS tokens. Besides, Smooth Love Potion (SLP), another ERC-20 token used in the Axie Universe, is transferred to users for "breeding" Axies. Through Axie's marketplace (marketplace.axieinfinitiy.com), 42,877 sales were fulfilled, including 42,634 Axies (i.e., the creatures of the Axie Infinity Universe). As of July 2021, the volume of ETH invested in the Axie Infinity Universe in lands and virtual items is estimated at 11,524 ETH. In order to overcome Ethereum scalability issues and to decrease the gas fees, Axie built over the Ronin network which is an Ethereum sidechain. During Q2 of 2021 Axies migrated to Ronin as the whole Axie Universe passed in "Origin Alpha" phase. A summary of Axie Infinity's profile is shown in Table 6.5.

Neon District presents a virtual game universe crafted by Blockade Games. Neon District is classified as a role-playing game where NFT assets (e.g., unique cards) are earned by players and evolved through gameplay. In brief, players battle an authoritarian regime in a dystopian

Table 6.5 Axie Infinity

Axie Infinity	
Type	Decentralized Gaming Ecosystem
Launched	2018
Marketplace	Operated under: marketplace.axieinfinity.com Current sales volume is estimated at 11,524 ETH
Token types supported	AXS: ERC-20 governance token used withing the Axie Universe for staking and payments (e.g., in the Axie NFT marketplace) ETH: Used to buy in-world NFTs such as Axies, lands (digital plots), items, and bundles. SLP: An ERC-20 token which is transferred to users when they breed Axies (i.e., the creatures of the Axie Infinity ecosystem) Axies: NFT tokens based on ERC-721 which represent the creatures of the Axie Infinity Universe. Land: Tokenized plots of land which act as homes and bases of operations for Axies.
Chains supported	Ethereum public blockchain, Ronin Ethereum sidechain
Community[a]	250,000+ active daily users 315,000 active monthly users

[a]Data collected from https://axieinfinity.com

Table 6.6 Neon District

Neon District	
Type	Decentralized Gaming Ecosystem
Launched	2019
Marketplace	Operated under: opensea.io/collection/neon-district Current trading volume is estimated at 847 ETH
Token types supported	NEON: In-game currency which is used for upgrading characters, buying gear, and/or cards. It could be acquired with ETH, or as a reward with the completion of certain tasks and missions within the game progression. ETH: Used to trade in-world NFTs (ERC-721) such as characters and cards
Chains supported	Ethereum public blockchain, polygon (L2)
Community[a]	3120+ active monthly users

[a]Data collected from https://dappradar.com

future, as part of the rebellion, leveling up their characters to earn in-game assets. Neon District was launched in late October 2019, and it runs over the Ethereum blockchain which is used for tokenizing in-game assets using the ERC-721 standard. Neon District's marketplace page on OpenSea[4] reports over a billion of unique assets. The universe of Neon District is released in seasons. Currently, Season 1 is ongoing, which features full single-player gaming. Players acquire NEON (the in-game currency) by accomplishing certain tasks and missions or by swapping ETH with NEON. NEON is used by players to acquire in-game assets like characters, gear upgrades, and cards. Considering the increased gas fees on Ethereum, the game allows users to link their Polygon wallet as an alternative to the Ethereum main net. Neon District's profile is summarized in Table 6.6.

Table 6.7 compares the profiles of the virtual worlds reported previously. The sample examined shows that half of the virtual worlds offers a decentralized gaming ecosystem and the rest decentralized virtual worlds. All of them support the Ethereum blockchain, but there are cases like The Sandbox and Axie Infinity that also support polygon and Ronin Ethereum sidechain, respectively. The marketplace of these environments is mainly available through OpenSea.io except the case of Axie Infinity that offers

[4]https://opensea.io/collection/neon-district.

Table 6.7 Virtual worlds profiles comparison

		Virtual world					
		Decentraland	The Sandbox	Somnium Space	Cryptovoxels	Axie Infinity	Neon District
Type	*Decentralized Virtual World*	x		x	x		
	Decentralized Gaming Ecosystem		x			x	x
	Launched	2017	2018	2018	2018	2018	2019
	Marketplace available through	OpenSea	The Sandbox	OpenSea	OpenSea	Axie Infinity	OpenSea
	Token	MANA	SAND	CUBET DAI	–	AXS SLP	NEON
	NFT	LAND	LAND ESTATE GAMES ASSET	WORLDS PARCELS	–	AXIES LAND	ETH to trade characters and cards
	NFT standards	ERC-721	ERC-721 ERC-1155	ERC-721	ERC-721	ERC-721	ERC-721
	Chains supported	Ethereum	Ethereum, Polygon (L2)	Ethereum	Ethereum	Ethereum Ronin Ethereum sidechain	Ethereum
	Trading volume (period: July 26 to August 14, 2021)	N/A	N/A	Ξ21.600[a]	Ξ17.400	Ξ90.000	Ξ847

[a]Ethereum Currency Symbol

its own marketplace. All virtual worlds examined use the ERC-721 NFT standard. In addition to this, The Sandbox also uses ERC-1155.

Artifacts Inferred from Blockchain-Based Metaverses

Reflecting on the aforementioned blockchain-based metaverse developments, this section summarizes their essential artifacts. These artifacts characterize a state-of-the-art virtual world where blockchain is an essential architectural layer for its sustainability.

- *Standardized tokens.* Blockchains offer a standardized mechanism for tokenization with the use of various standards, both for the creation of fungible (e.g., ERC-20) and non-fungible tokens (e.g., ERC-721). NFTs are encapsulated using smart contracts with certain attributes and functions (e.g., owner, approved address, authorized operator) to capture the unique identification of such objects and their metadata.
- *Economy.* The platforms offer an economy that is based on (i) tokenization of virtual land, (ii) tokenization of digital assets and experiences, and (iii) decentralized marketplaces. All virtual environments use both a fungible token, that acts as the in-game cryptocurrency, and several non-fungible tokens (ERC-721 or ERC-1155) to capture the unique and non-interchangeable assets of the virtual world. Through the embedded economy, users can own and monetize their creations and express themselves by interacting with the virtual world. Interactions can take various forms from creating and building to monetizing their land (e.g., entrance fee, renting). Most platforms offer several monetization opportunities such as tokenizing and selling their creations (e.g., wearables, tickets) directly from the metaverse environment or participating in various gamification activities (e.g., treasure hunts, events). Travel is also monetized in this space since such environments can simulate several physical boundaries of the real world, for example, improve the speed of the gaming environment or lift-off in-word restrictions like gravity. For example, in Somnium Space, avatars can walk at 4 mph, whereas cars can travel at 25 mhp. There is also the paid option of teleportation which happens instantly.

The creation of cars and teleports (or teleportation hubs) enables an enhanced user experience and additional venues for monetization for creators.

- *Minting of assets.* Platforms enable users to mint their own creations as NFTs. Such digital creations could be their digital avatars, land parcels, buildings, and/or other constructions. Users can even mint wearables for their avatars or even tickets for allowing users to participate in events. All assets are created as NFTs, made persistent over a p2p storage, and verified by a blockchain architecture.
- *Marketplaces.* Open marketplaces represent another artifact of blockchain-based metaverses where users can manage and trade their digital items (e.g., avatars, nametags, virtual parcels). For such metaverses, the marketplace is becoming a centerpiece of the metaverse's economy. Decentralized marketplaces are utilizing a p2p storage network to store the digital information alongside with ownership proofs that are recorded over a blockchain network.
- *Digital avatars.* Digital identity across metaverses is represented as tokens that are made persistent over a blockchain network to provide a trustworthy proof of ownership for avatars. Platform users are represented by digital avatars. Such digital avatars enable users to adopt an identity and express a personality. In general, digital avatars are represented as NFTs. As discussed in subsequent sections, the challenge remains *of how these avatars can become liquid and transferable across multiple blockchains.* The realization of a complete metaverse environment will require a seamless transfer of such identification objects, which remains a challenge that relates to interoperability.
- *DAOs.* By design, blockchains are characterized by decentralization and the removal of any central authority for their governance. Decentralized metaverses naturally inherit these characteristics of decentralized governance to maximize user engagement and activity. Using the native token of a virtual environment, holders can publish proposals or vote on existing ones that relate with the governance and evolution of the virtual world. In addition, token holders are presented with incentives to participate in the evolution of a virtual world or delegate their tokens to other voters that share the same ideology to

support or reject a certain proposal. The community in a blockchain-based metaverse drives policy upgrades and content creation.
- *Decentralized community*. Part of the native tokenomics of a blockchain-based metaverse is focused on growing the community of the virtual world. This is to ensure that the community is incentivized to further develop and evolve the project. A common growth model is embedded on the tokenomics of such platforms. For example, the revenue made from fees is then evenly distributed to various token holders (e.g., users, or ecosystem developers and gamers) that participate in the continuous growth of the ecosystem.

Features of a Blockchain-Based Metaverse

To move toward the creation of a realistic blockchain-based metaverse, the following essential features need to be considered:

- *Realism* relates to how realistic the generation of the virtual environment is for the user. What are the experiences presented to the user by the interactions with the virtual world and what kind of interfaces are used to interact with the virtual environment? Furthermore, this feature relates with the realism of the virtual environment; how the environment is actualized, what experiences are explorable by the users, and what are the means of expression or social interactions provided (Dionisio et al., 2013).
- *Ubiquity* refers to the layer responsible to safeguard the digital representation and ownership of the digital assets. It relates with the decentralized governance model offered by the underlying blockchain architecture. Such virtual worlds should be characterized by openness and fairness, where users collaboratively interact to evolve the virtual environment and make decisions that relate to its governance without the need of some central authority.
- *Interoperability* is concerned with the ability of moving digital assets, in the form of fungible or non-fungible digital objects, between virtual worlds in a seamless and instantaneous manner. The user should be abstracted from this process and the underlying blockchain networks

should be bridged in such a way that the history of the information is traceable and that the ownership of the digital asset is made persistent and can be verified as one-of-a-kind.

- *Scalability* refers to the constantly changing virtual reality environment where multiple users can interact in real time. The dynamic user interactions in a metaverse space are expected to generate large volumes of data. As the data volume increases, the need to analyze the data and infer new context is thus likely to increase as well. It is therefore important that the architectural layers on which a metaverse is settled are both reliable and secure. Blockchains can provide such a layer where the reliability of the data is preserved. At the same time, the generation of large volumes of data, and the digital representations of the virtual assets can be stored in p2p storage networks (e.g., IPFS (Benet, 2014)). On the other hand, the converge with artificial intelligence could provide a dynamic engine for creating enhanced diversity and rich content to the metaverse. For instance, data generated by user interactions can be used to forecast future behaviors or guide the decision-making on several actions from the metaverse space.
- *Tokenization* can provide a standardized methodology for new forms of information value creation. Tokenization refers to the process of converting the value of a tangible or an intangible asset (any tradable object) into a digital form (i.e., the token) that can be algorithmically generated, digitally represented, and traded over a blockchain network. A well-known standard for creating tokenized forms of virtual assets is the technical documents proposed by Ethereum developers under ERCs (Ethereum Request for Comments). The next section provides an overview of the various standards proposed under different blockchain implementations.
- *Liquid identity* relates with the adoption of a blockchain layer (or a sidechain) to empower users to uniformly self-manage and control their digital identities and private data. These digital identities can take the form of digital avatars where the ownership is verifiable by blockchain-enabled digital credentials. We envision that with the realization of interoperable blockchains, any type of virtual representation

(e.g., tokens, avatars) will become liquid and transferable between different chains.

Token Standards

An important aspect of a blockchain-based metaverse is the development and use of tokens. This section presents an overview of the token standards proposed by major blockchain protocols to support the generation of NFTs including (i) Ethereum blockchain, (ii) Efinity blockchain, (iii) Near blockchain, (iv) Flow blockchain, (v) Hedera Hashgraph, (vi) Bitcoin Cash Binance, and (vii) Binance smart chain.

Ethereum Blockchain

The Ethereum blockchain utilizes ERC standards to generate fungible and non-fungible tokens. Apart from ERC-20, ERC-721, and ERC-1155 that are the most frequently used, there are other ECR standards available as summarized in the bullet list below:

- ERC-20: This refers to the standard interface for fungible tokens. It defines the basic implementation for tokens within smart contracts.
- ERC-721: NFTs were initially proposed by the ERC-721 standard (Entriken et al., 2018) which denoted the two main aspects that differentiate NFTs from fungible tokens, that is, their uniqueness and nondivisibility. The ERC-721 requires a separate contract to be deployed for each token or collection.
- ERC-809: This standard is proposed to enable NFT owners to rent access to their NFTs, thus enabling rental agreements. Some functions have been taken from the ERC-721 standard.
- ERC-994: It can be considered as an extension to ERC-721 specifically designed to accommodate the requirements of the registration of land and physical property. A tree-like format is proposed to arrange NFTs and connect them with other contracts, allowing for the creation of complex conditional agreements.

- ERC-998: It extents the ERC-721 proposal by enabling the composition of any non-fungible token, and thus a complex composition of NFTs can be traded using a single transfer.
- ERC-1155: This standard enables the management of multiple token types (e.g., fungible and non-fungible) in a single deployed contract, in an attempt to decrease redundant bytecode on the Ethereum network.

Table 6.8 presents a summary of established and upcoming token standards for the Ethereum public blockchain. For a complete list of ERCs and their current status, the reader is referred to https://eips.ethereum.org/erc

Efinity Blockchain

Efinity blockchain was built by Enjin, and it aims to become the primary network for NFTs by supporting NFTs from any blockchain to offer a network that brings NFTs to everyone. The Enjin blockchain ecosystem seeks to build a scalable cross-chain token network, known as the Efinity blockchain, a Polkadot parachain that uses a Polkadot Relay Chain (Wood, 2016; Web3, 2020).

- Paratokens standard: Enjin developed a token standard, referred to as the "paratokens standard," for the Polkadot and Kusama[5] parachains. Through the paratoken standard, Efinity accepts tokens (both fungible and non-fungible) from any other chain including well-known Ethereum-based standards (e.g., ERC-20, ERC-721, ERC-1155).

Near Blockchain

The Near protocol is a proof-of-stake (PoS) blockchain that was developed in 2018 as a decentralized platform. Compared to Ethereum, it is faster and has lower gas fees. These characteristics have attracted the

[5] https://kusama.network/.

attention of many developers and users, especially in the NFT space. Near supports its own standards for token generation, including:

- NEP-171: Current NFT standard for the NEAR blockchain, inspired by the ERC proposals.

Table 6.8 Summary of established and prominent token standards

Proposal	Title	Type	Status	Fungibility	Token Interface
EIP-20	Token Standard	Standards Track—ERC	Final	Fungible	*Methods:* name(), symbol(), decimals(), totalSupply(), balanceOf(), transfer(), transferFrom(), allowance() *Events:* Transfer, Approval
EIP-721	Non-fungible token standard	Standards Track—ERC	Final	Non-fungible	*Methods—similar to ERC-20:* name(), symbol(), totalSupply(), balanceOf(), approve(), transfer(), transferFrom(), *Additional Methods:* ownerOf(), safeTransferFrom(), setApprovalForAll(), onERC721Received() *Requires:* ERC721Metadata, ERC-721 Metadata JSON Schema *Events:* Transfer, Approval, ApprovalForAll
EIP-809	Renting standard for rival, non-fungible tokens	Standards Track—ERC	Draft[a]	Non-fungible	*Methods—similar to ERC-20:* name(), symbol(), totalSupply(), balanceOf(), approve(), transfer(), transferFrom(), *Additional Methods:* reserve(), access(), settle(), checkAvailable(), cancelReservation() *Events:* Transfer, Approval, Reserve, Cancel

(continued)

Table 6.8 (continued)

Proposal	Title	Type	Status	Fungibility	Token Interface
EIP-994	Delegated non-fungible token standard	Standards Track—ERC	Draft[a]	Non-fungible	*Methods—similar to ERC-721:* ownerOf(), safeTransferFrom(), setApprovalForAll(), onERC721Received() *Additional Methods:* origin(), gets(), returns(), allows(), emitted() *Events:* Transfer, Approval, Reserve, Cancel
EIP-998	Composable non-fungible token standard	Standards Track—ERC	Draft[a]	Fungible and non-fungible	*Methods:* implements methods from ERC-20, ERC-721, ERC165, and ERC223 *Additional Methods:* rootOwnerOf(), rootOwnerOfChild(),ownerOfChild(), transferChild(), safeTransferChild(), transferChildToParent(), getChild() *Events:* ReceivedChild, TransferChild, TransferToParent, TransferFromParent
EIP-1155	Multi-Token Standard	Standards Track—ERC	Final	Fungible, non-fungible, and semi–non-fungible	*Methods—similar to ERC-20:* name(), symbol(), totalSupply(), balanceOf(), approve(), transfer(), transferFrom(), *Additional Methods:* safeTransferFrom(), safeBatchTransferFrom(), balanceOfBatch(), setApprovalForAll(), isApprovedForAll() *Events:* TransferSingle, TransferBatch, ApprovalForAll, URI

[a]This is a draft proposal (under development), as of August 19, 2021

- NEP-177: An interface for a non-fungible token's metadata.
- NEP-178: This NFT standard introduces an approval management system (e.g., approval management systems in ERC-721) which allows a set of users or contracts to transfer specific non-fungible tokens on behalf of the owner.
- NEP-181: Standard interfaces for counting and fetching tokens for an entire NFT contract or for a given owner. This standard adds essential functionality that is frequently required by marketplaces, and/or wallets when they need to show all tokens owned by a given account. The standard also has provisions to present statistics for all tokens included within a given contract.
- NEP-199: This standard provides an interface allowing non-fungible token contracts to request from financial contracts to pay-out multiple receivers, enabling flexible royalty implementations.

Flow Blockchain

Like Near blockchain, Flow uses a PoS consensus mechanism. Flow has its own standard for NFTs.

- Non-Fungible Token: The Flow blockchain supports NFT generation by providing a comparable standard to ERC-721 and ERC-1155. Each NFT on the Flow blockchain network is written using the Cadence programming language.

Hedera Hashgraph

Hedera is another blockchain that is based on PoS that achieves fast transaction speed and low fees. Hedera assists the generation of token through its token service.

- Hedera Token Service (HTS): Provides the ability to issue tokens (both fungible and non-fungible), which are native to Hedera adopting the same performance, security, and efficiency as HBAR (i.e., the utility token of the Hedera Hashgraph network), without a smart contract. Native tokens issued on HTS are minimizing upfront infrastructure costs, slow transactions speeds, complexity in managing governance, and regulatory obstacles (Baird et al., 2019).

Bitcoin Cash

Bitcoin Cash uses the Simple Ledger Protocol (SLP) to manage the issuance of tokens.

- Simple Ledger Protocol enables the creation, management, and transfer of NFTs on the Bitcoin Cash blockchain. Using this token system, custom token behavior could be embedded using the Bitcoin script programming language. Similar to the ERC-721 standard, the metadata for each token are stored off-chain. Each NFT created in SLP can have a unique token identifier, and collections of NFTs can be issued from the same address for easy classification.

Binance Smart Chain

The Binance Smart Chain, which is similar to the other chains reported above, has its own standard for tokens.

- BEP-721: Based on one of the first and most commonly used NFT standards of Ethereum (i.e., ERC-721), this standard allows the creation of NFTs on the Binance Smart Chain.

Other Chains

The improvement proposal framework introduced by the Ethereum community inspired other chains to create their own token standards.

- *Cardano:* The CIP-721[6] is proposed as the NFT standard for minting non-fungible tokens. Minting NFTs on Cardano requires the tokens to be linked to metadata with a unique link that is attached to the transaction where the token was created. This is different from the approach followed on Ethereum. In Cardano, token creation does not require a smart contract but is treated similarly to Cardano's native token.
- *Solana:* Minting NFTs on Solana requires the invocation of the Solana Program Library (SPL[7]) which provides on-chain code and common interface for minting fungible and non-fungible tokens. There is also the Metaplex Token Metadata contract[8] for supporting the linkage of metadata with SPL tokens.
- *Avalanche:* This layer-1 blockchain offers native capabilities of minting NFTs directly from its online wallet with the use of the NFT Studio.[9] The Avalanche's C-Chain runs the Ethereum Virtual Machine, and thus it supports all the ERC standards. On another note, Avalanche implements the Avalanche-Ethereum bridge[10] to enable a seamless bidirectional flow of tokens across the two ecosystems. Such attempts demonstrate how tokens of any type could become liquid from one blockchain network to another.

Research Perspectives and Open Challenges

As discussed in previous sections, the metaverse is defined as a shared, virtual, computer-generated space that is evolved by the collaborative actions of its users (i.e., content creators). The realization of a metaverse requires the convergence of a mixed reality that is composed of virtual and augmented reality over the Internet layer. We also argued that

[6] https://github.com/cardano-foundation/CIPs/blob/8b1f2f0900d81d6233e9805442c2b42aa1779d2d/CIP-NFTMetadataStandard.md.

[7] https://spl.solana.com/.

[8] https://docs.metaplex.com/nft-standard.

[9] https://docs.avax.network/build/tutorials/smart-digital-assets/wallet-nft-studio.

[10] https://bridge.avax.network/.

blockchains can provide an infrastructure that is ubiquitous and persistent for supporting the next generation of metaverses.

Developing a metaverse requires the representation of virtual and physical elements in a standardized manner. Blockchains by nature can provide the foundational layer for tokenizing all the things that need to be unique and nonreplicable. At the same time, the technology provides a unique way for creating digital representations and certificates of ownership with the use of NFTs. Furthermore, the open philosophy for creating the various fungible and non-fungible standards (e.g., ERC-20, ERC-721) allows the blockchain community to define new standardized token forms and develop a dynamic tokenization system. For example, the Ethereum community offers a unique life cycle for proposing such standards and approving them.

In this section, we discuss the various open challenges and research perspectives that pertain to (i) the creation of the metaverse, (ii) new innovative services and monetization opportunities, and (iii) regulation and alternative governance models that are likely to emerge in such virtual worlds.

Creation of the Metaverse

Interoperability. The current landscape of blockchain-based metaverses is still at the genesis stage and is composed of many fragmented, siloed, and independent virtual worlds. This landscape offers different perspectives to realism (e.g., social and psychological environment), scope, and user interactions. Although the majority of the virtual worlds are utilizing the same blockchain backbone for minting NFTs (securing their digital ownership and authenticity) and allow for the creation of the virtual characters or in-game assets (refer to Table 6.7), such environments are not interoperable. The realization of a cross-chain metaverse is currently a challenge and not yet realized.

To enable a "Universe" of metaverses, the following challenges need to be considered. Firstly, and as far as the technology part is concerned, the interoperability of blockchain protocols needs to be realized (Sunyaev et al., 2021). This will enable a unique and scalable infrastructure for building decentralized applications with immense capabilities. Imagine a blockchain layer where multiple blockchain protocols are communicating seamlessly with each other. Interoperability should therefore concern the transfer of smart contracts' states and allow users to be able to initiate transactions on other networks and transact with the deployment of contracts on other chains. Efinity[11] is an example of a cross-chain blockchain network for NFTs that is built on Polkadot[12] as a parachain. Another example is Flow (Hentschel et al., 2020) that enables a highly scalable blockchain architecture for NFTs and blockchain gaming by improving on consensus by splitting the responsibilities of each validator according to its type. On another note, interoperability should also be concerned with information sharing not only between public blockchain networks but also with private deployments. We further note that interoperability in blockchains is not only concerned with the protocol architecture but also with the challenges of having a shared economy, data ownership, and governance (Belchior et al., 2020).

Secondly, metaverses should be interoperable in terms of creating a global economy for both fungible and non-fungible assets. A user that is represented by a digital identity (e.g., an NFT avatar) should be able to be identified in Decentraland and at the same time using the same identity to teleport to The Sandbox ecosystem. The teleportation of any virtual asset should be seamless to the user. Similarly, minting virtual items on some chain should enable users to create shared experiences across multiple ecosystems and platforms. In other words, the *roaming* of characters and any virtual item should be made possible between independent virtual worlds. We argue that a seamless integration of the virtual worlds is likely to unlock several social and economic breakthroughs. Characters can teleport from one ecosystem to another and participate in various activities. For example, it should be possible for Decentraland users to visit a VR art exhibition in Somnium Space. Blockchain technology could provide the architectural layer for the integration of many virtual worlds under a "Meta-Universe." This will eventually build a utopian

[11] https://efinity.io/whitepaper/company.

[12] https://polkadot.network/.

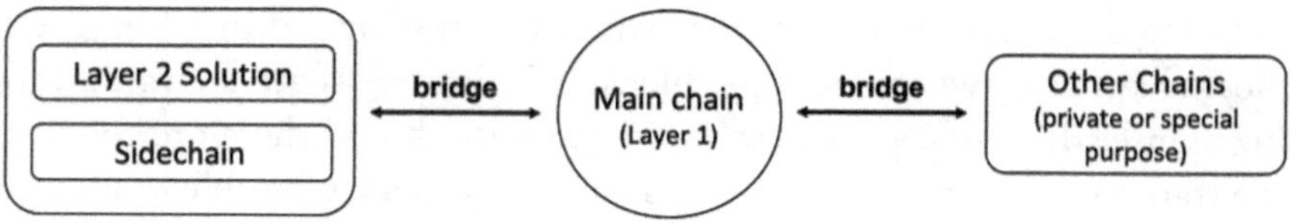

Fig. 6.2 Convergence of enabling technologies towards the Spatial Web

space that will realize the Spatial Web vision where physical interactions will be enhanced with the virtual dimension.

Gas fees. In a blockchain-enabled metaverse, all items (e.g., characters, virtual assets, in-game items) are registered as tokens on a blockchain network to provide a tamper-evident distributed ledger that ensures scarcity and allows users/players to own and trade their virtual assets. Due to the high throughput of transactions and in order to enable interoperability on blockchains and at the same time decrease gas fees, several projects are implementing their platforms utilizing high scalable layer-1 solutions (e.g., Avalanche, Solana), Ethereum layer-2 solutions (e.g., Polygon [previously known as Matic][13]), or sidechains (Gudgeon et al., 2020). For example, Axie Infinity is utilizing an Ethereum-based sidechain (i.e., Ronin[14]) to accommodate the high demand of issuing in-game transactions and transactions for minting, sharing of virtual assets with low transaction fees. Figure 6.2 proposes a blockchain stack for enabling interoperability between chains with the use of bridges. The sidechain enables users to deposit token transfers between Ronin and Ethereum. A blockchain bridge provides a bidirectional connection between different chains to allow for the transfer of data and/or tokens. They have been proposed as solutions to blockchain interoperability (e.g., Polkadot).

Visual environment. The creation of the next generation of metaverses will further enhance computer-generated visuals. This will enable a close to reality realistic environment for the user and further improve the user's experience. It is important for such environments to present a realistic environment to the user where the actions of a virtual avatar

[13] https://polygon.technology/.

[14] https://whitepaper.axieinfinity.com/technology/ronin-ethereum-sidechain.

simulate the user's physical actions. The degree of realism, which is embedded in a virtual world, is concerned with the sensory features offered by each ecosystem. In brief, these are concerned with richer visuals, detailed 3D modeling, realistic rendering, sound effects, and gesture-based interfaces.

Innovative Products and Services

NFT appraisals. Enabling real-time appraisals of individual NFTs or collections of NFTs (e.g., CryptoPunks[15]) is a challenge. Such appraisal models should consider several parameters to determine a close to realistic value of a given NFT. Technically speaking, the value of an individual NFT should consider at least the following: (i) its unique attributes and properties, (ii) the scarcity of individual attributes within a collection, (iii) demand that corresponds to the desire of ownership for a particular NFT, (iv) historic sales data, (v) floor price trend, (vi) the utility of the NFT, and (vii) the transferability of the ownership rights.

Another challenge relates with establishing a robust methodology for determining market capitalizations for entire NFT collections. NFTValuations[16] developed by the University of Nicosia proposes a robust methodology that builds on ML techniques to determine market capitalizations on an ecosystem basis. Currently, a beta version of the platform provides market capitalization data for CryptoPunks. Alternatively, UpShot[17] proposes the use of a prediction market that utilizes the wisdom of the crowd to incentivize people to predict the value of an NFT. A challenge that these platforms are likely to face is the high-risk exposure of these assets to the interest of the community, which, in reality, classifies such assets as highly volatile.

NFT oracles. Oracle services have been valuable in the decentralized finance (DeFi) space by enabling smart contracts to determine real-time price feeds of assets. For example, such Oracles have been proposed for

[15] https://www.larvalabs.com/cryptopunks. The main CryptoPunks contract can be found at: 0xb47e3cd837dDF8e4c57F05d70Ab865de6e193BBB.

[16] https://nftvaluations.com/about.

[17] https://upshot.io/.

the development of stable coins as well as to prevent arbitrage opportunities in various DeFi protocols. Similarly, Oracles that determine real-time appraisals of NFTs or forecast the value of NFTs could enable interesting and innovative open financial products and services. It is critical for the ecosystem to have an automated methodology to provide NFT appraisals that can be fed through Oracles to various smart contracts.

DeFi composability. DeFi indicates a movement of alternative financial services that are inclusive, fair, transparent, and composable. NFTs can be turned into liquid assets that can be used for providing, borrowing, and lending services. Drops[18] is a platform that allows users to use their NFTs as collateral to obtain thrustless loans. In general, Drops aims to bring more utility to NFTs by enabling idle assets to be used as liquidity to lending pools.

On another note, Pandora Finance[19] aims to bridge the gap between off-chain assets and the on-chain ecosystem by allowing asset owners to turn their real-world illiquid assets to a liquid state. There is a potential for innovative financial products and services by leveraging on the composability between DeFi and the NFT space. The ERC-1155 standard aims to enable fractional ownership of individual NFTs in an attempt to improve their liquidity. This will give the opportunity for micro-investors to own part of an NFT, including the royalties generated. Fractionalized NFTs can then be traded in decentralized exchanges (DEXes) like Uniswap.[20] An example of a platform that enables users to buy, sell, and mint fractions of NFTs is fractional art.[21] Overall, a new research dimension emerges from the composability of DeFi with NFTs as an expansion that goes beyond artwork into creating the next generation of tangible financial instruments.

Rarity tools. Many data analytic monitoring web services exist to monitor the market capitalization of cryptocurrencies. NFTs enabled a new generation of rarity tools that report real-time data on NFT collections. Such data include not only the market capitalization of each collection, but also estimates on market capitalization, sale volumes, total supply, number of

---

[18] https://drops.co/.

[19] https://pandora.finance/.

[20] https://uniswap.org/.

[21] https://fractional.art/.

owners, and so forth. An interesting feature of such services is the rarity score for each individual NFT based on the attributes of its collection. Rarity.tools[22] implements an example of a ranking of NFTs based on their rarity.

Indexing and search engines for NFTs. The ecosystem of NFTs is expected to grow, especially with the emergence of several metaverses. A challenge that remains open is how to search this space on individual NFT items or their collections. Implementing such a search engine will require an indexer to run on all chains and read data from smart contracts on the fly.

Marketplaces. We envision the new generation of NFT marketplaces that enable users to fractionalize their NFTs. Such marketplaces will also enable users to rent ownership rights on an NFT to other users or delegate the ownership of NFTs to investors who could then use the NFTs as part of their investment strategy (e.g., an NFT index fund).

Neobanks and NFT custody. Neobanks will be considering offering innovative services to NFT holders. Such services include custody of NFTs in digital vaults and offering high-yield products to users. A research challenge remains on what are the best techniques to provide a secure mechanism for the custody of NFTs or fractionalized tokens, and the cryptographic management of the private keys. At the same time, we are expecting a rise in the use of multi-NFT wallets for users to enable the self-custodianship of NFT assets cross-chain.

Business opportunities. In general, it is expected that the metaverse will create many business opportunities, especially for businesses that are interested in establishing deep customer relations and offer alternative user interaction experiences. Users will be offered an entire new environment for engaging with businesses, having full control of their private data and of their identities.

Monetization Opportunities

The emergence of metaverses with embedded crypto economies and participation incentives let people to socialize and earn money by monetizing their virtual assets (e.g., renting parcels of land) while at the same

[22] https://rarity.tools/.

time guaranteeing interoperability and genuine ownership. Other monetization opportunities relate with the organization of virtual events in the metaverse. Users can join the event using NFT tickets which demonstrate their entitlement to access the event. In general, anyone can generate NFT items without programming experience and mint them in some marketplace like OpenSea.[23] Such marketplaces directly connect creators and consumers without the need of any intermediary. Also, a smart contract could be utilized to govern the IP rights and distribute royalties to the creator automatically.

The creation of social tokens can enable the next generation of social platforms where creators are monetizing their creations and IP rights, as well as royalties are governed with the use of smart contracts over a transparent and decentralized blockchain network. This will enable the development of mini economies. For example, Pandora Finance (Vohra, 2021) permits users to tokenize their social skills with the use of NFTs and then trade them in their cross-chain DEX.

Play-to-earn (P2E) is the new trend in the metaverse gaming arena. Axie Infinity is such an example in which players from developing countries are sponsored to cover the costs of "breeding" Axies and play the game. In brief, Axie owners are lending their Axies to sponsored players that are then playing the game on their behalf to earn in-game reward tokens.[24] Such examples indicate how blockchain-based gaming enables an open P2E financial ecosystem.

DAOs and fractionalization of NFTs provide another monetization opportunity. Users that hold fractionalized ownership of NFT items get their royalties or rewards from selling an NFT. Furthermore, a fractionalized NFT can be governed by a DAO that will be responsible for its financial future and users are incentivized to participate in such a DAO with the use of a secondary token.

---

[23] https://opensea.io/.

[24] Tokens are received in Smooth Love Potions (SLP)—https://etherscan.io/token/0x37236cd05b34cc79d3715af2383e96dd7443dcf1.

Challenges on Governance, Generation, and Minting Processes

In this section, we present significant challenges associated with the governance, the generation, and the minting process of blockchain-based metaverse environments. These include (i) digital fingerprints, (ii) generation methods, (iii) token standards, (iv) regulation, and (v) taxation.

Digital fingerprints. This challenge relates to how to determine and verify the authenticity of each NFT. In most cases, a physical object is digitized and then pushed to some p2p storage network, whereas its digital fingerprint, which is generated by calculating the hash (e.g., SHA256) of its digital representation, is pushed on the blockchain (e.g., in a smart contract state or on the block using an OPcode). To verify the authenticity of the digital representation, one needs to calculate the hash of a given object and then compare it to the hash stored on the blockchain. Thus far, most digital fingerprints have been generated with the use of one-way hash functions (aka message digests). In computer vision, descriptors are used to describe the visual features of images, videos, and algorithms (Vassou et al., 2017). In this research direction, we suggest the utilization of such visual descriptors to provide a unique identification scheme based on the features that are used to describe each digital object. In cases where smart devices (e.g., VR glasses) are used to verify the authenticity of some visual information, having a visual descriptor will enable the verification algorithm to determine the feature vector that characterizes the object with a method that is invariant to rotation or sensitive to light conditions.

Generation methods. Avatar collections like CryptoPunks are created with the use of programmable generators[25] that are parameterized to generate unique collectible characters over a range of features in 2D. Each feature is unique, and its scarcity is determined as a parameter to the generation algorithm and according to the rareness degree. In a fully realistic metaverse environment, such digital objects can represent characters/avatars in 3D, virtual world objects or constructs, and in-game assets. A research challenge toward this direction relates with exploring various

[25] https://github.com/larvalabs/cryptopunks.

methodologies for programmable generators specifically designed for creating building blocks or items in a metaverse environment. The generators can be used for digitizing physical objects and annotating them with unique metadata or features. In addition, such generators can be used to evolve a virtual space dynamically if certain conditions are met. In addition, such generators could be driven by AI techniques. Lastly, visualization techniques, 3D modeling tools (e.g., 3DS Max[26]), and gaming engines (e.g., Unity[27]) currently used for the development of computer games could be further utilized and improved.

Token standards. The generation of fungible (ERC-20) and non-fungible tokens (e.g. ERC-721, ERC-1155) are following certain standard proposals that have been published by the community. It is expected that more standards will be proposed as part of accommodating unique properties and functions for virtual assets. Currently, several Ethereum virtual machine (EVM)-enabled blockchain networks (e.g., VeChain, Avalanche) and others like Bitcoin Cash, Solana, Cardano are publishing their own standards for minting NFTs.

Regulation. The rise of virtual worlds is generating a new virtual economy comprising many different virtual assets of intrinsic value. At the same time, the composability of NFTs with DeFi is likely to generate new investment opportunities in an open financial system. Evaluating the legal and regulatory risks in such an environment is a challenge. How is regulation reacting to this new environment? Some of the key legal questions that need to be answered include the following: How are NFTs categorized? How are intellectual property rights preserved? What anti-money laundering (AML) mechanisms should be in place? What are the sanction implications? What cybersecurity concerns exist? What are the state laws governing such virtual assets? Lastly, we highlight that the decentralized nature of NFTs and the lack of a standardized way to estimate their valuations is likely to create manipulation opportunities for AML. For example, NFTs could be potentially leveraged by illicit actors in masking the real value of financial transactions or other business activities.

---

[26] https://www.autodesk.eu/products/3ds-max/overview.

[27] https://unity.com/.

Taxation. The current legal framework in most jurisdictions treats royalties from IP (e.g., from art, books, software) as taxable property. In this space, sales from NFTs that encapsulate such royalties remain a gray area in terms of their tax treatments. With NFTs remaining below the radar, there is a high likelihood that financial crimes will deliberately use NFTs as a vehicle for money laundering and for conducting other illicit activities. Tax treatments from NFT sales, royalties, or other profits that relate with IP from NFTs should therefore be considered by governments.

Concluding Remarks

The vision of the Spatial Web will eventually eliminate the boundaries between digital content and objects from the physical world and enable new user interactions. Although we cannot predict whether and when this vision will reach maturity, several downstream technologies are pushing for its evolution. This chapter focuses on how DLTs, such as blockchains, can provide a ubiquitous layer to authenticate and decentralize information for the Spatial Web. More specifically, we discuss how blockchains can contribute to such an environment with providing an architectural layer for data integrity, and act as a standardization mechanism for creating and tokenizing virtual assets. Furthermore, this chapter presents an analysis of several blockchain-based metaverses (e.g., Decentraland, The Sandbox) and decentralized gaming platforms (e.g., Axie Infinity) in an attempt to understand their features, and how far blockchains, as a technology, could be utilized to support the vision of the Spatial Web—for the creation of a unified metaverse where physical reality is fused with the virtual world. Our analysis showed that blockchains can be considered as an enabler technology for the realization of the Spatial Web vision and that early signs of blockchain-based metaverses are examples of how the technology could be instantiated for the creation of virtual worlds with build-in immutability, authenticity, and digital ownership. The property of decentralization, offered by blockchains, spurs the hope that next-generation virtual worlds will be truly open and democratized. In addition, and considering the current status of blockchain-based metaverses, the chapter discusses several open challenges and research perspectives in an attempt to provide guidance on what needs to be considered to further evolve the space and push toward the realization of a metaverse that converges with the physical reality. Lastly, we consider and discuss opportunities that are likely to emerge in this space with the creation of new innovative products and services. The chapter contributes and enhances the existing body of literature on this interesting and complicated area by collecting, presenting, and analyzing rapidly evolving state-of-the-art technologies and environments like blockchain-based metaverse, NFTs, and virtual worlds. It also discusses main research perspectives and open challenges in this area.

References

Baird, L., Harmon, M., & Madsen, P. (2019). Hedera: A public hashgraph network & Governing Council. *White Paper, 1.*

Belchior, R., Vasconcelos, A., Guerreiro, S., & Correia, M. (2020). A survey on blockchain interoperability: Past, present, and future trends. arXiv preprint arXiv:2005.14282.

Benet, J. (2014). Ipfs-content addressed, versioned, P2P file system. arXiv preprint arXiv:1407.3561.

Berners-Lee, T., Cailliau, R., Groff, J. F., & Pollermann, B. (1992). World-wide web: The information universe. Internet Research.

Billen, R., Cutting-Decelle, A. F., Marina, O., & De Almeida, J. P. (2021). 3D City Models and urban information: Current issues and perspectives. edp Sciences.

Chaudhari, A. A., Laddha, D., & Potdar, M. (2019). Decentraland—A blockchain based model for smart property experience. *International Engineering Journal For Research & Development, 4*(5), 5.

Christodoulou, K., Paton, N. W., & Fernandes, A. A. (2015). Structure inference for linked data sources using clustering. In *Transactions on large-scale data-and knowledge-centered systems XIX* (pp. 1–25). Springer.

Cryptovoxels. (2021). A Blockchain Virtual World and Metaverse, Retrieved August 13, 2021 from https://www.cryptovoxels.com/.

Dionisio, J. D. N., III, Burns, W. G., & Gilbert, R. (2013). 3D virtual worlds and the metaverse: Current status and future possibilities. *ACM Computing Surveys (CSUR), 45*(3), 1–38.

Entriken, W., Shirley, D., Evans, J., & Sachs, N. (2018). Erc-721 non-fungible token standard. Ethereum Foundation.

Frey, D., Royan, J., Piegay, R., Kermarrec, A. M., Anceaume, E., & Le Fessant, F. (2008, March). Solipsis: A decentralized architecture for virtual environments. In *1st International Workshop on Massively Multiuser Virtual Environments*.

Gudgeon, L., Moreno-Sanchez, P., Roos, S., McCorry, P., & Gervais, A. (2020, February). Sok: Layer-two blockchain protocols. In *International Conference on Financial Cryptography and Data Security* (pp. 201–226). Springer.

Hentschel, A., Hassanzadeh-Nazarabadi, Y., Seraj, R., Shirley, D., & Lafrance, L. (2020). Flow: Separating Consensus and Compute–Block Formation and Execution. arXiv preprintarXiv:2002.07403.

Keller, J., & Simon, G. (2002). Toward a Peer-to-Peer shared virtual reality. In *Proceedings 22nd International Conference on Distributed Computing Systems Workshops* (pp. 695–700). IEEE.

Lyman, P., & Wakeford, N. (1999). 'Introduction: Going into the (Virtual) Field'. *American Behavioral Scientist, 43*(3), 359–376. https://doi.org/10.1177/00027649921955317

Lytras, M. Tsilira, A., & Themistocleous, M. (2003). Towards the semantic E-learning: An ontological oriented discussion of the new research agenda within the e-learning field. In the proceedings of *Ninth Americas Conference on Information Systems, (AMCIS 2003)*, Tampa, FL, USA, pp. 2985–2997. August 4–6, 2003.

Malandrakis, N., Potamianos, A., Iosif, E., & Narayanan, S. (2013). Distributional semantic models for affective text analysis. *IEEE Transactions on Audio, Speech, and Language Processing, 21*(11), 2379–2392.

Nakamoto, S. (2008). Bitcoin: A Peer-to-Peer electronic cash system. Retrieved August 12, 2017, from https://bitcoin.org/en/bitcoin-paper

Ordano, E., Meilich, A., Jardi, Y., & Araoz, M. (2017). Decentraland: A blockchain-based virtual world. *Technical Report*. Decentraland.

René, G., & Mapes, D. (2019). The spatial web: How web 3.0 will connect humans, machines, and AI to transform the world. Gabriel René and Dan Mape, ISBN: 0578562960.

Rymaszewski, M., Au, W. J., Wallace, M., Winters, C., Ondrejka, C., & Batstone-Cunningham, B. (2007). *Second life: The official guide*. John Wiley & Sons.

Ryskeldiev, B., Ochiai, Y., Cohen, M., & Herder, J. (2018, February). Distributed metaverse: creating decentralized blockchain-based model for Peer-to-Peer

sharing of virtual spaces for mixed reality applications. In *Proceedings of the 9th Augmented Human International Conference* (pp. 1–3).
Schnipper, M. (2017). Seeing is believing: The state of virtual reality. The Verge.
Somnium Space Ltd. (2021). Somnium Space—Economy Paper. Retrieved August 15, 2021, from https://somniumspace.com/files/Somnium%20Space%20Economy%20Paper.pdf
Sunyaev, A., Kannengießer, N., Beck, R., Treiblmaier, H., Lacity, M., Kranz, J., Fridgen, G., Spankowski, U., & Luckow, A. (2021). Token economy. *Business & Information Systems Engineering, 63*, 1–22.
Tapora, V. (2021). The metaverse—A new world for digital creatives. Retrieved August 15, 2021, from https://medium.com/hd-pro/the-metaverse-a-new-world-for-digital-creatives-9aabb55afaf6
Terpstra, G. A., & Huisinga, L. A. (2020). SmArt spaces: Restructuring art galleries as interactive portals. In *International Conference on Human-Computer Interaction* (pp. 411–418). Springer.
Vassou, S. A., Anagnostopoulos, N., Amanatiadis, A., Christodoulou, K., & Chatzichristofis, S. A. (2017, June). CoMo: A compact composite moment-based descriptor for image retrieval. In *Proceedings of the 15th International Workshop on Content-Based Multimedia Indexing* (pp. 1–5).
Vohra, P. (2021). Pandora protocol—Bridging real-world assets and open finance. Retrieved August 15, 2021, from https://docsend.com/view/b3mu733atjnee4np.
Wang, Q., Li, R., Wang, Q., & Chen, S. (2021). Non-fungible token (NFT): Overview, evaluation, opportunities and challenges. arXiv preprint arXiv:2105.07447.
Web Foundation. (2020). An introduction to Polkadot—Lightpaper. Retrieved August 15, 2021, from https://polkadot.network/Polkadot-lightpaper.pdf
Wood, G. (2016). Polkadot: Vision for a heterogeneous multi-chain framework. *White Paper, 21*.

7

Asset Tokenization of Real Estate in Europe

Max Zheng and Philipp Sandner

Introduction

Traditional real estate investments, as investments in real estate projects or existing real estate properties, especially in the commercial real estate sector, have proven to be very illiquid, complex, and high in transaction costs (Baum, 2020; Kalyuzhnova, 2018). Furthermore, the investment ecosystem has proven to be slow in transaction speed and settlement because there are many, and also partly, redundant intermediaries involved (Smith et al., 2019).

The primary purpose of some traditionally critical intermediaries is to verify and notarize a real estate purchase transaction. With the advent of

M. Zheng (✉)
Blockchain Founders Group GmbH, Neustadt, Germany
e-mail: max.zheng@blockchain-founders.io

P. Sandner
Blockchain Center, Frankfurt School of Finance & Management gGmbH, Frankfurt am Main, Germany
e-mail: p.sandner@fs.de

M. C. Lacity, H. Treiblmaier (eds.), *Blockchains and the Token Economy*, Technology, Work and Globalization, https://doi.org/10.1007/978-3-030-95108-5_7

blockchain technology, the traditional real estate sector could be hugely disrupted and changed in a revolutionary and innovative way.

On the one hand, blockchain technology, specifically the fractionalization of real estate through the tokenization of a particular real estate, makes the fractionalized real estate a very accessible investment. Therefore, any retail investor or anyone with low income could potentially own part of (i) a real estate asset, (ii) a real estate development project, or (iii) participate in the profits of any real estate in the form of rental income.

On the other hand, smart contracts could make processes more efficient. A smart contract is a set of predetermined rules and particular automation where the main purpose is to "serve as an immutable, event-recording ledger that facilitates trustless[1] P2P transactions" (Norta et al., 2018, p. 1). Hence, investors could potentially benefit from lower transaction costs, faster settlement times, as well as high transparency.

From the aforementioned opportunities and technological possibilities, it seems that the real estate market as we know it might experience a shift toward a much more digital infrastructure. If done correctly, market players such as real estate brokers, real estate investors, banks, real estate funds, or any other institution that is involved with real estate transactions could leverage blockchain technology in order to make (i) transactions more efficient and (ii) any real estate investment accessible and at the same time (iii) offer higher returns to investors by minimizing the frequency and magnitude of transaction costs.

Consequently, this paper analyzes the current market developments by showing what is being offered, how operations are carried out, and which business opportunities have evolved as of today. Furthermore, it will elaborate on the current regulatory environment in Europe by interpreting and analyzing the status quo with the help of experts' opinions. Lastly, an outlook will be provided on the challenges and future potential. This includes a summary of the results combined with a detailed analysis and interpretation.

---

[1] Norta et al. (2018) describe the term trustless transactions as those between at least two parties who agree on terms with a certain possibility of contractual deviation by the counterparty. One way is to include an intermediary in order to minimize this possibility. Another way would be to utilize smart contracts. Smart contracts have the ability to dis-intermediate the so-called trustless transaction.

Currently, blockchain technology is progressing at a rapid speed. This paper investigates the existing research gap and analyzes the influence of the current uncertainty within the insurance market. The purpose of this work is to provide an overview of the current market ecosystem of blockchain companies operating in the real estate sector, as well as exploring the respective jurisdictions they operate in. This paper also dives deeper into the current adaptation of blockchain applications in the field of tokenizing real estate. To pursue this, 12 experts' interviews were conducted and evaluated, which answered the following research questions (RQ):

RQ1: What are the conditions under which real estate asset tokenization makes sense?
RQ2: What do the current tokenized real estate offerings look like?
RQ3: What are the main benefits and how do they differentiate themselves from the existing methods of real estate financing/investing? What are the risks associated with this technology and this sort of offering?
RQ4: How do real estate tokenization companies currently utilize jurisdictions within the European Union and why did they choose their respective country of operation?

Furthermore, six leading companies that offer tokenized real estate were compared, and an analysis on how they operate and how their offerings are structured was carried out.

Blockchain Technology and the Theoretical Foundation

The white paper "Bitcoin: A Peer-to-Peer Electronic Cash System," written by Satoshi Nakamoto and published in 2008, is considered to describe the first application of blockchain technology (Nakamoto, 2008; Wandmacher & Wegmann, 2020; Sandner et al., 2020). In fact, the cryptocurrency Bitcoin sets the basis for blockchain technology and embodies the concept of a distributed ledger technology (DLT) (Wandmacher & Wegmann, 2020). Beck et al. (2017) state that the distributed ledger technology is a form of digital data structure which is cryptographically secured and governed by a consensus mechanism. One can define it as a digital register of records with a continuously expanding register of transactions (Beck et al., 2017; Andoni et al., 2019). One of the unique features of distributed ledger technology is the tamper resistance based on the cryptographic logic. Thus, it is considered a trustworthy technology because of the unbiased and incorruptible system (Nærland et al., 2017, as cited in Beck et al., 2017). As a matter of fact, any record that was registered in the system is stored in the decentralized ledger for all participating parties. This means that whenever a new record is added to the chain, the whole ledger is updated accordingly. Finally, this is visible for all participants and shows an updated database of a shared ledger (Kamble et al., 2019; Ølnes et al., 2017; Wang et al., 2019). As a result, blockchain technology offers ground for opportunities in the area of (i) ownership tracking of any kind with the highest transparency (Beck et al., 2017), (ii) asset management with regards to transactions of any financial product (Rawat et al., 2020), and (iii) operations and supply chain management (Cole et al., 2019).

On the contrary, blockchain technology faces challenges in the area of clarity, governance, data privacy, and data management. A lack of clarity within the technology is the result of Bitcoin being a very young and not yet fully understood technology, especially by professionals or big enterprises. Additionally, there is still low availability of skilled human resources needed in order to sustainably and thoughtfully deploy, control, and manage this technology. In fact, the lack and unavailability of knowledge restricts the adaptation of blockchain technology by enterprises (Upadhyay, 2020). When looking at the governance of blockchain technology, it is then clear that there are many different blockchain applications with widely varying governance structures. As a matter of fact, the technology itself aims to be decentralized so that there is no concentration of power and control. However, Okada et al. (2017) suggest that there is a certain importance of centralized decision-making and that there are blockchains which incorporate a degree of control of an authority. This makes sense as it can be beneficial in certain decisions to exclude or include a specific group of stakeholders. The results from experts interviews conducted by Ziolkowski et al. (2020) show that several industry experts evaluate the decentralization aspect as a potential hurdle in decision-making. In order to tackle this issue, the scholars suggest that, for example, certain decision types could be clearly distributed to the authorities in charge. Lastly, in the context of data privacy and data management, blockchain technology could face major issues regarding compliance measures on private data management (Ziolkowski et al., 2020). This is due to the fact that any public key can be traced publicly on the blockchain.

Blockchain-Based Smart Contracts

The concept of smart contracts is not new; in fact, the term "smart contracts" was already discussed by Nick Szabo in the 1990s (Kaulartz & Heckmann, 2016; Szabo, 1997). In the discussion, Szabo (1994, para. 1) describes a smart contract as a "computerized transaction protocol that executes the terms of a contract." Today, we can see that the form of smart contracts has transformed from its original definition. In particular, the emergence of blockchain technology has enhanced the efficiency of smart contracts immensely. According to Raskin (2017), the main issue was that the legal uncertainty surrounding smart contracts undermined its legitimacy. However, he states this is no longer the case with the introduction of blockchain technology. That is, blockchain solves the problem of "[interpreting] the contract in accord with the intentions of the parties" (Raskin, 2017, p. 317). In other words, smart contracts in application with blockchain technology enable the enforcement of predetermined terms of an agreement under the presumption of a specific trigger. Thus, the purpose of such an innovation was to cut costs from the need for human intermediaries and to make certain that the contracting parties have their terms and conditions met.

In his paper, "Can Smart Contracts Enhance Firm Efficiency in Emerging Markets?," Fandl (2020) argues that the lack of trust in the institutional environment of developing countries hinders economic growth through private transactions. However, he contends that blockchain technology and smart contracts could be a promising solution to this trust issue. This is because blockchain technology can enable a platform to be public and accessible to anyone. A smart contract executes a certain predetermined set of rules once certain conditions are reached. Therefore, smart contracts on the blockchain would not only make transactions transparent but this potentially eradicates all doubts regarding whether the contract's terms will be met or not. An example he provides to elucidate how blockchain and smart contracts can work hand in hand is that "failure to deliver goods by a set time will automatically trigger a default clause that transmits payment of liquidated damages to the injured party without the intervention of a judge or arbitrator." Indeed, the lack of trust could not only result in breached contracts but also the insecurity could possibly prevent a contract from being formed at all. Thus, considering that commercial real estate involves a large sum of money, smart contracts could eradicate concerns surrounding breaches.

Real Estate and Commercial Real Estate

Before diving into commercial real estate, it may be helpful to first evaluate why real estate can be a valuable investment. In their book, *Global Property Investment: Strategies, Structures, Decisions*, Baum and Hartzell (2012, p. 24) explain that real estate helps to diversify one's investment portfolio, which helps reduce risk while at the same time presents an opportunity for high returns. They state that since the acceptance of modern portfolio theory (MPT), asset allocation models reflect "strong prospective returns, coupled with low standard deviation of returns and a low correlation with equities and gilts (…)." However, in a paper about tokenization, Baum (2020, p. 9) reveals that "the actual allocation for institutional investors in 2019 was around 10%, around one quarter to one sixth of the optimized level" when, ideally, with regards to the MPT, property allocation should range between 30% and 60%.

One reason for this is the illiquidity aspect of real estate. According to Smith et al. (2019, p. 26), "most real estate transactions occur in private markets, where daily pricing and extensive information about an asset are not available." This means that not only are there transparency issues but this lack of transparency also creates high entrance barriers and high transaction costs. Smith et al. (2019) also talk about large minimum capital requirements, which essentially means that it is extremely difficult for low-income investors to participate in equity investments because they cannot reach the minimum requirements.

If real estate proved to be a difficult investment to participate in, commercial real estate proves to be even more challenging. Lizieri and Ward (2000, p. 1) explain that commercial real estate refers to "land and buildings owned by one party (an institutional investor, a specialist property company or private individuals) and let to another party," and thus, it is important to "distinguish commercial real estate from private residential markets, from owner occupied corporate real estate and from loans secured on property (such as mortgage backed securities)." This suggests that commercial real estate requires an even higher minimum capital investment than real estate, which then means that it is impossible for retail investors to participate in commercial real estate. Of course, this implies that those who do invest in commercial real estate can expect considerably high returns, potentially more than (residential) real estate (Ling & Naranjo, 2002).

Ultimately, the aforementioned experts and scholars claim that (residential) real estate and particularly commercial real estate investments can potentially be safe and offer high returns if the area does not face the issues it does. Until now, the current real estate investment utilized two methods through which people could participate in investment, namely, direct and indirect investment.

Current Methods of Investing in Real Estate

As mentioned in the previous section, there are two methods through which people partake in real estate, direct and indirect. Georgiev et al. (2003, p. 29) describe direct investments as involving "the acquisition and management of actual properties." That is, people with sufficient capital can directly purchase or sell real estate. However, as real estate is an illiquid asset class, most investors do not have enough money to participate directly, so they turn to indirect investments. Indirect investment "involves buying shares of real estate investment companies (such as REITs) or investing in the secondary mortgage market (such as in commercial mortgage-backed securities (CMBS) or CMBS pools)" (Georgiev et al., 2003, p. 29). A common financial instrument that these indirect investment vehicles use is the concept of securitization.

Securitization

According to Gaur et al. (2011), the concept of securitization received great momentum in the year 1970. In fact, any sort of financial liability can be securitized or, in other words, pooled together by an entity. This includes, for example, mortgages, receivables, and various types of debt. Typically for this process, a special purpose vehicle (SPV) is set up to purchase the underlying asset or debt instrument. The SPV then issues certain claims on the underlying asset which an investor can buy. The issuance of the securities usually guarantees the right for certain claims for the future cash flow (or other claims) generated by the holdings of the SPV (Gaur et al., 2011; Fabozzi & Kothari, 2007). The concept of securitization can therefore be a method for the financing of certain assets. Essentially, any rights or claims on cash flow of assets could be securitized and sold as such. This opens great potential for any financing activity, and many financing models for assets follow this principle (Rethmeyer, 2020). For example, in Germany, it would be possible to create a GmbH, which acts as an SPV that buys an asset. The SPV then issues claims on the equity growth of the asset, essentially being asset-backed securities. The SPV receives financing for its business activities, and the shareholders receive the underlying claim.

Tokenization of Assets/Rights

The term tokenization refers to the generation of a digital blockchain-based token that represents a security (Baum, 2020). Therefore, a firm issuing security tokens with the aim to raise funds is, by all means, initiating a security token offer (STO). In fact, any asset or right can be stored in the token. However, this depends on the prevailing regulatory framework in the country in which the token shall represent the security. This is because only when the regulator and the law system acknowledge the concept of a digital representation, the token can become effective by law.

With the law on "Token and TT Service Providers" (TVTG), Liechtenstein has established a legal framework for transactions based on "trustworthy technology" (TT) that applies for blockchain-based technology (Ministry for General Government Affairs and Finance, 2019). Essentially, Liechtenstein allows the tokenization of any rights and assets by invoking civil law. Accordingly, Sandner et al. (2019) and Prince Michael von und zu Liechtenstein (2019) state that under the "Token Container Model," introduced in the laws on TVTG, the asset or right that is being tokenized is digitally stored in a so-called token container. These token containers can then be transferred freely in the most transparent way possible with precise traceability. The government of Liechtenstein acknowledged the technology as trustworthy enough to allow equity share transactions to happen without any additional approval by a notary or lawyer. Token containers can hold all kinds of rights or even real assets such as real estate, stocks, bonds, gold, money, and basically anything of value. Although token containers that store securities are not a new type of security itself, the liability and duty applied to that specific security that is stored in such a container must still be obliged in its original form. With that being said, a tokenized asset (or right) does not change the duty, liability, or rule of any security. Specifically under the legal framework in Liechtenstein, the following rule applies: "the disposal over the token results in disposal over the right" (Nägele, 2019, p. 3).

Interview Results

This chapter presents the results from the expert interviews and also from research on current real estate tokenization use cases. The experts' surveys will be divided into four subchapters. Demographics and details about each interviewee and an interview summary can be found in Table 7.1.

Table 7.1 Participants of the experts' interview

Expert No.	Country	Industry	Job title
1	Switzerland	Tokenized Real Estate	CEO
2	Germany	Tokenized Real Estate	Founder & CTO
3	Germany	Tokenized Real Estate	CEO
4	Germany	Tokenized Real Estate	General Counsel
5	Germany	Tokenized Real Estate	Chairman
6	Germany	Tokenized Real Estate	Chairman
7	Luxembourg	Tokenized Real Estate Private Equity Fund	Managing Partner
8	Switzerland	Tokenized Real Estate & Tokenization Consultant	Founder & CEO
9	France	Independent Consultant	Advisor
10	Germany	Industry Expert & Blockchain Consultant	Advisor & Chairman
11	Italy	Crypto Assets Consultant	Advisor & Head of Crypto Division
12	Bulgaria	Real Estate Lawyer	CEO

Topic 1: Tokenization of Assets

This category assesses the key benefits of the concept of tokenizing assets with the help of blockchain technology. The experts were asked to evaluate and quantify the importance of aspects of blockchain technology. This was important to gain a better understanding of the application potential of the given aspect on the real estate tokenization market. The scale could be chosen between 0 being "not important at all" and 10 being "very important." Figure 7.1 shows that automation with smart contracts offers the biggest potential with a rather high evaluation of 7.69. The concept of fractionalization of real estate in the form of tokens and real-time settlement of transactions was valued at 7.29 and 6.8, respectively. Finally, other aspects in the field of tokenization of assets mentioned by the experts were timing, cost-efficiency, scalability, accessibility, liquidity, tradability, switching cost, knowledge about blockchain technology, and digital asset regulation.

The first question dealt with the concept of fractionalization of real estate in the form of tokens. The key point which most experts referred to was accessibility. In fact, the concept of fractionalizing an asset into

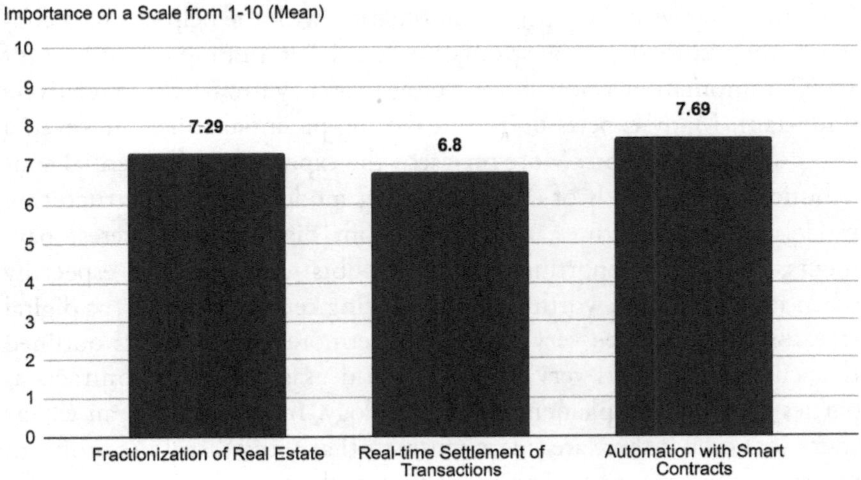

Fig. 7.1 Tokenization of assets—an evaluation of some key factors

small investable pieces allows any investor to realize any particular investment. As for the concept of fractionalizing itself, opinions were split. Some experts found it beneficial because fractionalization paired with blockchain technology could potentially ease cross-border investments and thus promote this very illiquid market. However, others say that fractionalization with blockchain technology is not new and compare the concept to existing models like exchange-traded-funds (ETFs) or similar models.

The second question was about the importance of real-time settlement for transactions of tokenized real estate. Here again, opinions were quite split. With a mean rating of 6.8, it can be evaluated as just a slightly important factor. The statement, "settlement is dependent on thresholds within the process and the process is just naturally very long" (Expert 6, 2020), sums up very well that many experts claim that settlement speed is still contingent on the traditional system. With that being said, this would simply mean that, for example, if a transaction needs to be approved by a lawyer, or if a physical signature is needed and waited upon, it would not matter if a real-time functionality exists because one process is dependent on the other.

Continuing with the aspect of automation with the help of smart contracts, the results show the strongest potential at a rating of 7.69 out of 10. The automation aspect shows a clear tendency toward being relatively important. Many experts point out the big potential it has; however, a few also express doubts. More precisely, the experts found potential contributions in the fields of capital-forming models, financial structuring models, token structures, automatic profit distribution, interest payments, and finally reporting systems. Doubts were expressed especially when it comes to the worthiness of digitizing certain processes, as digital transformation can be very costly. Furthermore, some experts outlined that currently there is very little real-world usage of smart contracts as parties must first implement this technology. In an example, an expert states that even if there are smart contracts that could distribute profits to investors, there must be a bank that accepts the smart contract.

Other important aspects that were mentioned by the experts dealt with liquidity, cost-efficiency, a marketplace for regulated trading of such securities, scalability, timing, and regulation. In summary, the experts expressed concerns about the ability to trade tokens on a secondary market. The current state does not offer such a marketplace, and this consequently raises the challenge of how to liquidate token assets. However, there are major cost savings associated with blockchain technology such as the underlying scalability of onboarding qualified shareholders from all over the world. Yet, once again, this is under the condition that regulations allow so. If the regulators from one country decide not to accept digital assets in the form of tokens, then this can be problematic for the investor. Finally, the question arises if now is the right time to implement blockchain technology for these respective firms.

Topic 2: Structure of the Real Estate Offering

This section sheds insights about current opinions on (i) the most interesting and also the most important locations to operate in when it comes to offering tokenized real estate and (ii) the underlying argumentation on why the respective country/jurisdiction was chosen.

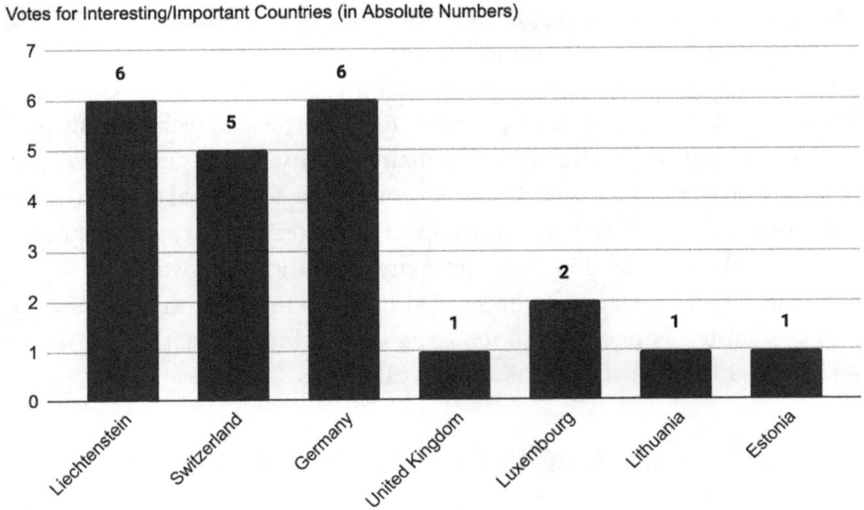

Fig. 7.2 Total number of votes for interesting/important countries to operate in (multiple choice was possible)

Figure 7.2 shows that the experts strongly tend to favor Lichtenstein, Germany, and Switzerland with the numbers of votes being 6, 6, and 5, respectively. The favorable situation is a result of two regulatory aspects. The first aspect includes a favorable legal framework for the token economy. Consequently, Liechtenstein is one of the few countries which allows security tokens to represent any equity or asset share of an asset. This is, of course, besides the existing authorization for tokens representing debt instruments or any other financial security. Moreover, Switzerland[2] is in a similar position and mostly referred to be the number one competitor of Liechtenstein. Germany, on the other hand, does not have such a flexible regulatory framework. It does, however, follow a very strict and stable token economy policy. Particularly, Experts 2, 5, and 6 stated that due to the fact that Germany follows such a strict regulation

[2] According to the DLT-Draft Bill (2019) that was dispatched by the Swiss Federal Council in December 2019, the token economy in Switzerland received clear guidance on what types of tokens are issuable. With a precise and very positive regulatory framework for crypto assets, Switzerland was henceforth considered a pioneer in developing an innovative market for crypto assets.

on digital token assets, this is to be specifically evaluated as positive. In fact, the experts believe that once the operating company succeeds within German regulations, it would succeed in most European countries. Nonetheless, this is not the case with, for example, a Liechtenstein prospectus aiming to be offered in Germany because, as Expert 6 says: "we could also just pick Liechtenstein and offer tokenized securities in Liechtenstein but if we want to passport these securities to, for example, Germany then we need to pass Germany regulations anyway."

Finally, we have experts who named Luxembourg, Estonia, Lithuania, and the United Kingdom as potentially interesting destinations to set up a legal operating entity for tokenized real estate.

Topic 3: Risk and Benefits of Tokenized Real Estate

This section will present insights about the timing and future potential of tokenized real estate, some real life examples that were mentioned by the experts, implications of risks and benefits, and, finally, the impact of tokenized real estate on the current market state.

Starting with the timing and potential of real estate tokenization, Fig. 7.3 shows that 8 out of 12 experts answered the question "Is now a good time to tokenize real estate?" with "yes," which, in this context, has two meanings. The first meaning is that now is a good time to tokenize real estate. The second meaning is that currently it is also a good time to deal with the topic of tokenization of real estate. Two experts claim that now is not an adequate time to tokenize real estate; however, in 1–2 years, the situation will become more suitable. Another two experts state that it will take more than 3 years for the infrastructure to be ready for the tokenization of real estate assets.

Essentially, advocates, who claim that now is a good time, provide several supporting arguments. First, they mention the affordability of blockchain technology in order to leverage and gain momentum in tokenizing real estate, which could lead to cost efficiencies. Second, they argue that the regulatory uncertainty, and thus, lack of regulation can be an opportunity for entering the market and gaining a first-mover

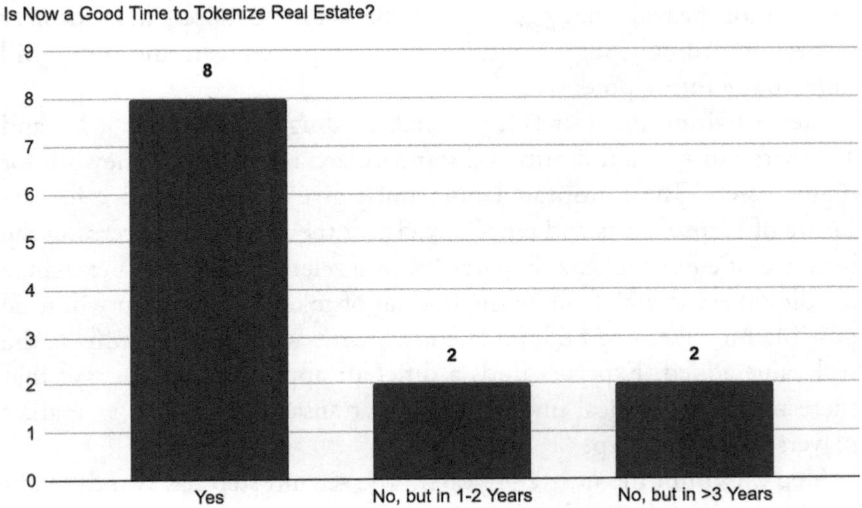

Fig. 7.3 An evaluation of the timing to start tokenizing real estate

advantage. And lastly, they anticipate that the promotion of any blockchain-based tokenization ideas can propel discussion and innovation.

However, critics argue that there are some implications of a bad timing to tokenize real estate. Implications could be, on the one hand, a missing digital land registry and the inability to issue asset-representing tokens which lead to only semi-tokenization of real assets. On the other hand, the current regulation is just not certain enough for practices such as *passporting* an investment prospectus of a real estate offering. Expert 10 also points out that now might be the right time to deal with the topic but not to tokenize real estate as tokens cannot be traded on a secondary market.

When looking at the future potential, there is a predominant opinion. Most experts think that once a standardized regulatory framework for the European Union has been established, the market around tokenized assets will thrive, progress, and experience a shift toward new ways to securitize assets. The most current European initiative is the "Markets in Crypto Assets (MiCa) regulation" that aims to set a European standard.

Despite the slightly different timelines the experts draw, there are some essential steps that most experts name. The following steps are necessary in order for the real estate tokenization market to be successful in the near future. Accordingly, steps 1 and 2 will be the prerequisite and step 3 will unleash the future potential:

Step 1 (within the next 1–3 years): According to Experts 3, 5, 10, and 11, there must be a uniform and standardized regulatory framework for digital assets. The European Union must give a clear directive for the future of crypto assets and especially clarify the situation concerning the issuance of equity tokens. Experts 1 and 6 refer to a regulated exchange for digital assets which allow the trading of tokens. Only then will it be possible for tokens to be liquidated, which is what they identify as the real value-added. Expert 9 finds a different approach, and he says that there must be a critical mass of relevant transactions as well as market players in the first step.

Step 2 (within the next 2–4 years): The second step has two different starting options. In the first situation, after having a standardized regulatory framework in Europe, the next logical conclusion would be to observe a critical mass of supply and demand being accumulated as well a certain transaction volume being processed. Expert 5 says that a digital land registry is necessary, particularly when dealing with equity tokens. Expert 6 suggests that, in the second step, the infrastructure can finally thrive and lead investment banks to join an ecosystem that allows placements to happen. This can potentially lead to greater reach and liquidity. Likewise, Expert 11 states that once regulatory certainty is ensured, more businesses will emerge. When looking at the second initial approach suggested by Expert 9, regulation will only change if there is a critical mass reached in the first place. Therefore, Expert 9 assumes that governments will initiate changes according to market movements. Finally, both Experts 9 and 10 agree that, after regulation has been implemented, businesses will need to adapt to the regulatory changes.

Step 3 (in >5 years): Step 3 deals with the future potential of how the tokenized real estate market could look like. Experts 1, 6, and 10 are confident about the fact that after around 5 years, there will be a major shift in how real estate offerings will prosper. Expert 1 believes that in the next 3–5 years, over 50% of all real estate offerings will be executed digitally. Experts 6 and 10 claim that after five years, real estate will experience a major transition toward the concept of tokenized assets.

Interestingly, Expert 8 imagines an online platform on a blockchain in which the relevant market participants of such transactions can interact with each other in the most transparent way possible.

Topic 4: Legal Challenges

The last section of the interview results presents the findings of experts' opinions about legal challenges. This chapter paid special attention to the most current Markets in Crypto Assets (MiCa) draft that was introduced by the European Commission in September 2020.

Experts 6, 8, 10, and 11 see the current MiCa regulations with respect to the licensing condition for certain asset-backed securities as a positive development. The main reason for this conclusion is that any progress made in the regulatory framework is to be evaluated as a positive development. Indeed, Expert 6 elaborates that when dealing with financial products, licensing should be applied and that not every company should be able to deal with asset-backed securities so easily. Expert 8 adds that, although specific licensing and operative requirement conditions might make it difficult for certain companies to operate, it is a necessary step in order to avoid fraudulent activities as experienced in the past (e.g. the wave of ICO scams). Interestingly, Expert 12 refers to the challenge of technology moving way faster than regulation and the risk of regulation not being able to keep up with the speed of technological progress.

Experts are concerned with two main issues when it comes to the role blockchain technology will play in terms of the transferability and purchase of tokens in the EU area. This issue deals with the fact that the driver might not be blockchain technology itself but regulation. This is because it is regulation that will enable the purchase and holding of digital assets. The second issue is that as long as BaFin[3] approves the prospectus, the major challenge will be the technological support of service providers in the respective country. Expert 6 presents an example with one of their own offerings, stating: "we [are] legally allowed to offer our product in 10 different EU countries. This is the prerequisite for

[3] BaFin is the financial regulatory authority for Germany: "The Federal Financial Supervisory Authority". In German: Bundesanstalt für Finanzdienstleistungsaufsicht.

EU-passporting. The absolute condition, however, is the sales of a technical product. Therefore, we are sort of dependent on the correct partnerships with placement providers that give us access to investors."

Real Estate Tokenization Use Cases in Europe

This subchapter will present research results on (i) companies that specialize in offering various tokenized real estate offerings and (ii) tokenization projects of single assets or entities.

Real Estate Tokenization Companies in Europe

This research conducted a comparative analysis over six major real estate tokenization companies wherein four variables were compared quantitatively and other "special rights" were compared qualitatively. The denoted "special rights" describe modifications in the debt instruments. Therefore, every tokenized real estate project was analyzed in detail. The analysis was based on a security prospectus offering from one of their listings in order to reasonably compare them among each other while following a quantitative and qualitative approach. Furthermore, this research identified tokenization platforms which offer tokenization as a service.

Accordingly, Tables 7.2 and 7.3 list and compare real estate tokenization companies. As a result, all security token offerings were, in fact, tokenized debt instruments. Due to the debt structure, every single project will be defined with different and individual contract terms. Therefore, some offer variable interest payments on the investment sum, while others offer fixed interest payments. For example, Bloxxter offers a guaranteed interest of 3% plus an additional open-end variable interest rate depending on the equity growth return of the property. Moreover, there is the possibility to offer voting rights. In fact, this accurately resembles the statements of Experts 1 and 6, saying that debt tokens are very flexible and that one can design the contract as close to equity shares as possible. The research further finds that 5 out of 6 companies are based in Germany with only one being based in Liechtenstein. Additionally, token

Table 7.2 Comparative table of real estate tokenization companies

Company name	Type of security token	Country/ Jurisdiction	Tradability	Special terms and conditions
Bloxxter	Debt token	Germany/BaFin	OTC, p2p	Guaranteed interest of 3%.
Crowdlitoken	Debt token	Liechtenstein/ FMA	OTC, DEX, p2p	N/A
Exporo	Debt token	Germany/BaFin	OTC, DEX, p2p	Return and specific rights dependent on listing.
Finexity	Debt token	Germany/BaFin	OTC, p2p	Return and specific rights dependent on listing.
iFunded/ iEstate	Debt token	Germany/BaFin	OTC	Fixed interest of 6%.
KlickOwn	Debt token	Germany/ BaFin	OTC, DEX, p2p	Return and specific rights dependent on listing.

holders will only be able to buy tokenized securities over-the-counter (OTC). Some offer the possibility to trade it via direct exchange (DEX) or via private trades among qualified investors. A qualified investor and shareholder must typically go through a know your customer (KYC) and anti-money laundering (AML) procedure. The results show that the fractionalization of assets allows to break down an asset into hundreds, if not thousands, of pieces. At the same time, blockchain technology allows the scaling of issuing fractionalized assets shares on the basis of very low additional costs. Therefore, companies can allow very small minimum investment sums resulting in low entrance barriers, especially for the targeted retail investors. The minimum investment sums range from €1 to €500.

Real Estate Single Asset/Entity Tokenization Projects in Europe

Table 7.4 lists single asset and entity tokenization projects. The results show three different single asset tokenizations, three tokenizations of funds, and one tokenization of a special purpose vehicle (SPV). Also,

Table 7.3 Comparative table of real estate tokenization companies

Company name	Analyzed prospectus (Link)	Minimum investment (€)	Website	Research comments
Bloxxter	Bloxxter prospectus	500	https://bloxxter.com/de	Only one offering listed.
Crowdlitoken	Crowdlitoken prospectus	100	https://crowdlitoken.com/	Could legally issue equity tokens.
Exporo	Exporo prospectus	1	https://exporo.de/	
Finexity	Finexity prospectus	500	https://finexity.com/	
iFunded/iEstate	iFunded prospectus	500	https://ifunded.de/en/	iFunded/iEstate does not offer tokenized debt yet, however, plans to do so.
KlickOwn	KlickOwn prospectus	10	https://www.klickown.com/	

Table 7.4 Comparative single asset/entity tokenization in Europe

Project name, website	Type	Country/ Jurisdiction	Size (€)	Research comments
Brickmark, https://brickmark.io/	Single asset tokenization	Germany/ BaFin	110 million	Debt token with 90% equity growth participation and 90% free cash flow participation.
Max Property Investment Group Plc, https://maxcrowdfund.com/en	Fund	The Netherlands/ AFM	750.000	Issued corporate bond share certificates with no guaranteed interest.
Peakside Capital Advisors, https://www.peakside.com/de/	Fund	Germany/ Bafin	200 million	Issuing equity token with a minimum investment of €50.000.
Property Schoenberg, https://property-schoenberg.com/	Single asset tokenization	Germany/ BaFin	850.000	Debt token with profit participation.
SAPEB AnnA, EquiSafe.io/	Single asset tokenization	France/ AMF	6.5 million	
Uavend Property and Leisure, http://www.uavend.com/	SPV	United Kingdom/ FCA	≈ 38.5 million	No public information about the type of security token offering STO.
WeInvest, https://www.weinvest-capitalpartners.com/	Fund	Luxembourg, CSSF	N/A	Real estate private equity fund without public information about fund size. WeInvest issued equity tokens of the fund.

investment project sizes range from €750,000 to €200,000,000 (note that the size of WeInvest was not disclosed publicly and therefore excluded). Moreover, tokenizations happened in Germany, the United Kingdom, the Netherlands, Luxembourg, and France. Besides the fact that, again, most projects were financed through debt issuance, WeInvest and Peakside Capital Advisors are the only two companies that claim to have issued equity tokens. Similar to the previously presented companies, the structure of the corresponding debt instrument can vary. Brickmark demonstrates that it is possible to have a "preferred equity"-like debt structure offering participation in equity growth as well as in the profits in free cash flow (S. Rind, personal communication, November 19, 2020). Certainly, with project volumes in the three-digit million range, the type of investors might be limited.

Discussion

In this section, the presented findings from the interviews are discussed against the theoretical foundations. It aims to examine the four research questions stated in the abstract.

Research Question 1: What Are the Conditions Under Which Real Estate Asset Tokenization Makes Sense?

Tokenization with the help of blockchain technology can have many implications that can benefit various business segments. This paper elaborates specifically on the potential benefits of the asset tokenization of real estate. The results from the interviews reveal that there are many aspects that can be of utmost importance for the real estate tokenization sector. Specifically, automation with the help of smart contracts shows a high potential for improvements in this field. The experts say that the function of distributing dividend payments in a fully automated way can enhance the cost-effectiveness of the whole business process. Another very important function is the reporting system of transactions happening on the blockchain. Expert 7 points out that their system has implemented a reporting system that tracks any transactions made on their online token management platform. The reporting system is based on smart contracts and is acknowledged by the government because the denotation of any transaction is immutable and fully traceable. The acknowledgment and the applicable laws in Luxembourg state that there is no need for additional approval by a notary for the transaction to be effective by law. As such, this resembles the example with the case of the Liechtenstein government considering that the government acknowledges the technology as reliable enough to be able to leave out intermediaries such as notaries. All these real-life examples are effective due to the fact that the blockchain can allow a platform to be fully transparent. A company specializing in the field of tokenizing assets has already proven that this can work on a private blockchain. The company Amazing Blocks AG, based in Liechtenstein, has tokenized its own equity on the Ethereum network. Its shareholders can be publicly seen on Etherscan.io, a platform that allows users to explore and search for any transaction made on the Ethereum blockchain. Hence, this is a very good example of how transparency can look on the blockchain, even though the main operations still take place on a private blockchain.

Given how blockchain technology works, it is also clear that it is very hard for hackers or any sort of manipulation to harm the system. In a worst-case scenario of manipulation, especially a private blockchain will not have any problems in comprehending or tracking transactions since there is an unfalsifiable transaction history on the blockchain. Moreover, the high adaptability of private blockchains allows the organization in charge to freely grant administrative roles and can thereby control authorizations for transactions.

In summary, since tokenization allows fractionalization of any assets as small as a thousandth of the original asset value, the experts say that this can potentially increase liquidity in the market. In fact, it allows any investor and especially low-income investors to participate in high-caliber real estate transactions. Hence, it not only provides greater liquidity but also gives any investor access to never existing investment opportunities. For the blockchain, this is a programming effort with high scalability results.

Research Question 2: What Do the Current Tokenized Real Estate Offerings Look Like?

In Europe, current offerings in tokenized real estate show very clear patterns. However, this research question must be examined from two sides. First, by looking at companies, and second, by looking at single asset or fund tokenizations. The company side shows that debt tokens seem to be the most feasible option as those were the only tokens being offered. This makes sense because 5 out of 6 of the companies are based in Germany and only in Germany can debt-based tokens be issued. Crowdlitoken, which is based in Liechtenstein, could potentially offer equity tokens but does not do so due to flexibility reasons in structuring the debt contract as delineated by Experts 1, 4, 5, 6, and 11. As a result, a very important measure for the investor to take would be to carefully compare the offering of what is available in the market as debt contracts may vary a lot. The results presented in tokenization use cases (see Table 7.2) show that "special terms and conditions" vary among guaranteed, variable, and fixed interest rates. Furthermore, some terms grant voting rights, while others do not. All these variations, as pointed out by Experts 3 and 4, can lead to retail investors losing sight of the details of this particular investment.

When looking at the single asset and fund tokenization side, we see a different pattern. Clearly, the investment sums can be far above the value of what is offered by companies that specialize in offering a wider range of tokenized real estate assets (e.g., Peakside Capital Advisors sized at €200 million or Brickmark issuing tokens worth €110 million). Usually, the investors of single asset or fund tokenizations are limited to a certain group of investors who may also have different investing preferences concerning the type of share to be acquired, namely debt or equity shares.

The former aspect can be seen in the example of Peakside Capital Advisors (see Table 7.4). The real estate fund, which issued equity tokens in a private placement, required the investors to invest a minimum amount of €50.000. The challenge here is the definition, inclusion, and exclusion of certain investors because then it might (or not) fall under regulations on private or public placements.

The latter aspect of investors' preference can be observed by looking at the offering's terms and conditions as well as by considering the experts' opinions. Table 7.4 shows that, on the one hand, contract terms can be designed very freely by offering, for example, profit participation, equity growth participation, or even voting rights. On the other hand, conditions can also differ by the type of token issuance. Based on the expert survey, professional investors typically prefer equity tokens because of higher returns, whereas retail investors prefer debt tokens because of the simplicity and convenience in terms of little active participation required.

Consequently, the study shows that a broad pool of investment opportunities can be created with blockchain technology. However, it might not yet be fully understood and accessible to retail investors. This has implications for the timing of these business activities, but the idea could potentially make commercial real estate investment opportunities available to everyone regardless of how wealthy they are.

Research Question 3: What Are the Main Benefits and How Do They Differentiate Themselves from the Existing Methods of Real Estate Financing/Investing? What Are the Risks Associated with This Technology and This Sort of Offering?

The main problem with investing in real estate is that this sector has proven to be very illiquid, complex, high in transaction costs, and this is true even more for commercial real estate investments which involve high entry barriers due to large upfront investment sums. The current options of direct and indirect investment in the real estate sector are limited. Current direct investments can be direct buyings of real estate properties. This, of course, involves high capital investments, which an average low-income individual does not have. Therefore, these groups are dependent on a loan provided by a bank in order to directly buy the underlying property. The other option for investing in real estate is by indirect investments in the form of buying shares in ETFs, real estate funds, REITs, or, if possible, by participating in private placements. Indirect, as the word implies, means that there is little control over what exactly the portfolio managers invest in. The investor can only choose by looking at the portfolio description but regularly has no voting rights. The concept of tokenization will now be contrasted with the current investing situation from the issuer's and the investor's perspective.

The concept of tokenization shows that transactions can be more efficient in terms of time savings and cost savings by leaving out intermediaries such as notaries or lawyers. Furthermore, blockchain technology allows any transaction to be perfectly traceable, under some regulatory frameworks in certain countries, which will be further elaborated in the next section, once an asset is tokenized, it can be freely transferred among certified and qualified investors on a private platform. In this way, there is no need to re-securitize any asset anymore and thus there is no need for any approval by a lawyer.

From an investor's point of view, tokenization allows direct investments and direct ownership of any tokenized real estate. Hence, tokenization enables accessibility and democratizes the current market state. The three main problems stated above can be solved, and the market could potentially include any investor to participate in real estate investments. Of course, the question remains, when the time will be right for this concept to fully mature.

Some experts state that there is great room for doubt in the area of regulation and still a very high lack of knowledge among market participants over blockchain technology and the concept of tokenization. Additionally, the issuance of equity representing tokens is just not allowed by major European countries such as in Germany, and, if allowed, then there is still lots of regulatory uncertainty over how digital assets are treated on a regulated market exchange. In fact, the nonexistence of a regulated digital assets exchange limits token holders in liquidating their assets, which makes experts rightfully assume that currently there is no liquidity created. They conclude that it might not be a good time to tokenize real estate but definitely a very good time to start dealing with the topic. Market players who want to establish a future position in the tokenized real estate industry can now benefit from a first-mover advantage and help build the infrastructure by acting as pioneers in this field. Finally, even though 8 out of 12 experts suggest that now is the right time to tokenize real estate, they add that certainly it is at its early stages of development and that there is still lots of potential for improvement and enhancement as elaborated above.

Research Question 4: How Do Real Estate Tokenization Companies Currently Utilize Jurisdictions Within the European Union and Why Did They Choose Their Respective Country of Operation?

The interview findings suggest that, although the technology is utilized for representing financial instruments on the blockchain, it does only provide marginal value at its current state. Most German-based companies are just displaying already existing debt constructs on the blockchain. In essence, as was also pointed out by the Experts 3 and 6, that is not new. This might be because under the current German legal framework, only the issuance of debt tokens is allowed.

However, when looking at single asset tokenizations, we have a very different situation. Table 7.4 shows that there are debts as well as equity tokenizations with a focus on the real estate sector, and we can see a perfect utilization of the concept of tokenization. It is thereby proven that it is possible to issue real equity tokens that are the equivalent to the current classical equity share.

When the experts were surveyed on why they set up the entity/project in their respective country, most experts preferred an environment where they are best connected to relevant parties. In fact, the starting barrier is much lower in an environment where the operators are well connected to regulators and key industry participants.

Thus, the answer to this research question is that currently, there are only a few market players who utilize crypto-friendly jurisdictions to their favor. Hence, companies fail to fully take advantage of jurisdictions with crypto-friendly regulations.

Conclusion

This section will summarize the previous findings and discussions. Then it will give theoretical and practical implications of the findings and point out some limitations of this work. This is followed by a suggestion for future research. Throughout the discussion, it is undoubtedly evident that blockchain technology has the potential to significantly impact the real estate industry. This paper outlined major inefficiencies and fundamental problems in the real estate asset class and provided an overview of how these problems are being tackled with the help of blockchain technology. A detailed analysis of the technology's features, benefits, and risks was conducted, and this analysis was verified through experts' opinions on current use cases. As a result, the outcome of this can be divided into two perspectives.

From a technological perspective, blockchain technology can enable intelligent automation with the help of smart contracts. The paper has identified that smart contracts can automate crucial processes such as the distribution of profits among investors for the respective asset. It could further be developed in a way to determine interest rate payments. Another feature of this would be the possibility to create an immutable reporting system. Due to the nature of blockchain technology, all transactions are recorded on a public ledger and can therefore be traced to their roots. Any fraudulent activity could be spotted and solved accordingly. This gives great potential to combat unauthorized financial transactions and helps in diminishing information asymmetry between relevant parties. The possibility and programmability of the Ethereum network allow a company to gain control over these specific actions. Consequently, it is possible to give certain users different roles within a private blockchain and thus control and authorize certain transactions.

From a business perspective, tokenization can be used to fractionalize any asset. The tokenized asset will then be displayed on the blockchain as a digital asset. The idea of fractionalizing an asset can create greater accessibility to investors because the digital asset itself has no limit to how small it can be fractionalized or by whom it can be acquired. In fact, the buyer could be a low-income individual based in Asia who could buy tokenized asset-backed real estate in Liechtenstein. Thus, with greater accessibility comes greater liquidity, at least in theory. The experts point out that there is still a big hurdle to overcome until blockchain technology and the concept of fractionalization of assets/fractional ownership can really take off. The main hurdle is that the current regulatory framework leaves room for uncertainty. There is no European-wide standard which makes it hard to execute a security prospectus offering with cross-border transactions. This is because all countries in which the offerings shall take place must accept the terms respective to the countries' applicable laws. Furthermore, there is no regulated exchange or secondary market in which tokenholders could potentially liquidate their tokens.

Hence, the great potential might only mature when these prerequisites are fulfilled. Accordingly, with consideration of the opinions of industry experts, it is reasonable to expect this to happen by around 2023. The most recent initiative of the European Commission and their draft on MiCa is the first step to achieve this goal. Once MiCa is set, new business opportunities will emerge.

References

Andoni, M., Robu, V., Flynn, D., Abram, S., Geach, D., Jenkins, D., McCallum, P., & Peacock, A. (2019). Blockchain technology in the energy sector: A systematic review of challenges and opportunities. *Renewable and Sustainable Energy Reviews, 100*(1), 143–174. https://doi.org/10.1016/j.rser.2018.10.014

Baum, A. (2020). Real Estate Tokenisation? The Future of Real Estate Initiative. Saïd Business School, University of Oxford Research. https://www.sbs.ox.ac.uk/sites/default/files/2020-01/Tokenisation%20Report.pdf

Baum, A., & Hartzell, D. (2012). *Global property investment: Strategies, structures, decisions.* https://www.researchgate.net/publication/288630809_Global_Property_Investment_Strategies_Structures_Decisions

Beck, R., Avital, M., Rossi, M., & Thatcher, J. B. (2017). Blockchain technology in business and information systems research. *Business & Information Systems Engineering, 59*(6), 381–384. https://doi.org/10.1007/s12599-017-0505-1

Bloxxter 1 GmbH. (2020, October 12). EU-Wachstumsprospekt. Bloxxter 1 GmbH. https://assets.ctfassets.net/tzwfn2nlmk5k/5sGlW7wDWN5ZB0pFHjkDAR/a522dfe5c519d6491879413eb7a321a5/Bloxxter_1_Zusammenfassung_Wertpapierprospekt.pdf

BrickMark AG. (n.d.). Homepage. https://brickmark.io/
Buterin, V. (2015, August 6). On public and private blockchains. Ethereum Blog. https://ethereum.github.io/blog/2015/08/07/on-public-and-private-blockchains/
Coinmarketcap. (2020, November 20). Crypto assets total market capitalization. Coinmarketcap. www.coinmarketcap.com
Cole, R., Stevenson, M., & Aitken, J. (2019). Blockchain technology: Implications for operations and supply chain management. *Supply Chain Management, 24*(4), 469–483. https://doi.org/10.1108/SCM-09-2018-0309
Crowdlitoken AG. (2020, April 6). Wesentliche Anlegerinformation. Crowdlitoken. https://crowdlitoken.com/wp-content/uploads/doc/kiid/KIID_CRT_DE.pdf
Equisafe. (2019, June 25). Throwback: First sale of building through blockchain technology in Europe completed on Equisafe platform €6.5 millions. Equisafe. https://www.equisafe.io/blog-posts/throwback-first-sale-of-building-through-blockchain-technology-in-europe-completed-on-equisafe-platform-eu6-5-millions
European Commission. (2020). Proposal for a regulation of the European Parliament and of the Council on Markets in Crypto-assets (MiCa), and amending Directive (EU) 2019/1937. European Commission. https://eur-lex.europa.eu/legal-content/EN/TXT/?qid=1600947409472&uri=COM:2020:593:FIN
Exporo GmbH. (2020, October, 21). Wertpapier-Informationsblatt. Exporo GmbH. https://assets.ctfassets.net/4xa6vepaoovq/66J06Zbt0XmmC1pfI8UHUa/dc5f8c7cf8dabc48b82ffadec80f0243/Wertpapierinformationsblatt_Exporo-Projekt-151-GmbH.pdf
Fabozzi, F. J., & Kothari, V. (2007). Securitization: The tool of financial transformation. *Yale ICF Working Paper No. 07-07*. https://ssrn.com/abstract=997079
Fandl, K. (2020, Spring). Can smart contracts enhance firm efficiency in emerging markets? *Journal of International Law and Business, 40*(3). https://scholarlycommons.law.northwestern.edu/njilb/vol40/iss3/2
Finexity AG. (2020, April 15). Basisinformationsblatt. Finexity. https://images.takeshape.io/b79f31a2-7325-4efd-9cef-65526ff6ab78/dev/9e0212f7-e701-475f-bb1a-4721d1bbf5aa/FINEXITY_neuprop040-2_BIB_HighRise.pdf
Finoa. (2018). The era of tokenization—Market outlook on a $24trn business opportunity. Medium. https://medium.com/finoa-banking/market-outlook-on-tokenized-assets-a-usd24trn-opportunity-9bac0c4dfefb

Fu, L. (2018, October 10). Peakside Capital launches its first tokenized RE fund. *Perenews*. https://www.perenews.com/peakside-capital-launches-first-tokenized-re-fund/

Gaur, V., Seshadri, S., & Subrahmanyam, M. G. (2011). Securitization and real investment in incomplete markets. *Management Science, 57*(12), 2180–2196. https://doi.org/10.1287/mnsc.1100.1155

Georgiev, G., Gupta, B., & Kunkel, T. (2003). Benefits of real estate investment. *The Journal of Portfolio Management, 29*(5), 28–33. https://doi.org/10.3905/jpm.2003.319903

iEstate GmbH. (2020, December 4). Vermögensanlagen-Informationsblatt. iEstate GmbH. https://ifunded.de/de/download/project/beautique-apartments/document/vermogensanlageninformationsblatt_pdf_7

Kalyuzhnova, N. (2018). Transformation of the real estate market on the basis of use of the blockchain technologies: Opportunities and problems. MATEC Web Conf. 212, 06004 (2018). https://doi.org/10.1051/matecconf/201821206004

Kamble, S., Gunasekaran, A., & Arha, H. (2019). Understanding the Blockchain technology adoption in supply chains-Indian context. *International Journal of Production Research, 57*(7), 2009–2033. https://doi.org/10.1080/00207543.2018.1518610

Kaulartz, M., & Heckmann, J. (2016). Smart contracts—Anwendungen der Blockchain-Technologie. *Computer Und Recht, 32*(9). https://doi.org/10.9785/cr-2016-0923

KlickOwn AG. (2020, February 25). Wertpapier-Informationsblatt (WIB). KlickOwn AG. https://www.klickown.com/file/Wertpapierinformationsblatt_Historisches_Lueneburg_Tokenbasierte_Schuldverschreibung.pdf

Ling, D. C., & Naranjo, A. (2002). Commercial real estate return performance: A cross-country analysis. *The Journal of Real Estate Finance and Economics, 24*(1/2), 119–142. https://doi.org/10.1023/a:1013938506550

Lizieri, C., & Ward, C. (2000). Commercial real estate return distributions: A review of literature and empirical evidence. https://core.ac.uk/download/pdf/1443073.pdf

Max Property Group B.V. (2020, April 1). Information document on Max Property Group Share Certificates (MPGS). Max Property Group B. V. https://maxcrowdfund.com/sites/default/files/mpgs-pdf-files/3_MPGS_Informatiedocument_20200401_UK.pdf

Ministry for General Government Affairs and Finance. (2019). Law on token and TT service providers; TVTG. Ministry for General Government Affairs

and Finance. https://www.naegele.law/files/Downloads/2019-07-12_BuA_TVTG_en_full_report.pdf
Nærland, K., Müller-Bloch, C., Beck, R., & Palmund, S. (2017). Blockchain to rule the waves—Nascent design principles for reducing risk and uncertainty in decentralized environments. *Proceedings of the 38th International conference on information systems*, Seoul, forthcoming.
Nägele, T. (2019). Executive summary of the "Tokens and TT Service Providers Law" AKA the "Liechtenstein Blockchain Act". https://www.naegele.law/downloads/TTTL_Summary.pdf
Nakamoto, S. (2008). Bitcoin: A peer-to-peer electronic cash system. Bitcoin.org. https://bitcoin.org/bitcoin.pdf
NASDAQ. (2020, November 20). Apple Inc. (AAPL). [Stock quote]. https://finance.yahoo.com/quote/AAPL/key-statistics?p=AAPL
Norta, A., Fernandez, C., & Hickmott, S. (2018). Commercial property tokenizing with smart contracts. *2018 International Joint Conference on Neural Networks (IJCNN)*. https://doi.org/10.1109/IJCNN.2018.8489534
Okada, H., Yamasaki, S., & Bracamonte, V. (2017). Proposed classification of blockchains based on authority and incentive dimensions. *2017 19th International Conference on Advanced Communication Technology (ICACT)*. https://doi.org/10.23919/ICACT.2017.7890159
Ølnes, S., Ubacht, J., & Janssen, M. (2017). Blockchain in government: Benefits and implications of distributed ledger technology for information sharing. *Government Information Quarterly, 34*(3), 355–364. https://doi.org/10.1016/j.giq.2017.09.007
Prince Michael von und zu Liechtenstein, H. S. H. (2019). The tokenization of assets and property rights. *Trusts & Trustees, 25*(6), 630–632. https://doi.org/10.1093/tandt/ttz051
Raskin, M. (2017). The law and legality of smart contracts. *Georgetown Technology Law Review*, N° 305.
Rawat, B. D., Chaudhary, V., & Doku, R. (2020). Blockchain technology: Emerging applications and use cases for secure and trustworthy smart systems. *Journal of Cybersecurity and Privacy, 1*(1), 4–18. https://doi.org/10.3390/jcp1010002
Rethmeyer, T. (2020). Introduction of a new asset class—Tokenized business processes as a new financing opportunity. Frankfurt School of Finance and Management.
Rind, S. (2019). Personal interview. Online communication.

Sandner, P., Lange, A., & Schulden, P. (2020). The role of the CFO of an industrial company: An analysis of the impact of Blockchain technology. *Future Internet, 12*, 128. https://doi.org/10.3390/fi12080128

Sandner, P., Nägele, T., & Gross, J. (2019, October 7). Liechtenstein Blockchain Act: How can nearly any right and therefore any asset be tokenized based on the Token Container Model? Medium. https://medium.com/@philippsandner/liechtenstein-blockchain-act-how-can-nearly-any-right-and-therefore-any-asset-be-tokenized-based-389fc9f039b1

ScalingFunds GmbH. (2019, September 9). ScalingFunds and Uavend to launch €35 million tokenised property in the U.K. ScalingFunds. https://www.scalingfunds.com/scalingfunds-and-uavend-to-launch-35-million-tokenised-property-in-the-u-k/

Smith, J., Vora, M., Benedetti, H., Yoshida, K., & Vogel, Z. (2019). Tokenized securities and commercial real estate. MIT Digital Currency Initiative, *Working Group Research Paper*. https://doi.org/10.2139/ssrn.3438286

Szabo, N. (1994). Smart contracts. Retrieved December 24, 2020, from http://www.fon.hum.uva.nl/rob/Courses/InformationInSpeech/CDROM/Literature/LOTwinterschool2006/szabo.best.vwh.net/smart.contracts.html

Szabo, N. (1997). The idea of smart contracts. Retrieved December 24, 2020, from http://web.archive.org/web/20140406003401/szabo.best.vwh.net/idea.html

The Federal Council (Switzerland). (2019). Vernehmlassung zum Bundesgesetz zur Anpassung des Bundesrechts an Entwicklungen der Technik verteilter elektronischer Register. https://www.newsd.admin.ch/newsd/message/attachments/59307.pdf

Upadhyay, N. (2020). Demystifying blockchain: A critical analysis of challenges, applications and opportunities. *International Journal of Information Management, 54*, 102120. https://doi.org/10.1016/j.ijinfomgt.2020.102120

Wandmacher, R., & Wegmann, N. (2020). Tokenization and securitization—A comparison with reference to distributed ledger technology. In Y. Thorhauer & C. Kexel (Eds.), *Facetten der Digitalisierung. Schriften der accadis Hochschule*. Springer Gabler. https://doi.org/10.1007/978-3-658-29870-8_8

Wang, Y., Han, J. H., & Beynon-Davies, P. (2019). Understanding blockchain technology for future supply chains: A systematic literature review and research agenda. *Supply Chain Management, 24*(1), 62–84. https://doi.org/10.1108/SCM-03-2018-0148

Ziolkowski, R., Miscione, G., & Schwabe, G. (2020). Decision problems in blockchain governance: Old wine in new bottles or walking in someone else's shoes? *Journal of Management Information Systems, 37*(2), 316–348. https://doi.org/10.1080/07421222.2020.1759974

8

Tokenization and Regulatory Compliance for Art and Collectibles Markets: From Regulators' Demands for Transparency to Investors' Demands for Privacy

Tom Barbereau, Johannes Sedlmeir, Reilly Smethurst, Gilbert Fridgen, and Alexander Rieger

Introduction

Thanks to the Internet, individuals and organizations can exchange digital information without centralized intermediaries or trusted third parties. *Distributed ledger technology* (DLT) and related innovations augment the Internet's potential; hence, it is now possible to transfer economic value, rights, and claims without a custodial intermediary such as a bank, financial institution, or stock exchange (Tapscott & Tapscott, 2018).

T. Barbereau • R. Smethurst • G. Fridgen • A. Rieger (✉)
SnT, University of Luxembourg, Luxembourg City, Luxembourg
e-mail: tom.barbereau@uni.lu; reilly.smethurst@uni.lu; gilbert.fridgen@uni.lu; alexander.rieger@uni.lu

J. Sedlmeir
FIM Research Center, University of Bayreuth, Bayreuth, Germany
e-mail: johannes.sedlmeir@fim-rc.de

M. C. Lacity, H. Treiblmaier (eds.), *Blockchains and the Token Economy*, Technology, Work and Globalization, https://doi.org/10.1007/978-3-030-95108-5_8

This new form of peer-to-peer economic exchange is accomplished via *tokenization*.

Tokenization allows people to trade via a distributed ledger a variety of ownership and access claims, licenses, and royalty rights as an alternative to conventional, paper-based exchange (Sunyaev et al., 2021). Tokenized claims can pertain to both physical and digital assets. Investors can trade tokenized claims to physical assets such as real estate, artworks, antique furniture, vintage cars, race horses, historical instruments, rare books, collectibles, customized machinery, and limited-edition fashion items (Whitaker & Kräussl, 2020). Investors, likewise, can trade tokenized claims to purely digital artworks like Beeple's "Everydays—The First 5000 Days" (sold by Christie's auction house for USD $69.3 million) or "The Pixel" by Pak (sold by Sotheby's auction house for USD $1.4 million) (ArtReview, 2021; Reyburn, 2021).

The tokenization trend began when Ethereum—a distributed ledger that is both public and permissionless—introduced support for general programming logic (Sunyaev et al., 2021). There are now broadly accepted standards such as Ethereum's ERC-20 for *fungible tokens*, ERC-721 for *non-fungible tokens* (NFTs), and ERC-1155 for either fungible or non-fungible tokens. ERC-20 tokens, alongside Bitcoin (BTC), are largely responsible for the popularity of fungible cryptocurrencies. NFTs, by contrast, each represent a unique instantiation of value; hence, NFTs are especially useful for claims that pertain to singular physical or digital objects, limited-edition products with unique serial numbers, and custom-made items (Whitaker, 2019).

The transfer of a token—either fungible or non-fungible—is achieved when a new record is appended to a distributed ledger's transaction history. Transactions typically contain details such as the wallet addresses of senders and receivers, the tokens that are transferred, and the transaction type. *Privacy-preserving* DLT solutions can purposefully omit transaction details from a publicly viewable ledger, either in entirety or in part. They aim to prevent the collection of identity information about the holders of particular wallets (Androulaki et al., 2020).

The privacy-preserving exchange of tokenized claims is potentially of interest to art and collectibles investors, who rely on high levels of discretion (Day, 2014); but for tokenized claims to become useful within regulated markets, additional documentation is required to identify market participants. Simply put, tokenized claims must comply with Anti-Money Laundering (AML), Counter-Financing of Terrorism (CFT), and Know Your Customer (KYC) laws. Europe's Fifth Anti-Money Laundering Directive (5AMLD) is especially pertinent, since it demands identification information and due diligence checks from art intermediaries. An array of digital document or certificate formats can be used for identification purposes, but to comply with laws such as Europe's General Data Protection Regulation (GDPR), natural persons' identity information must not be stored on a public ledger. If tokenized claims' transaction details or information about assets' permanent attributes is meant to be publicly viewable, then they can be stored *on-chain*, but natural persons' identity information must be stored *off-chain*.

Tokenized claims for digital art and collectibles achieved prominence in late 2017, when Dapper Labs' CryptoKitties became so popular that they congested the global Ethereum network. In 2021, tokenized claims for physical artworks gained attention. The family of Wladimir Baranoff-Rossiné (1888–1944) sold some of his artworks via Mintable, and the British artist Damien Hirst sold 10,000 unique physical artworks via Palm (Sullivan, 2021; Tarmy, 2021).

Tokenization offers art and collectibles investors a new way to achieve *fractional ownership* (Whitaker & Kräussl, 2020). The most common way, at present, for investors to achieve fractional ownership of high-value artworks is to purchase comparatively low-value shares of a securitized art fund. Liquid shares purchased on a secondary market thus provide an alternative to the primary art market's low liquidity. Tokenized fractional ownership extends this concept to a global pool of investors who can access a public ledger like Ethereum, so that investors are no longer obliged to register with a custodial broker or a company-owned stock exchange. There is, however, an important caveat. Regulatory developments are required to build a bridge between tokenized claims and custodied physical assets, so that the tokenized claims are legally binding and assets' custodians are liable in various jurisdictions.

In this chapter, we first compare two options for the fractional ownership of physical artworks and collectibles: securitized fractions traded via a company-owned exchange, and tokenized fractions traded via a global, public ledger. We then acknowledge the tension between regulators' demands for transparency and auditability and art investors' demands for privacy. We discuss regulatory requirements that pertain to the identification of art market participants and the storage of natural persons' identity information; then, in response, we encourage further research into digital certificates (stored off-chain), used in combination with *zero-knowledge proofs* (ZKPs) for selective disclosure. In sum, we endorse the prospective use of a *technology stack* for physical artworks and collectibles—a work-in-progress that combines DLT for tokenized claims and fractional ownership, off-chain identity information for regulatory compliance, and ZKPs for selective disclosure.

Tokenization for Fractional Ownership, Collateral, and Sponsorship

In 2020, demand for the fractional ownership of artworks and other luxury assets increased dramatically. Masterworks and Acquicent are notable examples. Masterworks attracted 10,000 new investors per month, and Acquicent enjoyed an 80% increase in sign-ups by potential investors (Kazakina, 2020).

Fractional ownership, acquired via secondary markets, is an alternative to the primary art market's high fees and low liquidity. The fee problems are caused by the fragility of the physical assets and the complicated acquisition and exchange processes (Campbell, 2008; Day, 2014). Between a buyer and a seller are dealers, auction houses, and gallerists who profit from high transaction costs. The buyer's premium charged by Christie's auction house, for instance, falls anywhere between 14.5% and 30.5%, depending on the location of the auction (Christie's Auction House, 2020).

Specific options for fractional ownership include shares of a single artwork, shares of an art fund, tokenized fractions of a single artwork, and tokenized fractions of an index fund. Fractional ownership—accomplished via shares or tokens—allows investors to participate in art markets without having to transport, store, or care for physical assets, and it enables investors who cannot afford high-value artworks to instead purchase comparatively low-value assets, namely the shares or tokens (Whitaker & Kräussl, 2020). Well-known Real Estate Investment Trusts (REITs) appeal to investors for similar reasons: investors do not have to act as caretakers for a particular property, they can acquire fractional ownership of a diversified property portfolio, and they can conveniently purchase and sell liquid shares of the REIT via online brokerage platforms.

Thanks to fractional ownership, the secondary art fund market, valued at an estimated USD $1 billion, has better liquidity than the primary art market, which is roughly valued at USD $60 billion (Deloitte, 2017). The art fund market dates to at least 1904, but it did not achieve prominence until the 1970s when the British Rail Pension Fund invested in artworks (Maneker, 2021b; Velthuis & Coslor, 2012). The Artemundi Global Fund is a recent financial success, for which transparent pricing data exists. From 2010 until 2015 (the fund's final year), the Artemundi Global Fund generated an average net annual return of 17% (Gylfason, 2020).

As for the fractional ownership of a single artwork, Masterworks already offers this option to investors. Masterworks' online platform allows art investors to build portfolios of shares and to then sell their shares on a secondary market created by the Masterworks' company-owned exchange. An art investment company named Maecenas revised this concept and used a DLT-based exchange instead of a company-owned exchange. Maecenas splits high-value artworks into tokenized fractions, using the ERC-20 fungible token standard. Buying a tokenized fraction of a single artwork (created via Maecenas) is thus comparable to buying a securitized fraction of a single artwork (created via Masterworks).

A non-custodial, Ethereum-based platform named NFTX extends this concept further. NFTX allows collectors of tokenized artworks and collectibles to create a tokenized index fund. The tokenized index fund is akin to a securitized art fund, but it is DLT-based. Fractions of the tokenized index fund created via NFTX can then be traded on non-custodial, Ethereum-based exchanges like Uniswap. The index fund tokens can also be staked via the NFTX platform to generate yield in the form of Ethereum's native currency (ETH). This is a genuinely new revenue stream for art investors.

Securitization and tokenization are similar in principle, but as noted, the medium of storage and exchange differs for each. Shares are registered on a proprietary exchange like the Nasdaq Stock Market (owned by Nasdaq, Inc.), whereas asset tokens are usually registered on an "unincorporated" distributed ledger (Zetzsche et al., 2017). If art investors purchase tokenized fractions instead of securitized fractions, they can purchase tokens directly from an asset's custodian, without necessarily requiring a brokerage or a company-owned exchange, and the transaction typically settles within minutes instead of days. By digitizing securitization's paper trail, tokenization reduces transaction costs (Sunyaev et al., 2021). This is a notable economic advantage.

Fractional ownership via secondary markets is not the only way to address the primary art market's lack of liquidity. Investors like Michael Steinhardt and Steven A. Cohen pledged artworks as collateral for loans of liquid cash from financial institutions. In 2011, Steinhardt nominated 20 paintings and drawings—some by Pablo Picasso and Jackson Pollock—as collateral for a loan from the JP Morgan Chase Bank (Weiss & Kazakina, 2011). Cohen entered into a similar agreement with Morgan Stanley at the end of 2015 (Goldstein, 2016). Since the volatility of blue-chip artworks is considered low, art-backed loans can secure low interest rates (Maneker, 2021b). An online, company-owned platform named NFTfi extended this concept of art as collateral to NFT-collateralized loans of fungible cryptocurrencies. The concept of art as collateral can potentially be extended to NFT-collateralized loans of cash from traditional financial institutions as well (Morante & Sofge, 2021).

In addition to benefits for investors, tokenization offers a potential advantage for artists and creators of collectibles, namely the ability to determine the resale conditions for their work and automatically receive portions of their work's resale values. At present, artists receive a portion of their work's initial sale value (together with galleries and auction houses), whereas they do not usually receive any profits from their work's resale events (O'Dair, 2019; cf. Maneker, 2021a). Artists' experiments with ledger entries and transaction conditions can be traced to Yves Klein's "Zones of Immaterial Pictorial Sensibility" from 1962 (Vikram, 2021).

A tokenized work's resale conditions can also be altered to suit artists' early sponsors or patrons, so that they too receive a portion of resale values via automated payments (Whitaker & Kräussl, 2020). Some people participate in art markets for reasons of aesthetic appreciation, emotional attachment, or moral support more so than investors' usual pecuniary concerns (Frey & Eichenberger, 1995; Gylfason, 2020). Tokenization thus offers sponsors, patrons, and supporters of art the prospect of permanent association—even pseudonymous association, if they wish—with artworks or art collections. It remains to be seen if this notion of *tokenized sponsorship* proves successful in comparison with the economic motives of increased liquidity and transaction-cost improvements.

For art and collectibles markets, tokenization entails not only benefits but challenges as well (O'Dair, 2019). For many of the technical challenges, there are experimental or nascent solutions. Excessive energy consumption, for example, is only an issue for a subset of distributed ledgers (Sedlmeir et al., 2020), and the performance of public ledgers like Ethereum can be improved via layer-2 solutions like *zk-rollups*, which allow for thousands of complex transactions per second (Schaffner, 2021). Privacy requirements are a more sensitive, ongoing challenge for DLT, especially for public ledgers (Platt et al., 2021; Preukschat & Reed, 2021).

If regulation requires participants in art and collectibles markets to register detailed transaction information on a public ledger, this might alienate investors that value discretion (Day, 2014; Oosterlinck, 2017). Discretion and anonymity are crucial for art investors, dealers, and auctioneers. So, too, is privatized knowledge. It enables investors to barter for the best deals, and it allows intermediaries, firstly, to protect key clients from competitors, and, secondly, to capitalize on research and insights about a given artefact and its market value to determine a margin between the acquisition price and the sale price. Private, interpersonal relationships and discretion are thus the heart and soul of the art market, not publicly viewable identity information and due diligence checks (Day, 2014; Runhovde, 2021). The tension is palpable.

Tokenized Claims for Custodied and Non-custodied Assets

Tokenized ownership, sponsorship, and access claims inspired a flurry of innovation in art markets and creative industries (O'Dair, 2019; Whitaker, 2019); but the liability of custodians that sell tokenized ownership claims is a complicated matter. This is in line with the ambiguous legal status of many DLT-based innovations (Zetzsche et al., 2017). Tokenized claims can pertain to digital artworks or physical artworks; they can be fungible (for fractional ownership of an artwork) or non-fungible (for complete ownership of an artwork); and they can pertain to custodied assets or else assets without a custodian. For investors interested in physical art and collectibles, only tokenized claims about custodied assets are relevant, whereas for investors interested in digital art and collectibles, both custodied assets (stored on a third-party server) and non-custodied assets (stored on-chain or on individuals' devices) are relevant.

If an investor purchases a tokenized ownership claim (NFT) for a digital artwork that is stored fully on-chain, then there is a direct link between the tokenized claim and the artwork's essential content. A conventional intermediary is not required to enforce the link between the claim and the asset. Although this level of control is desirable for some investors, the storage of large media files on a distributed ledger is expensive and impractical; hence, it is rare to find digital art stored fully on-chain. The Autoglyphs collection by Larva Labs is a notable exception. On 10 June 2021, Sotheby's auction house sold "Autoglyph #177" for USD $201,600 (Konrad, 2021). Autoglyph NFTs contain publicly viewable hex data plus instructions about how to render the hex data as a glyph image. This means that the artwork does not have to be stored off-chain as a high-resolution image file. The code that generates the glyph image is stored directly on-chain; hence, an Autoglyph NFT, as the name implies, is self-enclosed.

If a digital artwork exists as an image file stored off-chain, then the tokenized claim typically includes a link to the file's location and/or a cryptographic hash of the image file. The hash is akin to a digital fingerprint. It can be used to prove a match between a tokenized claim and a file stored anywhere off-chain. If the buyer of a tokenized claim wants to ensure that they can access the off-chain image file in the future, they could locally store a copy of the image file—perhaps even in the same wallet that stores the private key required to claim ownership of the token. In this case, the digital artwork would not require a custodian.

The same cannot be said for tokenized claims that pertain to custodied physical assets, since DLT cannot enforce a link between a tokenized ownership claim (on-chain) and the pertinent physical asset (off-chain). A trusted caretaker, curator, or other conventional intermediary is required to uphold the tokenized ownership claims that are stored on the distributed ledger and registered to an investor's digital wallet address. Examples of custodied physical assets with tokenized ownership claims include Pablo Picasso's "Fillette au beret" as well as the aforementioned works by Wladimir Baranoff-Rossiné and Damien Hirst (Sygnum Bank & Artemundi, 2021). Figure 8.1 provides an illustration of tokenized claims for custodied assets and tokenized claims for assets without a custodian.

It remains to be determined how various jurisdictions will treat tokenized ownership claims for physical assets. Tokenized ownership claims are not necessarily binding, and custodians of physical assets are not liable by default. For art investors, regulatory developments are thus of equal importance to the ongoing technological developments.

Most distributed ledgers are understood as *isolated networks*. Isolated networks are sometimes advantageous, and other times, they are not. For

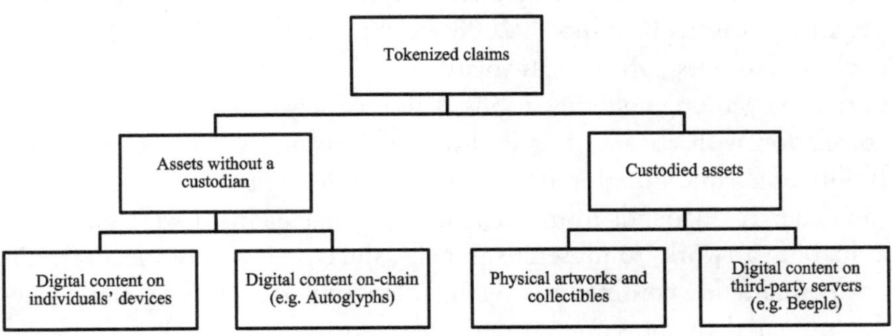

Fig. 8.1 Tokens for custodied assets and tokens for assets without a custodian

holders of fungible cryptocurrencies, to determine how many units of a cryptocurrency one owns, it is sufficient to read from the public ledger. Isolation, in this case, is not a problem, just as isolation is not a problem for owners of Autoglyph NFTs that are fully on-chain. If, however, one deals with tokenized claims for custodied physical assets, there must be a bridge between the DLT realm and the physical realm. If there is no bridge between these two realms, then investors risk buying a token that represents the ownership of nothing but the token itself.

For tokenized physical artworks, there is a need for evidence that attests to the asset's authenticity and condition as well as evidence that attests to the custodian's reputation. Without evidence of reputation, unethical owners of artworks can sell an 'exclusive ownership' token registered on Ethereum plus an 'exclusive ownership' token registered on a different ledger like Polkadot, with no intention to honor the promise. Investors face additional risks due to the fact that physical art is a *movable asset* that can be stolen or shipped across jurisdictions (Velthuis & Coslor, 2012; Meistere & di Torcello, 2018). For tokenized claims that pertain to physical assets, certifications issued by trusted third parties are irreplaceable, and regulation remains crucial.

Art Markets, AML/KYC Regulation, and Identification

Art appeals to investors for financial reasons as well as aesthetic or non-pecuniary reasons (Campbell, 2008; Velthuis & Coslor, 2012; Korteweg et al., 2016). First, art has less volatility and close to a non-changing rate of return over long holding periods. This is largely due to an artwork's low correlation with abstract financial instruments and the practical impossibility of a panic situation that incurs a double-digit decline. Second, art can generate dividends from efficient active management strategies, such as loaning artworks to museums. Finally, since art is a movable asset, it is not permanently confined to one jurisdiction, and its value is not always denominated in the same currency. A painting, diamond, or watch is easier to buy, sell, and move freely across jurisdictions than real estate. Art is thus "the ultimate offshore," since a physical artwork can be stored in one country while the buyer's money is stored in another country (Meistere & di Torcello, 2018).

Until very recently, art markets allowed participants to conduct high-value transactions with cash, a low level of regulatory oversight, and sometimes no identification checks. One case from the famous Panama Papers, leaked in 2016, illustrated how the art trade's anonymity allowed the Nahmad family to disguise their identity as the owner of an artwork involved in a legal restitution claim (Reyburn, 2016). In 2020, two Russian billionaires used a shell company to effectively obscure their identities as art investors, bypass United States' sanctions, and purchase over USD $18 million of artworks (Portman & Carper, 2020).

In response to identification problems such as these, regulators placed stricter demands on art markets. On 10 January 2020, Member States of the European Union enforced the Fifth Anti-Money Laundering Directive (5AMLD). The 5AMLD subjects intermediaries in the art market to the same requirements as banks, real estate agents, and notaries. For transactions (or a series of transactions) valued at €10,000 or more, art dealers must now register with a national government agency, and art investors must verify their identities and undergo customer due diligence (CDD) checks (Directive (EU) 2018/843, 2018). Similarly, on 1 January 2021, the United States extended the 1970 Bank Secrecy Act, so that the Act affects antiques and art dealers (National Defense Authorization Act for Fiscal Year 2021, 2020). Following these regulatory developments, KYC processes are more important for financial institutions that interact with art dealers, art galleries, art-secured loans, freeports, and auction houses' clients. The source-of-wealth (SOW) and source-of-funds (SOF) are also of increased importance and must now be identified.

If a financial institution advises a client who has an artwork as a SOF, the institution needs records, such as receipts, the auction catalogue's listed sale price of the artwork, sale prices of other works by the same artist (to check for major discrepancies), expert evaluations, and a confirmation that the work is not listed in databases such as Interpol's Stolen Works of Art Database or the FBI's National Stolen Art File (NSAF). Information about the permanent attributes of assets can be embedded in tokens. If this information is digitized, this will improve the efficiency of the database checks.

It is likewise possible, from a technical perspective, to store identity information about art market participants on a public ledger: one could use, for example, Ethereum's ERC-725 identity claims. Identity information stored on a publicly viewable ledger would, however, conflict with the art market's norms of discretion as well as laws like Europe's GDPR. A method that stores natural persons' identity information off-chain is thus required. Common options include paper-based documents or PDF files, but these options are not machine-readable and are therefore not the most efficient. For the off-chain storage of machine-readable identity information, common X.509 certificates can be used. So, too, can an emerging standard for digital identities named *verifiable credentials* (VCs) (Chadwick et al., 2019; Sporny et al., 2019). VCs can potentially be used in combination with a crypto-asset wallet, so that investors can control the exchange of both tokenized claims and off-chain identity information.

Digital Wallets for Tokenized Claims and Off-Chain Identity Information

Digital wallets are a promising area of research and development, following the European Commission's recent announcement of a Digital Identity Wallet (European Commission, 2021a). Today, it is already possible to use various Ethereum wallet applications to exchange both identity information (stored on-chain in machine-readable ERC-725 format) and crypto-assets (such as fungible tokens, NFTs, and Ethereum's native currency), but this option is not GDPR-compliant. It is also possible to use a *custodial* wallet offered by companies like Binance or Coinbase to exchange both machine-readable identity information (stored off-chain on company-managed servers) and crypto-assets. This option incurs *vendor lock-in*, which means that market participants cannot export their digital identity information or AML/KYC credentials in a standardized form that can be used with other intermediaries.

There is a third option, which is a work-in-progress: a *non-custodial* wallet that allows investors to control the exchange of standardized, machine-readable identity information (off-chain) as well as tokenized claims (on-chain) (Ramsey, 2020). The identity information, for this third option, can be stored in VC format on a device that is managed by the individual investor. The identity information does not have to be stored on a company-managed server. Developers refer to this non-custodial method of digital identity management as *decentralized* or *self-sovereign* (Preukschat & Reed, 2021).

VCs are a more flexible option for machine-readable identity information than X.509 certificates. The World Wide Web Consortium recommended VCs as a standard in 2019, whereas X.509 certificates were initially introduced in 1988 (Sporny et al., 2019). X.509 certificates are commonly used to identify servers, hence they are the backbone of today's World Wide Web. VCs extend the capabilities of X.509 certificates to identify natural persons and *smart devices*. VCs allow subjects to hold and present multiple certificates from different issuers; they can help ensure that semantic attributes are machine-readable across domain barriers; and they can be used in combination with ZKPs to satisfy natural persons' privacy requirements. The public keys of VCs' issuers can be registered on a DLT-based *public key infrastructure* (PKI) or else on a PKI managed by a certificate authority (Preukschat & Reed, 2021; Tobin, 2018).

Companies like Evernym and Trinsic as well as Linux's Trust over IP Foundation are notable developers of decentralized identity solutions. At present, these organizations do not offer a wallet app that allows investors to control the exchange of both off-chain VCs and on-chain tokens. This complex type of exchange would constitute a major advance for art investors that wish to comply with regulators' identification demands without significant privacy compromises. This type of exchange could also benefit members of the general population, who will perhaps in future hold *central bank digital currencies* (CBDCs) and exchange off-chain VCs in accordance with nascent digital identity policy frameworks from Europe and the Anglosphere (Gross et al., 2021; Neuerer, 2021).

The storage of VCs off-chain avoids the most egregious privacy problems, but this is not sufficient for art investors that want to selectively disclose just some information that is contained within VCs (to comply with regulators' transparency requirements). For these investors, ZKPs are required in combination with VCs stored off-chain.

Zero-Knowledge Proofs for Selective Disclosure

In the art market, there is a high demand for discretion, and consequently, there are informal requirements for the preservation of participants' anonymity (Day, 2014). On the other hand, regulators demand transparency and auditability of transactions. For a tokenization platform to achieve sustainable success, it must strike a balance between participants' demands and regulatory compliance. ZKPs can assist here.

Without ZKPs, DLT is not acceptable to privacy advocates. It does not make sense, simply put, to store private information on a public ledger. Likewise, it does not make sense to share a comprehensive list of private transactions with a global audience. It is not difficult to compile an individual wallet's transaction details, to link the on-chain transaction data with off-chain identity information (like KYC data from exchanges), and to thereby construct a comprehensive buyer/seller profile (Biryukov & Tikhomirov, 2019; Meiklejohn et al., 2013). Consequently, information stored on a distributed ledger should be considered personally identifiable. This is obviously not desirable for art and collectibles investors. Any decision to store information on a distributed ledger should thus be made with care.

A simplistic DLT-based tokenization platform will inevitably confront the so-called *verifier's dilemma.* If an entity wants to be sure that a statement about data is correct (e.g., a transaction is legitimate because the amount that the receiver gets is equal to the amount that the sender spent), one would intuitively expect that the entity needs to see the data and to independently compute the result of the algorithm (Luu et al., 2015). For complex statements, this can have negative consequences on performance, especially for public ledgers that have a high number of verifiers. Even more problematic is the amount of information exposed to the verifier. In most cases, the verifier is granted access to more information than is strictly required—often more than the entity that wants to prove the statement would like to reveal.

ZKPs can potentially solve the verifier's dilemma. With a ZKP, the prover can convince the verifier of a statement about the integrity of a computation without revealing the computation's result or any other information in excess of what they intended to prove (Goldwasser et al., 1989). Instead of receiving the data and recomputing the algorithm, the verifier will solely check an often-succinct proof that attests to the correctness of the prover's statement. Hence, ZKPs can strictly separate the visibility of data or a computation from the verification of its authenticity or correctness (Platt et al., 2021). Instead of revealing no information (and not being transparent) or revealing excessive information (i.e., sharing all data needed to replicate a computation), ZKPs allow a party to selectively disclose the information required and nothing in excess of this.

More specifically, ZKPs can allow investors to disclose basic things like proof of legal age or proof of a KYC check's completion. ZKPs can thus satisfy generic AML, CFT, and KYC requirements without forcing art market participants to disclose comprehensive identity information (Morais et al., 2019). This makes ZKPs attractive for art and collectibles investors, since they help balance discretionary demands and compliance requirements.

Proposed Technology Stack

We propose a technology stack that facilitates the exchange of tokens and identity information across various platforms and domains in a privacy-preserving manner (Fig. 8.2). It aims to avoid the problem of vendor lock-in (i.e., the provision of digital identity information and due diligence by a trusted third party that is platform-specific or application-specific). This, however, does not imply that market participants can remain isolated within the DLT realm and entirely avoid trusted third parties, regulators from various jurisdictions, or the physical realm. Trusted third parties act as custodians of the physical artworks and collectibles (or any other object that is tokenized), certify the authenticity of

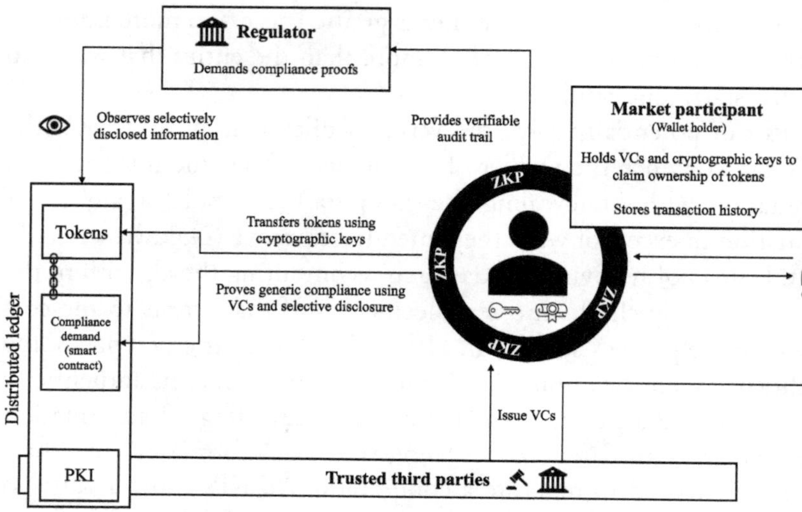

Fig. 8.2 Our proposed technology stack: DLT, VCs, and ZKPs

assets, and issue documents that are required by regulators. If a company-managed exchange acts as a trusted third party and assumes responsibility for the transaction of both ownership claims and compliance information, then vendor lock-in is the result. Investors would need to return to the same exchange in order for their claims to be recognized as valid and tradable, which undermines DLT's general ethos of interoperability (Sunyaev et al., 2021).

Our proposed DLT-based exchange involves a seller that holds tokens and identity-related VCs, as well as prospective buyers that also hold identity-related VCs. A trade between a buyer and a seller can occur under the following conditions:

1. The seller can use VCs (stored off-chain) to disclose to the prospective buyer important information about the physical asset (if this information is not already embedded within the token's smart contract, stored on-chain).
2. A smart contract can automatically demand generic compliance information (that is not specific to any jurisdiction). Both parties can then prove to the smart contract that they have satisfied this generic

compliance demand and thereby fulfilled the pre-requisites for the token transfer.

Generic compliance information may include the following: proof that one possesses a valid ID, proof that one is above a certain age limit, or proof of permission to engage in a particular transaction (issued by a trusted third party such as an accountant or a tax authority). Unique handling codes could also be registered as part of the transaction, which would enable various tax authorities to automatically recognize and categorize the transaction. If generic compliance information is not sufficient, sellers could hypothetically issue smart contracts that demand compliance information that is jurisdiction-specific. A smart contract such as this would only accept a transaction if a specific regulation's requirements were satisfied. This approach to software engineering is sometimes referred to as *compliance by design* (Kokash, 2014).

Selective disclosure (via ZKPs) can hide from a public ledger the identity of the tax authority's employee who signed the compliance-related VC demanded by the smart contract. For more specific privacy benefits, ZKPs can also be used to hide the addresses of the wallets involved in a token transfer, so that the only visible record consists of proof that the tokens spent coincide with the tokens received (Ben-Sasson et al., 2014). The transaction would thus consist of: (1) a ZKP for the transfer of the token (value), and (2) a ZKP that satisfies the automated request for generic compliance information, without revealing any identity information that is not required by various regulators. The supply of generic compliance information can potentially reduce a tokenization platform's risk of prohibition. This risk is serious, given the European Commission's recent position on "anonymous crypto-asset" transactions (European Commission, 2021b).

Outlook

In this chapter, we endorsed the prospective use of DLT for tokenized claims that pertain to custodied physical assets, digital certificates for off-chain identity management, and ZKPs for selective disclosure. We acknowledged the art market's recent regulatory challenges, specific to the identification of market participants and the off-chain storage of identity information. More broadly, we discussed a digitized paper trail as a viable alternative to the art market's inefficient and sometimes incomplete paperwork that is difficult to audit (Campbell, 2008).

Tokenized claims for physical artworks and collectibles are evidence of the increasing interest in tokenization, outside the limited domain of cryptocurrencies (O'Dair, 2019). Tokenization is becoming a powerful force for innovation, investment, and new or revised business models (Sunyaev et al., 2021; Treiblmaier, 2021). This is partly due to the reputation of distributed ledgers as "neutral" platforms that are beyond the control of any particular company or government (Fridgen et al., 2019). DLT offers investors and creators of artworks and collectibles the unique opportunity to exit single-provider, proprietary systems, and to interact with global stakeholders from previously disparate, closed systems. DLT potentially entails the creation of a global market wherein investors are not required to register with company-managed, custodial exchanges. The realization of this technological potential is, however, contingent upon regulatory developments in various jurisdictions.

The European Commission's recent policy package consists of four legislative proposals that greatly enhance the European Union's existing AML/CFT framework. Specifically, the policy package aims to "improve the detection of suspicious transactions and activities," which includes "transfers of crypto-assets." The policy package also strengthens due diligence checks and prohibits the use of "anonymous crypto-asset" transactions (European Commission, 2021b).

Tokenization thus entails new opportunities for art and collectibles markets as well as new regulatory challenges and unresolved conflicts. The most notable is the tension between investors' demands for privacy and regulators' requirements for transparency and auditability. In response to this tension, we suggested the use of digital certificates (stored off-chain for GDPR compliance) and ZKPs, so that transaction details and identity information can be selectively disclosed to regulators and financial institutions (for 5AMLD compliance). Although it is difficult to strike a balance between investors' and regulators' respective interests, we believe that this is possible with a technology stack that combines DLT-based tokenization, off-chain identity information, and ZKPs.

Although the proposed technology stack is a work-in-progress that is specific to art and collectibles markets, it could also be treated as a general prototype for the privacy-preserving exchange of NFTs, fungible tokens, digital currencies, and off-chain identity information. A successful technology stack for the art market could provide valuable insights about the design of a central bank digital currency (CBDC), since a CBDC system must also balance the requirements of privacy and auditability. The European Central Bank (ECB) recently proposed four work streams for their digital euro experiments. One stream investigated how AML/KYC procedures can be addressed in a setup that combines DLT, tokenization, and digital identity management (Gross et al., 2021).

We limited this chapter's scope to tokenization for art and collectibles markets, since this area of research and experimentation is not beholden to a central bank's vast array of stakeholders, nor is it subjected to the massive scalability requirements of a sovereign currency. We believe that the privacy-preserving exchange of tokenized art investments constitutes an opportunity for research that is both ambitious and appropriately limited.

References

Androulaki, E., Camenisch, J., Caro, A. D., Dubovitskaya, M., Elkhiyaoui, K., & Tackmann, B. (2020). *Privacy-preserving auditable token payments in a permissioned blockchain system*. 2nd ACM Conference on Advances in Financial Technologies (pp. 255–267).

ArtReview. (2021, April 15). Crypto-artist Pak's single grey pixel NFT sold for $1.36 million. *ArtReview*. https://artreview.com/crypto-artist-pak-single-grey-pixel-nft-sold-for-1-36-million-dollars/

Ben-Sasson, E., Chiesa, A., Garman, C., Green, M., Miers, I., Tromer, E., & Virza, M. (2014). Zerocash: Decentralized anonymous payments from Bitcoin. *IEEE Symposium on Security and Privacy, 2014*, 459–474. https://doi.org/10.1109/SP.2014.36

Biryukov, A., & Tikhomirov, S. (2019). Deanonymization and linkability of cryptocurrency transactions based on network analysis. *IEEE European Symposium on Security and Privacy (EuroS P), 2019*, 172–184. https://doi.org/10.1109/EuroSP.2019.00022

Campbell, R. (2008). Art as a financial investment. *The Journal of Alternative Investments, 10*(4), 18.

Chadwick, D. W., Laborde, R., Oglaza, A., Venant, R., Wazan, S., & Nijjar, M. (2019). Improved identity management with verifiable credentials and FIDO. *IEEE Communications Standards Magazine, 3*, 14–20. https://doi.org/10.1109/MCOMSTD.001.1900020

Christie's Auction House. (2020, September 21). *Financial information: Buying at Christie's.* Christie's. www.christies.com/buying-services/buying-guide/financial-information/

Day, G. (2014). Explaining the art market's thefts, frauds, and forgeries (and why the art market does not seem to care). *Vanderbilt Journal of Entertainment & Technology Law, 16*(3), 41.

Deloitte. (2017). *Art & Finance Report 2017*. Deloitte.

Directive (EU) 2018/843 of the European Parliament and of the Council of 30 May 2018 amending Directive (EU) 2015/849 on the prevention of the use of the financial system for the purposes of money laundering or terrorist financing, and amending Directives 2009/138/EC and 2013/36/EU, PE/72/2017/REV/1 (2018).

European Commission. (2021a, June 3). *Commission proposes a trusted and secure Digital Identity for all Europeans.* European Commission. https://ec.europa.eu/commission/presscorner/detail/en/ip_21_2663

European Commission. (2021b, July 20). Beating financial crime: Commission overhauls anti-money laundering and countering the financing of terrorism rules. *EC Press Release.* https://ec.europa.eu/commission/presscorner/detail/en/IP_21_3690

Frey, B. S., & Eichenberger, R. (1995). On the return of art investment return analyses. *Journal of Cultural Economics, 19*(3), 207–220. JSTOR.

Fridgen, G., Guggenberger, N., Hoeren, T., Prinz, W., & Urbach, N. (2019). *Opportunities and challenges of DLT (blockchain) in mobility and logistics.* Federal Ministry of Transport and Digital Infrastructure.

Goldstein, M. (2016, January 19). Morgan Stanley provides billionaire Steven Cohen with loan secured by art. *The New York Times.* https://www.nytimes.com/2016/01/20/business/dealbook/morgan-stanley-backs-billionaire-steven-cohen-with-loan-secured-by-art.html

Goldwasser, S., Micali, S., & Rackoff, C. (1989). The knowledge complexity of interactive proof systems. *SIAM Journal on Computing, 18*(1).

Gross, J., Sedlmeir, J., Babel, M., Bechtel, A., & Schellinger, B. (2021). *Designing a central bank digital currency with support for cash-like privacy* (SSRN Scholarly Paper ID 3891121). Social Science Research Network. https://papers.ssrn.com/abstract=3891121

Gylfason, G. (2020). *Aesthetic alpha: The economics of art investment*. Master of Science, University of Iceland. http://hdl.handle.net/1946/36884

Kazakina, K. (2020, September 5). Robinhoods of the art world lure scores of investors in pandemic. *Bloomberg*. https://www.bloomberg.com/news/articles/2020-09-05/robinhoods-of-the-art-world-lure-scores-of-investors-in-pandemic

Kokash, N. (2014). Integrating compliance management in service-driven computing: Conceptual models and automation architecture. In R. Ramanathan & K. Raja (Eds.), *Handbook of research on architectural trends in service-driven computing* (pp. 439–480). IGI Global. https://doi.org/10.4018/978-1-4666-6178-3.ch018

Konrad, A. (2021, March 18). He sold a digital 'cryptopunk' for $7.5 million. Now Figma CEO Dylan Field is ready to move into the 'metaverse.' *Forbes*. www.forbes.com

Korteweg, A., Kräussl, R., & Verwijmeren, P. (2016). Does it pay to invest in art? A selection-corrected returns perspective. *The Review of Financial Studies, 29*(4), 72.

Luu, L., Teutsch, J., Kulkarni, R., & Saxena, P. (2015). *Demystifying incentives in the consensus computer*. Proceedings of the 22nd ACM SIGSAC Conference on Computer and Communications Security (pp. 706–719). https://doi.org/10.1145/2810103.2813659.

Maneker, M. (2021a, March 15). NFTs are creating the opposite of everything they're meant to fix. *ARTnews.Com*. https://www.artnews.com/art-news/market/nfts-create-opposite-of-everything-they-are-meant-to-fix-1234586769/

Maneker, M. (2021b). Art lasts, markets pass: Can NFTs finally make art an asset class? *ARTnews.Com*. https://www.artnews.com/art-news/market/nfts-art-as-asset-class-1234590308/

Meiklejohn, S., Pomarole, M., Jordan, G., Levchenko, K., McCoy, D., Voelker, G. M., & Savage, S. (2013). *A fistful of bitcoins: Characterizing payments among men with no names*. Proceedings of the 2013 Conference on Internet Measurement Conference (pp. 127–140).

Meistere, U., & di Torcello, A. P. (2018). *The art market is increasing in transparency*. Deloitte Lithuania. https://www2.deloitte.com/lt/en/pages/finance/articles/art-market-increasing-transparency.html

Morais, E., Koens, T., van Wijk, C., & Koren, A. (2019). A survey on zero knowledge range proofs and applications. *SN Applied Sciences, 946*.

Morante, T. F., & Sofge, D. (2021, April 9). Non-fungible tokens (NFTs) as art loan collateral. *Business Law Today*. https://businesslawtoday.org/2021/04/non-fungible-tokens-nfts-art-loan-collateral/

National Defense Authorization Act for Fiscal Year 2021, 116, One Hundred Sixteenth Congress of the United States of America, Second Session, H.R. 6395 (2020).

Neuerer, D. (2021, July 11). *Digitalisierung: Union will mit digitalem Euro Facebook-Währung Paroli bieten*. Handelsblatt. www.handelsblatt.com

O'Dair, M. (2019). *Distributed creativity: How blockchain technology will transform the creative economy*. Palgrave Macmillan.

Oosterlinck, K. (2017). Art as a wartime investment: Conspicuous consumption and discretion. *The Economic Journal, 127*(607), 2665–2701.

Platt, M., Bandara, R. J., Drăgnoiu, A.-E., & Krishnamoorthy, S. (2021). Information privacy in decentralized applications. In M. H. U. Rehman, D. Svetinovic, K. Salah, & E. Damiani (Eds.), *Trust models for next-generation blockchain ecosystems*. Springer International Publishing.

Portman, R., & Carper, T. (2020). *The art industry and U.S. policies that undermine sanctions*. United States Senate, Committee on Homeland Security and Governmental Affairs.

Preukschat, A., & Reed, D. (Eds.). (2021). *Self-sovereign identity: Decentralized digital identity and verifiable credentials*. Manning.

Ramsey, R. (2020). An examination of the challenges posed by cryptocurrencies to AML/CTF regulation. *Amsterdam Law Forum, 12*(3), 20.

Reyburn, S. (2016, December 4). What the Panama Papers reveal about the art market. *The New York Times*.

Reyburn, S. (2021, November 3). JPG file sells for $69 million, as 'NFT mania' gathers pace. *The New York Times*.

Runhovde, S. R. (2021). In the dark, all art dealers are grey: Discretion and rationalisation in the Munch art market. *International Journal for Crime, Justice and Social Democracy, 10*(2), 1–14.

Schaffner, T. (2021). *Scaling public blockchains: A comprehensive analysis of optimistic and zero-knowledge rollups*. Master's Thesis, Center for Innovative Finance, University of Basel.

Sedlmeir, J., Buhl, H. U., Fridgen, G., & Keller, R. (2020). The energy consumption of blockchain technology: Beyond myth. *Business & Information Systems Engineering, 62*(6), 599–608.

Sporny, M., Longley, D., & Chadwick, D. (2019). *Verifiable credentials data model 1.0: Expressing verifiable information on the Web* (M. Sporny, G. Noble, D. Longley, D. C. Burnett, & B. Zundel, Eds.). World Wide Web Consortium.

Sullivan, P. (2021, July 23). A painting or an NFT of it: Which will be more valuable? *The New York Times*. https://www.nytimes.com/2021/07/23/your-money/nft-art-lebron-james-damien-hirst.html

Sunyaev, A., Kannengießer, N., Beck, R., Treiblmaier, H., Lacity, M., Kranz, J., Fridgen, G., Spankowski, U., & Luckow, A. (2021). Token Economy. *Business & Information Systems Engineering*, 1–22.

Sygnum Bank & Artemundi. (2021, July 15). *Sygnum Bank and Artemundi tokenize a Picasso on the blockchain.*

Tapscott, D., & Tapscott, A. (2018). *Blockchain revolution: How the technology behind Bitcoin and other cryptocurrencies is changing the world.* Portfolio/Penguin.

Tarmy, J. (2021, March 24). The line between NFTs and fine art gets even blurrier in new auction. *Bloomberg*. https://www.bloomberg.com/news/articles/2021-03-24/line-between-nfts-and-fine-art-gets-even-blurrier-in-baranoff-auction

Tobin, A. (2018). *Sovrin: What goes on the ledger?* Evernym.

Treiblmaier, H. (2021). The token economy as a key driver for tourism: Entering the next phase of blockchain research. *Annals of Tourism Research, 103177*. https://doi.org/10.1016/j.annals.2021.103177

Velthuis, O., & Coslor, E. (2012). The financialization of art. In K. Knorr-Cetina & A. Preda (Eds.), *The Oxford handbook of the sociology of finance*. Oxford University Press.

Vikram, A. (2021, May 5). The NFT's promise of control. *ARTnews.Com*. https://www.artnews.com/art-in-america/features/artists-nfts-control-market-1234591850/

Weiss, M., & Kazakina, K. (2011, October 18). Steinhardt pledges Picassos for real estate as art loans surge. *Bloomberg*. https://www.bloomberg.com/news/articles/2011-10-18/steinhardt-pledges-picassos-for-real-estate-as-art-loans-surge

Whitaker, A. (2019). Art and blockchain: A primer, history, and taxonomy of blockchain use cases in the arts. *Artivate: A Journal of Enterprise in the Arts, 8*(2), 21–47.
Whitaker, A., & Kräussl, R. (2020). Fractional equity, blockchain, and the future of creative work. *Management Science, 66*(10), 4594–4611.
Zetzsche, D. A., Buckley, R. P., & Arner, D. W. (2017). The distributed liability of distributed ledgers: Legal risks of blockchain. *University of Illinois Law Review, 4*.

9

Token-Based Insurance Solutions on Blockchain

Simon Cousaert, Nikhil Vadgama, and Jiahua Xu

Introduction

Insurance plays a vital role in dealing with risks and uncertainties in society. It provides us with financial compensation when we suffer from losses caused by various unfortunate events: from health impairment to job loss, from robbery to traffic accidents. As early as 2000 years ago, Indian, Chinese and Babylonian traders practiced methods of pooling risk (Dewan, 2008; Vaughan, 1996). For example, Chinese seafaring merchants pooled together their goods into a collective fund that would pay out if there was any damage to any of the members' ships (CB Insights, 2021). Today, the global insurance industry stands at taking in approximately 6 trillion USD of premiums. To put this number into context, this industry is larger than the overall economy of countries such as

S. Cousaert (✉) • N. Vadgama • J. Xu
Centre for Blockchain Technologies, University College London (UCL), London, UK
e-mail: nikhil.vadgama@ucl.ac.uk; jiahua.xu@ucl.ac.uk

M. C. Lacity, H. Treiblmaier (eds.), *Blockchains and the Token Economy*, Technology, Work and Globalization, https://doi.org/10.1007/978-3-030-95108-5_9

Germany and Japan. Despite the long history of insurance in society, the industry is required to constantly evolve to tackle, among other things,

1. the emergence of new risks, especially due to new technology development, such as cyber security breaches;
2. the transformation of existing risks, such as increasingly recurring natural catastrophes due to climate change;
3. shifts in consumer needs, such as rapid access to customized, on-demand insurance, quick claim management, as well as transparency in the insurance processes;
4. continuous advancement in techniques applied in insurance fraud.

Against this backdrop, there is a dire need for solutions that allow insurance policies to be flexibly designable, insurance holder and claim data to be easily manageable and insurance processes to be openly auditable. Bearing the nature of programmability, traceability and transparency, token-based insurance solutions built with blockchains are on the rise. In particular, the plethora of token models underpinned by smart contracts enables easy configuration of various products and services (Xu & Xu, 2022), as well as cost-efficient record-keeping of miscellaneous transactions and activities within the insurance business.

In the insurance industry, novel projects that utilize blockchain as an infrastructure range from those still at a proof-of-concept phase to those that have already gone into production. As an example of a start-up project, Claimshare (2021) combats double payouts for the same incident at different insurers, an issue that affects 5–10% of insurers' payouts. This project has won awards and partnered with Intel and KPMG (CB Insights, 2021). State Farm, the largest auto insurer in the United States, and the USAA (United Services Automobile Association) are using blockchain to settle subrogation claims between themselves in the property and casualty insurance sector. This system was announced as being in production in January 2021, helping automate and secure a previously manual process, thereby speeding up approximately 75,000 claims exchanged between these two companies (StateFarm, 2021). Finally, industry consortia have also been set up, such as B3i (the Blockchain Insurance Industry Initiative), incorporated in 2018 and owned by 21 global insurance participants—including Allianz, AXA, Generali, Zurich, Swiss Re—with over 40 companies as shareholders, customers and community members. With the vision for "better insurance enabled by frictionless risk transfer" (B3i, 2021a), B3i is creating insurance products on the blockchain and has released its first application that manages catastrophe excess of loss with a pipeline of new features expected to be added (B3i, 2021b).

The focus of this chapter is the area of novel token-based business models on blockchain. We explore how the insurance business can transform through the use of distributed ledger technology and tokenization. We first lay out the preliminaries of token-based insurance solutions; we then compare in detail three insurance protocols on blockchain, namely, Nexus Mutual, Etherisc and inSure; this is followed by a discussion on further challenges faced by token-based insurance solutions; we conclude the chapter with an outlook of the insurance industry in the token economy.

Preliminaries of Token-Based Insurance Solutions

In this section, we dissect major components of token-based insurance solutions—including core roles, main tokens and assets, key processes and operations—and discuss how these components are associated with each other. Figure 9.1 shows a stylized illustration of a general token-based insurance solution.

Roles

The token-based insurance model requires many actors, each of which has a vital role to play in the ecosystem. The main roles in this interplay include the insureds, the insurers, the underwriters, the reinsurers, the claim assessors and, finally, a decentralized autonomous organization (DAO) responsible for governance.

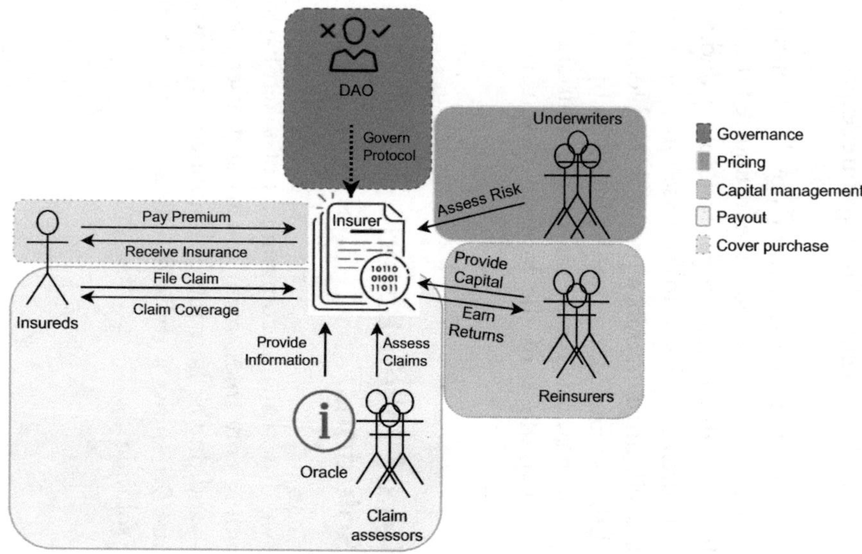

Fig. 9.1 Different actors and actions of a stylized token-based insurance solution

Insureds

Insureds are protection seekers, the target consumers of insurance products and services. They pay premiums—in the form of some cryptocurrency designated by the insurance platform (see section "Payment Token" for further details)—to alleviate the potential negative impact on future hazards. The insureds are financially compensated—again in the form of some cryptocurrency—if the hazard occurs.

Insurer

The insurer's role is typically played by the insurance protocol, which consists of smart contracts that can hold premiums paid in tokens and redistribute funds to insureds with approved claims. For a mutual insurance protocol, insureds are simultaneously owners of the protocol and are entitled to the protocols' premium surplus after claim payout deductions.

Underwriters

Underwriters assess risk levels of uncertain events. If empirical data on the occurrences of a risk event is available, conventional actuarial models are applicable for risk evaluation. This computation can be performed automatically by the protocol itself. In this case, the same party can undertake the insuring and underwriting roles: the protocol. Absent historical statistics, underwriting can be achieved through the wisdom of the crowd. In this case, a group of platform users can express their view on the riskiness of an event by staking their tokens with a quantity of their choice. Should the risk event occur, their stake will be contributed to the cover; otherwise, the users will be awarded, proportionate to their stake, with part of the protocol's premium income.

Reinsurers

Absent reinsurers, an insurance protocol's payout capacity is limited to premiums received. Reinsurance increases an insurance protocol's solvency through an additional layer of financial guarantee. In the decentralized space, the role of the reinsurer is typically assumed by risk-taking investors, who likely share part of the protocol's profit as a form of reinsurance premium, but, expectedly in rare cases, can also suffer losses (Karpischek et al., 2016). In that sense, users who stake tokens on risk events can also be deemed to be reinsurers to a certain extent. Indeed, they inject additional capital to the insurance payout pool and suffer loss when a certain level of risk events is exceeded but earn returns otherwise. With the contribution of their funds, they reduce the capital required by other contributors, thereby reducing the insurer's risk exposure.

Claim Assessors

For certain insured risks, a smart contract can automatically assess the legitimacy of claims by reading data feeds provided by oracles. It is possible to distinguish between centralized oracles and decentralized oracles. Centralized oracles are controlled by a limited number of entities. Data can be fed in through manually emitted transactions or automatically through cross-platform protocols such as Chainlink (2021). Decentralized oracles are typically operated through on-chain protocols, such as price oracles provided by decentralized exchanges with automated market-making protocols (Xu et al., 2022). For claims that are difficult to evaluate automatically, the assessors can be a group of users who express their approval or objection toward the claim with the voting power proportionate to their token holding (usually designated governance tokens). With the voting method, a well-designed incentive and penalty scheme must be in place to encourage honest assessment and deter malicious vote manipulation (Braun et al., 2022).

Decentralized Autonomous Organization

Many new token-based insurance solutions have a decentralized autonomous organization (DAO) as a key component in governing the protocols. DAO is a collective noun referring to everyone eligible to participate in a protocol's governance. Eligibility is often represented by the holding of governance tokens. The decentralized nature of tokens means that no single entity controls the mechanics and economics behind a token. Still, those decisions are made by a community organized around the set of rules imposed by the token (Cointelegraph, 2021). The DAO operates using smart contracts that establish the rules. People with a stake in the DAO are often rewarded with voting rights, frequently in the form of a governance token. Thus, a governance token holder often has a say in how a DAO-governed protocol should change elements like protocol parameters, budgeting and treasury expenditures. In its ultimate form, a change to the DAO is proposed by a community member and voted upon by the governance token holders, after which the proposal gets implemented or not. A DAO can consist of the insurers, insureds, underwriters, claim assessors and governance token holders.

Assets and Tokens

Different from workflows of traditional insurance, token-based insurance solutions are underpinned by a multitude of digital assets and tokens. A permissionless and public blockchain allows anyone to transact and verify transactions with these tokens. As discussed further in this chapter, the token economics (or "tokenomics") defines the utility of each token and the ways the token can be used to incentivize positive behavior in the network.

Payment Token

Most protocols have a designated token for premium payments. The designated premium token can be the same as the denominating currency of a potential payout (e.g. SURE in InsurToken). If they differ, the insureds can often purchase cover in a desired payout currency, usually a widely adopted cryptocurrency such as ETH or DAI (e.g. Nexus Mutual). For user-friendliness, some protocols (e.g. Etherisc) also allow cover to be purchased directly in fiat currency. While different currencies can be accepted, some protocols (e.g. Nexus Mutual) convert all payments in the back-end into a designated token for the ease of accounting, mostly via a decentralized exchange (BraveNewDeFi, 2021b).

Insurance Token

An insurance token represents a certificate of cover obtained by the insured in return for the premium payment. The insurable risk covered by a policy is usually non-transferable, and hence naturally, undividable. Therefore, an insurance policy can be represented by a non-fungible token (NFT), corresponding to the exact risk covered by the policy. However, not every insurance protocol employs insurance tokens. Some protocols rely on immutable on-chain transaction records as proof of cover (such as Nexus Mutual), while others implement hybrid bookkeeping systems with a central database to record insurance purchases. Despite the indivisibility of insurable risk, the beneficiaryship of a policy may be fractionalized and transferred. As such, a tokenized insurance policy would be easily tradable on a blockchain-based secondary market (e.g. fidentiaX, 2021).

Governance Token

In line with decentralization principles, blockchain-based insurance protocols typically employ governance tokens for a distributed sovereignty. First and foremost, governance token holders have voting rights on issues related to protocol-level rules, such as updating the pricing scheme or adding a new insurable risk. Certain protocols also grant governance token holders the voting rights to approve or reject a claim. Governance tokens sometimes also represent ownership of the protocol, where token holders share the profit and loss of the protocol. This representation can be achieved by algorithmically setting the price of the tokens such that the market capitalization of the governance token corresponds with the total funds locked in with the insurance pool contracts (e.g. Nexus Mutual). Governance tokens are sometimes also used for payments, which automatically makes insureds governance token holders, thereby entitling them to a share of the protocol ownership that changes depending on premiums paid and insurance payouts received. Mutual insurance protocols often take this approach.

Processes and Operations

The workings of a specific solution are tied to its processes and operations. The unique selling proposition of a protocol is often embedded in the different use cases that it offers to customers. This section seeks to generalize a set of processes and operations frequently observed in token-based insurance solutions.

Cover Purchase

Insureds can purchase cover against risks using tokens or currencies permitted by the protocol for premium payment (see section "Payment Token"). Insureds can customize the cover by specifying parameters such as the amount insured and coverage period. Depending on the protocol specifications, insurable risks may include:

Financial risks Insurance can cover negative price movements of a crypto asset below a certain reference price. When purchasing such a type of insurance along with the crypto asset, a user is buying the equivalent of a put option where the underlying asset's price is floored.

Security risks Insurance can cover malicious attacks targeting protocols that are underpinned by smart contracts. This type of coverage can provide insurance against the situation where a hacker discovers and exploits a security loophole of a decentralized finance (DeFi) protocol, moving funds from the protocol's smart contract to their address and causing losses on the side of protocol users.

Off-chain hazards Insurance can cover unanticipated, unfortunate events such as flight delays. Oracles are needed to feed data of events that are external to the blockchain into the smart contract (Braun et al., 2021).

Pricing

Depending on the protocol, premiums are set either actuarially using historical data or based on the community's collective view. In the case where users stake tokens to signal their belief on the risk level (see section

"Underwriters"), the less risky a user believes a contingency to be, the more tokens the user is willing to stake. A higher number of tokens staked in a risk pool reduces the cover price, which correspondingly reflects a lower risk level. In short, pricing of an insurance cover pivots on underwriters' work: all other things equal, the riskier the underwriting result of an event shows, the higher the premium. In addition, the price of a particular insurance cover is also positively correlated with the total amount insured and the coverage period.

Payout

Insurance payouts can either be triggered automatically or processed manually through individually filed claims. In the former case, once information on the occurrence of the events is fed into the insurance smart contract, the payout function is activated, and the affected insureds are immediately compensated. For off-chain risk events, the provision of external data is done by oracles. In the latter case, the legitimacy of a claim is determined with human judgement by the protocol team or a group of claim assessors and through a poll with all eligible protocol participants.

Capital Management

Insurance protocols can have a capital model that determines the minimum capital to be held, a metric often set to similar standards as EIOPA's Solvency II (EIOPA, 2020), which ensures a confidence level of 99.5% in solvency over one year. Generally, there are two types of cash flows. First, insureds purchase coverage by paying a premium to a capital pool and the capital pool pays customers in case there is an accepted claim. Second, the funds in the capital pool can be invested to generate returns (BraveNewDeFi, 2021a). In the unlikely event that the reserves in the capital pool are completely depleted, capital from other sources must be employed. The governance token holders would likely make this decision. Out of the six biggest insurance protocols listed on Coinmarketcap (2021), there have not yet been any known instances of insolvency, and no concrete procedure of how to handle such a situation has been documented.

Governance

A governance token holder has a say in how to shape the protocol. In its ultimate form, a change to the protocol is proposed by a community member and voted upon by governance token holders. A decision is never made by only a select group of developers but rather by the whole community that holds voting rights. Governance token holders can take part in underwriting, assessing and deciding on larger changes to the entire insurance protocol.

Comparison of Existing Decentralized Insurance Protocols

This section compares three major insurance protocols by market capitalization: Nexus Mutual, Etherisc and inSure (Table 9.1).

The dominant market position of these protocols indicates a certain level of industry recognition. With a heterogeneous pool of actions, these protocols each have their unique take on a generalized framework.

Nexus Mutual

Nexus Mutual is a decentralized insurance protocol. The platform token, NXM, has several functionalities, including governance, the ability to purchase cover and the ability to vote on claims. The first version of the application went live on the Ethereum mainnet in May 2019. As of August 2021, the protocol has an active cover amount of over 500 million USD (Nexus Mutual Tracker, 2021). Customers of Nexus Mutual can insure themselves against three main types of risks: the risk of a yield token losing its peg ("yield token cover"), the risk of protocol failures ("protocol cover") and the risk of hacks or halted withdrawals on exchanges or custodial wallets ("custody cover"). Customers can pay in ETH or DAI to buy a cover, which gets automatically converted to NXM by the smart contracts. Bought covers are not tokenized but kept by a central system. If a customer suffers a loss and believes this loss qualifies for the bought cover, they can file a claim. The cost of filing a claim is integrated into the initial

Table 9.1 Comparison between major token-based insurance solutions

Protocol	Native token	Market cap (million USD)	Native token functionality	Tokenized cover	Claim assessment	Capital model
Nexus Mutual	NXM	815.8	– Governance – Cover purchase – Claim assessment	No	Decentralized, through NXM holders	Based on EIOPA Solvency II, 99.5% confidence
inSure	SURE	108.4	– Governance – Cover purchase – Claim assessment	Yes, SURE token itself	Centralized and decentralized, through auditing companies and SURE holders	Based on EIOPA Solvency II, 99.9% confidence
Etherisc	DIP	25.0	– Reward risk taking – Monetizing services	Yes, via Risk Pool tokens	Depends on product	Based on EIOPA Solvency II, 99.99% confidence

Market cap equals native token price times its circulating supply, data retrieved on 31 August 2021 from https://coinmarketcap.com/

amount paid for the cover. After the claim is correctly filed, the outcome is determined by "claim assessors", NXM holders who stake a portion of their NXM. Assessors acting in good faith are rewarded. Those who act fraudulently can be punished by having part of their staked NXM burned. With the help of "Incentivai", a machine learning algorithm that checks user behavior, the advisory board of Nexus Mutual determines whether or not an act is "fraudulent" (Nexus Mutual, 2021).

A final functionality of the NXM token is its use in a process called "risk assessment". "Risk Assessors" can stake NXM in a specific cover of which they believe the risk of an eventual payout is small. This extra capital decreases the premium for that specific cover. Through staking, Risk Assessors earn proportional rewards in NXM equivalent to 50% of the cover premium paid by insureds. This way of incentivizing investors allows the Nexus Mutual protocol to attract more capital. In the event of a payout, the Risk Assessor loses some or all of their deposit. The protocol capital requirements are determined by a capital model that borrows heavily from EIOPA's Solvency II (Karp & Melbardis, 2017). The price of NXM is determined depending on the reserves in the capital pool and the required funds, which, in turn, affects the whole ecosystem.

Etherisc

Etherisc is a protocol that allows anyone to create their insurance products by providing common infrastructure, product templates and insurance license-as-a-service. At the moment, two insurance products have been launched: Crop Insurance and Flight Delay Insurance. Other applications such as Hurricane Protection and Crypto Wallet Insurance are either in the design or prototype phase (Etherisc, 2021). The platform token, DIP, is a core element in the overarching protocol and incentivizes and rewards platform users for bringing risk to the network and building and maintaining products. Specifically, the token is used to buy insurance products, reward users for updating risk models (similar to the Risk Assessors in Nexus Mutual), reward those that provide reliable data/oracles and reward a multitude of other stakeholders. Next to the platform token, Etherisc introduces Risk Pool Tokens, the tokenized versions of insurance products, allowing a token marketplace where participants can purchase and redeem tokenized covers. The combination of a "risk pool" and a "reinsurance pool" ensures that long-tail events are covered and that there is always enough capital to pay claims. The required capital is also calculated based on the EIOPA Solvency II model, but Etherisc imposes a 99.99% confidence level instead of 99.5%.

inSure

inSure is a decentralized insurance protocol that focuses on protecting traders' portfolios against scams, devaluations and stolen funds. The company launched its first features in 2019 and is currently fully operational and progressing on making the assessment and payment processes fully automated. The platform token, SURE, has multiple functionalities, including governance, claim assessments and the ability to purchase cover. Customers of inSure buy cover by buying SURE tokens. This model differs from the Nexus Mutual cover, where one buys specific covers with the NXM token. SURE tokens are the cover, which means they are transferable. The insured buys a certain number of SURE tokens to insure oneself corresponding with a specific inSurance plan (inSure, 2021a). After acquiring and holding SURE tokens for seven days in their wallet, the insured is covered against multiple risks up to a certain level, depending on the insurance plan. If a customer's portfolio is affected by a scam, devaluation or stolen funds, they can file a claim. That claim is voted upon by auditing companies and SURE holders if there is a challenge to the consensus of the auditing companies. It is not clear whether these parties are incentivized for correct behavior. As of August 2021, there remains a lack of publicly available documentation on inSure's capital model. There is a capital pool and a "surplus pool". The capital pool's goal is to support business development. The surplus pool accrues money by collecting premiums paid by customers and is intended to cover all claims. When the surplus pool cannot cover all claims, the capital pool will be used to cover the shortfall.

Other Insurance-Related Solutions on Blockchain

Besides the peer-to-peer coverage applications listed in the previous section, other protocols also have a relation to the insurance industry, but are not deemed to be insurance specific in the conventional sense. Example applications are insurance marketplaces, financial markets that allow hedging positions and protocols offering protection to borrowers against liquidation of collateral.

fidentiaX

fidentiaX is a marketplace for life insurance trading on blockchain. The company raised funds through an ICO (initial coin offering) in late 2017, where the platform's native FDX were distributed to investors in exchange for ETH. On fidentiaX, insureds list their life insurance policy that interested buyers can bid for. The winning buyer pays the insured a lump sum while the insured transfers the beneficiaryship of the policy. After the transaction, the buyer takes over the premium payment and is entitled to receive the maturity benefit of the insurance policy (Braun et al., 2020). The platform is still in the prototype phase. As per the design, three types of tokens are intended to be employed on the platform: (1) ERC-20-based tokens to represent insurance policies, (2) FDX for bidding and (3) stablecoin for payment.

Opyn

Options in financial markets can be utilized for multiple purposes, but in the context of insurance, they function as instruments that can hedge risk. Opyn is a DeFi option and insurance platform that provides protection and hedging instruments for DeFi deposits and ETH risk. The first version of the Opyn protocol offered protection for USDC and DAI deposits on Compound (Perez et al., 2021). The current second version of the Opyn protocol allows anyone to buy, sell and create options on any ERC20 asset.

These options are cash-settled European options, whose exercise date coincide with their expiration date. Opyn option products can be created with oTokens, an ERC20-compatible contract that represents the option product. The protocol states that over 1 billion USD notional volume of options have been traded with over 20,000 trades. Its core developers and investors currently govern the platform.

Backd

Backd provides assurance to users of lending protocols such as Compound and Aave (Xu & Vadgama, 2022). Backd describes itself as "reactive liquidity", preventing undercollateralized loans from becoming liquidated. Backd aims to increase the capital efficiency of asset borrowing in DeFi, where borrowers do not need to exceedingly overcollateralize their loan position in fear of automatically triggered liquidation. Instead, borrowers delegate fund management to the Backd protocol, which tops up collateral whenever a loan position is on the verge of being liquidated, while using the excess capital for yield farming, an investment activity in DeFi (Cousaert et al. 2022).

Discussion

Still, in its infancy, the token-based insurance space is very early within its evolution. While the blockchain industry is witnessing a huge wave of interest due to the booming DeFi industry, DeFi projects are currently dominated by lending protocols and decentralized exchanges. Nexus Mutual, with a total value locked (TVL)—the quantity of tokens secured in the DeFi application's smart contracts—of half a billion USD as of August 2021 (DefiLlama, 2021), prides itself as the largest token-based insurance project but ranks only 24th of all DeFi projects by TVL. Despite the immaturity of the token-based insurance sector and the lack of attention received relative to other DeFi areas, many benefits can already be seen. Indeed, some challenges remain unsolved and have not been tested. In this section, we briefly explore these.

Benefits

Efficient Risk Transfer

Conventionally, systemic risks can be transferred to the capital market: for instance, exposure to catastrophe risk can be packaged and sold in the form of CAT bonds. Similarly, risks can be easily passed on to the capital market with tokenization and thus reduce or even render moot capital requirements on the insurer's side. By shifting the risk completely onto the capital markets, blockchain-based insurance protocols can act solely as a risk bundling and dividing machine, thus evading regulation applied by conventional insurance companies. Tokenization also makes secondary sales easier. If a purchased cover is tokenized, customers can create a secondary market for insurances. In that case, buying and selling commonly issued covers can be handled outside of a specific ecosystem. A centralized layer on top of issuing the covers complicates the selling and transferring of insurance for those who want to monetize their policy or simply move their funds or activities to another address. Tokenizing purchased cover would address these issues. Fungible tokens can be used to set up a secondary market on a decentralized exchange such as Uniswap for people to trade their purchased cover. If the cover is highly personalized or unique, a non-fungible token will offer similar advantages, although a more specialized market will be needed.

Transparency

In case all aspects from the purchase of cover to claims and payout are on a blockchain means the entire insurance process is visible end-to-end. This transparency enables participants in the ecosystem to investigate for themselves whether a protocol is trustworthy. Indeed, the growth and success of a protocol depend on good behavior from its community concerning the entire underwriting and claims assessment processes—in stark contrast to traditional insurance products where this trajectory is opaque, which often leads to poor customer experience. Oracles are also utilized to provide relevant information for the assessment of claims.

These oracles can also be decentralized in nature, meaning that there is further transparency in how information relevant to a claim is handled, where this information has come from and what relevant references have been used.

Security

Security within a token-based insurance protocol is strengthened through several technological and systematic features. Starting with technological features, without discussing the security features of a blockchain system and smart contracts in detail—one of the main points is that the working code of these protocols is visible for anyone to audit. This transparency can help create a secure system whereby faults in a protocol are easily spotted and corrected. Such an environment also inspires trust in a protocol itself as users (who can read the code) are confident in the performance and behavior of the system. With respect to security in the sense of trusting the process of underwriting and claims management, the decentralized autonomous organizations (DAOs) that manage these protocols are composed of governance token holders who are able to vote on the management and direction of the protocol. This decentralized approach can help improve the ecosystem's security as the community is incentivized to act in the best interests of the protocol to support an increasing token price. A secure protocol features a good design with a strong incentive for correct reporting and a strong disincentive for fraudulent behavior. As such, whenever an incident occurs, and a customer files a claim, holders of the platform token can use their vote to decide whether that claim is justified and if that incident falls under the bought cover.

The security of a protocol is dependent on the token design that creates functionalities to optimize the operational efficiency of the service. For example, the token can be used to incentivize correct behavior and disincentivize fraud, reward participants for the correct pricing of the insurance services, or reward people outside of the network for providing reliable data through oracles or manual processes.

Customization and Agility

Tokens can have many functions programmed into them, which do not rely on single entity intermediaries for overseeing and maintaining those functions, as they are automatically enforced by the smart contracts which can be updated or enhanced through community governance processes. In the context of insurance protocols, tokens and smart contracts can be used to improve cover customization, connecting insurers and insureds faster. In addition to customization, there is a great deal of agility in how insurance protocols can deal with claims through their community governance systems, and indeed agility in the direction of the protocol itself. Insurance protocols operating as DAOs with governance tokens can upgrade themselves, thus altering the practices for underwriting and claims through invoking voting of governance token holders to pass decisions. This gives these new protocols agility in evolving and responding to changes in their markets in a way that traditional insurance players just cannot do.

Challenges

Lack of Contingency Plan for Insolvency

Existing protocols do not seem to have any contingency plan for insolvency in place. Although most protocols follow the Minimum Capital Requirements (MCR) standards from EIOPA's Solvency II to a certain extent, there is simply not enough data for confident actuarial modeling of the risks insured. According to the UK Financial Services Compensation Scheme (FSCS), there have been 38 insurance defaults within the traditional insurance sector since 1985 that the FSCS has been involved with (FSCS, 2021). In the UK, if an insurer becomes insolvent, the FSCS will cover up to 90% of an insured's claim (subject to certain limits and eligibility of the policy). In addition to protecting insureds through government insurance schemes, an efficient reinsurance market enables traditional insurance players to diversify risks. Within the token-based insurance sector, this reinsurance or government backed insurance does not exist and contingencies from protocols have not been elucidated.

Low Competition and Participation

One could argue that there is a monopoly player within this sector: Nexus Mutual stands as the largest player, with other projects not having seen many projects built on top of their protocols (e.g., Etherisc with only Crop Insurance and Flight Delay Insurance) or with little participation (e.g. inSure). Between March and August 2021, only ten insurance claims were raised on inSure (inSure, 2021b). Out of these, only one was approved. The other nine were rejected due to not meeting policy requirements. Furthermore, the participation in voting was extremely low, with many claims not receiving any votes. These protocols are indeed new and evolving. In the case of Etherisc, many new insurance products have been designed and are awaiting licensing. In the case of inSure, their roadmap still includes several features to be built to increase participation in the protocol (running through to 2022).

Fragile Incentive and Penalty Mechanism

Just like insurance companies, a DAO exhibits a reluctance to approve claim requests. Understandably, since a DAO has the incentive, at least in the short run, to retain funds within the protocol whenever possible instead of disbursing them to cover an individual's loss. In the long run, one may argue that persistent reluctance to approve claims will result in diminishing attraction of the protocol to end users, which will subsequently lead to a depreciation of protocol tokens and thus a devaluation of a DAO's token holding. This negative consequence would discourage a DAO from blindly rejecting all incoming claims to ensure the user base, and hence, the value of the protocol. Therefore, theoretically, at equilibrium, a DAO should exert sufficient discretion to scrutinize claims. On the one hand, opportunistic and fraudulent claims are screened out to ensure the profitability of the protocol. On the other hand, legitimate claims are needed to get compensated to ensure users' welfare. Unfortunately, current insurance protocol users have exhibited a short-term orientation which the pseudonymous nature of blockchain applications may have exacerbated. Fraudulent behavior is also an issue from both claimants and voting members. Looking at inSure, several claims filed incorrect reference events that did not occur. On Nexus Mutual, there is at least one incident where an insured submitted a false claim and then subsequently voted for it (Nexus Mutual, 2021).

Centralization

By definition, a decentralized protocol should be designed to operate, evolve and grow even after the original development team and the protocol foundation has disbanded. However, current insurance protocols exhibit centralization in many ways. First, most protocol teams take full charge in either the pre-screening of claims or the ultimate judgement on the legitimacy of claims, representing a concentration of power and a single point of failure. Second, existing voting schemes might trigger the so-called Matthew effect. Specifically, users who hold a lot of wealth will influence the voting result to their favor, compounding the accumulation of wealth and power. Protocols as such are thus vulnerable to majority attacks, where a user or a group of colluding users holding a significant proportion of the governance token supply can submit false claims and vote in favor of them, pocketing profit from the protocol.

Conclusion and Outlook

In this chapter, we have described how many players are using blockchain technology and tokens to create novel insurance products that utilize new technology and business models to cover new types of risk and improve customer experience. Tokens seek to facilitate flexibly designed and openly auditable insurance policies, which is in stark contrast with traditional insurance products. However, the new token-based insurance industry is at a nascent stage. We have discussed many of the benefits and challenges that face this fledgling industry, and the success or failure of this industry ultimately depends on secure and sound protocol design and practical tokenomics.

In the current stage of the industry, there have been many protocols and DeFi projects that have come to the fold but have quickly disappeared, either due to poor and insecure protocol design or simply due to business models where the tokenomics have not garnered a community to develop them. Nexus Mutual is the leading project in the space, and others are still slowly emerging. As interest in the whole DeFi sector increases and as the exchange and lending sub-sectors mature, the insurance sector is likely to gain increased attention. Nexus Mutual boasted over 1.2 billion USD in cover at its peak in 2021 and currently has active cover of approximately 200 million USD out until January 2022. For a new platform with a niche insurance product, these are promising numbers. The Minimum Capital Requirements have also been greater than 100%, reaching as much as 200% at times in 2020. Of the 95 claims made to date, 18 were accepted and paid out over 10 million USD (Nexus Mutual Tracker, 2021). Although these claims currently relate to DeFi and Smart Contract risk, more conventional consumer use case products are also developing and slowly emerging, as we have seen in the case of Etherisc. As the DeFi movement increases in size, more attention from new adopters will turn to these new insurance products as well.

Finally, the blockchain itself and the use of tokens have seen use in the traditional insurance sectors, with many proof-of-concept projects taking place and being delivered to consumers. This development is still at an early stage, and inevitably, as the exploration and use of blockchain as an infrastructure in the traditional insurance industry increases, so will the use of tokens. This moment may be the inflection point for the token-based insurance industry to challenge traditional insurance markets.

Acknowledgments The authors thank Niklas Häusle, Vincent Piscaer, Juan Ignacio Ibañez, Matthew Sheridan, and the editors Horst Treiblmaier and Mary C. Lacity for their valuable comments.

References

B3i. (2021a). *B3i—The blockchain insurance industry initiative*. Retrieved August 23, 2021, from https://b3i.tech/home.html

B3i. (2021b). *What we do—B3i*. Retrieved August 23, 2021, from https://b3i.tech/what-we-do.html

Braun, A., Cohen, L. H., & Xu, J. (2020). fidentiaX: The tradable insurance marketplace on blockchain. *Harvard Business School Case*, 219–116.

Braun, A., Häusle, N., & Karpischek, S. (2021). Decentralized autonomous risk transfer on the blockchain. In *The Routledge handbook of FinTech* (pp. 69–78). Routledge. Retrieved August 23, 2021, from https://doi.org/10.4324/9780429292903-7

Braun, A., Häusle, N., & Karpischek, S. (2022). *Governance of Decentralized Autonomous Organizations*. Retrieved 17 June, 2022, from https://doi.org/10.2139/ssrn.3760531

BraveNewDeFi. (2021a). *Glossary & appendices—Nexus mutual*. Retrieved August 23, 2021, from https://nexusmutual.gitbook.io/docs/welcome/glossary-and-appendices#defined-terms

BraveNewDeFi. (2021b). *NXM token*. Retrieved August 23, 2021, from https://nexusmutual.gitbook.io/docs/users/understanding-nexus-mutual/nxm-token

CB Insights. (2021, August 2). *How blockchain is disrupting insurance*. Retrieved August 23, 2021, from https://www.cbinsights.com/research/blockchain-insurance-disruption/

Chainlink. (2021). *Blockchain Oracles for hybrid smart contracts*. Retrieved August 23, 2021, from https://chain.link/

ClaimShare. (2021). *ClaimShare home page*. Retrieved August 23, 2021, from https://claimshare.intellecteu.com/

CoinMarketCap. (2021). *Top insurance tokens by market capitalization*. Retrieved August 23, 2021, from https://coinmarketcap.com/view/insurance/

Cointelegraph. (2021). *What is a decentralized autonomous organization, and how does a DAO work?* Retrieved August 23, 2021, from https://cointelegraph.com/ethereum-for-beginners/what-is-dao

Cousaert, S., Xu, J., & Matsui, T. (2022). SoK: Yield Aggregators in DeFi. *IEEE International Conference on Blockchain and Cryptocurrency (ICBC)*. https://doi.org/10.1109/ICBC54727.2022.9805523

DefiLlama. (2021). *Nexus mutual protocol: TVL and stats*. Retrieved August 23, 2021, from https://defillama.com/protocol/nexus-mutual

Dewan, N. (2008). *Indian life and health insurance industry*. Gabler. Retrieved August 23, 2021, from 10.1007/978-3-8349-9788-3

EIOPA. (2020). *Solvency II*. Retrieved August 23, 2021, from https://www.eiopa.europa.eu/browse/solvency-2_en

Etherisc. (2021). *Etherisc—Decentralized insurance*. Retrieved August 23, 2021, from https://etherisc.com/

FSCS. (2021). *Insurance insolvencies*. Retrieved August 23, 2021, from https://www.fscs.org.uk/what-wecover/insurance/insurance-insolvencies/

fidentiaX. (2021). *fidentiaX—World's 1st marketplace for tradable insurance policies*. Retrieved August 23, 2021, from https://www.fidentiax.com/

inSure. (2021a). *Crypto & DeFi insurance plans*. Retrieved August 23, 2021, from https://insuretoken.net/plans.html

inSure. (2021b). *inSure Snapshot page*. Retrieved August 23, 2021, from https://snapshot.org/#/insuretoken.eth

Karp, H., & Melbardis, R. (2017). *Nexus mutual: A peer-to-peer discretionary mutual on the Ethereum blockchain*. Retrieved August 23, 2021, from https://nexusmutual.io/assets/docs/nmx_white_paperv2_3.pdf

Karpischek, S., Mussenbrock, C., Brukhman, J., & Bernstein, R. (2016). *Etherisc: A decentralized insurance and reinsurance marketplace*. Retrieved August 23, 2021, from https://etherisc.com/files/etherisc_whitepaper_0.3_en.pdf

Nexus Mutual. (2021). *Claims assessment*. Retrieved August 23, 2021 from https://nexusmutual.gitbook.io/docs/welcome/faq/claims-assessment#have-any-claims-assessors-had-their-nxm-stake-burned-for-fraudulent-voting-during-the-claims-assessment-process

Nexus Mutual Tracker. (2021). *Nexus mutual tracker*. Retrieved August 23, 2021, from https://nexustracker.io/

Perez, D., Werner, S. M., Xu, J., & Livshits, B. (2021). Liquidations: DeFi on a Knife-edge. *Financial Cryptography and Data Security*, 457–476. https://doi.org/10.1007/978-3-662-64331-0_24

StateFarm. (2021, January 26). *Blockchain Solution Solves State Farm®, USAA Subrogation Challenge*. Retrieved August 23, 2021, from https://newsroom.statefarm.com/blockchain-solution-solves-state-farm-usaa-subrogation-challenge/

Vaughan, E. J. (1996). *Risk management*. Wiley.

Xu, J., Paruch, K., Cousaert, S., & Feng, Y. (2022). *SoK: Decentralized exchanges (DEX) with automated market maker (AMM) protocols*. https://doi.org/10.48550/arXiv.2103.12732

Xu, J., & Vadgama, N. (2022). From Banks to DeFi: The Evolution of the Lending Market. In N. Vadgama, J. Xu, & P. Tasca (Eds.), *Enabling the Internet of Value* (pp. 53–66). Springer. https://doi.org/10.1007/978-3-030-78184-2_6

Xu, T. A., & Xu, J. (2022). A Short Survey on Business Models of Decentralized Finance (DeFi) Protocols. *Workshop Proceedings of Financial Cryptography and Data Security*. https://doi.org/10.48550/arxiv.2202.07742

10

Revisiting Blockchain Token Sales: How Crypto Companies Raise(D) Money

Esther Nagel and Johann Kranz

Introduction

Start-up financing has been a topic of practical and academic relevance for decades. Just as the start-ups' business models, their chosen funding mechanisms often take on innovative, state-of-the-art forms. Crowdfunding, namely, the collection of funds from many parties, often in small denomination, became popular for fundraising as platforms such as Indiegogo and kickstarter.com emerged in 2008 and 2009, respectively. The phenomenon of crowdfunding reached new momentum with the emergence of blockchain technology (BT). Crypto companies started to embrace BT's tokenization affordance by creating and issuing

Note: earlier versions of this chapter's contents were published in the journal *Business and Information Systems Engineering* (BISE) 2019 and in the proceedings of the conference *European Conference on Information Systems (ECIS) 2020.*

E. Nagel (✉) • J. Kranz
LMU Munich, Munich, Germany
e-mail: nagel@bwl.lmu.de; kranz@bwl.lmu.de

M. C. Lacity, H. Treiblmaier (eds.), *Blockchains and the Token Economy*, Technology, Work and Globalization, https://doi.org/10.1007/978-3-030-95108-5_10

company-specific tokens to buyers all over the world. Attracted by numerous design options around arising token standards, a regulatory void, the absence of intermediary costs, conventional investor oversight and profit shares, as well as a bullish cryptocurrency market, start-ups raised more than USD 20 billion through token sales (TSs) in the years 2017 and 2018. In 2018, an average of 482 token sales opened every day. While these TSs collected USD 12.75 million on average, a large share of the sum went to few, big projects such as EOS, an operating system for decentralized applications (dApps), which collected USD 4.1 billion, and the messenger app Telegram, which raised USD 1.7 billion (PWC, 2018; Coindesk, 2018).

Blockchain technology's decentralized, immutable, and transparent nature allows issuers to cut out many of the intermediaries present in traditional venture financing, such as banks, venture capital firms, or payment providers (Haas et al., 2015; Sunyaev et al., 2021). The benefits that occur through TSs are summarized in Fig. 10.1. Owing to low investment barriers and an aim to attract a large number of investors, TSs were often seen as a vehicle to democratize start-up funding. Besides these features, TS differ from traditional crowdfunding and other forms of entrepreneurial financing, such as business angel or venture capital investments, in several important ways. For investors, TSs are associated with higher asset flexibility and liquidity, since tokens can be bought in

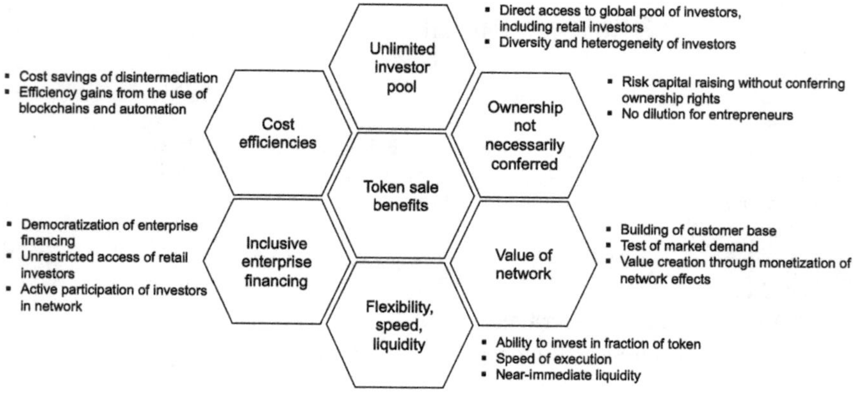

Fig. 10.1 Benefits of token sales. (Illustration adapted from OECD, 2019)

fractions as desired and can usually be traded on crypto exchanges after a TS. Additionally, rights can be associated with the token, ranging from access to or discounts for services and products to profit or voting rights. For issuers, TSs offer a relatively easy and fast way to raise capital, to economize on fees otherwise charged by intermediaries, and to unilaterally specify investment terms. However, economic and regulatory uncertainties and rising marketing and consulting costs soon started to increasingly exacerbate the execution of TSs (Amsden & Schweizer, 2018). From a buyer's perspective, established trust-building intermediaries are largely absent and high information asymmetries complicate due diligence, a situation that has been exploited by several fraudulent TSs (Kaal & Dell'Erba, 2017; Amsden & Schweizer, 2018).

In this hyped setting of the years 2017 and 2018, we first conducted research on token sales. In Kranz et al. (2019), we introduce token sales as a new form of crowdfunding and research field in the information systems discipline. Through a description of the TS ecosystem, market designs, and technological implications, we derive a research agenda along the dimensions *design and features*, *measurement and value*, *management and organization*, and *regulations and legal*. One recurring issue we observed was the role of trust in TS. While blockchain is sometimes denoted as a "trustfree technology" (Beck et al., 2016), Hawlitschek et al. (2018) assess a trust frontier when transactions involve real-world interactions in lieu of purely virtual representations. The authors state a need for trusted interfaces in blockchain-based decentralized markets. In Nagel and Kranz (2020), we aim to shed light on the nature of technological artefacts embedded in TS processes, and on how they work as interfaces for overcoming the trust frontier. We find that while some factors equally create trust in traditional crowdfunding and in TSs, TSs give rise to new trust-building technological artefacts (e.g., code hosting services, crypto exchanges) or increase the importance of existing artefacts (e.g., social media platforms).

In this chapter, we revisit the main findings of the aforementioned studies. The next sections summarize the initial TS process and its accompanying activities. We will then consider the scope and roles of trust-building technological artefacts in TS. Finally, we aim to highlight recent developments in crypto company funding and the TS phenomenon. TSs prove to be a highly dynamic concept, continuously responding to technological, organizational, and environmental factors. We therefore also include recent developments, including the shift to security token offerings (STOs), initial exchange offerings (IEOs), and the rise of decentralized finance (DeFi) start-up and funding activity. We end this chapter with a summary and outlook on crypto company funding.

From Blockchain Technology to Token Sales

A blockchain refers to a shared databank that uses cryptography and a decentralized consensus mechanism to enable peer-to-peer transactions. In a TS, the issuing entity generates cryptographic tokens which can be bought by investors. The change of ownership is registered on the blockchain, a distributed ledger that allows for decentralized and immutable transaction recording (Beck et al., 2017; Notheisen et al., 2017). New transactions, grouped in blocks, are only added to the blockchain after so-called miners have verified their legitimacy. In the most common consensus mechanism, called proof-of-work, miners compete to solve a hash function (e.g., SHA-256) to approve a block of transactions for which they get remunerated. Once a miner has found the correct solution to the non-invertible hash function and the majority of network participants agree with the proposed solution, the block can be added to the chain. Beyond "maintaining a coherent set of facts between multiple participating nodes" (Swan, 2015, p. 4), consensus mechanisms also secure the distributed ledger from attacks and prevent double spending of cryptographic assets.

The Token Sale Ecosystem

Smart contracts play a central role in the implementation and execution of an Initial Coin Offering (ICO). A smart contract is source code stored on the blockchain. It defines a set of rules for the interaction of two or more parties. The terms defined in a smart contract are automatically executed if the prespecified conditions are met. In the case of an ICO, these rules concern settings such as token price or sale duration. Most ICOs have built upon the Ethereum blockchain protocol (Buterin, 2014). In contrast to the Bitcoin blockchain, Ethereum enables (quasi) Turing complete smart contracts. Issuers use smart contracts to generate (a process also called minting) and allot tokens with a set of customized properties. Once the ICO goes live, the smart contract is activated and can receive funds from investors, mostly in the form of cryptocurrencies such as Bitcoin or Ether. Upon reception of these funds, smart contracts issue a corresponding number of tokens to the investor and transfer the received funds to the issuer's wallet. These transactions are verified by miners and stored on a blockchain. After a TS, the tokens can be listed on crypto exchanges such as Binance, Coinbase Exchange, or Huobi Global to be traded by token holders. Figure 10.2 illustrates the ecosystem of a TS.

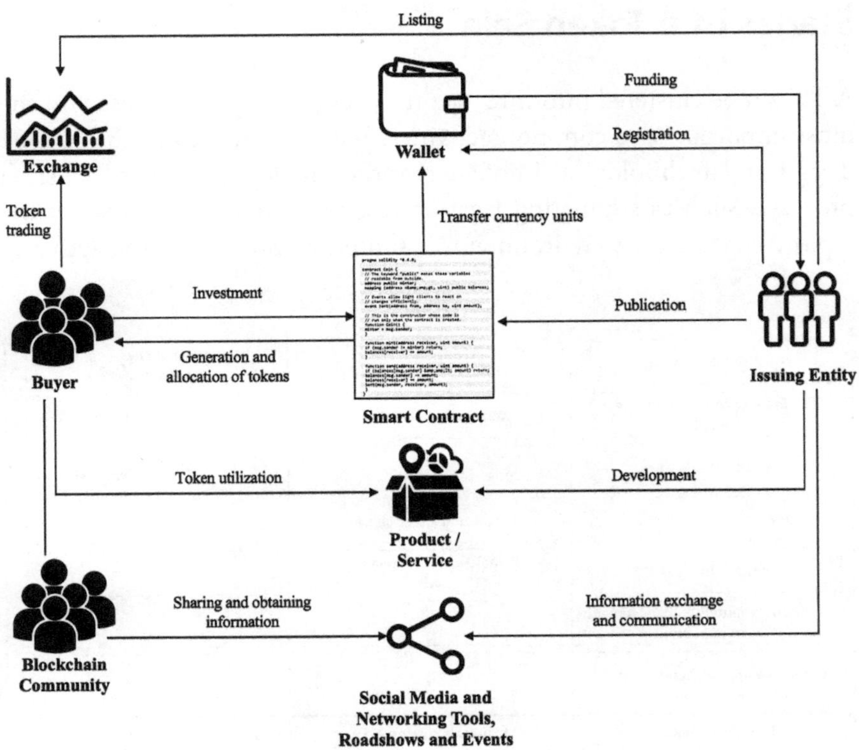

Fig. 10.2 The token sale ecosystem (Kranz et al., 2019)

As depicted in Fig. 10.2, in a TS, an issuer sells proprietary blockchain-based digital crypto tokens in exchange for a direct payment, usually in a cryptocurrency (Barsan, 2017; Rohr & Wright, 2018). The rights given to token holders are specified in a whitepaper that is published on the issuing organization's website. The token issuing organization also must determine a token design model and issuing structure in accordance with regulatory rules and business considerations. Token sale consultants support the issuing team in legal, marketing, and business development decisions or advise TS buyers (Fahlenbrach & Frattaroli, 2019; Kranz et al., 2019). The properties of tokens differ widely. Tokens can be tied to access rights to in-application offers, governance powers, or profit shares (Adhami et al., 2018).

Stages of a Token Sale

A TS can be clustered into three main stages (see Fig. 10.3) based on the most important and common activities. We concentrate on TSs' market design and technological implementation and less on issuers' internal processes such as stipulating legal or vesting structures. Because of the rapidly changing TS environment, it should be noted that the activities

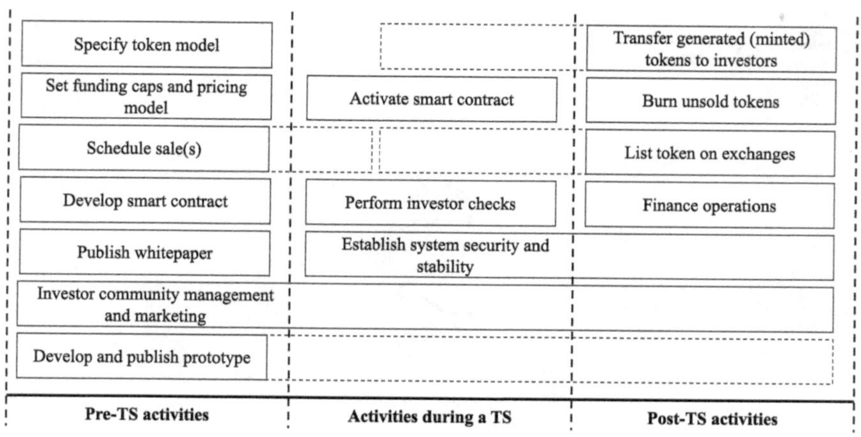

Fig. 10.3 Process of a token sale (Kranz et al., 2019)

and their timing vary considerably between TSs. Our focus is on the most typical TS configurations. In lieu of traditional intermediaries, a myriad of technology artifacts connects different stakeholders and is thus used to enable and support TSs.

Pre-TS Activities

In the pre-TS stage, issuers select a market design from various options and determine a token model that aligns with the issuers' business model and strategy and with the investors' interests. First, issuers determine a token type. There are four main types. *Donation tokens* are not linked to any rights or claims for a future product or service and are used to gather funds for idealistic entrepreneurial ideas or causes. *Currency tokens* serve as virtual currencies on the issuers' blockchain protocol and can be used to pay for products or services. They are often used when TS issuers set up a new blockchain protocol. *Utility tokens* serve as "digital coupons" which can be redeemed for issuers' offerings or to gain access to a platform or application. In most early TS, utility tokens were issued because of regulatory issues and product popularization (Pietrewicz, 2018; Adhami et al., 2018). Finally, *security tokens* are tokens that give investors rights to a pro-rata share of future profits, for example, dividend or revenue share. A subcategory of security tokens are *equity tokens*, which additionally provide control or voting rights. Due to their resemblance to securities, for which strict regulatory rules exist, security tokens are the most disputed token type from a regulatory perspective (SEC, 2017; BaFin, 2018).

Second, in the majority of TSs, issuers set caps on the maximum supply of tokens that can be generated in a TS and specify the value of a token. Some TSs do not limit the supply of tokens, which allows issuers to raise an unlimited amount of funding. However, token oversupply can have negative implications for token valuation and issuer reputation. In capped TSs, issuers determine a lower and/or upper limit of funding. In the case of a lower limit, a so-called soft cap, the invested funds are paid back to investors if the defined soft cap is not reached. A hard cap defines the maximum amount of funding an issuer seeks to raise. Once this limit is reached, no more investments are accepted by the smart contract. A variant of the hard cap model is "collect and return", in which a hard cap exists, but additional investments beyond the hard cap are accepted by the smart contract. In this case, after the TS, the tokens are distributed to investors by the ratio of the hard cap to the total received funds. Excess funding is redistributed to investors accordingly. To ensure a broad token distribution, issuers can use a "dynamic ceiling" model in which the hard cap is divided into multiple (hidden) mid caps. In this way, the TS proceeds into multiple, isolated rounds to avoid dominance of major investors. Another market design option for issuers to remain key token holders is to limit the circulating supply of tokens by holding back a certain share of tokens.

Third, issuers set the pricing model. In case of capped token sales, fixed prices may be set either arbitrarily by the token issuing entity, or, less commonly, a floating price is determined by an auctioning model. In Dutch auctions, the issuing entity allocates its tokens to the highest bidders and the token is charged at the lowest accepted bid's price. In a reverse Dutch auction, only a specified share of overall tokens is offered per day and the price per token declines with every day that the TS is active, until the defined funding goal is reached.

Fourth, another market design option important for TSs is the schedule of token sales. Many issuers run one or multiple rounds of exclusive TS pre-sales before opening the TS to the public in a main sale. In pre-sales, selected investors have the opportunity to buy tokens at significantly lower prices than in the main sale. Pre-sales allow issuers to attract renowned key investors, explore demand, create attention for the main sale, and test and finance the main sale. A disadvantage is that pre-investors have an incentive to sell discounted tokens at regular prices as soon as the main sale launches or the token becomes tradable, respectively. Token issuing entities may therefore impose one or multiple lock-up period(s) in which newly acquired tokens must not be traded. It can be observed that an increasing number of TSs refrains from main sales due to the lower regulatory requirements pre-sales are subjected to. For instance, the messaging service Telegram canceled its main sale after achieving the funding goal in two rounds of private sales. In pre-sales, investors are granted rights to the future token through a Simple Agreement for Future Tokens (SAFT, see www.saftproject.com).

Once issuers finalize these design options, the issuing entity develops a smart contract which administers funds and tokens during the TS. It is programmed to receive cryptocurrencies from investors, to send them to the digital wallets of the issuing entity, and to transfer the equivalent number of tokens to investors. The tokens typically follow Ethereum's ERC-20 token standard (Vogelsteller & Buterin, 2015) which allows developers to create customized and standardized tokens with relative ease. ERC stands for "Ethereum Request for Comments", the command protocol of the Ethereum blockchain, which runs on programming language Solidity, which is similar to java script. The ERC-20 token standard includes all specifications required for a TS and ensures that tokens will be compatible with generic third-party transaction services and applications. The issuer can specify the TS by setting parameters, such as total token supply, burning rules, funding goal and duration, freezing options, and token value bound to a cryptocurrency like Bitcoin or Ether. Based on this information, the token price and transaction fee for miners—referred to as gas on the Ethereum blockchain—are calculated. Newer token standards, such as ERC-223 and ERC-777, aim at addressing shortcomings of ERC-20 by automatically canceling invalid transfers or offering improved handling mechanisms.

After determining the token design, TS issuers generally publish information about the token design, business model, technological solution, and the venture's roadmap in a whitepaper. Issuers distribute these whitepapers using their own website and social media platforms such as Reddit, Bitcoin Talk, or Cryptocointalk. In the absence of auditing intermediaries and content regulation, whitepapers are crucial for overcoming the substantial information asymmetries between issuers and investors. One must bear in mind, though, that whitepapers are fully written by issuers. Given the high regulatory uncertainty involved in TSs, whitepapers provide information on the token sales' terms and conditions, which specify the issuing party and its place of business, timing and pricing of the token sale, use of the raised funds, and other rights and obligations associated with the token. Whitepapers also explain how to pay for the issuers' token, detailing a TS's smart contract address and a recommended gas limit. Therefore, whitepapers are a main source for investors' due diligence.

To allow investors to assess issuers' technological solution and the status quo of its implementation during the pre-TS stage, many issuers partly or fully publish their prototype's source code on a web-based hosting service (e.g., GitHub), often in an alpha or beta version. Some issuers additionally offer bounties for code auditing and bug detection in the TS's smart contract. A further important source of information is the blockchain community's sentiment, as articulated on social media (e.g., Reddit, Slack, Telegram, Facebook, Twitter). Issuers also use these channels for direct and indirect communication with the community and potential investors. To increase community interest and support, issuers frequently use so-called "airdrops" and "bounty programs" which offer token-based rewards for performing social media campaigns like Twitter posts using the TS's hashtag, blog posts, or other promotional activities for the TS. TS-related websites (e.g., Coindesk) are another important resource for investors, as they offer ratings, news, and schedules on forthcoming TSs.

Activities During a TS

The actual TS starts with the activation of the smart contract. On average, TSs last 41 days (Kostovetsky & Benedetti, 2018), during which issuers are in charge of marketing, investor relations, and support. Before investors can send money to the smart contract and participate in the token sale, an increasing number of ICO issuers requires them to register themselves ("whitelisting"). Whitelisting complies with Know-Your-Customer (KYC) and Anti-Money-Laundering (AML) policies and thus protects issuers from regulatory scrutiny and blocks illegal investors who use TSs for money laundering or "pump and dump" behaviors.

In the actual TS, investors send funds, usually cryptocurrencies such as bitcoin or ether, to the smart contract, which transfers the currency units to the digital wallets of the issuing entity. These wallets do not actually store the currency units (this is done on the blockchain), but they store one or more public and private keys which are needed to send and receive cryptocurrencies. A wallet's data file contains the private key, a 256-bit number, which is only known to the owner, and a corresponding public key, which is needed to prove ownership of cryptocurrencies and to facilitate transactions.

To ensure a safe transfer and storage of funds, an errorless smart contract is crucial. In addition, the security and stability of wallets and information regarding the TS are issuers' top priorities, as hackers can use vulnerabilities to compromise the TS. For instance, the CoinDash TS lost an estimated USD 7 million in investments after cyber-attackers manipulated the smart contract address posted on the issuer's website. Thus, security precautions include professional audits of wallet and website code, smart contract verification, and two-factor authentication. As wallets are a main target of hackers, issuers use multi-signature wallets, which require more than one private key for authentication and special hardware for a secure deposit of private keys to prevent the invested funds from theft.

Post-TS Activities

In the post-TS stage, the smart contract transfers tokens to investors' wallets. Unsold tokens are mostly "burned" to decrease the number of tokens in circulation and to increase token valuation. Further, token burning ensures that the distribution of tokens between investors, issuers, and other entities remains as communicated in the whitepaper. A key advantage for TS investors compared to conventional venture investments is the high liquidity of tokens. To facilitate an easy exchange of tokens, the token should be listed on crypto asset exchanges. However, getting listed on top-tier exchanges is difficult as exchange operators focus on tokens with high trade volumes and charge considerable amounts for a listing. To get listed, the token should also follow a common standard, like Ethereum's ERC-20 token format, which allows easy integration on exchanges. However, even if a token gets listed on an exchange, it may get delisted at a later point due to low trading volumes, technical issues, or suspicions of fraud.

Based on the received funds and the investor network established through the TS, issuers further develop the product or service and integrate the token in their offering. To fund these efforts, the issuer may liquidate some of the received funding into fiat currencies. Similar to traditional investor relations, token holder and community management continues to be a key priority for issuers to keep investors informed and well-disposed so as to increase user and token demand. Although rare, issuers may also perform subsequent TSs to raise more money.

Trust—A Problem in Token Sales?

While TSs offer various advantages to issuers and buyers, buyers face high levels of risk due to the decentralized nature and technologic novelty underlying TSs in addition to risks known from established types of crowdfunding (Bannerman, 2013; Werbach, 2018). Risks related to technological vulnerabilities, buyers' impeded due diligence abilities, and fraud have given reason for distrust in this new form of peer-to-peer venture funding model (Amsden & Schweizer, 2018; Kaal & Dell'Erba, 2017). In extreme cases, so-called exit scams have occurred, wherein the collected funds were stolen and the founders "disappeared" (Elendner et al., 2016; Kaal & Dell'Erba, 2017). In this case, the blockchain features of pseudonymity and decentralization turn into an escape route for scammers. Thus, studying how trust is established between market participants in such an environment is of special interest. Dowlat and Hodapp (2018) estimate that only 8% of TS tokens move on to trade, and that only half of these tokens will do so successfully.

Building upon extant research, Nagel and Kranz (2020) suggest that technological artefacts arise to mediate between the interacting parties and help bridge the *trust frontier* in TSs. In the space of time between March 2018 and November 2019, the authors conducted 22 interviews with TS consultants, TS issuers, and TS buyers to investigate by which technological artefacts (Iivari, 2007) trust through ability, integrity, and benevolence (Mayer et al., 1995) is created in start-ups that seek to raise capital by blockchain-based crowdfunding. The following section describes the study setup and findings.

Overcoming the Trust Frontier in Token Sales

For this study, Nagel and Kranz (2020) follow the definition of trust by Mayer et al. (1995, p. 712) as "the willingness of a party to be vulnerable to the actions of another party based on the expectation that the other will perform a particular action important to the trustor, irrespective of the ability to monitor or control that other party." Therefore, trust allows involved parties to overcome the uncertainty and risk inherent to interactions (Jones & George, 1998). According to the framework provided by Mayer et al. (1995), trust stems from a trustor's set of beliefs (in the case of a TS the buyer) in regard to qualities commanded by the trustee (in the case of a TS the issuer). The authors refer to these beliefs as factors of perceived trustworthiness or attributes of trust. They propose three such factors. Ability refers to the trustee's competence to fulfil the behavior as expected. Benevolence refers to the trustee's interest in the trustor's well-being. Integrity presumes that the trustee follows a set of desirable principles.

Blockchain technology is renowned for being "trustless" (Swan, 2015), meaning that users can interact irrespective of mutual trust and at the absence of intermediaries or central authorities. Most blockchains use a proof-of-work consensus mechanism that eliminates the need for a third-party notary or intermediary, and the incorruptible and transparent nature of record keeping negates the possibility of manipulations. Once confirmed, blockchain-stored transactions are irreversible. No party can revise confirmed transactions (Wright & De Filippi, 2015). These technological features make up blockchain technology's trust-free property. However, it is important to note that this logic postulates a self-contained or closed ecosystem (Glaser, 2017). It ceases to apply for more "complex phenomen[a] with socio-technical characteristics" (Hawlitschek et al., 2018, p. 59). The more human interaction a blockchain-based transaction involves, the less a completely "trust-free" logic applies (Hawlitschek et al., 2018).

To illustrate this dilemma, Hawlitschek et al. (2018) extend the blockchain engineering framework proposed by Glaser (2017) for the case of decentralized sharing economy markets. In the framework, the environment layer refers to the effective socio-economic and legal environment. The other lower layers are strongly technology-based. The infrastructure layer contains the hardware and protocol layers. The application layer refers to the blockchain-based service, which is based on one or more smart contracts. The agent layer is the virtual action space for humans and computers. In real-world interactions, the behavioral layer arises. In this layer, actual behavioral patterns occur. The authors assess a *trust frontier* that separates the virtual space from the actual physical world. For blockchain systems to successfully replace trust in platform providers, this frontier needs to be overcome through trusted interfaces, such as complementary technological artefacts (Glaser, 2017).

Nagel and Kranz (2020) find that the interviewees were well aware of the risks associated with TSs and ways buyers' vulnerabilities are exposed, often expressing wary attitudes. Across interviews, interviewees mentioned that the intangibility of TS processes, the high number of scams, and the novelty and complexity of blockchain technology complicate trust-building. One of the interviewees summarized the situation as "You need to believe a lot to invest in a token sale". Another interviewee raised concerns against the term "investors" for token buyers, stating, "You have nothing, you completely depend on the goodwill of the issuer". Yet, over the course of the interviews, the authors identified several technological artefacts that are deeply embedded in the TS process and influence perceived *ability*, *benevolence*, or *integrity*. Table 10.1 presents the findings concerning key challenges of trust formation in the context of TS and the role technological artefacts claim for each attribute of trust.

The identified artefacts can be summarized in three groups according to the archetypes of technological applications proposed by Iivari (2007) (Fig. 10.4). First, Nagel and Kranz (2020) assess a group of *informating technological artefacts*. This group includes the project website and whitepaper as well as rating platforms. Second, they find a group of *mediating technological artefacts* that bridge the trust frontier in TSs. This group comprises social media platforms and code hosting services. Third, crypto wallets and crypto exchanges are summarized in the cluster *automating technological artefacts*. The following paragraphs describe how these artefacts are applied in TSs and in which ways they influence the perceived trustworthiness.

Table 10.1 Summary technological artefacts at the trust frontier of TSs

Attributes of trust	Key challenges in the context of TS	Critical technological artefacts for trust formation
Ability	Difficulty to assess issuing team's ability in terms of technical and entrepreneurial competence. Successful execution of most TS projects requires excellence in programming, business planning, and company-building	• Team and advisor credentials provided through website and whitepaper as well as professional social media platforms • State of product development and profile information accessible on code hosting services
Benevolence	In a market driven by complexity, speculation, and high expectations in terms of speed and outcome, issuers need to communicate project progress and extensively respond to the community in a satisfactory way	• Tone and speed of information on social media platforms • Listing on crypto exchange(s) • Application of standards for coins and other infrastructure
Integrity	In absence of clear regulation, buyers rely on issuers to act according to accepted norms. Technological artefacts grant transparency and information exchange	• Disclosure of project and TS code on code hosting services • Social media platforms provide community sentiment and allow for fact-checking concerning team and advisor background

Similar to studies on traditional crowdfunding, we find that informating and mediating technological artefacts influence trust perception in a crowdfunding project (Ahlers et al., 2015; Belleflamme et al., 2013; Hui et al., 2014; Mollick, 2014). In traditional crowdfunding, the platform bundles services, such as crowd activation, customer support, issuer-buyer communication, project risk scoring, and compliance evaluation (Haas et al., 2015; Macht, 2014). For TSs, in contrast, this technological artefact is not convertible, and the authors find that a plethora of technological artefacts provides buyers and issuers with analogue and advanced

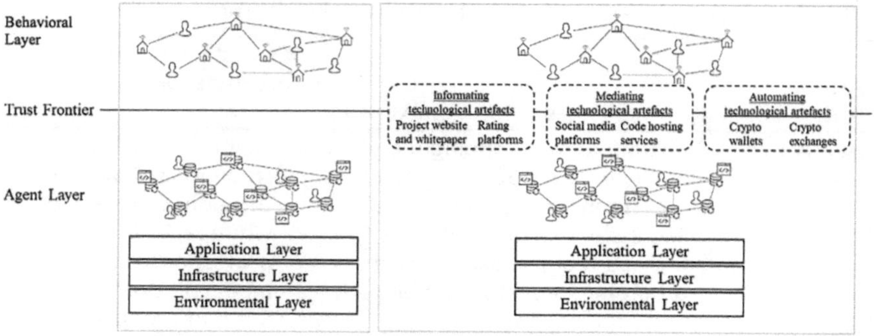

Fig. 10.4 Extended Blockchain Engineering Framework (*left*; based on Hawlitschek et al., 2018) and identification of technological artefacts at the trust frontier in TS (*right*)

interfaces. This evolution is especially striking for social media platforms. The key informants emphasized the importance of a community movement to create attention, favorable attitudes, and trust for TSs. Extant literature on intermediated crowdfunding highlights the significance of community efforts (Hui et al., 2014; Lu et al., 2014; Saxton & Wang, 2014) and community benefits (Belleflamme et al., 2014). Yet, the data suggests an even stronger effect of these artefacts in TSs. A reason may be that in blockchain-based crowdfunding, the community assumes critical due diligence tasks and exchanges information and opinions on social media platforms. The community is further directly engaged in the inspection and refinement of the source code hosting platforms, a further particular technology artefact in TS. In blockchain-based crowdfunding, the community of highly active and engaged users performs tasks that are comparable to those of traditional intermediaries in start-up investing (Beck, 2018).

Nagel and Kranz (2020) further identify automating technological artefacts, including crypto wallets, and crypto exchanges as distinct technological artefacts in TSs. These artefacts reflect the strong technological embeddedness of blockchain-based crowdfunding models, and have great impact on trust perceptions in TSs, for instance, by allowing for transparency, asset security, and flexibility through the option to exchange previously bought tokens. Yet, especially the emerging role of crypto exchanges as TS launch platforms indicates that the range of technological artefacts may not suffice to bridge the trust frontier of this decentralized market (Hawlitschek et al., 2018). The analysis of informating and mediating technological artefacts showed that while the key informants have reservations due to paid and fraudulent content, the artefacts provide an infrastructure for trust formation, especially when used between trusted peers and in a standardized form (Hoffman, 1998). Yet, centralized TS launch platforms may signal a development toward reintermediation (Balyuk & Davydenko, 2019). We find this area especially futile for future research, as findings will be relevant for other industries that are currently disrupted by blockchain technology (Pazaitis et al., 2017).

New Forms of Token Sales and Alternative Funding Vehicles

These insights on technological artefacts in TSs have proven a good indicator for subsequent developments. A review of most recent TSs confirms a growing role of technological artefacts, such as increased significance of crypto exchanges for TS launches. In this section, we trace the evolution of TSs. First, we describe changes in the funding volumes and funding origins for blockchain start-ups. Striking observations include a stall in the number and volume of TSs while VC funding hit record levels. Second, we explain the extant scope of TS forms. As TS regulations and processes changed, so did their denominations. Utility-token-issuing initial coin offerings (ICOs) were increasingly replaced by digital security offerings (DSOs) and security token offerings (STOs) or launched via a crypto exchange in the form of an initial exchange offering (IEO). Using exemplary TSs, we will refer to each of these forms and point out how the market and its actors have matured.

The quantity and volume of TSs has dropped significantly since a peak in 2018, the year in which the Telegram and EOS token sales pushed monthly funding volumes to up to 5.8 billion (Strategy &, 2020). Yet, even in 2019, the yearly volume surpassed USD 4 billion. It is important to note though that the Bitfinex TS was the year's main funding lever,

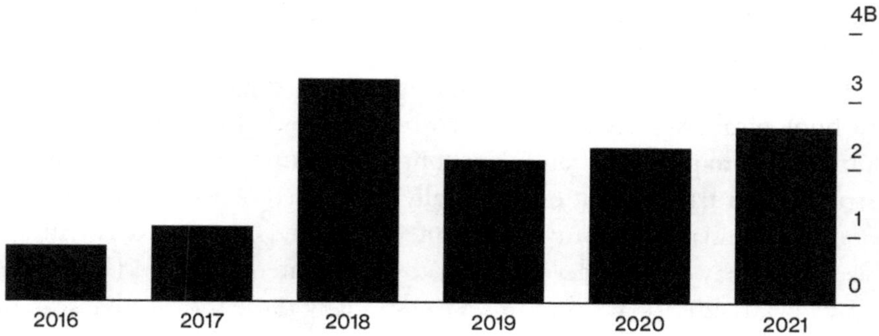

Fig. 10.5 Venture capital funding in blockchain start-ups in USD (CB Insights, 2021)

accounting for more than USD 1 billion. Other notable TSs were those of Kinesis (USD 194 million) and GCBIB (USD 143 million).

At the same time, VC funding in blockchain start-ups is steadily increasing since a drop from the 2018 value (Fig. 10.5). By the end of the first quarter of 2021, 129 blockchain start-ups raised USD 2.6 billion, exceeding the 2020 total of USD 2.3 billion in 341 deals. One driver of this development is the emergence of specialized crypto VC funds like Pantera Capital, FBG Capital, Alameda Research, and Coinbase Ventures. Coinbase Ventures, for instance, was funded in 2018 with the aim of providing funding for early-stage crypto companies (blog.coinbase.com, 2018). The company has since made more than 122 investments (crunchbase.com, 2021). More mature crypto companies have also actively raised funding through initial public offerings (IPOs). For instance, the online discount brokerage Robinhood launched an IPO in July 2021 at the electronic stock exchange NASDAQ. Since 2020, funding in crypto companies has focused on those that offer DeFi applications and solutions (Chen & Bellavitis, 2020).

Parallel to these developments, token sales still occur. For instance, the decentralized derivatives trading protocol Vega raised USD 43 million from more than 21,000 unique participants in July 2021. The token sale excluded buyers from the United States and Canada due to regulatory restrictions. The collected money is supposed to go toward improvements of its mainnet. The protocol had previously closed a USD 5 million in October 2019 and USD 5 million funding round in March 2021.

Contributors included venture capital and trading firms as well as individual investors.

In summary, TSs have changed significantly over time. Initial coin offerings (ICOs) were the earliest form of TSs. ICOs were barely regulated and gave issuers full control over the TS structure, as described in the section *Stages of a Token Sale*. Oftentimes, the issuing companies were at an early stage and used the proceeds to develop the platform on which the issued tokens could be employed. Buyers in ICOs are granted limited protection due to lack of regulation. This form of TS has been heavily disputed as many issuers claimed to offer unregulated utility tokens that did indeed meet criteria of securities.

As a response, so-called security token offerings (STOs) gained in popularity, especially from 2019 onward (Lambert et al., 2021). With jurisdictions increasingly adjudging issued tokens as assets, equity, or debt security of the issuer, the sales of such tokens became subject to local disclosure documentation and diligence requirements. Many ICOs have ex-post been determined to sell investment products, rendering them illegal, and many scholars argue that STOs will replace ICOs due to regulatory uncertainty (Mazzorana-Kremer, 2019). Tokens in STOs can represent a range of illiquid assets, including company shares, real estate, or intellectual property rights. While only five STOs were conducted in 2018, 55 STOs took place in 2019 (Miglo, 2021). It is important to consider that, beside blockchain start-ups, increasingly established institutions conduct corporate directly issued security token offerings. Notable are, for instance, the STO by the Austrian Government with Austrian government bonds in October 2018 at USD 1.4 billion and Bank of China's STO of tokenized bonds that raised USD 2.8 billion in December 2019 (Strategy &, 2020).

As explored in the previous section, the absence of intermediaries posed challenges to the trust relationship between issuers and buyers in TSs. Buyers' struggle to perform proper due diligence gave rise to the so-called initial exchange offerings (IEOs), of which the relative share in TSs considerably increased in the second half of 2019 (Strategy &, 2020; Anson, 2021). In an IEO, issuers sell their tokens via a virtual asset exchange that has vetted the offering beforehand. Besides this regulated environment, the asset exchange will also act as a trading platform for buyers. Advantages of IEOs include the exchange's established user base, leading to heightened reach and reputation of the TS. In addition, initial decentralized exchange (DEX) offerings (IDOs) are strongly related to IEOs with the difference that IDO tokens are offered via decentralized exchanges. Such decentralized exchanges can be decentralized versions of commonly centralized exchanges. For instance, the marketplace Binance operates the platforms Binance Launchpad for IEOs and the platform Binance DEX for IDOs. Such decentralized platforms propose a return to the initial decentralized approach to TSs, tokens, and coins.

Summary

The goal of this chapter was threefold. In the first sections, we delineate how TSs are designed from an economic and technological perspective and which activities and transactions among heterogeneous actors occur using different technology artifacts. Because of blockchain technology's decentralized nature, TSs provide a largely disintermediated funding mechanism that could diminish barriers inherent to traditional venture financing and other types of investment. Many regard TSs as a democratization of venture funding and advancement of crowdfunding, since investors can participate in projects with little means and supervision (Rohr & Wright, 2018). Equally, issuers can collect capital without giving away equity and at relatively low costs (Conley, 2017). However, the disintermediated nature and technological novelty of TSs pose various challenges for issuers, investors, and regulators alike (Kostovetsky & Benedetti, 2018). In light of an array of fraudulent TSs, regulatory authorities struggle to find a balance between guarding against risks and empowering innovation (Lagarde, 2018).

From a business perspective, we refer to research that shows how technological artefacts can counter the distrust raised from fraudulent TSs. Nagel and Kranz (2020) explore how informating, mediating, and automating technological artefacts help overcome the trust frontier (Hawlitschek et al., 2018) in TSs. Based on exploratory interviews with key informants, the authors find that TSs span a complex web of heterogeneous actors who perform a series of social and technical activities. The use of the plethora of technologies by heterogeneous actors in TSs offers an exciting context for many research opportunities in IS. One important indication of this research is the trend toward regulated forms of TSs, at times via an intermediating exchange platform.

This impression is confirmed in the last section of this chapter, which describes recent developments in how blockchain start-ups raise funding. We observe that, while the hype surrounding TSs has stalled, they are prospering in regulated forms and have been subject to progressive institutionalization. In combination with other funding vehicles, including VC firms and IPOs, blockchain companies are strengthening their relevance and building a flourishing token ecosystem. Especially the upcoming trend toward DeFi (Chen & Bellavitis, 2020) has given new dynamics to crypto company financing. IS research is continuing to keep up with advances in forms of TS execution. While the analysis of TS success factors and legitimation strategies remain of interest (e.g., Bruckner et al., 2020; Shaikh & Joseph, 2020), the observed developments are likely to challenge new research questions on the interplay of ever-varying market actors and technological artefacts in TSs.

References

Adhami, S., Giudici, G., & Martinazzi, S. (2018). Why do businesses go crypto? An empirical analysis of initial coin offerings. *Journal of Economics and Business, 100*, 64–75.

Ahlers, G. K., Cumming, D., Günther, C., & Schweizer, D. (2015). Signaling in equity crowdfunding. *Entrepreneurship Theory and Practice, 39*(4), 955–980.

Amsden, R. & Schweizer, D. (2018). *Are blockchain crowdsales the new 'gold rush'? Success determinants of initial coin offerings*. Working paper. Concordia University.

Anson, M. (2021). Initial exchange offerings: The next evolution in cryptocurrencies. *The Journal of Alternative Investments, 23*(4), 110–121.

BaFin. (2018). *Initial coin offerings: Hinweisschreiben zur Einordnung als Finanzinstrumente*. Retrieved September 25, 2018M from https://www.bafin.de/SharedDocs/Downloads/DE/Merkblatt/WA/dl_hinweisschreiben_einordnung_ICOs.pdf?__blob=publicationFile&v=2

Balyuk, T., & Davydenko, S. A. (2019). *Reintermediation in FinTech: Evidence from online lending. Working paper*. Emory University.

Bannerman, S. (2013). Crowdfunding culture. *Journal of Mobile Media, 7*(01), 1–30.

Barsan, I. M. (2017). Legal challenges of initial coin offerings (ICO). *Revue Trimestrielle de Droit Financier (RTDF), 3*, 54–65.

Beck, R. (2018). Beyond bitcoin: The rise of blockchain world. *Computer, 51*(2), 54–58.

Beck, R., Avital, M., Rossi, M., & Thatcher, J. B. (2017). Blockchain technology in business and information systems research. *Business and Information Systems Engineering, 59*(6), 381–384.

Beck, R., Stenum Czepluch, J., Lollike, N., & Malone, S. (2016). *Blockchain–the gateway to trust-free cryptographic transactions*. Proceedings of the Twenty-Fourth European Conference on Information Systems (ECIS).

Belleflamme, P., Lambert, T., & Schwienbacher, A. (2013). Individual crowdfunding practices. *Venture Capital, 15*(4), 313–333.

Belleflamme, P., Lambert, T., & Schwienbacher, A. (2014). Crowdfunding: Tapping the right crowd. *Journal of Business Venturing, 29*(5), 585–609.

blog.coinbase.com. (2018). Introducing Coinbase ventures. Retrieved July 2, 2021, from https://blog.coinbase.com/introducing-coinbase-ventures-c67865a1d2fe

Bruckner, M., Straub, A., & Veit, D. (2020). *Initial coin offerings, how do investors decide? A systematic literature review*. Proceedings of the Americas Conference on Information Systems (AMCIS).

Buterin, V. (2014). *A next-generation smart contract and decentralized application platform*. White Paper. Retrieved January 14, 2018, from https://www.ethereum.org/pdfs/EthereumWhitePaper.pdf/

CB Insights. (2021). Blockchain funding is at an all-time high—Here's what's driving the boom, Retrieved July 10, 2021, from https://www.cbinsights.com/research/blockchain-tech-funding/

Chen, Y., & Bellavitis, C. (2020). Blockchain disruption and decentralized finance: The rise of decentralized business models. *Journal of Business Venturing Insights, 13*, e00151.

Coindesk. (2018). *Coindesk ICO tracker*. Retrieved October 3, 2018, from https://www.coindesk.com/ico-tracker/

Conley, J. (2017). *Blockchain and the economics of crypto-tokens and initial coin offerings*, Retrieved July 5, 2018, from http://www.accessecon.com/Pubs/VUECON/VUECON-17-00008.pdf

Crunchbase.com (2021). *Coinbase Ventures*. Retrieved July 20, 2021, from https://www.crunchbase.com/organization/coinbase-ventures.

Dowlat, S., & Hodapp, M. (2018). *Crypto asset market coverage initiation: Network creation*. Satis Group (Satis Group).

Elendner, H., Trimborn, S., Ong, & Lee, B. T. M. (2016). *The cross-section of crypto-currencies as financial assets: An overview*. Discussion Paper. Leibniz Information Center for Economics.

Fahlenbrach, R., & Frattaroli, M. (2019). *ICO investors*. Working paper. European Corporate Governance Institute-Finance.

Glaser, F. (2017). *Pervasive decentralisation of digital infrastructures: a framework for blockchain enabled system and use case analysis*. Proceedings of the 50th Hawaii International Conference on System Sciences (HICSS).

Haas, P., Blohm, I., Peters, C. & Leimeister, J. M. (2015). *Modularization of crowdfunding services—Designing disruptive innovations in the banking industry*. Proceedings of the Thirty-Sixth International Conference on Information Systems (ICIS).

Hawlitschek, F., Notheisen, B., & Teubner, T. (2018). The limits of trust-free systems: A literature review on blockchain technology and trust in the sharing economy. *Electronic Commerce Research and Applications, 29*, 50–63.

Hoffman, R. R. (1998). Whom *(or what) do you (mis) trust?: Historical reflections on the psychology and sociology of information technology*. Proceedings Fourth Annual Symposium on Human Interaction with Complex Systems.

Hui, J. S., Greenberg, M. D., & Gerber, E. M. (2014). *Understanding the role of community in crowdfunding work*. Proceedings of the 17th ACM Conference on Computer-supported Cooperative Work & Social Computing.

Iivari, J. (2007). A paradigmatic analysis of information systems as a design science. *Scandinavian Journal of Information Systems, 19*(2), 111–117.

Jones, G. R., & George, J. M. (1998). The experience and evolution of trust: Implications for cooperation and teamwork. *Academy of Management Review, 23*(3), 531–546.

Kaal, W. A., & Dell'Erba, M. (2017). *Initial coin offerings: emerging practices, risk factors, and red flags*. Verlag CH Beck (2018), U of St. Thomas (Minnesota) Legal Studies Research Paper (pp. 17–18).

Kostovetsky, L, & Benedetti, H (2018). Digital tulips? Returns to investors in initial coin offerings. Retrieved July 10, 2018, from https://ssrn.com/abstract=3182169

Kranz, J., Nagel, E., & Yoo, Y. (2019). Blockchain token sale. *Business & Information Systems Engineering, 61*(6), 745–753.

Lagarde, C. (2018). *A regulatory approach to fintech*. Finance and Development, vol June 2018.

Lambert, T., Liebau, D., & Roosenboom, P. (2021). Security token offerings. *Available at SSRN, 3634626*.

Lu, C.-T., Xie, S., Kong, X., & Yu, P. S. (2014). *Inferring the impacts of social media on crowdfunding*. Proceedings of the 7th ACM International Conference on Web Search and Data Mining.

Macht, S. (2014). Reaping value-added benefits from crowdfunders: What can we learn from relationship marketing? *Strategic Change, 23*(7-8), 439–460.

Mayer, R. C., Davis, J. H., & Schoorman, F. D. (1995). An integrative model of organizational trust. *Academy of Management Review, 20*(3), 709–734.

Mazzorana-Kremer, F. (2019). Blockchain-based equity and STOs: Towards a liquid market for SME financing? *Theoretical Economics Letters, 9*(5), 1534–1552.

Miglo, A. (2021). STO vs. ICO: A theory of token issues under moral hazard and demand uncertainty. *Journal of Risk and Financial Management, 14*(6), 232.

Mollick, E. (2014). The dynamics of crowdfunding: An exploratory study. *Journal of Business Venturing, 29*(1), 1–16.

Nagel, E., & Kranz, J. (2020). *Exploring technological artefacts at the 'trust frontier' of blockchain token sales*. Proceedings of the 28th European Conference on Information Systems (ECIS).

Notheisen, B., Hawlitschek, F., & Weinhardt, C. (2017). *Breaking down the blockchain hype–towards a blockchain market engineering approach*. Proceedings of the 25th European Conference on Information Systems (ECIS).

OECD. (2019). Initial coin offerings (ICOs) for SME financing. Retrieved June 15, 2021, from https://www.oecd.org/finance/ICOs-for-SME-Financing.pdf

Pazaitis, A., De Filippi, P., & Kostakis, V. (2017). Blockchain and value systems in the sharing economy: The illustrative case of Backfeed. *Technological Forecasting and Social Change, 125*, 105–115.

Pietrewicz, L. (2018). Emerging trends in entrepreneurial finance: The rise of ICOs. *Studia i Materiały, 27*(1/2), 65–78.

PWC (2018) Initial coin offerings—A strategic perspective, Retrieved July 20, 2018, from https://www.pwc.ch/en/publications/2018/20180628_PwC%20S&%20CVA%20ICO%20Report_EN.pdf

Rohr, J., & Wright, A. (2018). Blockchain-based token sales, initial coin offerings, and the democratization of public capital markets. *Hastings LJ, 70*, 463.

Saxton, G. D., & Wang, L. (2014). The social network effect: The determinants of giving through social media. *Nonprofit and Voluntary Sector Quarterly, 43*(5), 850–868.

SEC. (2017). *Chairman Jay Clayton: Statement on cryptocurrencies and initial coin offerings*. Retrieved September 24, 2018, from https://www.sec.gov/news/public-statement/statement-clayton-2017-12-11

Shaikh, F. A., & Joseph, D. (2020). *Pitching it right: Legitimation strategies in initial coin offerings*. Proceedings of the 28th European Conference on Information Systems (ECIS).

Strategy &. (2020). 6th ICO/STO Report. Retrieved July, 15, 2021 from https://www.pwc.com/ee/et/publications/pub/Strategy&_ICO_STO_Study_Version_Spring_2020.pdf

Sunyaev, A., Kannengießer, N., Beck, R., Treiblmaier, H., Lacity, M., Kranz, J., Fridgen, G., Spankowski, U., & Luckow, A. (2021). Token Economy. *Business & Information Systems Engineering, 63*(4), 457–478. https://doi.org/10.1007/s12599-021-00684-1

Swan, M. (2015). *Blockchain: Blueprint for a new economy*. O'Reilly Media.

Vogelsteller F., & Buterin, V. (2015). *ERC 20 token standard*. Retrieved July 28, 2018, from https://github.com/ethereum/EIPs/blob/master/EIPS/eip-20.md

Werbach, K. (2018). Trust, but verify: Why the blockchain needs the law. *Berkeley Tech. LJ, 33*, 487.

Wright, A., & De Filippi, P. (2015). Decentralized blockchain technology and the rise of lex cryptographia. Available at SSRN 2580664.

11

Ensuring Safety and Security in Blockchains: A Private Capital Markets Example

Daniel Conway, Kiran Garimella, and Oscar A. Jofre

The Digital Ecosystem

Modern digital ecosystems have acquired a distinct identity, similar to a singularity (Kurzweil, 2017), due to the increasing technological sophistication of the application of internet technologies, reducing cost of computing power and storage, and increasing bandwidth. Powering them are APIs (Application Programming Interfaces), analytics, machine learning, and the data, the new oil. On the non-technical side, the world has,

D. Conway (✉)
University of Arkansas, Fayetteville, AR, USA
e-mail: DConway@walton.uark.edu

K. Garimella
University of South Florida, Tampa, FL, USA
e-mail: KGarimella@usf.edu

O. A. Jofre
KoreConX, Toronto, ON, Canada
e-mail: Oscar@KoreConX.com

M. C. Lacity, H. Treiblmaier (eds.), *Blockchains and the Token Economy*, Technology, Work and Globalization, https://doi.org/10.1007/978-3-030-95108-5_11

partly as a result of technological advances and partly as a result of ideological shifts, become much more global in nature. Everyone and everything are much more intertwined than ever. In 1980, Milton Friedman stated that no one person could make a pencil, rather the components and assembly were the result of efforts from around the world. This conversation, known as "I Pencil", introduced many to the opportunities, reality, and challenges of global commerce. Today, many products, from the pencil retailers to small kiosks in malls depend on the efficient functioning of a global supply chain. This begs several questions. What are some of the characteristics of the modern digital ecosystem? What are their implications for the design of business blockchains? Finally, how does all this impact their safety and security?

Characteristics of Digital Ecosystems

Modern digital ecosystems are driven by the interplay of technology and business that enable and motivate each other. When technology provides enabling capabilities, established businesses and entrepreneurs look for ways to leverage these new capabilities for competitive advantage (Chung et al., 2020). On the other hand, innovation in business, ranging from complex derivatives, partnerships, unbundling of services, and changing trends in capital markets (such as crowdfunding and the move from initial public offerings (IPOs) to private placements) motivate innovation and adoption of new technologies. In this section, we briefly cover some important business drivers followed by the technical drivers that are shaping the new digital ecosystems. In the next section, we explore their implications for blockchains.

The Business Drivers of Digital Ecosystems

According to the World Trade Organization (2021), the world is continuing to grow more interconnected and global trade continues to expand in the long term. This increasing globalization places enormous burdens on traditional information systems, not only on local storage and computing but also in providing end-to-end visibility of transactions, people, goods, and assets. What happens to transactions during the handoff? How can we be sure that the data from one system flows into the other system without alteration? Quite often, the data is transferred by manual rekeying of data. The potential for errors and fraud is substantial. Anan et al. (2020) detail reconciliation problems and highlight the concerns regarding trust within both domestic transactions across multiple jurisdictions.

Besides the economic drivers of digital ecosystems, there are also ideological drivers to contend with. Distrust of governments, central banking systems (such as the US Federal Reserve), and the role of intermediaries are powerful ideological factors. Privacy scandals by social media have poured oil over the fire. On the business side, responsible behavior is prized (at least in the long term!) over unjust and inequitable practices (Epley & Kumar, 2019). All of these concerns can be packaged into one powerful concept: *trust.* The following questions require provably credible answers:

- Can I trust the parties to the transaction?
- Can I trust that the assets represented by the transaction are actually present and authentic?
- Can I trust that the transactional data is correct?
- Can I trust that the financial and contractual terms have been met?
- Can I trust that the transaction is regulatorily compliant?

The Technology Drivers of Digital Ecosystems

The data explosion is the main driver of technology innovation, running the gamut of Big Data for handling large volumes of data (of which, according to Forbes (Marr, 2019) about 90% is unstructured) to machine learning for analysis, understanding, and predictions. Fortunately, this is all accompanied by rapidly decreasing cost of storage, leading to an increase in computing power. For example, today's cell phones have over 100,000 times the processing power of the Apollo computers (Kendall,

2021)—one giant leap for technology! The final ingredient for the perfect storm is the Cloud. More and more companies are moving their data and computing infrastructure into the cloud. Digital ecosystems are best served by the considerably cheaper expense of the cloud where the participating companies can host their applications and data and utilize machine learning algorithms (all of which are open sourced and therefore free).

Implications for Ecosystem Blockchains

The modern economy enhances the scope of risk beyond the confines of individuals and companies. Driven by globalization and the availability of exponentially increasing data at decreasing cost, much of it freely available, companies have no choice but to be participants in a global web of business relationships. One aspect of this increasing interconnectedness is the loss of direct control over the business processes. Another is the need for having trust in all the participants; the more removed they are, the greater the need for trust and assurance.

A useful model for analyzing organizations is the people-process-technology model. The task of keeping these three components working together within a company becomes magnified as the company grows and expands its reach and scope into multiple countries. Growing a company requires forming many partnerships which, by the nature of the relationship, are decoupled at varying degrees. Correspondingly, the need for stronger mechanisms to ensure the safety and security of assets and transactions also increases (see Fig. 11.1).

Until the advent of blockchains, companies in the ecosystem had only two ways to ensure that all the participants and their assets remain safe and secure: point-to-point integration of systems, which remains fairly expensive without absolutely ensuring the integrity of transactions (especially transitively), or to insist that all the companies be on the same ERP system, which is not only expensive but untenable unless there is one company that can dominate the ecosystem.

In either case, companies have to incur enormous expense and perhaps even lose their branding. In a largely decoupled ecosystem, participants

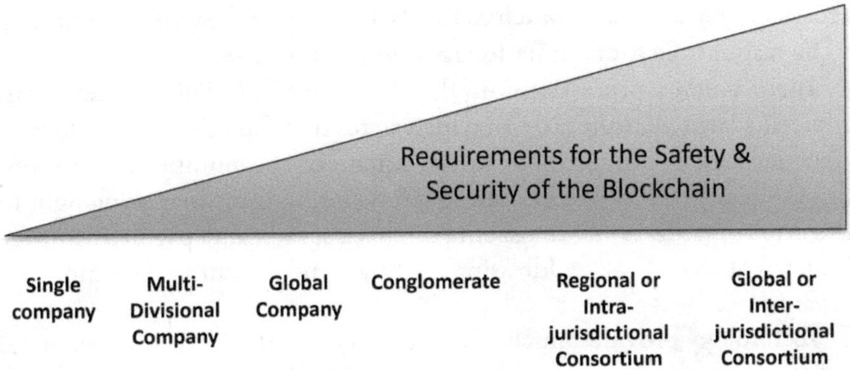

Fig. 11.1 Safety and security requirements of assets and digital tokens

want to keep their own branding, channels, and contacts. They are worried about their value proposition becoming commoditized.

Initially, much of the attention and improvements in safety and security have been in the context of single organizations. Ecosystems are naturally more complex. The more decoupled an ecosystem, the stronger should be the mechanisms for safety and security.

Globalization drives special requirements for blockchains, in general, and for their safety and security, specifically. Authenticity of assets must be preserved across jurisdictions. The standards of identity verification differ.

Challenges for Safety and Security

Moving from single entities to ecosystems increases the existing risks exponentially and introduces new risks. In a large digital ecosystem, organizations are the visible universe. Inter-organizational space, to borrow an analogy from physics (NASA, 2020), is the invisible universe that is made up of dark matter (i.e., unidentified and unverified entities) and dark energy (invisible transactions). In keeping with the analogy, this dark "stuff" comes into existence at an exponential rate compared to the growth of the actual entities and keeps pushing the entities of the digital ecosystem farther apart, much as the dark matter and energy is presumed to be responsible for an inflationary physical universe.

There are no protections in the dark space of digital ecosystems. Metcalf's law (Metcalfe, 2013), which states that the value of an information network is proportional to the square of the number of its users, drives the urgency of incorporating safety mechanisms that bring light to the inter-organizational transactions. This is a radical departure from the traditional way of addressing safety and security within the organization.

Technology provides much of the security, but the inter-organizational space requires an expanded definition of security and safety. The larger ecosystem consists of participants and interactions that are coupled in various strengths (strongly or loosely).

Decentralization Versus Distributedness

One common area of confusion in the discussion on blockchains is around decentralization, which is conflated with the extent of distribution of nodes (what we call "distributedness"). The notion of "centralization" has the connotation of control and power, as understood by the usage of "Central Party" (in politics) and "Central HQ" (in companies). However, distributedness relates to physical or virtual separation of coordinated computing power, storage, and other resources. Figure 11.2 illustrates these concepts.

Safety and Security

To better illustrate the challenges related to safety and security in a digital ecosystem, we utilize an example from the private capital market ecosystem currently in use by KoreConX and its blockchain, KoreChain. The private capital market ecosystem is complex due to many factors, including complexities which traverse from different jurisdictional regions. These complexities include accommodating different forms of identity,

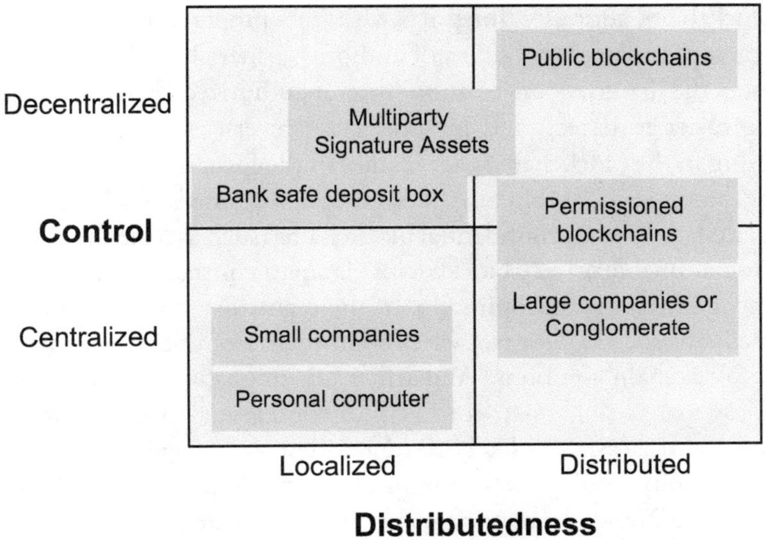

Fig. 11.2 Centralization versus distributedness

sensitivity to privacy requirements, reporting standards and mandates, governance, and regulations regarding transactions.

Safety and Security: An Expanded Perspective

Like blockchain itself, the terms "safety" and "security" are terms consisting of many components. Security is often summarized with the CIA triangle, meaning confidentiality, integrity, and availability. Like many technologies, blockchain addresses some existing security issues and results in new issues.

Blockchain addresses availability by being Distributed Denial of Service (DDOS) resistant, accomplished by distributing copies across multiple regions, server operating systems, and physical facilities, thus avoiding the risks associated with technology monoculture (Geer et al., 2003). Distributed and proof of work was demonstrated before the introduction of blockchain by Rosenthal with Stanford's digital preservation initiative "Lots of Copies Keep Stuff Safe" (LOCKSS.org).

Blockchain addresses integrity with the property of immutability. Given appropriate distribution of authority, generally <51%, blockchain changes the integrity conversation from unauthorized changes to changes being easier to detect, and in some cases reverse. Confidentiality, still evolving in the blockchain space, comes in the form of none (transparent blockchains such as bitcoin), private permissioned blockchains (i.e., Hyperledger Fabric), confidential blockchains (such as Monero or Zcash), or programmable privacy blockchains via smart contracts (Secret Network or Incognito). It is our opinion that the regulatory risk for confidential blockchains such as Monero will prevent them from being used in enterprise blockchain solutions. And while not impossible, the difficulty of building manageable smart contracts for confidential blockchains such as Monero and Zcash will likely restrict widespread usage as a solution to confidentiality needs. The future of programable privacy solutions such as the Secret Network are unclear and more promising, as smart contracts would not need to be done external to the Cosmos ecosystem.

Safety and security is traditionally associated with authentication (login credentials, multi-factor authentication, biometrics, etc.), authorization (access rights), and protection against malware. For the purpose of the token economy, we need a much more comprehensive view of safety and security to include dynamic identity verification, risk management, governance, transactional integrity, validation of people and process, and well-behaved smart contracts. Blockchain provides the core infrastructure of the initial creation of records, forming consensus, and storing immutably. Additional functionalities include privacy, auditability, non-repudiation, and recourse.

An expanded treatment of safety and security also requires addressing the special challenges and requirements of the various types of participants. On public blockchains, participants are offered the same set of security options. Any additional needs the participants might need would be on their own. On private blockchains, participants are heterogeneous as they have different requirements regarding privacy and security.

Components of Safety and Security for Blockchain

Private capital market ecosystems are typically dispersed across various geographies and are subject to different regulations. They may operate in different business cultures that define how they collaborate, exchange information, repose trust, have expectations, and are motivated by incentives. Configuration of the elements of decentralization of the ecosystem, such as number of endorsers or validators, certificate authorities, and service providers have implications for governance and data quality. While blockchains do provide the basic infrastructure for consensus and immutability, the entities performing the consensus must of course be legitimate. This highlights the need for specific requirements for the various types of participants.

Specific Requirements for Participants

Issuers (the company that is raising capital through issuance of shares) struggle with two major concerns: raising capital in a compliant way and managing shareholders in a compliant way. The greatest concern is that the issuer might inadvertently run afoul of regulatory requirements causing the legal and accounting fees to mount or possibly expose the company to penalties imposed by tax or regulatory authorities. The lack of a common method for investors to view the issuer's offering documents (Offering Memorandum or Private Placement Memorandum) and other investment details is a continuing obstacle for true transparency. The absence of standardization between the reporting and communication profiles of one capital markets platform to another contributes to the investor confusion, as the expectations of shareholders are colored by their experience with the differing platforms and tokens. Issuers also waste a lot of time and money by cobbling together a variety of tools to manage shareholder documents and communications. Notifications and reports to shareholders, in particular, must be provided in a way that's non-repudiable and auditable.

For investors, there's a persistent concern that some offerings are operating in a regulatory gray area. This may leave shareholders more vulnerable to fraud at worst and uncertainty at best. Investors need the assurance of due diligence that that has been performed on the company. For example, there were two highly visible cases of fraud prosecuted by the SEC against a diamond mining company and a real estate initial coin offering (ICO) (Bitcoin News, 2017), where due diligence was not performed and the use of funds were deemed to be inappropriate. Some of these frauds are preventable through better due diligence (Alois, 2016).

Shareholders should be treated equally with other shareholders (i.e., no preferential treatment to some shareholders) in dividend payments, revenue sharing, and voting when those rights are part of the subscription agreement. Finally, investors do not want to risk losing their digital securities entirely due to error-prone code and complete exposure on the open platforms, where hackers have full visibility to the code and can therefore explore vulnerabilities in traffic as well as conduct adverse analysis of transaction traffic.

There is a significant personal and professional risk for management and board members in being associated with a non-compliant offering. They need to monitor and trace all corporate activity with the assurance that the data is immutable and that it has been added to the chain only in accordance with established protocol or smart contract. Since much of management's reporting obligations to the board are not stipulated by law, directors on the company board can be uninformed about critical data. Management also requires stronger internal controls for securities transactions; however, implementing such controls can be costly to design, implement, and monitor. Inadequate safety and security expose the management and board to liability, legal action, penalties, and loss of time and reputation.

Attorneys, accountants, and auditors require comprehensive and trustworthy data that is available easily, traceable in an automated way, and assured of non-tampering. They are also responsible for recourse and recovery in case of errors, omissions, or fraud.

Broker-dealers have a fiduciary responsibility for conducting due diligence on the company, its offering, and running KYC (Know Your Customer) ID verification, AML (anti-money laundering) checks, and suitability on investors. They are required to maintain copies of all such checks and ensure they are not tampered with.

Functional Requirements

Safety and security within digital business ecosystems need to address concerns of authenticity of assets and participants, their identity, risk management, governance, transactional integrity, process validation, finality, and privacy.

Authenticity

The top public blockchains are typically a buzzing hive of activity where the digital assets are passed back and forth often at dizzying speeds, from an hour (bitcoin) to thousands per second (Polygon and EOS). While keeping track of this activity, it is easy to ignore the gorilla in the room (http://www.theinvisiblegorilla.com/). The "gorilla" in blockchains is the authenticity of the participants and of the digital instruments. Blockchains are lauded for their ability to cryptographically seal the transactions, but so far they have not addressed the issue of verifying the authenticity of the participants or that of assets themselves. Private blockchains such as Hyperledger allows a step toward digital identity by supporting X.509 V3 digital certificates, though they are administered locally.

Public Key Infrastructure (PKI) allows for the creation of data identifiers (DI) and the self-signing of them as well, and there is substantial activity in the DI space today. This allows for organizations to uniquely create identifiers for everything and digitally sign them to authenticate origin. Multisignature can enhance this identification and authenticity effort, though authenticity is a much more fundamental concept that subsumes the concept of identity.

The following fictional story illustrates this very well:

> *A Chinese trader was engaged in the trading of canned sardines. His clerk managed the warehouse containing these cans. One day, delayed at work and hungry, the clerk helped himself to a can of sardines. When he opened it, he was astonished to find that it was full of sawdust and asked his boss about it. "Ah," said the wily trader, "Cans are for trading, not for eating."* (Saut, 2019)

Identity

Identity is a manageable problem in centralized environments, since there is typically a small set of entry points for any person (or business entity) and the roles that the person plays are known. For example, a supplier can send an email, log into the corporate ERP, or arrive in person. In a distributed or decentralized system, the situation is complicated by the fact that individuals and business entities interact with the ecosystem in unpredictable ways.

One aspect of identity impacts transactional integrity in the financial world, and that is anti-money laundering (AML). The validation of identities and money transactions are time-bound; KYC-class ID verification typically expires after some duration (depending on the type of financial transactions and jurisdictions) or under some conditions (when KYC data changes). AML verification is done per transaction. Identity is dynamic since it includes not just static identity (such as name, date of birth, social security number, etc.) but also location identity (address), social identity (phone, email, and social media), financial identity (bank and credit card accounts), and financial transactional identity (movement of money, property, and securities transactions). The financial world requires, at a minimum, KYC and AML that includes checks against sanctioned lists which must be done not just once but continually for each transaction.

Risk Management

Risk management for an organization is a complex and dynamic challenge made all the more difficult by ongoing complications associated with digital transformation. The other side of the coin of risk management is safety and security. The components of safety and security designed to benefit organizations have evolved over decades and continue today as new risks emerge. These components run the gamut from the technical to the organizational and regulatory. A study by Deloitte (Santhana, 2021) describes standard risks such as strategy, business continuity, reputation, and information security. Blockchain technology forces us to think of non-standard risks of value transfer and smart contracts.

Governance

Risk management is intimately tied to governance, which concerns itself with four critical questions: Are we doing the right things, are we doing them the right way, are we getting them done well, and are we getting value? In digital ecosystems, we move from centralized governance to a shared governance model, ranging from an informal code of ethics to a formal Governance Committee.

Transactional Integrity

We define a transaction to be an atomic action that includes at least two participants who have a party-counterparty relationship and an action they perform. Public blockchains address the integrity of transactions from a technical perspective (such as ensuring that the cryptographic hashes match). However, business ecosystems have to go beyond this to address the issue of business integrity.

Process Validation

Process validation extends the notion of transactional integrity into an end-to-end process. This extension is non-trivial, since a series of valid transactions can still yield an outcome that was unanticipated and, in many cases, lead to adverse consequences. A good example is the notion of end-user certificates in arms deals, dramatically described in Frederick Forsyth's "Dogs of War" (1974).

While transactional integrity in business blockchains addresses both technical and business validation, processes require technical and business validation for a series of steps. Trust needs to flow through processes in a transitive way. For example, if transaction T_{AB} between parties A and B is valid, and transaction T_{BC} between parties B and C is also valid, then the end-to-end transaction T_{AC}, indicating the sequence of transactions T_{AB} and T_{BC}, should also be valid.

Finality

An important element of transactions is the assumption of finality. The public chains assure probabilistically asymptotic finality which, for all practical purposes, is adequate. However, financial services require a stronger guarantee of finality; indeed, they require certainty in finality of transactions, which should be deemed "settled". The traditional financial institutions build in adequate processing time to ensure that batch processes have completed, records have been posted, and funds have been settled between the intermediaries (such as payment gateways, escrow accounts in banks, broker dealers, and companies). In the public markets, this is typically a T+3 settlement period, where T is the time required to complete the workflow and add three days. People generally do not subscribe to the notion of probabilistic settlement (even if proven to be practically adequate), while they feel more comfortable with guaranteed finality (even if that cannot be achieved in some circumstances). To demonstrate this dramatically, we ask our students if they would be willing to accept an employment contract that promises to pay their salary every pay period with a probability of 0.95. So far, we have not had any takers!

Privacy

Privacy and confidentiality is a major concern for most people, especially so in the wake of social media scandals. Several are recapped in PC World's article about the topic (Griffith, 2018). Securities transactions are in general not entitled to complete privacy for regulatory reasons, but they do need to be private to only those entities that are parties to the transaction and to those who have fiduciary responsibilities for those transactions. Additionally, many countries require data to be stored in their own jurisdiction.

Enhancing the Safety and Security of Ecosystem Blockchains

Participating in a digital ecosystem, as we have seen, increases the risk to participants on many fronts, such as privacy, confidentiality, non-repudiation, and immutability. In addition, there is also the risk of an entity losing its identity, branding, and value-proposition. Without that assurance, participants will not trust the blockchain ecosystem and deem it as safe.

Blockchains that power the business ecosystems must address safety and security in a much more comprehensive way, going beyond technical security. In public blockchains, the participants are relatively homogenous in the way they interact and transact on the chain, in that there is no restriction to participation. In a business setting, this is not true. The participants are much more diversified, variously empowered, subject to information asymmetries, and possess differing economic power. The level of participation is governed by the role of the participant.

While every industry has its own specific needs, participants can be broadly classified into the following categories: retail individuals, producers, suppliers, service providers, intermediaries, and regulators. We will focus on the private capital markets to serve as an example of the nuances of safety and security requirements in blockchains.

We will use the example of KoreConX's KoreChain, built on Hyperledger Fabric, a permission-based blockchain. The KoreChain, deployed in twenty-three countries across five Cloud platforms with an annual processing capacity of ten billion transactions, has been in production mode for more than a year; moreover, its smart contract infrastructure allows the creation of a multitude of financial assets, ranging from securities, debt instruments, derivatives, asset-based non-fungible tokens, and stablecoins (Kore Protocol, 2021). For this reason, we use the KoreChain to provide practical examples of how some of the issues of safety and security in ecosystem blockchains are being addressed. We are confident that these ideas can be used by other enterprise blockchains.

We use a failure surface vector to guide the discussion, realizing that not all these components of safety and security are applicable to all the

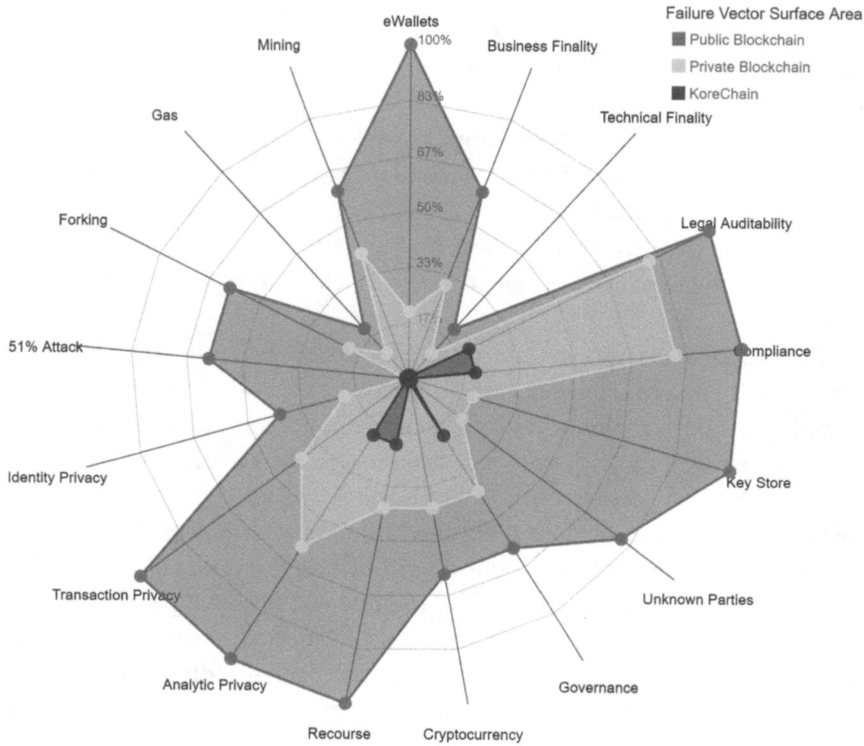

Fig. 11.3 Technical safety and security

blockchains. In Fig. 11.3, we have depicted a radar (or spider) chart of the failure vector surface of blockchains, broadly generalized into public, private, and a production-level blockchain for the global private capital markets (the KoreChain).

Technical Safety and Security

Mining: Miners operate the blockchain. The risk in this case is related to unauthorized parties having access to private financial data and that non-compliant transactions will not be accepted. For example, if an option cannot be executed for 270 days from issue, then the miners must guarantee that the transaction is rejected until the appropriate time has passed. The issue of gaining adoption with miners and providing them incentives, or of dealing with rogue miners, is eliminated in the KoreChain since the specialized and highly regulated nature of private capital transactions prevents entities or individuals that who are not party to the financial transaction or have any fiduciary responsibility cannot participate.

Gas Fees: The transaction costs of validating financial transactions on the KoreChain are subsumed by the regulated participants independent of the transactions themselves. This fee-agnostic participation ensures that the participants have no incentive to manipulate fees or cause inadvertent throttling of transactions. Trading (of securities) is filled with a lot of uncertainty, which increases in thinly traded markets that do not have mature liquidity mechanisms such as market-makers. Presence of gas fees and mining incentives, typically paid in volatile cryptocurrency, adds another layer of uncertainty which is not really necessary.

Forking: There are two varieties of forking risk in blockchains. One is beneficial forking due to the normal process of creating blocks, where transient forks are created all the time; eventually, one fork of the chain wins and the other forked chains wither and die. Similar to this normal process of forking, system upgrades that are agreed to by the miners also cause a fork (known as a hard fork), but this is expected and planned. The other way forking happens is due to a contentious hard fork which happens either in case of widespread disagreement between miners or due to a malicious takeover attempt. The KoreChain prevents this because of a strong governance framework and consensus policies that prevent any takeover attempt by validators, since each validator has a specific role and the role limits the types of validations that can be performed on the KoreChain.

51% Attack: This type of attack happens when 51% of the hashing power is achieved by one miner or a cabal of conspiring miners, explicitly created to attack, disrupt, and break off from the main chain. At the time of this writing, Bitcoin SV is under 51% attack (Gkritsi, 2021). The question of attack does not arise on the KoreChain due to the nature of the participants who have no incentive to mount such an attack. The digital assets in capital markets are non-bearer instruments that cannot function as payment instruments; in other words, they are non-fungible. Governance and non-fungibility remove incentives for 51% attacks. If they do occur, they are easily traceable and compensating entries can be added to restore any damages. All of this is completely done in a compliant way and is fully auditable. The parties who agree to correct any wrongdoing are all registered and regulated.

Cryptocurrencies: Successful cryptocurrencies suffer from their own success since they are worth stealing. Generally speaking, mature blockchains (such as the bitcoin network) are virtually unbreakable. However, the surrounding layers—applications and e-wallets—are not as secure, and that's where the thefts occur. This problem is not present in the KoreChain since it has no native cryptocurrency and is not powered by any other cryptocurrency.

Sutton's law states that when diagnosing, one should first consider the obvious (Cadogan, 2020). This is a generalization of the bank robber Willi Sutton's famous reply to a reporter who asked him why he robbed banks. *"Because,"* replied Sutton, *"that's where the money is."*

If there is no fungible currency or bearer instruments worth stealing, the incentive to break in for economic gain is reduced. No such disincentives exist on public blockchains that are driven by cryptocurrencies.

Data security: Data on mature blockchain is immutable and cannot be tampered with easily. However, the data is accessible for reading. Unless key parts of the data are encrypted, reading the data is valuable enough for criminal use, ranging from adverse analysis to sophisticated front-running of trades to arbitraging across multiple exchanges (McIntosh, 2020). While this is just as true in the public markets, these behaviors cause distrust in the public markets, with the net result being minimal participation in the stock markets (Guiso et al., 2008). This is especially true of the younger generation (Gamm, 2015). The KoreChain addresses this issue by encrypting sensitive information on the chain and ensuring that only authorized parties with a need to know (as part of their fiduciary duties) are able to execute GET requests to retrieve this sensitive data.

eWallet: An eWallet (or e-wallet) is a digital store of digital assets (most often, cryptocurrencies). The major problem of e-wallets is that they require some technical savviness to operate comfortably; when the wallet is not easily usable, and its technology is not well-understood, broad adoption will be challenging. Wallets are not safe by themselves, since they can be stolen or hacked, which now forces people to keep hardware-based cold wallets (i.e., not connected to the internet). Unfortunately, this introduces several failure modes: forgetting the password or passkey, hardware errors, or dependence on the wallet manufacturer's software.

e-Wallets offer no advantage in the capital markets when it comes to securities. More generally, non-bearer instruments do not require the type of safety measures that are necessary for securing fungible, bearer instruments such as currencies, fiat, or crypto. For this reason, KoreChain does not require any e-wallets, since all securities are managed by an SEC-registered transfer agent. This offers double protection, since losses can be recovered, and illegal or unauthorized transfers of securities are not possible.

Functional Safety and Security

We now proceed with the functional components of safety and security in blockchains, with a focus on the KoreChain as an example of how a production-level permissioned blockchain for the global capital markets digital ecosystem addresses these concerns. We begin with authenticity and identity since the integrity of assets, entities, and people is the most vulnerable entry point into the blockchain. We see many business models where, to take an extreme example, someone wants to put cherries on the blockchain. The question remains, how do we know it's a real cherry and not a plastic imitation? If the cherry-picker says so, how do we know that the cherry-picker is real?

In financial assets and transactions, the problem is easier to address since the financial instruments are created only by regulated parties (a requirement of the KoreChain) and asset-backed tokens and stable coins require escrow accounts and audits. In contrast, public blockchains, through complete open participation, allow anyone to create an unlimited number of digital assets with complete flexibility on governance and interpretation of value, including non-bearer instruments (which have considerable protections in the traditional regulated world) and bearer instruments (which have practically no protections).

Authenticity

The authenticity of financial assets on the blockchain can be assured by tightly controlling the production of assets to be driven by regulatory compliance and corporate law. For example, securities are created only upon verified registration and SEC-approved offerings. The subscription agreements are cryptographically secured and immutably associated with the digital securities; additionally, investors sign their own copies of the agreements. The original offering is also locked in with the securities themselves. For all other digital assets such as asset-based tokens and stable coins, only legally approved contracts are securely linked to the tokens or coins.

Identity

The private capital markets have numerous participants such as issuers, broker-dealers, securities lawyers, custodians, secondary market operators, compliance officers, transfer agents, and others. All such entities are regulated by various regulatory bodies, such as the Securities and Exchange Commission (SEC), the Financial Industry Regulatory Authority (FINRA), and State bar associations in the United States. For other entities, such as investor acquisition firms and KYC ID & AML providers, there are multiple checks including KYC and good standing checks. The most critical participants in the capital markets are the investors and shareholders. Their ID is verified and their transactions are submitted to AML only by the FINRA-registered compliance officers.

The next level of identity verification is that of keeping the verification fresh. This needs to be done periodically as KYC IDs are valid only for a limited period of time, typically six months to a year for securities and depending on the jurisdiction. Another reason for redoing the KYC is if any changes are made to essential ID information (address, phone, email, etc.). Investors also need to be subject to suitability checks and accreditation requirements. All of these can change any time but monitoring for such changes and redoing the KYC ID verifications is a huge factor in building trust for other participants. Every financial transaction itself is of course subject to AML checks.

Governance

Public blockchains are open and allow any and all to create and transact tokens and smart contracts on their own. Smart contracts are also susceptible to trace vulnerabilities, which include indefinitely locked funds, leakage to arbitrary users, and being terminated (Nikolic et al., 2018).

Privacy

While capital market transactions cannot be truly private (in particular, when there is an audit or a regulatory requirement for disclosure), transactions are required to be hidden from participants who are not parties to the transaction or to those who have no fiduciary responsibility for those transactions. Moreover, most countries impose data to be stored within their own jurisdictions. KoreChain addresses this need through the creation of country-based channels so that all KoreNodes that participate within a country have segregated data. Cross-jurisdictional transactions are possible only through sharing data on a need-to-know basis to participants or entities who are licensed to work in those jurisdictions.

Process Safety and Security with Smart Contracts

All blockchains have two main functions, broadly speaking: handling data and handling processing. Smart contracts handle transaction processing using the data on the chain. Just as the data is distributed and immutable, so are the smart contracts.

Smart contracts are subject to tremendous risks in public chains, but the most critical flaw in smart contracts on the public blockchains is that they are neither smart nor contracts. They are not smart in the sense of artificial intelligence; they are basically stored procedures. While this is expected to improve with the use of full Turing languages, immutability of code on a blockchain makes adaptive learning challenging as only the data in a smart contract would change, rather than the logic itself. Smart contracts are definitely not contracts in the sense of legal contracts. The term "contract" has a technical meaning in software engineering, where it means an interface specification that guarantees to produce stated results if the corresponding inputs are provided, and that the requesting party need not worry about how the service itself is implemented; additionally, the service provider agrees to preserve the integrity of the interface (i.e., the service request specification) even when they upgrade or add functionality to their service code. By no means is such a "contract" a legal contract.

This fundamental misunderstanding coupled with inadequate governance of the code quality of "smart contracts" has led and continues to lead to significant losses which, unfortunately, or rarely recoverable besides providing no recourse to the party that incurs the losses.

AI implies some degree of contextual awareness and improved automatic decision-making. KoreChain defines its KoreContracts as true smart contracts, in that they maintain the beneficial properties of blockchain such as immutability, while being aware of the context of a transaction and the regulatory restrictions related to execution of the code. They are smart because they incorporate well-defined code as well as operating under a protective umbrella of AI technologies that perform continual audit with multiple levels of validations. KoreContracts are also efficient implementations of legal contracts since they are built on the six legal doctrinal principles that can be proven: offer and acceptance, competence, unforced, due mutual consideration, moral and legal intent, and enforceable (KoreConX, 2018).

Finally, KoreContracts are fully Ricardian. All clauses in a contract are separably represented and every transaction has immutable references to specific clauses, called their enabling contractual clauses. Some transactions even have references to enabling contractual clauses from two or more KoreContracts.

KoreChain strengthens the safety and security of the blockchain by providing the infrastructure to create truly smart contracts that are fully referenceable, provably enabled by legal contracts, auditable, and legally defensible. While all of this doesn't make KoreContracts fool-proof, these capabilities considerably strengthen trust in the KoreChain.

What Happens When Things Go Wrong

There is nothing on earth that is 100% safe and secure. As Clint Eastwood said in the movie, The Rookie (1990), *"If you want a guarantee, buy a toaster."* Public blockchains do not address this problem by deliberate design. However, business transactions are subject to errors, omissions, inadvertent loss, and fraud. Lack of mechanisms to deal with these inevitable eventualities causes major distrust among lay participants. The key is to maintain immutability, yet deals with the issues that might impact trust. One approach consists of three moats of security mechanisms: prevention, detection, and recovery (see Fig. 11.4).

Prevention

The outermost moat is that of prevention. Since the KoreChain is permissioned, participants require special keys and certificates to access the chain. The KoreProtocol (the specification for interacting with the KoreChain and designing KoreContracts) also requires further authenticating information in real time during transactions. Furthermore, sensitive data is encrypted, and key exchange is done securely through public key cryptography using a secure messaging layer that is part of the KoreChain itself, which means all messages are encrypted and their request-response interactions are logged for non-repudiation and auditability. All participants on the KoreChain are regulated entities and KYC ID and AML verifications are performed by these entities on the owners of digital assets (such as investors and shareholders) and their transactions. Finally, the KoreContracts are designed only by authorized parties, their execution is overseen not only by the general consensus mechanism

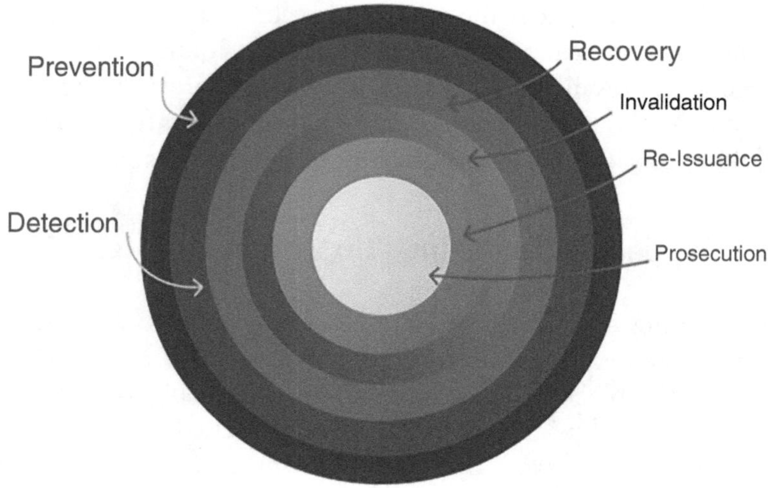

Fig. 11.4 Moats of Security Mechanisms

but also AI-based monitoring, and they are built on legal doctrinal principles.

Detection

As mentioned before, none of this can guarantee an error-free or fraud-free ecosystem. Therefore, KoreChain has the next moat of security: detection. Various reports and auditing mechanisms complement the normal due diligence practiced by each of the regulated parties (which they are legally obligated to do).

When errors or fraud is detected, it is essential that there be some legal recourse and recovery, the lack of which is one of the biggest obstacles to widespread adoption of cryptocurrencies based on public blockchains.

Recovery

When errors or fraud are detected, there's nothing that public blockchains can do without causing massive feuds. In the poster child case of the DAO Hack on Ethereum, Siegel (2016) describes how the organization decided to turn back time and hard fork the blockchain so that none of the transactions that occurred after a particular time would be part of the record. This act remains controversial today, as it is only possible with centralized control similar to the central banking system used today. In other cases, such as the hack of the Dignity coin, and over 1660 others, the blockchain is permanently destroyed (99Bitcoins, 2021).

Erasure or modification of data is impossible in any blockchain. Instead, compensating entries are made to recover and provide restitution in the KoreChain. Each of such entries requires notes or reasons for entries, linkage or reference to the original transactions, and only regulated parties can approve such correcting entries. First, the existing securities are invalidated on the KoreChain; next, they are re-issued in the correct form. This is possible since digital assets on the KoreChain are all deemed to be both non-fungible and non-bearer instruments. In case of fraud, there is a final step—the assembly of data and reports to provide evidence to regulators in case of prosecution.

Conclusion

Safety and security take on a wider meaning and scope in blockchain applications that support large digital ecosystems associated with the token economy. As it is still an evolving effort in the SEC-regulated space despite decades of effort and volumes of output, we don't expect it to be a trivial effort in this new token economy. The key will be to learn what features of safety and security have been effective in the regulated world and evolve those concepts into an economy where the regulation components can be implemented in true smart contracts and with equivalent trust-building characteristics. This journey will also be without final destination in that there will always be new risks and changing economic incentives at play. A key will be architecting a system that both discourages bad behavior by making it more expensive to attack than the reward of doing so, as well as a system that identifies mitigatable attacks.

By incorporating both technical and functional components of safety and security in the design of ecosystem blockchains and in their management, we can build stronger blockchains that foster trust in the ecosystem. Permissioned blockchains are in a position to architect their blockchain applications to meet the unique needs of their digital ecosystems. Since such flexibility is inexpensively available within permissioned blockchains, digital business ecosystems are advised to design their blockchain applications by using the framework we present for a comprehensively safe and secure digital ecosystem that is trusted by all of its participants.

References

99 Bitcoins. Dead Coins. (2021). Retrieved August 4, 2021 from https://99bitcoins.com/deadcoins/

Alois, J. D. (2016). Crowdfund insider. Whatever happened to the ascenergy crowdfunding fraud case? Retrieved August 1, 2021 from https://www.crowdfundinsider.com/2016/08/89353-whatever-happened-ascenergy-crowdfunding-fraud-case/

Anan, L., Barrett, A., Mahajan, D., Nadeau, M.-C., & McKinsey & Company Global Banking Practice. (2020). McKinsey on payments. Retrieved August 1, 2021 from https://www.mckinsey.com/~/media/mckinsey/industries/financial%20services/our%20insights/mckinsey%20on%20payments%2031/mckinsey-on-payments-issue-31.pdf

Bitcoin News. (2017, 30 September). *SEC charges 'real estate and diamond' ICO with fraud*. Retrieved August 2, 2021 from https://news.bitcoin.com/sec-charges-real-estate-and-diamond-ico-with-fraud/

Cadogan, M. (2020, November 3). *Sutton's Law*. Retrieved August 2, 2021 from https://litfl.com/suttons-law/

Chung, V., Dietz, M., Rab, I., & Townsend, Z. (2020). *McKinsey quarterly ecosystem 2.0: Climbing to the next level*. Retrieved August 3, 2021 from https://www.mckinsey.com/business-functions/mckinsey-digital/our-insights/ecosystem-2-point-0-climbing-to-the-next-level#

Epley, N., & Kumar, A. (2019). How to design an ethical organization. *Harvard Business Review*, 144–150.

Forsyth, F. (1974). *The dogs of war*. Viking Press.

Gamm, S. (2015). *TheStreet. Why millennials don't trust wall street or investing in stocks*. Retrieved August 1, 2021 from https://www.thestreet.com/investing/why-millennials-dont-trust-wall-street-or-investing-in-stocks-13135109

Geer, D., Bace, R., Gutmann, P., Metzger, P., Pfleeger, C. P., Quarterman, J. S., & Schneier, B. (2003). *Cyber insecurity: The cost of monopoly*. Retrieved 1 October, 2021, from https://cryptome.org/cyberinsecurity.htm

Gkritsi, Eliza (2021). BSV Suffers 51% Attack: Report. Retrieved August 5, 2021 from https://www.coindesk.com/markets/2021/08/04/bsv-suffers-51-attack-report/#:~:text=A%2051%25%20attack%20occurs%20when,have%20mined%20the%20same%20block

Guiso, L., Paola, S., & Luigi, Z. (2008). Trusting the stock market. *The Journal of Finance, LXIII*(6).

Kendall, G. (2021). The conversation: Would your mobile phone be powerful enough to get you to the moon? Retrieved August 1, 2021, from https://theconversation.com/would-your-mobile-phone-be-powerful-enough-to-get-you-to-the-moon-115933

Kore Protocol. (2021). Empowering private capital markets. Retrieved August 1, 2021, from https://www.koreconx.com/infrastructure-management/

KoreConX. (2018). The three fallacies of smart contracts. Retrieved August 1 2021, from https://www.koreconx.com/three-fallacies-smart-contracts/

Kurzweil, R. (2017). Futurism: Ray kurzweil claims singularity will happen by 2045. Retrieved August 1, 2021, from https://www.kurzweilai.net/futurism-ray-kurzweil-claims-singularity-will-happen-by-2045

Marr, B. (2019). *What is unstructured data and why is it so important to businesses? Any easy explanation for anyone*. Forbes. Retrieved August 1, 2021, from https://www.forbes.com/sites/bernardmarr/2019/10/16/what-is-unstructured-data-and-why-is-it-so-important-to-businesses-an-easy-explanation-for-anyone/

McIntosh, R. (2020). *Financial magnates. Crypto market manipulation is still alive and well, says orbs' Ilan Sterk*. Retrieved August 2, 2021, from https://www.financemagnates.com/cryptocurrency/interview/crypto-market-manipulation-is-still-alive-and-well-says-orbs-ilan-sterk/

Metcalfe, B. (2013). Metcalfe's law after 40 years of ethernet. *Computer, 46*(12), 26–31.

NASA Science. (2020). *Universe: Dark energy, dark matter*. Retrieved August 1, 2021, from https://science.nasa.gov/astrophysics/focus-areas/what-is-dark-energy

Nikolic, I., Kolluri, A., Sergey, I., Saxena, P., & Hobor, A. (2018). *Finding the greedy, prodigal, and suicidal contracts at scale*. Retrieved August 1, 2021, from https://arxiv.org/pdf/1802.06038.pdf

Santhana, P. (2021). *Deloitte perspectives. Blockchain risk management: Risk functions need to play an active role in shaping blockchain strategy*. Retrieved August 2, 2021, from https://www2.deloitte.com/us/en/pages/advisory/articles/blockchain-risk-management.html

Saut, J. (2019). *Raymond james advisor perspectives. Trading sardines?!* Retrieved August 1, 2021, from https://www.advisorperspectives.com/commentaries/2019/03/27/trading-sardines

Siegel, D. (2016). CoinDesk. Understanding the DAO attack. Retrieved August 3, 2021, from https://www.coindesk.com/understanding-dao-hack-journalists

World Trade Organization. (2021). World trade primed for strong but uneven recovery after COVID-19 pandemic shock. Retrieved August 1, 2021, from https://www.wto.org/english/news_e/pres21_e/pr876_e.htm

12

Utilizing Non-fungible Tokens for an Event Ticketing System

Ferdinand Regner, André Schweizer, and Nils Urbach

Introduction

Blockchain technology is a radical innovation with the potential to challenge or even replace existing business models relying on third parties for trust (Beck & Müller-Bloch, 2017). The concept of blockchain was

This chapter is based on Regner, F., Schweizer, A. and Urbach, N. (2019) NFTs in Practice—Non-Fungible Tokens as Core Component of a Blockchain-based Event Ticketing Application, Proceedings of the 40th International Conference on Information Systems (ICIS 2019), December 15–18, Munich, Germany. Please have a look at this paper for further methodological details.

F. Regner
Investment Natives e.U., Wien, Austria
e-mail: office@investmentnatives.com

A. Schweizer
qbound GmbH, Gilching, Germany
e-mail: andre.schweizer@qbound.io

N. Urbach (✉)
FIM Research Center, Project Group BISE of Fraunhofer FIT, Frankfurt University of Applied Sciences, Frankfurt am Main, Germany
e-mail: nils.urbach@fim-rc.de

M. C. Lacity, H. Treiblmaier (eds.), *Blockchains and the Token Economy*, Technology, Work and Globalization, https://doi.org/10.1007/978-3-030-95108-5_12

introduced in 2008 through the release of the Bitcoin whitepaper (Nakamoto, 2008) and was primarily used as the technology behind cryptocurrencies during its first years. In 2014, with the Ethereum protocol, a second generation of blockchains was introduced, with the feature to program and execute software—so-called smart contracts—on all participating blockchain nodes. Consequently, any user is enabled to create and deploy programs on a shared global infrastructure (Buterin, 2014; Wood, 2014). This has led to the realization of new concepts designed to simplify human interaction and collaboration on a large scale across several industries (e.g. supply chain management, international payments, international trade finance, energy markets, and notary services) (Christidis & Devetsikiotis, 2016; Guggenberger et al., 2020; Wüst & Gervais, 2017). Particularly, the use cases of Initial Coin Offerings (ICOs) that reinvented crowdfunding through the use of blockchain and its ability to tokenize assets has drawn public attention (Bachmann et al., 2021). The spectacular success of ICOs, where globally an estimated 19 billion USD has been collected, has been enabled by the ERC-20 standard (OECD, 2019). This standard, which specifies a common interface for fungible tokens that are divisible and not distinguishable, was mutually agreed on by the developer community to ensure interoperability (Vogelsteller, 2015).

In contrast, non-fungible tokens (NFTs) differ from fungible tokens in two important aspects. Every NFT is unique and cannot be divided or merged (Voshmgir, 2018). This new form of token was first introduced with the ERC-721 standard in late 2017 (Entriken et al., 2018). ERC-721 deviates significantly from the ERC-20 standard as it extends the common interface for tokens by additional functions to ensure that tokens based on it are distinctly non-fungible and thus unique (Entriken et al., 2018). For practitioners, these distinct properties of NFTs enable a variety of new use cases. It particularly improves the tokenization of individual assets which is not feasible with fungible tokens, as they cannot digitally represent uniqueness. Thus, practitioners have conducted a multitude of experiments in the past months using NFTs to represent digital goods such as virtual gaming assets and digital artwork—a market of USD 28 billion as of April 2021 (CoinGecko, 2021).

However, aside from the existence of early experimental use cases, a deeper understanding of NFTs would be beneficial from the viewpoint of research in three main aspects. First, solidified descriptive knowledge about the general characteristics of NFTs and the differences from fungible tokens enables a better understanding of the benefits and resulting opportunities. Second, improved prescriptive knowledge about the process of designing and evaluating applications based on NFTs benefits both researchers and practitioners. Third, increased awareness of practical challenges enables future researchers to better focus on solving these challenges. However, in-depth investigations of NFTs by academic researchers touching these aspects are still scarce. Further, the current body of knowledge lacks best practices, development project experience, and insights into blockchain-based software development (Delmolino et al., 2016). We aim to bridge that gap in research by demonstrating the applicability of non-fungible tokens in a specific domain and answering the following research question:

What are the benefits and challenges of using NFTs on Ethereum?

We answer the question by following a design science research (DSR) approach and developing the use case of an event ticketing system. Doing so, we present a new way to create, manage, transfer, and track ownership and usage rights involved. We have chosen tickets as an illustrative example because (1) current solutions typically face problems such as fraud, counterfeiting, and limited control over secondary transactions (Waterson, 2016); (2) due to heavy reliance on third parties for trust there is a potential for disruption through blockchain technology (Beck & Müller-Bloch, 2017); and (3) the use case is limited in scope and thus suited for DSR prototype building. Therefore, we design and implement a prototype based on NFTs for a decentralized, blockchain-based event ticketing system that aims to replace existing centralized ticket applications. By evaluating the prototype and its use, we gain valuable insights, discover challenges, and draw conclusions that enable both a technical-oriented and management-oriented audience to benefit from it. The creation and evaluation of a prototype are central activities of the DSR approach we follow, which has been taken several times by IS researchers when dealing with blockchain use cases (Beck et al., 2016; Notheisen et al., 2017; Lockl et al., 2020). Further, building an instantiation in a specific domain is a well-recognized practice when confronted with new technology (Hevner et al., 2004). Lindman et al. (2017) specifically propose the development and analysis of blockchain-based prototypes using a DSR approach. As thorough evaluation is key to prove the correctness and applicability of the resulting prototype, we follow an iterative build and evaluate approach (Hevner, 2007; Gregor & Hevner, 2013). Further, we draw on extant literature and expert interviews to assess the suitability of the artifact for its intended purpose and to gain insights into the benefits and challenges of NFTs.

Background

Blockchain and Non-fungible Tokens (NFT)

Blockchain first gained popularity as the protocol behind the cryptocurrency Bitcoin, which was introduced in 2009 at the peak of the financial crisis (Nakamoto, 2008; Zohar, 2015). Aside from this first instantiation and the use case of cryptocurrencies, a broader range of applications emerged—a development that is mainly attributed to the possibility to run pieces of software code on a blockchain (Beck et al., 2016). These so-called smart contracts, a term coined by Nick Szabo in 1994, allow parties that do neither know nor trust each other to securely perform transactions. The correct execution is ensured by a consensus protocol that runs on all participating nodes of the underlying blockchain and provides consistency (Szabo, 1994; Glaser, 2017; Sillaber & Waltl, 2017).

The first and most popular blockchain protocol, which supports a virtual machine with which Turing-complete scripting languages can be executed, is Ethereum, which was first introduced in 2014 (Buterin, 2014). As Ethereum is a public, permissionless blockchain protocol, it allows any user to create and deploy programs on its shared global infrastructure (Wood, 2014). A vibrant community has evolved that runs a multitude of pieces of software code (smart contracts) on the Ethereum blockchain. To foster interoperability, the community agreed on multiple application-level standards—so-called Ethereum Requests for Comments (ERCs) (Ethereum Foundation, 2018). The most well-known standard, called ERC-20, specifies a standardized interface for fungible tokens which have been widely used to provide holders with certain access or governance rights, and to facilitate ICOs, a form of crowdfunding (Vogelsteller, 2015; Rohr & Wright, 2017). The popularity of ICOs, which raised over USD 7 billion in 2017 and more than USD 13 billion in 2018, has contributed to the global popularity of tokens in general (OECD, 2019). A search on Etherscan, a popular Ethereum blockchain explorer, returns over 435,000 token contracts deployed on the public Ethereum main chain (Etherscan, 2021), indicating that tokens represent an important component for blockchain use cases. While fungible tokens, such as tokens based on the ERC-20 standard, have gained great popularity, a new class of tokens was introduced in late 2017 with the ERC-721 standard. The ERC-721 standard specifies a standardized interface for so-called non-fungible tokens (Entriken et al., 2018). The motivation behind the creation of this new standard was that a crucial difference between fungible tokens and non-fungibility tokens exists. The term fungible refers to the interchangeability of each unit of a commodity with other units of the same commodity, that is, two parties could swap the same amount without any gain or loss. While fungibility is an essential feature of any currency, non-fungibility is the opposite as every token is distinguishable and thus cannot be divided or merged (Merriam-Webster, 2018; Voshmgir, 2018). This also has implications for tracking the ownership of tokens as each NFT needs to be tracked separately. The ERC-721 standard specifies that every NFT has a globally unique ID, is transferable, and can optionally include metadata. NFTs were created for a specific purpose—to represent ownership over digital or physical assets (Entriken et al., 2018). While the concept of "colored coins" as a representation of real-world assets on the Bitcoin blockchain has been discussed before the advent of Ethereum, with the creation of the ERC-721 standard, this idea has first been realized (Wang, 2017).

The first application based on NFTs to reach widespread adoption was a virtual online game called CryptoKitties. The most expensive NFT that represented ownership of a virtual cat was sold for over USD 100,000 in late 2017 (Tepper, 2017; Muzzy, 2018). A second wave of public interest in NFTs started with the launch of NBA Top Shot in 2020, which has already achieved $390 million in sales of NBA moments. Multiple artists have begun to tokenize their artworks and sell NFTs via auctions; most famously the artist Beeple gained USD 69.3 million at the auction of an NFT in 2021 (PitchBook, 2021). The market capitalization of NFTs totals an estimated USD 28 billion as of April 2021 (CoinGecko, 2021). Yet, despite the public craze, rigorous studies dealing with the topic remain scarce. Thus, we treat NFTs as a potentially valuable building block and utilize a specific use case to check if this assumption is valid and to gain theoretical and practical insight on usage, benefits, and challenges.

Event Ticketing Systems

Tickets represent a mechanism to demonstrate entitlement to access to any event such as sports or culture. They come in many forms, ranging from physical paper to electronically readable codes on paper or chips embedded in smart cards or wristbands (Waterson, 2016). Tickets can be bought on the primary market directly from the event organizer or from authorized sellers such as appointed agents, mostly for a fixed price. Secondary markets also exist, with the notable difference that any price can be charged and buyers and sellers often directly engage in business or rely on secondary ticket sale platforms, which typically take 25–30 percent of secondary sales in fees (Waterson, 2016). The status quo is not satisfactory for the two central stakeholders—the event organizer and the customer—as multiple complaints at consumer protection agencies show (McMillan, 2016; Courty, 2017; NZ Herald, 2017). Consumers have to trust third parties when buying tickets on secondary markets and thus face the risk of purchasing fraudulent or invalidated tickets, which are counterfeits or might be cancelled (The Australian Government the Treasury, 2017). Using QR-codes or barcodes, which encode information, but do not encrypt it, is not sufficient to make tickets truly tamper-proof. Further, consumers lack the capability to validate if the barcode on their ticket is valid. In various cases, the same barcodes have been sold multiple times or have been obtained by extracting it from pictures of a ticket posted online (Tackmann, 2017). The problem of ticket fraud is quite substantial: An estimated 12 percent of ticket buyers get scammed, which amounts to an estimated yearly damage of USD 2 bn (Waterson, 2016; Leonhart, 2018). Ticket prices on secondary markets are taken to extremes, partially through the use of bots which automatically drive up prices to earn a profit by reselling them at the highest possible markups (Courty, 2017). The problems in secondary markets in the domain of ticketing are prototypical and apply to many other industries. Current literature suggests that industries with heavy reliance on third parties for trust are a potential target for disruption through blockchain technology (Beck & Müller-Bloch, 2017).

Research Method

To design, implement, and evaluate a blockchain event ticketing system prototype, we follow a DSR approach. DSR, which historically originated from engineering, involves the creation of an artifact which has not existed previously and serves a meaningful purpose (March & Smith, 1995). In the DSR context, the creation of a prototype represents an instantiation of a blockchain-based IT artifact (March & Smith, 1995). Through artifact instantiation, we demonstrate both feasibility of the design process and the designed product and enable researchers to learn about the effect of the artifact on the real world and its appropriate use (Hevner et al., 2004). This approach has been taken several times by IS researchers when dealing with new aspects of blockchain technology (Beck et al., 2016; Notheisen et al., 2017; Schweizer et al., 2017).

Hevner et al. (2004) list seven guidelines for applying DSR in the IS space: It requires the creation of an innovative artifact that fulfils a specific purpose (1) for a specified problem domain (2). It is crucial to thoroughly evaluate the artifact with respect to providing a solution to the specified problem (3). A clear and verifiable contribution such as solving an unsolved problem or solving a known problem in a more effective or efficient manner is also mandatory (4). It requires rigorous definition, formal representation, coherence, and internal consistency of the artifact

(5). Through the creation of the artifact, we construct a problem space along the process and a method to find an effective solution for it (6). Finally, we must communicate the results effectively (7). In Table 12.1, we map our approach to meet these seven guidelines.

Prototype Design and Development

Problem Statement and Derivation of Design Objectives

Our literature analysis revealed the current problems in the event ticketing industry. To recap our findings, the status quo is not satisfactory for the two central stakeholders—the event organizer and the attendee, as multiple complaints at consumer protection agencies show (McMillan, 2016; Courty, 2017; NZ Herald, 2017). Following the relevance cycle laid out by Hevner (2007), we additionally validated our findings by interviewing the CEO of a ticketing firm, who contributed valuable expert knowledge and confirmed our preliminary findings. Based on these findings and additional literature, we derived the desired design objectives for the prototype. Compliant to the relevance cycle proposed by Hevner (2007), we defined our design objectives and subsequent acceptance criteria for the evaluation of the research results based on Hevner et al. (2004). Table 12.2 lists the design objectives and the proposed evaluation criteria and methods.

Fundamental Design Decisions

A well-designed system architecture provides the roadmap for the subsequent development process (Nunamaker et al., 1990). Before trying to apply a blockchain-based solution right away, we first ensured that our fundamental design decisions are well grounded. Thus, we followed the decision model by Wüst and Gervais (2017), which helps to decide if the use of blockchain technology is useful for a specific scenario. It guides the user through sequential decision criteria in the form of questions. As

Table 12.1 Mapping of DSR guidelines by Hevner et al. (2004) and our contributions

Guideline	Contribution
(1) Design as an artifact	Our prototype instantiates an NFT-based artifact that allows trust-free creation, management, and transactions of event tickets.
(2) Problem relevance	We address a research gap in scientific literature regarding the question whether NFTs are suited to represent scarce digital assets. Additionally, we tried to gain insight into the benefits and challenges of the use of NFTs, which are yet to be determined by researchers. Regarding the use case of event tickets, we aim to address the problems of fraud, lack of trust, lack of control over secondary market transactions, low transparency, and high dependence on intermediaries.
(3) Design evaluation	To evaluate the prototype in terms of functionality, formal completeness, consistency, accuracy, reliability, and efficiency, we follow the approach of Hevner et al. (2004), who stated two main goals: (1) the solution works (proof by construction), and (2) characterize the environments in which it works (illustrative scenarios).
(4) Research contributions	Our contribution is to demonstrate the usefulness of NFTs in the domain of event tickets with scientific rigor. Through artifact instantiation, we demonstrate both feasibility of the design process and the designed product and enable researchers to learn about the effect of the artifact on the real world and its appropriate use (Hevner et al., 2004). Additionally, we aim to lay the foundation for further research and higher-order theory of NFTs and blockchain application development (Gregor, 2006; Glaser, 2017).
(5) Research rigor	We closely follow the guidelines by Hevner et al. (2004) regarding the DSR process in IS. Additionally, we draw on best practices by other IS researchers that have dealt with similar approaches when evaluating new aspects of technology (Beck et al., 2016; Notheisen et al., 2017; Schweizer et al., 2017). To determine if our artifact design is complete, we follow a strategy of satisficing, meaning the solution needs to be satisfactory regarding solving the requirements and constraints of the problem we state for the selected use case (Hevner et al., 2004).

(*continued*)

Table 12.1 (continued)

Guideline	Contribution
(6) Design as search process	We follow an iterative build and evaluate approach. To further assess the suitability of the artifact for its intended purpose and gain insights into the benefits and challenges, we additionally draw on extant literature on both the application and solution domain, as suggested by Hevner et al. (2004), and perform semi-structured expert interviews (Schultze & Avital, 2011). As peer-reviewed literature is scarce in this new area of research, we also make use of publicly accessible Internet sources such as open-source code repositories, whitepapers, and blog articles, which strengthens our domain knowledge and ensures the recency of this paper.
(7) Communication of research	We aim to provide clear information to both the management-oriented and technically oriented audiences. The former benefits from our reasoning about benefits and challenges, while for the latter we publish the entire source code of the project on GitHub, including all formal tests. This enables technical researchers and practitioners to replicate our work and/or build on it.

the key question, namely, if all interacting parties can inherently be trusted, was clearly answered with no, a blockchain solution is advisable according to the model. Since we positively answered the follow-up question if publicly available verification is necessary, the selected implementation is built on a public permissionless blockchain. Our design objectives provided a valuable guideline to select a blockchain with desired features. The Ethereum blockchain is a public and permissionless blockchain that supports smart contracts and has the largest community of developers and rests on more than 9000 nodes (as of August 2021) that run the network without a central point of failure (Etherscan, 2021). These properties enabled us to build an automated application that inherits the key features of the underlying blockchain such as decentralized trust, integrity, transparency, non-repudiation, and availability. Ethereum developed its own high-level programming languages which are compiled into bytecode that can be run on the Ethereum virtual machine; its most popular being Solidity which features a JavaScript-like syntax (Tikhomirov, 2018). Thus, we chose to develop the smart

Table 12.2 Design objectives

Design objective	Description	Evaluation
1. Digitization 1.1. Digital storage of all data 1.2. Digital exchange of all data	Portability for tickets independent from a physical medium should be achieved (Fujimura et al., 1999). All data has to be stored and exchanged in a purely digital way (Nærland et al., 2017).	Validation of efficacy and completeness though simulation and descriptive methods.
2. Control over secondary market transactions 2.1. Managing transactions 2.2. Price caps 2.3. Charging transaction fees	The event organizer should be able to manage ticket transactions and earn transaction fees from any paid ticket transfer among attendees. Management policies should be determined by the ticket issuer (Fujimura et al., 1999). This includes pausing all transactions and capping ticket prices for secondary market transactions.	Functional analysis of the prototype to assess efficacy and reliability through testing and simulation.
3. Independence 3.1. Decentralization 3.2. Trustfulness	No centralized broker or authority should be assumed to sell tickets (Fujimura et al., 1999). Event organizers should be able to conduct business independent of intermediary parties.	Assessment of efficacy and validity through testing and descriptive evaluation.
4. Security 4.1. Availability 4.2. Integrity 4.3. Privacy	A secure environment is characterized by the accessibility of resources (availability), the authenticity of data (integrity), and the prevention of access to illegitimate users (privacy) (Vacca, 2013).	Consistency and reliability should be verified using testing, simulation and descriptive evaluation.
5. Validation 5.1. Verifiability of ownership	To increase trust in the integrity of the system, ticket ownership should be verifiable in a simple way at any time.	Functional testing and simulation to assess the reliability.

(continued)

Table 12.2 (continued)

Design objective	Description	Evaluation
6. Transparency 6.1. View current ticket ownership 6.2. Access to transaction history	Ticket transaction history should be fully transparent. Current ownership status and any state change, from the creation and transfers between attendees to the end of the lifecycle, should be publicly viewable.	Analysis of accuracy and completeness through simulation and descriptive methods.
7. Automation 7.1. No manual interaction required after setup	The event organizer should not be required to perform any manual action after an initial setup. Any policies set by the organizer should be enforced automatically.	Functionality and reliability should be assessed through testing and simulation.
8. Cost Efficiency 8.1. Efficient cost structure	The fixed and variable costs of the system should be economical from the event organizers point of view.	Assessment of efficiency through simulation.

contract code for the prototype in Solidity. We relied on the development framework Truffle, which contains tools for the deployment of contracts and the testing library Mocha as well as ganache-cli, which provides a local Ethereum blockchain for testing (Truffle, 2019). Additionally, Infura provides access to public Ethereum test networks such as Ropsten without requiring us to set up our own full Ethereum node (Consensys, 2019). This toolkit proofed essential for efficient development, which is characterized by being test-driven and quick iterations (Janzen & Saiedian, 2005). Each of these choices is popular in the blockchain community, with more than 1 million users each (Mougayar, 2018). We used NFTs as the fundamental core component of our prototype, as they contribute to fulfilling our design goals thanks to their properties of uniqueness, indivisibility, and transferability (Entriken et al., 2018). We reused the well-tested, audited, and community-reviewed implementation of the ERC-721 standard by OpenZeppelin, which we extend with additional functions needed for our specific use case (OpenZeppelin, 2019).

Resulting Prototype

Adhering to the design objectives and design choices we had specified, we built a prototype that addresses the concerns of both the event organizer and the attendees. Following the DSR cycle laid out in the previous section, we took to an interactive approach and started with a basic design to resolve a highly simplified and abstracted problem. After evaluation of the preliminary results and performance of unit tests, we refined the requirements and the design needed to solve them respectively. The resulting prototype should be viewed as a basic implementation that focuses on core features necessary to meet the design goals we specified. The only two entities participating in the simplified process are the event organizer and the event attendees. They conduct business solely by interacting with the smart contract—the need for a middleman is eliminated completely. The only requirement for the two parties is to own an account on the Ethereum blockchain, funded with some of its native cryptocurrency Ether, to interact with the smart contract. The sequence of interactions can be split in three phases:

(1) Setup phase: First, event organizers deploy a smart contract for a specific event. Initial parameters, such as the name of the specific event, an initial ticket price, a maximum price factor for tickets, the event start datetime, the maximum amount of tickets available, and an initial transaction fee for secondary ticket transactions, are provided to the *constructor()* as specified in the contract deployment script. The event organizer is the owner of the smart contract and thus can change these parameters later by interacting with the smart contract, in addition to withdrawing its balance and pausing transactions of tickets at any time.
(2) Primary market: After contract deployment, event attendees can buy tickets until the supply limit is reached by sending a transaction containing Ether to the payable function *buyTicket()*. The function first checks if the amount transferred is sufficient and then calls the internal function *createTicket()* which "mints" a new NFT that acts as the virtual representation of a ticket. Each ticket is unique as its ID can only exist once per contract and its ownership can be verified at any

time by calling the function *checkTicketOwnership(id)*. The total number of tickets owned can be obtained by calling *balanceOf()*.

(3) Secondary market: Ticket owners can offer their tickets for resale by calling the function *setTicketForSale()*. They can use the function *setTicketPrice()* to charge any price that does not exceed the maximum price as defined by the event organizer. Any user with access to a blockchain-enabled web browser can purchase tickets from current ticket owners once approval has been given by the ticket owner through the call of *approvedAsBuyer()*. The buyer can now transfer the required amount of cryptocurrency to the payable function *buyTicketFromAttendee()*, which finally transfers the ticket to the buyer. The transaction fee set by the event organizer is automatically deducted and kept by the contract, where it can be withdrawn only by the contract owner. Once the event has started, the modifier *EventNotStarted()* will prohibit the use of any setter functions. Thus, no more tickets can be created or transferred after the time specified in *eventStartDate*. The organizer can call *setTicketToUsed()* to validate a ticket at the venue.

While the scope of this prototype does not feature a front-end for retail users, its full compatibility with the ERC-721 standard enables users to use any compatible wallet or NFT-marketplaces like OpenSea to facilitate peer-to-peer transactions in an easy manner (OpenSea, 2019). The prototype is deployed on the Ethereum test network Ropsten and thus allows any user with access to an Ethereum node to invoke the smart contract and use it. The source code of the implemented prototype including instructions for deployment is publicly available on GitHub (https://github.com/ratio91/NFT-event-tickets).

Evaluation and Discussion

For the evaluation, we linked back our resulting prototype to the design objectives and the evaluation criteria (see Table 12.2). Our evaluation is not limited to a single activity conducted at the end of the build phase, but rather represents an iterative process and encompasses multiple methods and perspectives (Pries-Heje et al., 2008).

Testing and Experimental Evaluation

For a thorough analysis of our prototype's functionality, structure, formal completeness, consistency, and quality, we relied on algorithmic white box testing, such as unit tests (Hevner et al., 2004). To refine and optimize our prototype, we followed a test-driven approach and iterated between testing and improving (Janzen & Saiedian, 2005). We utilized the Truffle framework containing the Mocha testing library and Chai assertion library for structural testing, unit tests, and functional tests (Truffle, 2019). To ensure the consistency and quality of each public function and all modifiers our prototype contains, we wrote several unit tests. Additionally, we created a series of integration tests to simulate the complete workflow, allowing us to test the formal completeness and functionality of our prototype. In total, we created 33 tests within 289 lines of JavaScript code to ensure that our prototype behaves correctly during state changes. A successful test run with artificial data, simulating the fully automated completion of the entire process as laid out in the previous section, thus serves as proof of construction, and shows that our solution works (Nunamaker et al., 1990). In addition to running tests and performing simulations, we also used the code linter Solhint and fixed all reported issues (Protofire, 2019). To avoid security holes and potential defects in our code, we searched recent literature covering security issues for smart contracts, as reported in Atzei et al. (2017) and Fröwis and Böhme (2017), and amended our code where necessary (e.g. setting some public functions to private). To allow other researchers or practitioners to verify our prototype and to enhance it further, we open sourced the entire project.

Expert Evaluation

To assess our artifact and discuss different scenarios regarding implications for our prototype and NFTs in general, we selected nine experts with different backgrounds based on their previous knowledge of NFTs and event ticketing. We introduced all experts to our research beforehand and followed a semi-structured interview guide (Holstein & Gubrium,

1995). We digitally recorded the interviews and analyzed them afterwards according to scientific standards (Schultze & Avital, 2011). Our interviews consisted of two main parts and typically lasted about 30 minutes. First, we focused on the recommended descriptive evaluation approach of assessing an artifact's efficacy and utility through the creation of illustrative scenarios around it (Hevner et al., 2004; Akoka et al., 2017). We discussed the suitability of our prototype regarding our specified design objectives and invited the interview partners to come up with realistic scenarios and explore the implications of our prototype. Second, we also asked open questions to allow for an in-depth discussion of the general aspects of NFTs such as: How can the implications NFTs have on the use case be generalized? What do you see as the main benefits of NFTs? In your perspective, what disadvantages does the use of NFTs have? What challenges remain and how could they be addressed in the future? Depending on the technical background of the interviewee, we also included analytic questions regarding the perceived fit of our prototype into existing technical IS architecture (Hevner et al., 2004).

Design Objectives Evaluation Results and Discussion

DO1—Digitization: Our simulation reveals that the whole workflow can be processed without the need for any physical representation of the data. Full digitization is achievable in principle, especially for the process of buying and selling tickets. However, fallback mechanisms are advisable to include less sophisticated users such as generating QR-codes that encode the ID of the ticket. The user could then decide whether to print out the ticket or show it digitally on the phone.

DO2—Secondary Markets: NFTs enable us to embed logic in digital assets such as event tickets themselves, rather than embedding logic in the applications that control assets. The prototype shows that embedding business rules for transferring event tickets works and enables event organizers to stay in control of the process, set price limits and charge ticket sellers a defined fee. A hard-coded logic is superior to governance or regulation that requires the monitoring of actual user behavior and enforcement of rules by human actors (Waltl et al.,

2019). It is much easier to collect a fee from the seller of a ticket if it is automatically deducted or to prevent transactions altogether, rather than requiring the seller by law to obey certain rules (Davidson et al., 2018). Thus, we consider the prototype as both more effective and more efficient than currently existing ways to control secondary market transactions. The only weakness we discovered is a scenario, where users circumvent the system altogether by transferring the private key of an Ethereum account that owns an event ticket itself, rather than exchanging the ticket within the system. This could be prevented by the implementation of KYC measures, which verify the identity of a user of a specific blockchain address. KYC itself is a hot topic among practitioners and researchers at the moment and could also be realized using a blockchain-based system (Kumar et al., 2020).

DO3—Independence: To become independent of intermediaries, event organizers and event attendees require a system that operates in a trust-free way. Using blockchain technology, users can trust the rules which are enforced automatically and cannot be manipulated (Beck et al., 2016). As every Ethereum node processes and validates transactions independently, the only trust required is in the underlying blockchain protocol (Glaser, 2017). However, trustlessness is not only a property of the platform but also of every individual smart contract (Fröwis & Böhme, 2017). Our interview partners generally agreed that independence from intermediaries can be achieved and the design objective is met. However, several experts highlighted that the most realistic use case for our NFT-based prototype would be the integration with existing platforms to benefit from the aggregation of users. Existing dependencies on intermediaries are replaced with a new dependence on technical intermediaries such as smart contract developers.

DO4—Security: Our literature research revealed that the security of a blockchain-based system is dependent on the general security of the underlying blockchain protocol and the security of individual smart contracts. The former faces security risks such as a 51% attack, where a single entity holds the majority of computing power (Choi et al., 2016). The latter faces security risks that originate from coding errors, a fact that we acknowledged at the beginning of our process and tried to mitigate as good as possible. The use of well-audited code from

OpenZeppelin as a basis for our implementation is an effective measure to reduce the attack surface of our smart contracts. Despite these measures, it cannot be ruled out that the application is vulnerable. Penetration tests by security professionals would be a valuable contribution (Vacca, 2013). Operational errors, such as the redeployment of new smart contract versions, open further possibilities for human error. Yet, a scenario where users are misled to interact with an outdated or even a fraudulent version of the smart contract, instead of the valid one, could be imagined and poses a problem. Additionally, the account security of the event organizer could be compromised in case the private key securing it is obtained by a malicious party. Thus, trust in the security measures taken by the event organizer is critical for the overall security of the system. We tried to limit the potential damage of such a scenario by effectively restricting the options of the owner to change parameters and pause transactions. Ownership of tickets itself would still be protected in such a case, thanks to the use of NFTs, which embed rules to only give current owners certain permissions (Entriken et al., 2018). NFTs also help to ensure integrity as they guarantee the uniqueness of tickets by design. The prototype does not provide a high level of privacy for users, as the Ethereum blockchain is public and uses pseudonymous identities. Researchers have shown that with limited effort, privacy based solely on pseudonymity can be overcome (Tschorsch & Scheuermann, 2016). Several interviewed experts indicated potential legal issues as data privacy laws might be breached. Aside from integrity and privacy, availability is a key factor of a secure system (Vacca, 2013). The Ethereum blockchain which is the protocol used as the basis for our prototype ensures virtually no downtime (Vermeulen et al., 2018).

DO5—Validation: Verifying the ownership of tickets worked fine in our simulations. Due to the transparency of all transactions conducted with the smart contract, users are able to verify the correctness of their actions at any time (Beck et al., 2016).

DO6—Transparency: As the transaction data is immutably stored on the blockchain, a record of ticket ownership is maintained. The open nature of the Ethereum blockchain allows anyone to view and thus verify the current owner of a ticket at any given time. However, viewing ownership only returns the Ethereum account or smart contract owning a ticket. Due to the pseudonymous nature of the blockchain, no details on user identities are known, unless effort is taken to uncover the true identity behind the account or perform KYC to identify users beforehand (Cai et al., 2018). To achieve full transparency KYC is necessary as any entity can own multiple Ethereum addresses. Higher transparency would be met with resistance by many event organizers due to fear of uncovering illegal side deals, such as withholding special contingents of tickets not visible for the public that are dealt behind closed doors for special favors.

DO7—Automation: As our simulation successfully showed, the event organizer is free from the need to take any manual action after the initial deployment of the smart contract. However, in case of errors being made in the setup phase, the event organizer can only correct these by sending transactions to the smart contracts which costs transaction fees. Thus, the organizer needs to properly fund the account in advance.

DO8—Cost efficiency: Simulating the deployment of the prototype showed that the expected gas amount required of 5 million gas costs about 0.01 Ether. The corresponding amount in fiat currency such as USD or EUR depends on the current exchange rate, which is highly volatile (Rimba et al., 2018). At the time of our simulation, it corresponded to about 20 USD (EthGasStation, 2021). Rising Ether prices could increase the costs substantially and lower cost efficiency. For event attendees, transaction fees for each interaction with the smart contract are substantially lower. However, despite lower costs, the fact that users are constantly reminded that any interaction with the prototype comes with a small fee might lead some users to prefer a centralized solution, where prices are more hidden instead (Beck et al., 2016).

Discussion of General Benefits and Challenges

A key benefit of NFTs is that they represent uniqueness better than any blockchain-based instruments before. They can help to make assets programmable and enhance liquidity and security. Even for assets with certain fungible aspects, a better differentiation can be achieved if NFTs are used rather than fungible tokens. Thanks to these benefits, NFTs enable new use cases for blockchain technology and have the potential to improve existing blockchain systems by simplifying them. Two main use cases can be distinguished. First, tokenization of digital goods is a perfect fit for NFTs as they can guarantee authenticity and uniqueness. Tickets could be considered as a bundle of rights and thus the tokenization of rights in general could be considered a viable use case for blockchain-based systems and specifically NFTs. During research of gray literature, we found several use cases that provide further evidence that NFTs are useful, such as the enablement of ownership in digital art (0xcert, 2018). Second, NFTs are ideally suited to represent physical assets in the digital sphere. A resulting increase in the transparency of ownership benefits regulators. However, to bridge the gap between the physical and the digital world, additional components such as intelligent sensors are also necessary.

Yet, using NFTs poses several challenges. As they are nothing more than a standardized piece of software code executed on a blockchain, they are highly dependent on the properties of the underlying blockchain protocol. As one expert explained, "anything you can do with NFTs is enabled by Ethereum, and everything you cannot do is not enabled by Ethereum". One of the most notable challenges of public blockchains like Ethereum is their limited scalability. However, we found that solutions that overcome this challenge already exist, such as using layer 2 networks (Schaffner & Schaer, 2021). If this issue is resolved, NFTs should be extremely scalable, as tests revealed that a single contract can handle 2^128 NFTs without problems (Entriken et al., 2018). Another challenge is the design dilemma of private versus public blockchain (Corten, 2017). Multiple researchers have shown that privacy is not guaranteed as it is possible to make sense out of pseudonymous data on public blockchains, where transparency and public access is a key feature (Tschorsch & Scheuermann, 2016). Yet, development of new promising technologies such as zero-knowledge proofs (ZKP) is ongoing and will solve this issue in the future (Koens et al., 2018). ZKP is a cryptographic method allowing to prove to another party certain properties without revealing them (e.g. proving that you're of a certain age, without revealing your actual age) (Koens et al., 2018). Proof that privacy is feasible for NFTs has been achieved by EY, which used ZKPs in combination with NFTs to facilitate private equity transactions (Khatri, 2018). Further, NFTs lack easy accessibility for retail users as they are a backend component and do not provide a user-friendly interface.

The requirement of paying gas for each function call, which is priced in Ether, complicates the use of blockchain-based systems even for experienced users (Rimba et al., 2018). Thus, users are required to purchase cryptocurrency upfront to pay transaction fees, even in case the business model would generally not charge the retail users (Cai et al., 2018). However, a EIP (Ethereum Improvement Proposal) called "Gas Stations Network", enabling smart contracts to pay the gas costs instead of the user, shows that this problem can be resolved (Weiss et al., 2018). Not only the price of gas fluctuates but also the price of the cryptocurrency. Ether is highly volatile (Rimba et al., 2018). This makes it very hard for retail users to calculate costs based on fiat currencies such as USD. A potential way to overcome this challenge is to use decentralized stablecoins such as DAI that try to resemble the value of fiat currency and thus free users from the currency risk and mental effort of fluctuating exchange rates (Ito & O'Dair, 2019).

Another important challenge for the use of blockchain-based systems in general is limited legal enforceability (Christidis & Devetsikiotis, 2016). While token owner can rely on authenticity, legal ownership and consumption of the rights represented by NFTs are a different matter. For a blockchain-based system to be truly trustless, legal correctness and legitimacy within the current institutional environment are required (Hawlitschek et al., 2018). Further, as NFTs are a very young phenomenon, people who understand NFTs are very scarce and the language used in the blockchain space is very technical and generally not well understood by the public.

During the construction of the artifact, we revealed a typical issue for NFTs regarding the creation of tokens. Unlike for fungible tokens, for NFTs, it is not possible to create many tokens right away. Minting NFTs one by one is cumbersome and inefficient since it requires lots of computational power and thus high gas costs occur. One solution we found and applied is to create the tokens only when demanded and paid for by buyers. This strategy is called "user-mintable" tokens (Stehlik & Vogelsang, 2018). Another challenge is the two-stepped process of approving transactions before the actual transaction can happen (Entriken et al., 2018). While a solution that is commonly used is to transfer NFTs temporarily to a marketplace contract that takes care of the transactions, this approach has some disadvantages. The fact that token ownership is temporarily transferred away from the owner poses a problem for some use cases and security can be negatively affected. What is more, every additional transfer costs gas and reduces efficiency. Further, the nature of smart contracts generally makes it easy to extend the system with new features. However, upgrading existing smart contracts bears multiple technical and operational risks and costs money. Relying on development frameworks like OpenZeppelin and Truffle significantly simplifies upgrade procedures and reduces risks.

Summing up, NFTs enable new beneficial ways to digitally represent digital and physical assets. Yet, many challenges remain to be solved. NFTs are based on blockchain technology which is still in its infancy and not yet ready for a mass market of retail users, who demand simplicity, user-friendly interfaces, and legal clarity. These demands cannot be solved by NFTs but need to be addressed on the level of the underlying blockchain protocols and legal institutions. Further, public knowledge about NFTs is still scarce. Given these challenges, we expect the role of NFTs to be restricted to a backend component rather than being directly visible for retail users. Nonetheless, we consider NFTs a highly valuable component for blockchain-based systems with the potential to enable many more practical use cases apart from the one discussed in this paper.

Conclusion

We have investigated NFTs as an emerging phenomenon and evaluated NFTs as a core building block for a blockchain-based event ticketing system. We followed a design science approach based on the guidelines of Hevner et al. (2004) and iteratively developed a prototype. Through the process of designing, building, and evaluating the NFT-based prototype, we were able to generate several relevant findings regarding benefits and challenges of the new token type. We found that NFTs can help to overcome the weaknesses of existing non-blockchain event ticketing systems, such as susceptibility to fraud, lack of control over secondary market transactions, and validation of ownership. Further, our findings indicate that the use of NFTs currently poses several challenges, mostly inherited from the underlying blockchain protocol. Since we have shown that work on solutions to overcome these challenges is currently in progress, we propose further research to re-assess the state of these challenges in the near future.

Before highlighting the contributions of our research, we must consider its limitations. First, by considering a specific use case in detail and following a rigorous research process to draw generalizable implications from it, we may have missed on certain insights that might have been discovered in different use cases. The use case itself is limited to a strongly simplified model of requirements for an event ticketing system and does not capture the role of other stakeholders and related processes in detail. Our architectural choices may narrow down the generalizability further (Koens & Poll, 2018). Second, despite our attempt to address the issues of user experience, legal implications, as well as technical and operational risks, we acknowledge their limited role in this study (Governatori et al., 2018). To reveal more insight into user acceptance of a system based on NFTs, we thus suggest complementary studies on other use cases of NFTs, including extensive field experiments with retail users and legal experts as key parts. Therefore, our findings should merely be perceived as a preliminary step toward a better theoretical and practical understanding of NFTs.

Despite these limitations, our research is one of the first scientific attempts to address the questions if NFTs are useful in practice and how they can help to improve existing systems in real-world domains. The valuable insights we generate for practitioners are threefold: First, we highlight the differences between NFTs and fungible tokens and provide best practices for the development and evaluation of systems using NFTs. Second, we demonstrate the usefulness of NFTs for the use case of event tickets and provide proof by construction through a successful implementation of a working prototype (Hevner et al., 2004). Third, we elaborate on the consequences of its use and highlight practical challenges. In addition to these practical insights, we add descriptive knowledge to an emerging field of research where scientific studies are scarce. We extend and complement existing studies in the literature on blockchain technology by adding new best practice approaches on how to build and evaluate a blockchain-based system using DSR (Glaser, 2017). Finally, our research serves as a foundation for future theoretical and practical research on NFTs, enables other researchers to draw on its findings and design principles, and lays the foundation for higher-order theory development (Gregor, 2006).

References

0xcert. (2018). NFT Spotlight #3—KnownOrigin, the non-fungible art platform. Retrieved from https://0xcert.org/news/nft-spotlight-3-knownorigin/

Akoka, J., Comyn-Wattiau, I., Prat, N., & Storey, V. C. (2017). *Evaluating knowledge types in design science research: An integrated framework* (Lecture Notes in Computer Science). Springer International Publishing.

Atzei, N., Bartoletti, M., & Cimoli, T. (2017). A survey of attacks on Ethereum smart contracts (SoK). In M. Maffei & M. Ryan (Eds.), *Principles of security and trust* (pp. 164–186). Springer.

Bachmann, N., Drasch, B., Fridgen, G., Miksch, M., Regner, F., Schweizer, A., & Urbach, N. (2021). Tarzan and chain: Exploring the ICO jungle and evaluating design archetypes. In *Electronic markets*. Springer.

Beck, R., & Müller-Bloch, C.. (2017). Blockchain as radical innovation: A framework for engaging with distributed ledgers as incumbent organization. In *Proceedings of the 50th Hawaii International Conference on System Sciences (2017)* (pp. 5390–5399).

Beck, R., StenumCzepluch, J., Lollike, N., & Malone, S. (2016). Blockchain—The gateway to trust-free cryptographic transactions. In *Twenty-Fourth European Conference on Information Systems (ECIS), İstanbul, Turkey, 2016* (pp. 1–14). Springer Publishing Company.

Buterin, V. (2014). A next-generation smart contract and decentralized application platform. http://buyxpr.com/build/pdfs/EthereumWhitePaper.pdf

Cai, W., Wang, Z., Ernst, J. B., Hong, Z., Feng, C., & Leung, V. C. M. (2018). Decentralized applications: The Blockchain-empowered software system. *IEEE Access, 6*, 53019–53033.

Choi, S., Smolander, K., Park, S., Yli-Huumo, J., & Ko, D. (2016). Where is current research on blockchain technology?—A systematic review. *PLOS ONE, 11*(10), 1–27.

Christidis, K., & Devetsikiotis, M. (2016). Blockchains and smart contracts for the internet of things. *IEEE Access, 4*, 2292–2303.

Coingecko. (2021). CoinGecko Q1 2021 Cryptocurrency Report. https://landing.coingecko.com/q1-2021-report/

Consensys. (2019). Infura—scalable blockchain infrastructure. https://infura.io/

Corten, P. A. (2017). *Blockchain technology for governmental services: Dilemmas in the application of design principles.*

Courty, P. (2017). *Ticket resale, bots, and the fair price ticketing curse.* http://web.uvic.ca/~pcourty/FPT1005.pdf

Davidson, S., Novak, M., & Potts, J. (2018). *The cost of trust: A pilot study.* https://ssrn.com/abstract=3218761

Delmolino, K., Arnett, M., Kosba, A. E., Miller, A., & Shi, E. (2016). Step by step towards creating a safe smart contract: lessons and insights from a cryptocurrency lab. In J. Clark, S. Meiklejohn, P. Y. A. Ryan, D. S. Wallach, M. Brenner, & K. Rohloff (Eds.), *Financial cryptography and data security, Christ Church, Barbados* (Vol. 9604, pp. 79–94). Springer.

Entriken, W., Shirley, D., Evans, J., & Sachs, N. (2018). ERC-721 non-fungible token standard. https://eips.ethereum.org/EIPS/eip-721

Ethereum Foundation. (2018). Ethereum improvement proposals. https://eips.ethereum.org/

Etherscan. (2021). Token tracker. https://etherscan.io/tokens

EthGasStation. (2021). ETH gas station. https://ethgasstation.info/calculatorTxV.php

Fröwis, M., & Böhme, R. (2017). In code we trust? In J. Garcia-Alfaro, G. Navarro-Arribas, H. Hartenstein, & J. Herrera-Joancomartí (Eds.), *Data Privacy management, cryptocurrencies and blockchain technology* (pp. 357–372). Springer International Publishing.

Fujimura, K., Kuno, H., Terada, M., Matsuyama, K., Mizuno, Y., & Sekine, J. (1999). Digital-ticket-controlled digital ticket circulation. In *Proceedings of the 8th Conference on USENIX Security Symposium—Volume 8* (p. 18). USENIX Association.

Glaser, F. (2017). Pervasive decentralisation of digital infrastructures: A Framework for blockchain enabled system and use case analysis. In: *50th Hawaii International Conference on System Sciences (HICSS-50), Waikoloa Village, Hawaii*, January 4–7, 2017 (pp. 1543–1552).

Governatori, G., Idelberger, F., Milosevic, Z., Riveret, R., Sartor, G., & Xu, X. (2018). On legal contracts, imperative and declarative smart contracts, and blockchain systems. *AI and Law, 26*(4), 377–409.

Gregor, S. (2006). The nature of theory in information systems. *MIS Quaterly, 30*(3), 611–642.

Gregor, S., & Hevner, A. R. (2013). Positioning and presenting design science research for maximum impact. *MIS Quaterly, 37*(2), 337–355.

Guggenberger, T., Schweizer, A., & Urbach, N. (2020). Improving inter-organizational information sharing for vendor managed inventory: Towards a decentralized information hub using blockchain technology. *IEEE Transactions on Engineering Management, 67*(4), 1074–1085.

Hawlitschek, F., Notheisen, B., & Teubner, T. (2018). The limits of trust-free systems: A literature review on blockchain technology and trust in the sharing economy. *Electronic Commerce Research and Applications, 29*, 50–63.

Hevner, A. R. (2007). A three cycle view of design science research. *Scandinavian Journal of Information Systems., 19*(2), 87–92.

Hevner, A. R., March, S. T., Park, J., & Ram, S. (2004). Design science in information systems research. *MIS Quarterly, 28*(1), 75–105.

Holstein, J. A., & Gubrium, J. F. (1995). *The active interview*. SAGE Publications.

Ito, K., & O'Dair, M. (2019). A critical examination of the application of blockchain technology to intellectual property management. In H. Treiblmaier & R. Beck (Eds.), *Business transformation through blockchain: Volume II* (pp. 317–335). Springer International Publishing.

Janzen, D., & Saiedian, H. (2005). Test-driven development concepts, taxonomy, and future direction. *Computer, 38*(9), 43–50.

Khatri, Y. (2018). EY reveals zero-knowledge proof privacy solution for Ethereum. https://www.coindesk.com/ey-reveals-zero-knowledge-proof-privacy-solution-for-ethereum/

Koens, T., & Poll, E. (2018). What blockchain alternative do you need? In J. Garcia-Alfaro, J. Herrera-Joancomartí, G. Livraga, & R. Rios (Eds.), *BT—data privacy management, cryptocurrencies and blockchain technology* (pp. 113–129). Springer International Publishing.

Koens, T., Ramaekers, C., & Van Wijk, C. (2018). *Efficient zero-knowledge range proofs in Ethereum*. https://t.co/RDwESNOvjR?amp=1

Kumar, M., Nikhil, Y., & Anand, P. (2020). A blockchain based approach for an efficient secure KYC process with data sovereignty. *International Journal of Scientific and Technology Research, 9*(1), 3403–3407.

Leonhart, M. (2018). About 12 percent of people buying concert tickets get scammed. https://www.cnbc.com/2018/09/13/about-12-percent-of-people-buying-concert-ticketsget-scammed-.html

Lindman, J., Tuunainen, V. K., & Rossi, M.. (2017). Opportunities and risks of blockchain technologies—A research agenda. In: *Proceedings of the 50th Hawaii International Conference on System Sciences* (pp. 1533–1542). Waikoloa, United States.

Lockl, J., Schlatt, V., Schweizer, A., Urbach, N., & Harth, N. (2020). Toward Trust in Internet of Things (IoT) ecosystems: Design principles for blockchain-based IoT applications. *IEEE Transactions on Engineering Management, 67*(4), 1256–1270.

March, S. T., & Smith, G. F. (1995). Design and natural science research on information technology. *Decision Support Systems, 15*(4), 251–266.

McMillan, C. (2016). Secondary ticketing: the problem and possible solutions, explained. https://inews.co.uk/culture/music/secondary-ticketing-problems-solutions/

Merriam-Webster. (2018). Fungible synonyms, fungible antonyms. https://www.merriam-webster.com/thesaurus/fungible

Mougayar, W. (2018). The blockchain's magical million users club. http://startupmanagement.org/2018/11/20/the-blockchains-magical-million-users-club/

Muzzy, E. (2018). CryptoKitties isn't about the cats. https://medium.com/@everett.muzzy/cryptokitties-isnt-about-the-cats-aef47bcde92d

Nærland, K., Müller-bloch, C., Beck, R., & Palmund, S. (2017). Blockchain to rule the waves—Nascent Design principles for reducing risk and uncertainty in decentralized environments abstract. In: *Thirty Eighth International Conference on Information Systems, South Korea 2017.*

Nakamoto, S. (2008). *Bitcoin: A peer-to-peer electronic cash system.* https://bitcoin.org/bitcoin.pdf

Notheisen, B., Cholewa, J. B., & Shanmugam, A. P. (2017). Trading real-world assets on blockchain. *Business & Information Systems Engineering, 59*(6), 425–440.

Nunamaker, J. F., Chen, M., & Purdin, T. D. M. (1990). Systems development in information systems research. *Journal of Management Information Systems, 6*(4), 89–106.

NZ Herald. (2017). The great ticket mark-up—how fans are paying through the nose. https://www.nzherald.co.nz/entertainment/news/article.cfm?c_id=1501119&objectid=11833817

OECD. (2019). Initial coin offerings (ICOs) for SME Financing. https://www.oecd.org/finance/initial-coin-offerings-for-sme-financing.htm

OpenSea. (2019). OpenSea. https://opensea.io/

OpenZeppelin. (2019). OpenZeppelin. https://openzeppelin.org/

Pitchbook (2021). Emerging spaces: Nonfungible tokens. https://my.pitchbook.com/emerging-spaces/456

Pries-Heje, J., Baskerville, R. L., & Venable, J. R. (2008). Strategies for design science research evaluation. *European Conference on Information Systems (ECIS 2008)*, Paper 87.

Protofire. (2019). Solhint—Solidity Linter. https://protofire.github.io/solhint/

Rimba, P., Tran, A. B., Weber, I., Staples, M., Ponomarev, A., & Xu, X. (2018). Quantifying the Cost of Distrust: Comparing Blockchain and Cloud Services for Business Process Execution. *Information Systems Frontiers, 22*, 1–19.

Rohr, J., & Wright, A. (2017). *Blockchain-based token sales, initial coin offerings, and the democratization of public capital markets* (Cardozo Legal Studies Research Paper No. 527). *SSRN*.

Schaffner, T., & Schaer, F. (2021). Scaling public blockchains—A comprehensive analysis of optimistic and zero-knowledge rollups. https://wwz.unibas.ch/fileadmin/user_upload/wwz/00_Professuren/Schaer_DLTFintech/Lehre/Tobias_Schaffner_Masterthesis.pdf

Schultze, U., & Avital, M. (2011). Designing interviews to generate rich data for information systems research. *Information and Organization, 21*(1), 1–16.

Schweizer, A., Schlatt, V., Urbach, N., & Fridgen, G. (2017). Unchaining social businesses—blockchain as the basic technology of a crowdlending platform. In: *38th ICIS*.

Sillaber, C., & Waltl, B. (2017). Life cycle of smart contracts in blockchain ecosystems. *Datenschutz Und Datensicherheit—DuD, 41*(8), 497–500.

Stehlik, P., & Vogelsang, L. (2018). *Privacy-enabled NFTs: User-mintable, non-fungible tokens with private off-chain data*. https://eips.ethereum.org/EIPS/eip-721

Szabo, N. (1994). Smart contracts. https://bit.ly/2rLG2Nr

Tackmann, B. (2017). *Secure event tickets on a blockchain* (Lecture Notes in Computer Science) (Vol. 10436, pp. 437–444). Springer.

Tepper, F. (2017). People have spent over $1M buying virtual cats on the Ethereum blockchain. https://t.co/Ea718is6M5

The Australian Government the Treasury. (2017). *Ticket reselling in Australia*. www.itsanhonour.gov.au

Tikhomirov, S. (2018). Ethereum: State of knowledge and research perspectives. In A. Imine, J. M. Fernandez, J.-Y. Marion, L. Logrippo, & J. Garcia-Alfaro (Eds.), *Foundations and practice of security* (pp. 206–221). Springer International Publishing.

Truffle. (2019). Truffle suite. https://truffleframework.com/

Tschorsch, F., & Scheuermann, B. (2016). Bitcoin and beyond: A technical survey on decentralized digital currencies. *IEEE Communications Surveys and Tutorials, 18*(3), 2084–2123.

Vacca, J. R. (2013). *Computer and information security handbook.* (J. R. Vacca, Ed., 2nd edn.). Morgan Kaufmann.

Vermeulen, E., Fenwick, M., & Kaal, W. (2018). Why blockchain will disrupt corporate organizations: What can be learned from the "digital transformation". *The Journal of the British Blockchain Association, 1*(2), 91–100.

Vogelsteller, F. (2015). ERC: Token standard #20. https://github.com/ethereum/EIPs/issues/20

Voshmgir, S. (2018). Fungible tokens vs. non-fungible tokens. https://blockchainhub.net/blog/blog/nfts-fungible-tokens-vs-non-fungible-tokens/

Waltl, B., Sillaber, C., Gallersdörfer, U., & Matthes, F. (2019). Blockchains and smart contracts: A threat for the legal industry? In *Business transformation through Blockchain: Volume II* (pp. 287–315). Palgrave Macmillan.

Wang, Y. (2017). Designing privacy-preserving blockchain based accounting information systems. *SSRN Electronic Journal.*

Waterson, M. (2016). *Independent Review of consumer protection measures concerning online secondary ticketing facilities.* https://bit.ly/2wLvnrB

Weiss, Y., Tirosh, D., & Forshtat, A. (2018). EIP 1613: Gas stations network. https://eips.ethereum.org/EIPS/eip-1613

Wood, G. (2014). *Ethereum: A secure decentralisedgeneralised transaction ledger.* Ethereum Project Yellow Paper, 1–32.

Wüst, K., & A. Gervais. (2017). Do you need a blockchain? *IACR Cryptology EPrint Archive*, 1–7.

Zohar, A. (2015). Bitcoin: Under the hood. *Communications of the ACM, 58*(9), 104–113.

13

Saving the Oceans with NFTs

James Allen Regenor and Eric D. Achtmann

House of Cards

Following nearly two years under COVID lockdown, the world has emerged to a flurry of climate disasters across the globe and, indeed, news of impending climate collapse. Flooding in Europe and China has eradicated whole towns and, as of mid-July 2021, over 34,000 wildfires burned in the United States and Canada.[1] In Siberia alone, 40 million acres burned this year (yes, Siberia—an area 1.7 times the United States covered with once-frozen tundra separating one of the world's largest methane sources from exiting to the atmosphere). In the Amazon, an area the

[1] https://fas.org/sgp/crs/misc/IF10244.pdf

J. A. Regenor (✉)
Boston, MA, USA

E. D. Achtmann
Buffalo, NY, USA
e-mail: eric.achtmann@globalcapitalx.com

M. C. Lacity, H. Treiblmaier (eds.), *Blockchains and the Token Economy*, Technology, Work and Globalization, https://doi.org/10.1007/978-3-030-95108-5_13

size of the United Kingdom is ablaze,[2] while parts of the Pacific Northwest reached sustained temperatures typically felt in the world's deserts. Once watered parts of California are beginning to resemble parched Lake Mega-Chad in the Saharan Bodélé Depression and hydroelectric plants lay fallow.[3,4,5] This week's news alone brought to light fears of an impending stalling of the Gulf Stream, Atlantic Overturning Meridional Circulation (AMOC)[6] which would drastically and irreversibly change global weather—plunging the parts of North America and Europe into arctic temperatures and causing deadly drought across Southeast Asia.[7] And, as a direct and macabre attribution, it is estimated that humans have caused the extinction of 83 percent of the plant and animal life on the planet to date.[8] It goes without saying that "something is seriously, seriously wrong here".

None of this was unexpected. Already in 1979 Jay Forrester's "Limits to Growth" predicted in detail these developments[9] and, for the climate deniers, recently released studies performed by big oil going back 50 years have confirmed the same[10]—and made the causal link between human behavior (e.g., the burning of fossil fuels) and planet threatening climate change. In July, a UN panel announced that irreparable damage has been done and that humanity's best hope through immediate concerted measures is to prevent the "worst" from happening, while the "bad" is already taken as a given. Accelerated by climate change is the collapse of the ecosystems which feed us—already weakened by human ignorance, neglect, hubris, and greed.

---

[2] https://www.youtube.com/watch?v=osBJoLZaWKQ

[3] https://www.businessinsider.com/take-a-look-at-lakes-that-dried-up-california-drought-2021-6?op=1

[4] https://www.rt.com/news/270688-mega-chad-lake-sahara/

[5] https://www.cnbc.com/2021/08/06/california-shuts-down-major-hydroelectric-plant-amid-severe-drought.html

[6] https://en.wikipedia.org/wiki/Atlantic_meridional_overturning_circulation

[7] https://www.theguardian.com/environment/2021/aug/05/climate-crisis-scientists-spot-warning-signs-of-gulf-stream-collapse

[8] https://www.globalcitizen.org/en/content/humans-destroyed-83-of-wildlife-report/

[9] https://www.thenation.com/article/archive/limits-growth-book-launched-movement/

[10] https://www.thenation.com/article/environment/big-oil-knew-climate-crisis/

The same society which receives the rewards of technology must, as a cooperating whole, take responsibility for control. To deal with these new problems will require a new conservation. We must not only protect the countryside and save it from destruction, we must restore what has been destroyed and salvage the beauty and charm of our cities. Our conservation must be not just the classic conservation of protection and development, but a creative conservation of restoration and innovation. Its concern is not with nature alone, but with the total relation between man and the world around him. Its object is not just man's welfare, but the dignity of man's spirit. US President Lyndon B. Johnson, February 23, 1966

Nobody Sees the Oceans' Tears

At the forefront of this ecological collapse are the world's oceans which account for approximately 71 percent of the World's surface area. Directly, 10 percent of the world's population depends on fisheries for their livelihoods, and 4.3 billion people are reliant on fish for 15 percent of their animal protein intake.[11] Indirectly, countless creatures and ecosystems—including humanity—depend on the sustenance of the world's oceans.

Inspired by these facts, The Salacia Project ("TSP" or "Salacia") is a result of hearing the klaxons sounding the alarm of the impending failure of marine ecosystems. Every person on earth is affected by the oceans. From food sources or weather patterns generated by the currents, the health and vitality of the marine ecosystems should be a concern of everybody. The Salacia Project is a gateway project based on four premises:

1. *Our oceans are unique, irreplaceable, and essential to life.* They literally provide the air we breathe. In fact, the oceans produce over half of the world's oxygen and absorb 50 times more carbon dioxide than our atmosphere. They also regulate our climate and weather patterns.[12]
2. *Our oceans are under assault.* Ten human-driven factors are primary drivers in the destruction of our life-giving oceans. These include (1) overfishing and irresponsible fish farming, (2) ghost fishing, (3) gar-

[11] http://www.fao.org/news/story/en/item/248479/icode/

[12] https://oceanservice.noaa.gov/facts/why-care-about-ocean.html

bage, (4) acidification, (5) dead zones, (6) mercury pollution, (7) offshore drilling, (8) whaling and shark-finning, (9) ocean warming, and (10) destruction of habitats and reefs.[13,14] Already, the oceans have become home to five floating garbage "gyres", some larger than Texas and Germany.[15] The plastic pollution in our oceans alone could outweigh fish by 2050 if things don't change.[16] Below the surface and in some of the most fish-populated areas, disintegrating nuclear submarines are becoming the "slow moving Chernobyl", with catastrophic potential that threatens entire ecosystems.[17]

3. *Lacking accountability is at the root of the problem.* According to the World Wildlife Foundation ("WWF"), the global plastic pollution problem has been created in one generation. The WWF suggests that by creating system-wide accountability through the full plastic container manufacturing value chain, the problem can be arrested.[18] The issue is tricky because the production and materials are often far upstream from the actual point of use and disregard where the pollution occurs so an "it's not my problem, I didn't throw it in the water" mentality prevails and neither incentivizes reduction of unnecessary or harmful products and waste, nor responsible sustainable production using biodegradable alternatives. For example, before considering if paper, bamboo, or metal straws can replace plastics, we need to pose the question whether the prolific use of straws—a major source of pollution—is even necessary. Using blockchain provenance to track and trace plastic pollution from on production to pollution will enable governments and consumers to hold the whole value chain to account.
4. *Application of modern technology can help to change behavior.* Modern technology is as much the root of the problem as it can be a part of the

---

[13] https://apnews.com/article/oceans-coral-reefs-us-news-ap-top-news-corals-488c25b18b6349988feb791420a24370

[14] http://www.worldoceansday.ca/education-resources/top-11-issues-affecting-oceans

[15] https://response.restoration.noaa.gov/about/media/how-big-great-pacific-garbage-patch-science-vs-myth.html

[16] https://www.greenpeace.org.au/blog/oceans-attack-can-help/

[17] https://www.bbc.com/future/article/20200901-the-radioactive-risk-of-sunken-nuclear-soviet-submarines

[18] https://wwf.panda.org/wwf_news/?344071/Accountability-can-reverse-plastic-pollution-crisis-says-WWF-report

solution. While technology alone has never solved a problem, its application has solved many. Doing so in a responsible, judicious matter is the key.

Herein lies a critical concept. Specifically, [mother] nature is both complex and efficient. Since the Precambrian era ca. 600 million years ago, increasingly complex life has inhabited this planet.[19] The relationships, interactions, and processes which govern this life—from the galactic to the sub-atomic—transcend our ability to understand. Even with the spectacular scientific advances of late, we have only scratched the surface, and one could argue that we have no more perspective of the complexities of nature than a fruit fly has of the New York Stock Exchange. It is the epitome of hubris and unconscious incompetence that would lead humanity to believe that it can "fix" nature—or bend it to its will. In fact, recent history is replete with examples where Man has sought to "correct", "improve", or even outsmart nature with catastrophic consequences including Stalin's 1930s bid to reduce world hunger by releasing the Kamchatka "King" crab into western regions with catastrophic effect for global northern marine environment,[20] European canalization of waterways leading to destructive flooding,[21] or the damaging unbalancing of entire ecosystems through the systematic killing of predators in the United States (e.g., Yellowstone National Park).[22] Ultimately, we are forced to try to reverse these ill-conceived and short-sighted initiatives with 20:20 hindsight—and varying degrees of success. Consequently, and as provocative as it may sound, nature is not the problem. Humans and their behavior are. Hence, we are well advised to address our own issues, before trying to counsel Mother Nature.

To better apply technologies to restore the vitality and health of marine ecosystems, understanding what behavior shifts that have the greatest

[19] https://en.wikipedia.org/wiki/Precambrian

[20] https://morningstaronline.co.uk/a-2057-stalins-crab-all-set-to-take-over-the-northern-seas-1

[21] https://climate-adapt.eea.europa.eu/metadata/adaptation-options/rehabilitation-and-restoration-of-rivers

[22] https://www.nps.gov/yell/learn/nature/wolf-restoration

impact on pollution allows governments and NGOs to focus on those groups and/or elements of the value chain.[23]

While innovation and technology cannot correct the damage it has caused at the hands of humans, it can help to change human behavior and localize the impact of often non-local events. For technologies to be helpful, they should leverage four key characteristics to produce the desired outcomes (see Fig. 13.1), specifically:

a. *Archive* events in terms of objective criteria (e.g., who, what, where, when, and how). Failure to archive events runs the risk of acknowledgement of their very existence. "If a tree falls in the forest…."[24]
b. *Assess*—Once an event is archived, its impact must be assessed in terms of objective criteria which are meaningful for all stakeholders over the short and long term (e.g., lives, health, cost).
c. *Ascribe*—With the assessment of impact and application of forensics, it becomes possible to identify patterns, processes, and causality.
d. *Address*—Once causality has been established, problems can be addressed through preventative and corrective measures.

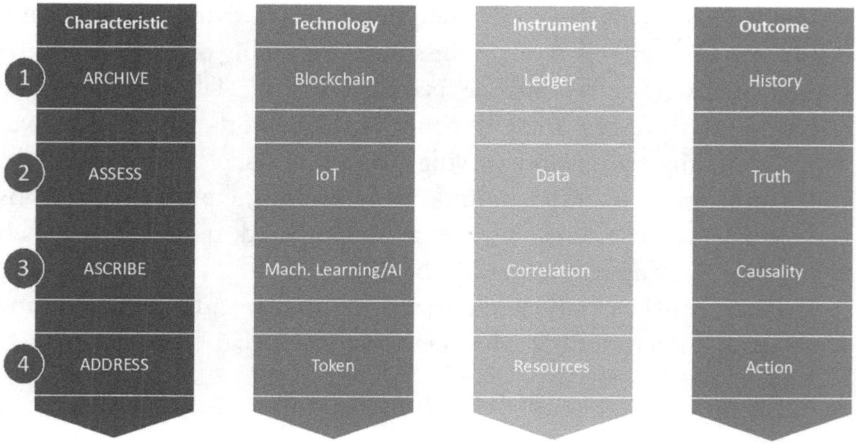

Fig. 13.1 Technology Levers (Courtesy: Salacia.io)

[23] https://deloitte.wsj.com/articles/the-human-side-of-tech-driving-behavioral-change-1522900929

[24] https://en.wikipedia.org/wiki/If_a_tree_falls_in_a_forest

The convergence of blockchain, IoT, AI, and NFTs is critical to weave a data fabric layer essential to gaining a strategic understanding of the problem while applying knowledge learned from the data sets to create tactically executable solutions. There are many battles to be waged in this fight. Having a common architecture allowing for data visualization within a data integrity framework created with a blockchain distributed ledger is critical to having truth and transparency in the historical records required to identify causality. Those records aid in the development of strategies and incentives to shift behaviors of people, governments, and corporations in a positive direction.

To sustain an environment suitable for man, we must fight on a thousand battlegrounds. Despite all of our wealth and knowledge, we cannot create a redwood forest, a wild river, or a gleaming seashore. But we can keep these we have. Lyndon B. Johnson February 23, 1966

What Is the Salacia Project?

President Johnson's words are both inspirational and prescriptive in the development of the Salacia Project, "…a creative conservation of restoration and innovation. Its concern is not with nature alone, but with the total relation between man and the world around him". The Salacia Project is a call to action, a call to examine, understand, and reverse the profound negative impact humankind is having on the oceans.

Salacia Project draws its name from the muse of Neptune and the protectress of the sea. The mission of the Salacia Project is to create a community focused on leveraging technology to restore the vitality and health of the oceans and marine ecosystems. Functionally, Salacia is a platform to pool community, technology, and resources to generate BlueTech solutions and to promote the education needed to raise awareness of the relation between human behavior and the catastrophic developments our oceans are experiencing. Like most startups, each of these BlueTech solutions is yoked with the need to raise funds. Salacia Project will create revenue flow by minting collectable digital assets in the form of non-fungible tokens ("NFT"). In startups, this yoke manifests itself in the tension that exists between the allocation of resources between fundraising and technology development. Salacia Project will lighten the yoke by availing resources to the BlueTech Projects in the form of minds, hands, funds, and time. Salacia will use the platform to promote activities to educate and raise awareness of the impact humankind is having on the oceans and marine ecosystems, and to generate a resource stream via NFT sales.

The Salacia Project is a direct result of this renewed awareness in the importance of climate tech (i.e., BlueTech, GreenTech). In the past year close to 300 companies have made a commitment to achieve Net Zero emissions before 2050.[25] Corporations are now realizing the market value of being a good global corporation—and global stakeholder.

> *In January of last year, I wrote that climate risk is investment risk. I said then that as markets started to price climate risk into the value of securities, it would spark a fundamental reallocation of capital. Then the pandemic took hold—and in March, the conventional wisdom was the crisis would divert attention from climate. But just the opposite took place, and the reallocation of capital accelerated even faster than I anticipated. Larry Fink, CEO of BlackRock, Letter to CEOs, 2021*

Corporations moving to Net Zero will have a positive impact on the climate, which, in turn, will have a positive impact on the oceans and marine ecosystems, but is that enough? Pausing to reflect: 2050 is 29 years from now and a lot of irreparable damage will occur until then.

The Salacia Project provides individuals and corporations a means to act now—to do more than sitting by idle waiting for somebody else to take action to save the oceans and marine ecosystems.

> *To sustain an environment suitable for man, we must fight on a thousand battlegrounds. Despite all of our wealth and knowledge, we cannot create a redwood forest, a wild river, or a gleaming seashore. But we can keep these we have. Lyndon B. Johnson February 23, 1966*

---

[25] https://www.forbes.com/sites/dishashetty/2021/03/24/a-fifth-of-worlds-largest-companies-committed-to-net-zero-target/?sh=60ccee44662f

Riding the Third Wave of Blockchain Innovation

The first wave of blockchain and cryptocurrency innovation was the Initial Coin Offering ("ICO") craze where hundreds of different companies and individuals released tokens in an adrenaline-fueled speculative frenzy. Few of those projects ever took shape.

Some enterprise projects emerged from the first wave, whereby TradeLens and the IBM Food Trust[26] are current impactful examples.

Today, the second wave of innovation is hitting the beach—Decentralized Finance ("DeFi"). Traditional financial institutions have begun to leverage blockchain technology and the attributes of cryptocurrency technologies to create decentralized finance tools for banks and traditional financial institutions. Startups are creating innovative peer-to-peer financial tools to which the banks are now responding.

Salacia Project is riding the most recent, third "NFT" wave as it builds momentum. NFTs are being used to create value across multiple verticals from digital representations of physical items, collectibles, unique digital art, or as a source of provenance for fine wines and gems. The Salacia Project is using NFTs in a collectible digital asset schema. The Salacia Project NFTs benefit from market value creation based on the scarcity of the collectible much like traditional sports trading cards (see Fig. 13.2).

What type of market value is possible? Today, CryptoPunks has a market cap of nearly $2 billion[27] and estimates of CryptoKitties market value exceed $400 million. Are other projects utilizing crypto in an altruistic manner? There is a project called AMACOIN positioned to save the rainforest.[28]

The origin of the AMACOIN was possible by converting the title of tangible assets, such as a commodity resource, to a smart asset via the AMACOIN token. This conversion leads to more precise definitions of

[26] https://www.ibm.com/blockchain/solutions/food-trust

[27] https://www.prnewswire.com/in/news-releases/cryptopunks-market-capitalization-nearly-2--billion-860065110.html

[28] https://medium.com/@amazoniansgreencoin/the-cryptocurrency-that-will-help-to-save-the-amazon-5538a80e6dda

Fig. 13.2 Examples of Salacia Project Collectable NFTs (Courtesy: Salacia.io)

tradable assets, and it also benefits from the blockchain's state-of-the-art transparency concerning the natural resource and commodity markets. Under globally recognized certification standards, the EBCF[29] will enhance the adoption of AMACOINs to anyone who wants to create a better world. Our Amazonian coins are not just superficial numbers on a blockchain: they stand for an actual concrete asset within the Amazonian rainforest.[30]

The Salacia Project shares the same altruistic DNA as the AMACOIN Project. The difference between collectable digital assets like CryptoKitties or CryptoPunks and Salacia Project is the benefactors of the revenue stream. The revenue stream for the Salacia Project provides resources for new and existing conservation and environmental projects.

[29] https://www.ebcf.org

[30] https://medium.com/@amazoniansgreencoin/the-cryptocurrency-that-will-help-to-save-the-amazon-5538a80e6dda

Resources Provided by the Salacia Project

1. *Minds*: Salacia intends to bring the leading technologists and academics together to solve the wicked problems facing our marine ecosystems.
2. *Hands*: Salacia will create a venue for individuals and communities to come together to work on projects together. A benefit of working as a team to solve a problem is a sense of ownership. Salacia will provide hands-on opportunities for people to be involved in the solution.
3. *Money*: Through the sales of collectable NFTs, Salacia will generate revenue that can be used to fund research, innovation, existing projects, and prizes awarded for solving wicked problems. A recent example is the X Prize where "SpaceShipOne crossed the finish line in an eight-year, $10 million space race Monday, winning the Ansari X-Prize with its second spaceflight in less than a week. Along the way, the world's first privately developed spacecraft also broke a 41-year-old altitude record and created a new astronaut".[31]
4. *Time*: Salacia hopes to accelerate solution development and employment by providing BlueTech company with resources. So much of a company's development time is wasted as it searches for resources.

There are many examples of wicked problems being solved when a community unites to tackle them. The best recent example is the 2015 Hyperloop Challenge. SpaceX launched the competition and called on students to submit design proposals for the Hyperloop, which works by shooting pods through a vacuumed-sealed tube. SpaceX then selected 30 teams to participate in the competition, which had its first run in January. SpaceX awarded prize money to many teams, but ultimately Technical University of Munich[32] took home the win thanks to achieving the top speed overall of any team to run in the finals.[33]

Salacia endeavors to leverage past successes for future gains and will follow this model.

---

[31] https://www.nbcnews.com/id/wbna6167761

[32] https://www.yahoo.com/entertainment/big-winners-elon-musks-hyperloop

[33] https://techcrunch.com/2019/07/21/team-tum-wins-spacex-hyperloop-pod-competition-with-record-288-mph-top-speed/

To be impactful in restoring the health and vitality of the oceans Salacia runs parallel lines of effort. First, to understand cause, scale, and potential solutions of the harms, Salacia uses NFTs as prize money for solutions generated from Hackathons and prize competitions. Second, education and awareness are needed in both commercial and consumer markets to prevent escalation or continuation of the harm. Salacia is funding aggressive marketing and education programs in concert with local government entities and existing conservation organizations. Third, many existing conservation and environmental organizations are doing great work and could scale with resources. Salacia helps existing organizations maintain and expand their current charters. Fourth, leveraging new and existing tech, Salacia restores the vitality of marine ecosystems. Last, Salacia is focused on protecting and preserving the vibrant ecosystems not yet harmed by humankind. An aggressive education and monitoring system will be created by the Salacia Project.

Also envisioned is the ability for corporations to participate by offering Salacia NFTs as part of their loyalty programs or their employee incentive programs. Corporations would also get a secondary benefit by being able to show they are participating in BlueTech development, conservation, and environmentalism. This participation could also become part of their calculus for their Environment, Social, and Governance ("ESG") scoring. It is anticipated in the future, ESG scoring will have an impact on interest rates from lenders. It will have an impact potentially on contracts from government organizations. ESG scoring requirements could become part of the requirements of government contracts and there could be flow down requirements.

As investors are making investment decisions based on ESG data presented by corporations, the SEC has said they will audit corporation's ESG claims. The SEC recently stated, "The staff will continue to examine firms to evaluate whether they are accurately disclosing their ESG investing approaches and have adopted and implemented policies, procedures, and practices that accord with their ESG-related disclosures".[34] Salacia collectables will provide a transparent manner for SEC examination.

[34] https://www.sec.gov/files/esg-risk-alert.pdf

To keep operating cost low, the Salacia Project is leveraging existing technology by utilizing the exchange provided by OpenSea platform. Moreover, the Salacia Project is utilizing existing digital wallets such as Coinbase wallet or many others to provide visibility of your non-fungible token collections. It is anticipated people will want to highlight their response to the call action by displaying the different and rare NFT tokens they acquire.

Salacia Project Roadmap

Figure 13.3 depicts the Salacia Project's roadmap.

Conclusion

Since the advent of industrialization and with wanton abandon for the delicate natural balance which took tens of millions of years to attain, humanity has caused—directly or indirectly—the extinction of over one million species[35] on our planet and destruction of over 70 percent of the

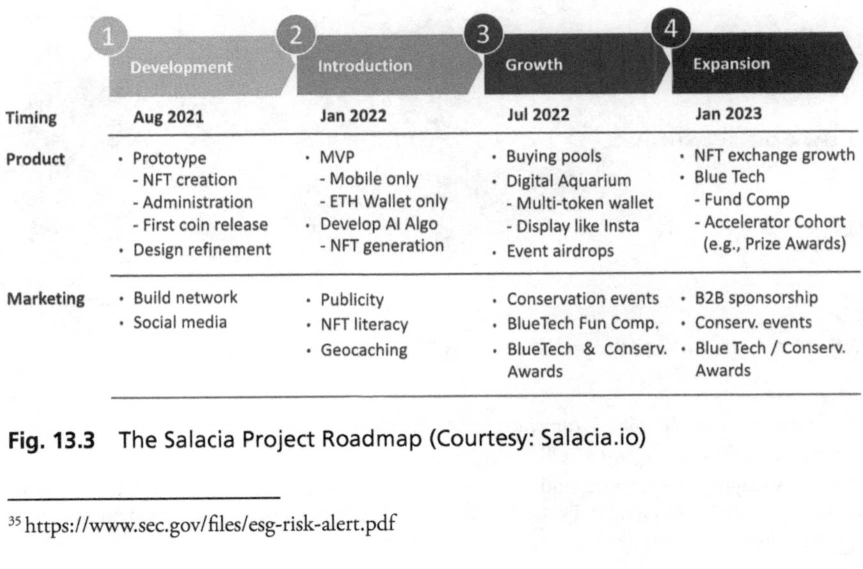

Fig. 13.3 The Salacia Project Roadmap (Courtesy: Salacia.io)

[35] https://www.sec.gov/files/esg-risk-alert.pdf

biosphere[36]—a macabre achievement surpassing the comet strikes which eradicated the dinosaurs.

Mother Nature does not discern among borders, parties, race, or socio-economic standing. This ecological collapse taking place in our marine eco-systems is forcing a rapid transition from a world of quarterly earnings and "drill baby drill"[37] to "if you are not part of the solution, you are part of the problem". The boat is sinking for all irrespective who sits nearest to the hole. Further, as the system becomes increasingly non-linear and unstable, "wait and see" or "let's average extreme perspectives"[38] are non-starters.

New technologies must be leveraged to create applications like The Salacia Project. New virtuous cycles are needed as the call to action is sounded (Fig. 13.4).

The Salacia Project is one small effort to raise awareness, fund BlueTech, and provide a venue for people, corporations, and governments to make a difference as they answer the call to action.

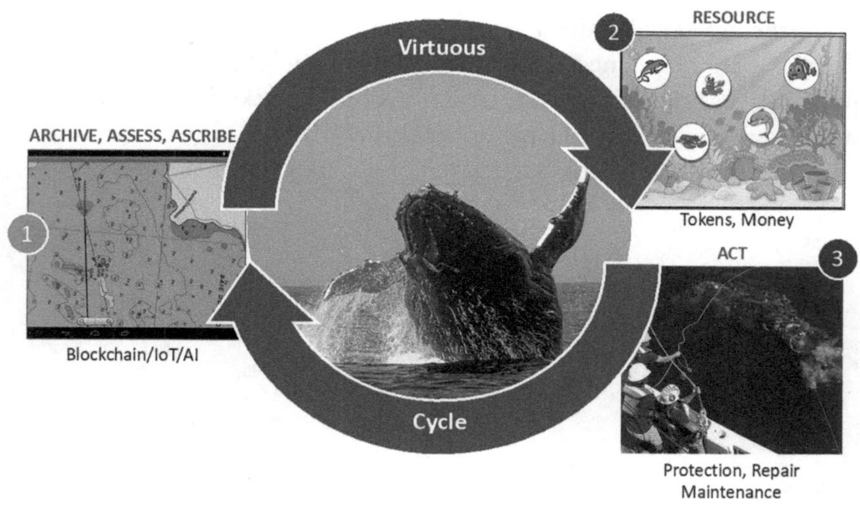

Fig. 13.4 The Salacia Project's Virtuous Cycle (Courtesy: Salacia.io)

[36] https://www.ncbi.nlm.nih.gov/pmc/articles/PMC7157458/

[37] https://en.wikipedia.org/wiki/Drill,_baby,_drill

[38] Note: Averaging two extreme (and often unrealistic) perspectives does not produce an accurate result and, in fact, can produce a result which has no bearing on reality (e.g., otherwise known as "garbage in, garbage out").

Correction to: Recovering from Blockchain Missteps and Myths with Coopetition

Dale Chrystie

Correction to:

Chapter 2 in: M. C. Lacity, H. Treiblmaier (eds.), *Blockchains and the Token Economy*, Technology, Work and Globalization, https://doi.org/10.1007/978-3-030-95108-5_2

The Author has provided belated corrections to the title of this chapter. The corrections to the chapter title have been carried out as follows:

Recovering from Blockchain Missteps and Myths with Coopetition

The updated original version of this chapter can be found at https://doi.org/10.1007/978-3-030-95108-5_2

M. C. Lacity, H. Treiblmaier (eds.), *Blockchains and the Token Economy*, Technology, Work and Globalization, https://doi.org/10.1007/978-3-030-95108-5_14

Appendix: Overview of Blockchain Technologies

Mary C. Lacity and Horst Treiblmaier

For readers new to blockchain technologies, we provide this brief overview to quickly bring readers up to speed so they can understand the innovations described by authors of this collection.

In short, blockchains are software; they are peer-to-peer systems for validating, time-stamping, and permanently storing transactions on a shared *distributed ledger*. Digital assets, represented by *tokens*, exist only in digital form, and come with rights of use. Ownership over the asset is proven using cryptographic private-public key pairs. *Consensus algorithms* determine the procedures for validating transactions, updating the ledger, and keep the ledger in sync and the network secure. Most blockchains also use *smart contracts* that apply rules to automatically execute

M. C. Lacity
Sam M. Walton College of Business, University of Arkansas,
Fayetteville, AR, USA
e-mail: mclacity@uark.edu

H. Treiblmaier
School of International Management, Modul University Vienna,
Vienna, Austria
e-mail: horst.treiblmaier@modul.ac.at

M. C. Lacity, H. Treiblmaier (eds.), *Blockchains and the Token Economy*, Technology, Work and Globalization, https://doi.org/10.1007/978-3-030-95108-5

transactions based upon pre-agreed conditions (Lacity, 2020). From this brief explanation, a blockchain application comprises multiple components, each of which is examined in more detail.

Distributed ledger. Fundamentally, a blockchain application comprises a *distributed ledger* and a network of independent nodes to manage copies of the ledger. The ledger is often structured as a chain of blocks but alternative structures such as directed acyclic graphs are also possible. Each block comprises header information and the sequenced transactions. The block header includes a pointer to the previous block of transactions, forming a chain of sequenced blocks over time that extends all the way back to the first block, called the 'genesis block'. A blockchain is an append-only database that grows with every block. The contents of each block, once they are deep enough in the chain, are basically immutable (Treiblmaier, 2019).

Tokens. The distributed ledger tracks transactions of digital asset exchanges among trading partners. Digital assets can represent *fungible tokens*, where each token is interchangeable because they are identical for practical purposes and thus fully interchangeable. Bitcoins, litecoins, and ether are examples of fungible tokens. Digital assets can also represent *non-fungible tokens* (NFTs), whereby each token is unique and can have a different value than others of its kind. CryptoKitties, an NFT launched on Ethereum in 2017, popularized NFTs (Wong, 2017). NFTs have opened new opportunities for value creation and exchange. As of October 2021, Mike Winkelman—the artist known as Beeple—has the highest price paid for an NFT at $69 million for a digital collage of this work (Kastrenakes, 2021).

People often question: What makes these tokens valuable? Price is determined by market demand relative to supply. People demand tokens for a variety of reasons, such as the desire to support a project or community, to access services that require tokens, and the anticipation that the token will increase in value. Scarcity of tokens, relative to the demand, drives up value (Zur & Lacity, 2021). As an example of a fungible token that is scarce, Bitcoin's software capped the total monetary supply at 21 million bitcoins and has an automatic monetary distribution schedule (Nakamoto, 2008). The last bitcoin will be released in the year 2140 and after that no more of them will be created. Each NFT is scarce because it is one of a kind. Whether Beeple's digital collage increases or decreases in value remains to be seen, but its uniqueness certainly contributes to its value.

How does one prove ownership over a tokenized asset? In a blockchain network, the ownership of a digital asset is proven using public-private key pairs. Each private-public key pair is a mathematical mate such that it is impossible to figure out the private key if one only has access to the public key. In the future, however, quantum computing might be able to break several popular cryptography systems, which might then be replaced by post-quantum cryptography. Private keys are stored in *digital wallets* off a blockchain; public keys are stored on the distributed ledger. To transfer an asset, the sender uses the private key from her digital wallet to authorize the transfer of the asset from her public address to the recipient's public address. The asset will remain linked to the recipient's address on the distributed ledger until the recipient decides to use his private key to transfer the value to another address.

Consensus. A consensus algorithm ensures that the copies of the ledger stay in sync. The nodes in the network constantly check to make sure no party tampers with the records after the fact. If anyone cheats, the other parties' nodes automatically ignore it. Decentralization thus secures the ledger. With no central honeypot of value, a hacker would need to overtake more than 50 percent of the network to try to control the ledger.

The consensus algorithm also determines which node is allowed to add a new block to the top of the ledger. A proof-of-work algorithm uses a competition among nodes to determine which node creates the next block. A proof-of-stake algorithm requires nodes to lock away some amount of cryptocurrency as insurance that the node behaves honestly. Members with the highest 'stake' (i.e., having the largest account balances) are giving priority in the selection algorithm. Proof-of-authority is a consensus mechanism that pre-authorizes nodes with the authority to validate and add transactions to a distributed ledger. The algorithm takes turns selecting a leader from among the list of authorized nodes. These are just three examples of consensus algorithms; there are many more such as proof-of-activity; proof-of-capacity; proof-of-elapsed time; proof-of-listening; and proof-of-luck (Lacity, 2020).

Consensus algorithms can be classified into four types based on who is authorized to transact in the network, and who is authorized to operate a validator node (see Table A.1). Rights of participation are either open to the public or private; rights of validation are either permissionless (anyone may operate a validator node) or permissioned (an individual or institution needs permission or must be selected/voted upon to run a validator node).

Thus far, individuals, projects, and startups have been the primary adopters of public-permissionless blockchains. Several incumbent enterprises, particularly those in financial services, began to examine the blockchain landscape when Bitcoin was about five years old. Industry consortia like R3, founded in 2014, were started to help incumbent enterprises understand the threats and opportunities of the token economy. Most consortia explored private-permissioned blockchains. The first enterprise blockchain applications went live when Bitcoin was already nine years old, in 2018, with the IBM Food Trust for tracing food and TradeLens for tracing shipping containers. Businesses largely chose private networks to meet scalability, confidentiality, and regulatory compliance requirements that public blockchains could not yet provide. Private networks require infrastructure investment and agreements on business rules, data, and decision-making rights, which can be slow and costly. Ultimately, enterprises may embrace public blockchains for certain use cases. EY, Microsoft, and ConsenSys are also proponents of public blockchain networks. They released the Baseline Protocol, which uses zero-knowledge proofs, to provide confidential transactions on Ethereum.

Smart contracts. A smart contract—a concept developed by Nick Szabo (1997, 1998)—is a piece of software that stores rules for negotiating the terms of an agreement, automatically verifies the contract and then executes the terms. Ethereum was the first major blockchain to include full smart contracting capabilities, thus escalating blockchains from peer-to-peer payment systems to platforms that can execute machine-to-machine agreements. Among others, smart contracts have been deployed for lotteries, voting, crowdsourcing, asset sharing, asset tracking, real estate, insurance, identity management, bidding, rating, gaming, and gambling. One special kind of smart contact is called a Decentralized Autonomous Organization (DAO):

Table A.1 Types of blockchain networks

		Who can operate a validator node?	
		Permissionless *(Anyone)*	Permissioned *(Requires permission, selection, or election)*
Who can submit transactions?	**Public** *(Anyone)*	**Public-permissionless** Examples: • Bitcoin • Ethereum • Monero • EOS (node validators)	**Public-permissioned** Examples: • Ripple • EOS (block producers)
	Private (*requires keys to access*)	**(Virtual) Private-Permissionless** Example: • Baseline Protocol allows for confidential transactions on public networks	**Private-permissioned** Examples: • MediLedger • IBM Food Trust • TradeLens

The idea of a DAO is to create a completely independent entity that is exclusively governed by the rules that you program into it and 'lives' on the chain. This is more than using the blockchain to manage a company: instead, the code is the entire company. And it cannot be stopped.

—Henning Diedrich (2016), author of *Ethereum: Blockchains, Digital Assets, Smart Contracts, DAOs.*

Think of a decentralized autonomous organization as a completely digital 'company' with no managers or employees (Lacity, 2020).

Conclusion

We'll have succeeded in our overview if readers can comprehend the meaning the following definition of a blockchain application:

> A blockchain application is a peer-to-peer system for validating, time-stamping, and permanently storing transactions on a shared *distributed ledger. Tokenized assets* native to each blockchain application exist only in digital form and come with rights of use. *Cryptography* and *consensus* algorithms are used to validate transactions, to update the ledger, and to keep the ledger in sync and network secure. Most blockchains also use *smart contracts* that apply rules to automatically execute transactions based upon pre-agreed conditions. (Lacity & Van Hoek, 2021, pp. 110–111)

References

Diedrich, H. (2016). *Ethereum: Blockchains, digital assets, smart contracts, decentralized autonomous organizations*. Wildfire Publishing.

Kastrenakes, J. (2021). Beeple sold an NFT for $69 million through a first-of-its-kind auction at Christie's. *The Verge*. Retrieved August 2, 2021 from https://www.theverge.com/2021/3/11/22325054/beeple-christies-nft-sale-cost-everydays-69-million

Lacity, M. (2020). *Blockchain foundations for the internet of value*. Epic Books/University of Arkansas Press.

Lacity, M., & Van Hoek, R. (2021). What we've learned so far about blockchain for business. *Sloan Management Review, 63*(3), 48–54.

Nakamoto, S. (2008). Bitcoin: *A peer-to-peer electronic cash system.* https://bitcoin.org/bitcoin.pdf

Szabo, N. (1997). View of formalizing and securing relationships on public networks. *First Monday.* firstmonday.org

Szabo, N. (1998). Secure property titles with owner authority. Retrieved August 14, 2021 from https://nakamotoinstitute.org/secure-property-titles/

Treiblmaier, H. (2019). Toward more rigorous blockchain research: Recommendations for writing blockchain case studies. *Frontiers in Blockchain, 2*(3), 1–15.

Wong, J. I. (2017, December 4). The Ethereum network is getting jammed up because people are rushing to buy cartoon cats on its blockchain. https://qz.com/1145833/cryptokitties-is-causing-ethereum-network-congestion/

Zur, C., & Lacity, M. (2021). *The emergence of Web 3.0: Tokenization and the internet of value.* Blockchain Center of Excellence White Paper, University of Arkansas. https://cpb-us-e1.wpmucdn.com/wordpressua.uark.edu/dist/5/444/files/2018/01/BCoE2021_02_POST.pdf

Index[1]

[1] Note: Page numbers followed by 'n' refer to notes.

M. C. Lacity, H. Treiblmaier (eds.), *Blockchains and the Token Economy*, Technology, Work and Globalization, https://doi.org/10.1007/978-3-030-95108-5

FSC
www.fsc.org
MIX
Papier | Fördert
gute Waldnutzung
FSC® C083411

Kolibri 360 GmbH
Ferdinand-Jühlke-Straße 7
99095 Erfurt, Deutschland
produktsicherheit@kolibri360.de